D1558403

MTEL:
COMMUNICATION
& LITERACY
SKILLS

MTEL: COMMUNICATION & LITERACY SKILLS

LEARNINGEXPRESS ®

NEW YORK

Copyright © 2011 LearningExpress, LLC.

All rights reserved under International and Pan-American Copyright Conventions.
Published in the United States by LearningExpress, LLC, New York.

Library of Congress Cataloging-in-Publication Data:
MTEL: communication & literacy skills.
      p.   cm.
ISBN-13: 978-1-57685-769-4
ISBN-10: 1-57685-769-7
    1. Teachers—Certification—Massachusetts.   2. Teaching—Massachusetts—Examinations—Study
guides.   I. LearningExpress (Organization)
LB1763.M4M74 2011
371.1209744—dc22
    2010026505

Printed in the United States of America

9 8 7 6 5 4 3 2 1

First Edition

ISBN 978-1-57685-769-4

For more information or to place an order, contact LearningExpress at:
  2 Rector Street
  26th Floor
  New York, NY 10006

Or visit us at:
  www.learnatest.com

CONTENTS

CONTRIBUTORS

The following individuals contributed to the content of this book.

Gregory C. Benoit is a writer and editor living in Rhode Island. He holds a BA in English from Connecticut College, and an MA in Medieval Literature from the University of Connecticut. He spent 12 years teaching college-level English, writing, and literature, and also worked for many years as a newspaper editor and freelance photographer.

Wim Coleman and **Pat Perrin** usually write collaboratively. Their books for young readers appear in school and public library collections, on required and recommended school reading lists, and in the Renaissance Learning Accelerated Reader and Scholastic Reading Counts quiz programs. Their plays, articles, and stories have been published in *AppleSeeds* and *READ* magazines, and they have written testing materials for several major companies. Wim has degrees from Drake University in Theater, Literature, and Education. Pat's degrees are in English (Duke), Liberal Studies (Hollins), and Art Theory and Criticism (U.Ga.).

Judith Hicks was a classroom teacher in Compton, California and has been a teacher educator in the United States and abroad for eight years. She holds a Reading Specialist credential, and she has contributed to a variety of textbook and curriculum projects. She is currently pursuing a PhD in Education at Stanford University.

Mike Segretto has been an assessment writer for ten years while also creating a wide assortment of informational and entertainment material for various online sites and print publications. He holds a degree in film and English from Hofstra University.

HOW TO USE THIS BOOK

CHAPTER SUMMARY

In order to gain a teaching position in the public schools of Massachusetts, you will first need to get a Massachusetts teaching certificate, referred to as a teaching license. Regardless of what subject area you intend to teach, you will need to pass the Massachusetts Tests for Educator Licensure, commonly known as the MTEL program, in order to become licensed. The purpose of this book is to help you gain that teaching license, and its focus is especially on helping you to pass the MTEL Communication and Literacy Skills (01) Test. By the time you're finished with this book, you will be fully prepared to gain the teaching position of your dreams!

This book will help you to prepare fully for the process of gaining your Massachusetts licensure and becoming a teacher. In it, you'll find:

- a chapter discussing the benefits of teaching in Massachusetts
- a chapter explaining the various requirements for teaching in Massachusetts and the different licenses available
- an overview of the MTEL program, with general information about the many subject area tests offered
- an in-depth explanation of the MTEL Communication and Literacy Skills Test, which every candidate must pass to receive licensure in Massachusetts

- a full-length diagnostic pretest
- reading and writing skills review chapters
- two additional full-length practice tests

You should begin with Chapter 1, which discusses the teaching career in general. This will help you to understand what it means to be a teacher, and specifically what it means to teach in Massachusetts. It gives you a good idea of what to expect in the Massachusetts public school system, and it will help you to solidify your thinking and expectations regarding the profession as a whole.

Chapter 2 gives you more specific information on what is required of all Massachusetts teaching candidates. You will also learn what is needed if you do not presently live in Massachusetts and how to attain licensure in the most effective manner. This chapter also introduces you to the MTEL program, which is the focus of the remainder of the book.

After Chapter 2, you should take the diagnostic pretest. After you have taken the test, use the corresponding evaluation tables to identify your strengths and weaknesses. This will be a great help in targeting your review later, as it will show you the areas that you might need to strengthen.

Once you have completed the pretest and evaluated your results, move on to Chapters 3 and 4. Chapter 3 gives you a wealth of information on the many subject matter tests offered in the MTEL program, and you will be able to determine which ones you will be required to take to get your license. Chapter 4 goes into even greater depth on the Communication and Literacy Skills Test, which most teaching candidates must pass. You will have your pretest results in hand and can focus on which areas of these tests will most require your attention.

Even if you intend to teach a subject that does not rely heavily on writing skills, such as math, you will still need to be fully competent in your communication abilities. Remember that the Communication and Literacy Skills Test is required of most candidates, regardless what subject they intend to teach, and that test focuses entirely on these skill sets. Furthermore, most of the subject area tests also have open response questions that require you to write a short essay in your own words. So spend as much time as needed on Chapters 7 and 8 to review your reading and writing skills in order to strengthen your communication skills.

After you have fully reviewed these chapters, take the first of the two practice tests. Use the evaluation tables to compare your results with the pretest; you will undoubtedly find that you have improved greatly. You may then return to the relevant chapters in this book to practice some more. Remember that communication skills are like any other skill: you must practice if you want to improve.

Finally, take the second practice test when you feel ready. You will find that your results have improved greatly since the pretest, and you will have a clear idea of what to expect when you sit down to take the MTEL.

The MTEL and You

You already have two valuable tools for passing the tests—this book and your own determination. Now the rest is up to you. Remain disciplined, follow your study schedule, and do not give up. Most importantly: practice, practice, practice. Plenty of practice will improve your skills and build your confidence.

Good luck!

MTEL:
COMMUNICATION
& LITERACY
SKILLS

MAKING THE DECISION TO BECOME A TEACHER

CHAPTER SUMMARY

Teaching is more than a job; it's a way of life. What's more, your choice to become a teacher will have a greater impact than you might think—you'll be influencing hundreds or even thousands of other people through your efforts. In this chapter, you will learn what to expect from a career in teaching—what it is, and what it isn't—and you'll gain some insight from others who teach. You will also learn about the benefits of teaching in Massachusetts in general, and in Boston in particular.

Teaching Is a Career

You've probably heard the old saying: "The three reasons to become a teacher are June, July, and August!" This is an amusing slogan, but it belies the truth of teaching. Summer holidays might prove a nice benefit for some, but the work and responsibility required during the teaching months more than offset it.

Teaching is not a 9 to 5 sort of job. Most of the time, you take work home with you to continue in your personal time. You will be reading essays, grading tests, creating lesson plans, designing bulletin boards and other classroom learning aids, and engaging in countless other tasks involved in the day-to-day rigors of teaching. Then there's your own personal development: a teacher needs to be always learning, always expanding horizons, always keeping up to date on the latest information both in your own field and in teaching in general. You will spend time meeting with parents, attending faculty meetings, taking part in courses and seminars, and sometimes even working toward a graduate degree.

Teaching is not just a job; it's a career, and as such it requires a professional attitude and commitment.

Teachers Are Professionals

Many jobs allow an employee to call in sick on a moment's notice. After all, the work will still be there tomorrow, and missing a day is no big deal. But that is not the case for teachers; when a teacher is absent, the classes still must be taught, and that means that someone else must cover for you when you're out. It can also mean that your lesson planning gets set back during your sick time, costing you lost days that can never be regained.

Your students also depend on you, and a teacher quickly realizes that he or she is responsible to many more people than just the principal or school board. Students look to their teachers as role models, and this means that a professional teacher is accountable both inside the classroom and outside. In this sense, a teacher is never off duty; students who meet you in the grocery store still expect you to behave in a professional and courteous manner.

As already stated, being a professional teacher also requires you to be a professional learner. Physicians must stay up-to-date on the latest medical research and medical developments if they are to serve their patients faithfully, and the same is true with teachers. Students expect their chemistry teachers, for example, to be current on recent studies in the field, and every field has the same requirement: constant learning.

Teaching Is Caring

Many career paths don't involve much interaction with other people. A research scientist, for example, might spend the day peering through a microscope and making calculations—but this is not the case for teachers! The field of teaching is dependent on interacting with other people, since it is other people that you're trying to teach.

Take a moment and reflect on some of your favorite teachers throughout your own schooling. What set them apart from the rest? Why do these people come immediately to mind? If you think it through, you will discover that your favorite teachers had an impact on your life because they took time to pay attention to you, they made an effort to help you understand, they were willing to go beyond the call of duty for your sake—in short, they cared about you.

Teaching involves more than simply imparting knowledge to others. You will be a listener, a mediator, a disciplinarian, a role model—a friend.

Teachers Are Skilled Communicators

Effective teachers are able to express their thoughts and ideas clearly, both in writing and when speaking. What's more, a good teacher must learn to be comfortable speaking in front of large groups of people. This will take place inside the classroom, of course, but it will also be necessary when speaking with parents, when meeting with other educators, and in many other settings. Writing skills will also be vital, even if you are teaching in a field that is not writing intensive. You will be called on to create clearly expressed lesson plans, communicate with parents and administrators, write comments and critiques on your students' work, even make written presentations that will be read by your professional colleagues. Good vocabulary, spelling skills, grammar, and writing mechanics will be essential.

Your communication skills will also tie together with the need to care that we discussed previously. You will find yourself called on to explain to a mother, for example, that her daughter is failing your class because she isn't turning in her homework. Such communication needs to be more than simply clear—it needs to be tactful!

Benefits of Teaching in Massachusetts

We began this chapter by emphasizing the work involved in teaching, but we must not overlook the many benefits that come to those who teach in Massachusetts. For starters, your efforts and caring affect many lives—many more lives than you might think. You influence your students in ways that will last the rest of their lives, and beyond them you also influence people whom you might never meet. Members of your students' families will be influenced by your teaching and your example; people in the community will be affected by your presence in Massachusetts; even your fellow educators will be influenced by your professionalism and zeal to learn.

You can also be proud to say that you are a teacher in Massachusetts, because our state has one of the finest public school systems in the United States, ranked at number two for the nation in 2009 by *U.S. News and World Report* magazine![1] The state is constantly working to improve the academic environment in its public schools, for both students and educators alike.

Other advantages to teaching in Massachusetts include the salary and benefits. Massachusetts schools rate in the top eight states for highest average salary. According to the Washington, D.C. Job Source, Massachusetts teachers average nearly $60,500 per year. For comparison, here are average salaries for various regions of the nation:

STATE	AVERAGE SALARY
Arizona	$45,772
Florida	$46,930
Montana	$42,874
Texas	$46,179
Washington	$49,884

[1] http://www.usnews.com/articles/education/high-schools/2009/12/09/americas-best-high-schools-state-by-state-statistics.html; accessed May 25, 2010.

Health insurance and retirement benefits are also advantages. School districts usually offer multiple options to consider for health insurance, from personal and family plans to health maintenance organizations (HMOs) and preferred provider organizations (PPOs). The Massachusetts system provides retirement, death, and disability benefits to eligible teachers and administrators.

Finally, Massachusetts offers a wide diversity of locations and opportunities for teachers, whether you want to be in a small town, in the suburbs, or in an urban school environment. The northwestern portion of the state offers the rolling mountains of the Berkshire region, while the eastern portion offers some of the nation's finest ocean beaches. The state's urban areas, such as Boston, Worcester, and Springfield, offer all the attractions of the nation's largest cities, from arts and entertainment to fine dining. And the entire state is rich in American history, from the site of the Boston Tea Party to the famed ride of Paul Revere. Whatever your tastes in lifestyle and environment, you'll find a niche in Massachusetts.

Teaching in Boston

If you are looking for a more vibrant (and sometimes more challenging) teaching environment, you might want to consider targeting the schools within the Boston region. Teaching and living in the greater Boston area offers opportunities—both in teaching and lifestyle—that other regions cannot provide. There is a wide diversity of landscape and natural beauty, ranging from ocean beachfront to teeming metropolis, all within the small radius commonly referred to as "the hub" of Boston. The city offers some of the nation's best in technology, finance, fashion, educational institutions, and the arts. Sports fans love the accessibility of their favorite teams, and those more athletically inclined can participate in the world-famous Boston Marathon. The richness of Boston's higher educational offerings provides opportunities for further study in any field imaginable. And, of course, the city offers an abundance of American history which would require a lifetime to exhaust.

Teachers in the Boston region also face challenges that other districts do not offer. For example, approximately 21% of Boston students will drop out of school before graduating. This creates a unique opportunity to change the lives of students who might otherwise be at risk of losing all interest in furthering their education. However, it also presents the challenge of teaching a greater number of students who may not be interested in learning.

Another trend facing Boston public schools is declining enrollment and lower average scores on standardized testing. Are these trends associated with the high incidence of dropouts in the system? One of the challenges that you would face if you teach in Boston would be to identify the causes of these and other similar problems, then to devise solutions. Your career in the Boston school system may be more challenging than in other parts of the state—and the rewards and satisfaction may also be far greater.

As a teacher in the Boston system, of course, you would still be free to live in one of the many surrounding towns which offer a more rural or suburban setting. The subway system, known as the T, is extensive and easy to use—far easier than many other urban mass transit systems. Thousands commute to and from the downtown area every day, avoiding the traffic and tension found on the highways.

Special Financial Incentives for Boston Teachers

In addition to the rewards and challenges already noted, teaching in the Boston region can provide you with several very attractive financial rewards. First and foremost is the possible cancellation of your student loans!

Many Boston schools qualify for the Federal Perkins Loan Cancellation program, which provides up to 100% forgiveness on your student loans if you meet certain criteria. Visit http://studentaid.ed.gov to learn more.

Many of the colleges and universities around Boston also offer reduced tuition—up to 40% off—to Boston teachers pursuing a Master's degree. Call the Boston public school system for more information at (617) 635-9639.

Why I Teach

"It's exhilarating! And it can be frustrating, too. But even on my worst days, I can find something to be encouraged by. Overall, I wouldn't trade it for anything!"
—Janet P., Worcester

"Teaching is like any other art, I think. You have to work hard, you have to always be trying something new. Sometimes you're proud of the final product; sometimes you see flaws in it. A teacher needs to be realistic or she'll lose sight of the goal."
—Rebecca J., Chicopee

"It's kind of like being a parent, actually. . . . The students imitate you, they tease you, they disobey you—you name it, if kids do it, they'll do it. But when my 'kids' graduate I always get choked up."
—Dave K., Norwood

"June, July, and August, right? Ha! Let me tell you about my summers. I take a week off in June to go camping with my family, but when we get back summer school classes start. I spend three evenings a week teaching judo at the Y, and most weekends I'm correcting summer school homework. Summers have nothing to do with it. I teach because I love it, plain and simple."
—Simon W., Andover

"I began my teaching career fresh out of college—a long time ago, but it doesn't seem like it. I remember being frightened at first, some of the older students seemed intimidating, but I think that was mostly because I wasn't that much older than they were. Anyway, that went away soon enough and then I started to hit my stride. After a while, teaching sort of becomes part of who you are—almost like it's part of your personality. I've never regretted a minute of it."

—Dr. James Q., retired superintendent of schools

"There's nothing like seeing one of your students suddenly 'get it.' I call those my 'ah-ha' moments, when someone in the classroom all of a sudden starts getting excited about what we're studying. Yes, it's a lot of work to get there, but man it's worth it when you do!"

—George P., Dracut

"I spend a lot of time mentoring, although it doesn't seem like that's what I'm doing. Every year, I find a few students who are thinking about dropping out. You can tell—it's like they're not paying attention to what's going on inside the classroom, but to what's going on outside. Usually seems to hit around the time they get their driver's license. Something about that pull of independence, I suppose. Anyway, keeping them in school is what I find most rewarding."

—Donna O., South Boston

"I teach because it's what I do best. What else can I say?"

—Pete G., Pepperell

"I love teaching in Boston. There's just so much energy in downtown, it carries inside the classrooms, too. I taught for a while in Pennsylvania, and there were things there I don't have here—a different lifestyle and some great friendships—but I get charged up every morning as soon as I get on the T, and my students respond to my enthusiasm."

—Patricia L., Boston

CHAPTER 2 ▶ TEACHING IN MASSACHUSETTS

CHAPTER SUMMARY
The state of Massachusetts requires that all public school teachers be licensed by the state board of education. In this chapter, you will learn about the various types of licenses available and how to obtain them, and about both traditional and alternative routes to becoming certified in Massachusetts.

Massachusetts Licensure

Massachusetts licensure is required for all who teach in any Massachusetts public school. There are four types of teaching license available:

- Temporary
- Preliminary
- Initial
- Professional

The **Temporary** license is issued only to candidates who have experience teaching in public schools in another state. It is valid only for one calendar year, intended to give teachers time to attain the **Initial** license. To be eligible, you must have at least three years of teaching experience under a valid license from a state that has reciprocity with Massachusetts: that license or teaching certificate must be comparable to the Initial license issued in Massachusetts. Many states have reciprocity with Massachusetts, enabling experienced teachers to make use of the Temporary license. Visit www.doe.mass.edu/edprep/nasdtec.html for a list of states whose licensure is compatible.

The **Preliminary** license is issued to candidates who do not meet the requirements for the Temporary license and who have not completed the Approved Educator Preparation (EdPrep) program, which will be discussed in more detail. It is valid for five years, allowing a hired teacher time to fulfill the EdPrep and other requirements. To be eligible, you must hold a Bachelor's degree, and you must pass the necessary tests on the MTEL. There may be additional requirements for some teaching fields.

The Initial license is issued to candidates who have completed the EdPrep program. It is valid for five years, but unlike the Preliminary license it can be extended once for an additional five years if necessary. To be eligible, you must hold a bachelor's degree, you must pass the necessary tests on the MTEL, and you must have completed an approved EdPrep program.

The **Professional** license is issued to those who have at least three years' teaching experience under an Initial license. Most educators will begin teaching with either the Preliminary license or the Initial license, moving on to gain the Professional license after gaining experience in the Massachusetts schools system.

The **Preliminary** and **Initial** licenses require the following:

- possession of a bachelor's degree
- completion of an approved educator preparation program (Initial license only)
- passing score on the Communication and Literacy Skills test (see Chapter 4)
- passing score on any subject matter knowledge tests required for the field sought (see Chapter 3)

- evidence of sound moral character
- other requirements specific to various teaching fields; visit www.doe.mass.edu for more information

For detailed information on what a particular license in your subject area will require, visit www4.doemass.org/elar/licensurehelp/LicenseRequirementsCriteria PageControl.ser.

Approved Educator Preparation (EdPrep) Programs

The Massachusetts Department of Education (DOE) requires its teachers to have a mastery of *pedagogical skills*, those areas of expertise that make an effective educator, such as the use of age-appropriate instructional strategies, the ability to assess the degree of a student's understanding and progress, the ability to clearly communicate new areas of knowledge, and so forth. These are the skills that are taught in college-level programs designed to prepare the teachers of tomorrow.

The EdPrep requirement can be met by completing any of the following:

- a teacher preparation program from an approved college or university
- the Alternative/Practice-Based Licensure Program
- the Performance Review Program

Teacher preparation programs at specified colleges and universities are available throughout Massachusetts. Visit www4.doemass.org/elar/licensurehelp/HigherEdOrganizationsPageControl.ser for a complete list.

The **Alternative/Practice-Based Licensure Programs** are nondegree programs intended specifically to prepare candidates to meet the EdPrep requirement for Initial licensure. These programs are accelerated and somewhat advanced, including an emphasis on field-based work, and frequently consist of a series of intensive seminars or courses focused on the Massachusetts Professional Standards for Teachers, pedagogical skills, and an assessment of a candidate's performance in the teaching setting. More information can be found at www.doe.mass .edu/edprep/district.html.

The **Performance Review Program** is overseen by an independent company called Class Measures. It is intended for experienced teachers rather than candidates who have no field experience. To qualify for this program, you must:

- hold a Massachusetts Preliminary Teaching License in any teaching field except:
  - early childhood
  - elementary
  - library
  - students with moderate or severe disabilities
  - deaf and hard-of-hearing
  - visually impaired students
  - academically advanced
  - reading specialist
  - speech, language, or hearing disorders
- have at least three full years of employment in the role of the Preliminary licensee, as well as documented seminars, courses, and relevant experience
- be employed in a district in which there is no Massachusetts-approved district-based program for obtaining an Initial license or in which the approved program is not available (including out-of-state districts)
- be recommended by the principal of all schools in which you have taught
- complete a competency review if you teach in a field that does not have a subject matter test available on the MTEL

Traditional Routes to Certification

Most teacher candidates will have attained their bachelor's degree at a college or university that offers a certified program in teacher education, such as those accredited by the National Council for Accreditation of Teacher Education (NCATE). Within Massachusetts, many colleges and universities offer approved educator preparation programs which are certified by the state of Massachusetts. For a complete list of colleges and universities offering these programs, visit www.doe.mass.edu/educators/directory.html or phone (781)338-6600.

Alternate Routes to Certification

Teaching candidates who hold a bachelor's degree but have not completed a certified educator preparation program can pursue either the Preliminary or Initial license through the following programs.

Post-Baccalaureate Programs offer access to the Initial license through at least two semesters of course work at the college or university level. These programs generally also include some type of field-based experience or internship in a school district. Some programs culminate in a master's degree, while others allow the candidate to meet the requirements without pursuing the full graduate degree.

Teacher of Record post-baccalaureate programs are approved preparation programs that have been designed by public school districts, often in partnership with a college or university. Candidates are hired as a "teacher of record" under a Preliminary license and are assigned a team of mentors for additional support and supervision. Additional course work and seminars are required to complete this path to licensure, as well as a final assessment at the end of the program. This method is popular for those seeking to change their career, as well as candidates who already hold a bachelor's degree but lack the educator-preparation coursework, since it allows a candidate to fulfill those requirements while working in the teaching field.

The **Performance Review Program**, already discussed in this chapter, is designed for candidates who have completed a program that is not certified by the Massachusetts DOE.

Fees and Refunds

There is a $100 fee for any first-time application for licensure, plus an additional $25 fee for each additional subject area or level. For example, applying for History grades 8–12 would cost $100, and an additional license for English grades 8–12 would be another $25. All fees are nonrefundable, even if you are denied licensure for some reason.

Testing Information

The Massachusetts DOE requires both subject area knowledge and pedagogical skills of all its teacher candidates. The pedagogical skills are assessed and strengthened through the EdPrep programs listed previously, while a candidate's subject area knowledge is assessed through the Massachusetts Tests for Educator Licensure (MTEL).

For most candidates, the MTEL portion of licensure will consist of at least two tests: the Communication and Literacy Skills test, which all candidates must pass; and one or more specific subject area tests, determined by the field or fields of teaching you intend to enter. The Communication and Literacy Skills Test is discussed in detail in Chapter 4, and the subject area tests are discussed in Chapter 3.

The MTEL tests are criterion-referenced, which means that your scores will be determined by how you match up with specific scoring rubrics. This is a different method from that used in some standardized tests, which compare your results against the results of all the other people taking the test. The specific rubrics used to determine your scores are discussed in Chapters 3 and 4.

Further Information

Further information on the requirements for teaching in Massachusetts can be obtained from:

- Massachusetts DOE Information Line: (781)338-6600
- Massachusetts DOE website: www.doe.mass.edu
- MTEL website: www.mtel.nesinc.com

CHAPTER 3

OVERVIEW OF THE MTEL PROGRAM

CHAPTER SUMMARY

The Massachusetts Tests for Education Licensure (MTEL) program consists of a broad array of tests designed to assess your qualifications for teaching in any given field. This chapter outlines the various tests available, helping you to determine which ones you will be required to take. You will also learn what is involved in taking the test, either on paper or on a computer, and what to expect on the day of the test.

About the MTEL

The Massachusetts Tests for Educator Licensure (MTEL) dates back to 1998 and consists of an overall test of communication and literacy skills, as well as a wide variety of subject matter tests. The program was designed to ensure that Massachusetts teachers can communicate effectively with students, parents, and other educators, and also to ensure that they are knowledgeable in their specific area of teaching.

Most of the MTEL tests consist of both multiple-choice questions and open-response questions, the latter requiring candidates to write their responses in their own words. Tests for languages other than English also assess listening and reading comprehension and the ability to write and speak fluently in that language. The specific areas of MTEL testing are as follows.

Communication and Literacy Skills Test (01)

All areas of Massachusetts teaching licensure will require that candidates take the Communication and Literary Skills Test. This important topic is discussed fully in Chapter 4.

General Curriculum (03)

The General Curriculum test is divided into the following two subtests, both of which are required if you take it:

- **Multi-Subject Subtest:** This test includes 55 multiple-choice questions and 1 open-response question. The open-response question will require you to spend 20 to 30 minutes to prepare an adequate response. The multiple-choice questions determine 90% of your score, and the open-response question determines the remaining 10%.
- **Mathematics Subtest:** This test includes 45 multiple-choice questions and 1 open-response question. The open-response question will require you to spend 20 to 30 minutes to prepare an adequate response. The multiple-choice questions determine 90% of your score, and the open-response question determines the remaining 10%.

Academic (Pre-K to 12) Subject Matter Tests

Candidates wishing to teach in prekindergarten through grade 12 will be required to take the Communication and Literacy Skills Test plus at least one specific subject matter test. These tests consist of multiple-choice questions and open-response ques-

tions, designed to assess proficiency and depth of understanding on the given subject.

Each subject matter test includes 100 multiple-choice questions and 2 open-response questions. Each open-response question will require you to spend 20 to 30 minutes to prepare an adequate response. The multiple-choice section counts for 80% of your score, and the open-response questions count for 20% each.

The subject matter tests include the following, with test numbers in parentheses. (For an up-to-date list of tests, visit www.mtel.nesinc.com.)

- Academically Advanced (52)
- Biology (13)
- Business (19)
- Chemistry (12)
- Early Childhood (02)
- Earth Science (14)
- English (07)
- Foundations of Reading (90)
- General Science (10)
- Health/Family and Consumer Sciences (21)
- History (06)
- Latin and Classical Humanities (15)
- Mathematics (09)
- Mathematics (Elementary) (53)
- Mathematics (Middle School) (47)
- Mathematics/Science (Middle School) (51)
- Middle School Humanities (50)
- Music (16)
- Physical Education (22)
- Physics (11)
- Political Science/Political Philosophy (48)
- Reading Specialist (08)
- Speech (44)
- Technology/Engineering (33)
- Theater (45)
- Visual Arts (17)

Foreign Language Subject Matter Tests

These language tests are broken down as follows:

- **French and Spanish:** This test includes 100 multiple-choice questions and 2 open-response questions. One open-response question is written, and the other is given orally. The multiple-choice questions determine 70% of your score, and the open-response questions determine the remaining 30%.
- **German and Italian:** This test includes 55 multiple-choice questions and 2 open-response questions. One open-response question is written, and the other is given orally. The multiple-choice questions determine approximately 67% of your score, and the open-response questions determine the remaining 33%.
- **Chinese (Mandarin), Portuguese, and Russian:** This test includes 55 multiple-choice and short-answer questions and 4 open-response questions. One open-response question is oral, and the other three are written. The multiple-choice and short-answer questions determine approximately 33% of your score, and the open-response questions determine the remaining 67%.

Adult Basic Education Test (55)

This subject matter test includes 100 multiple-choice questions and 2 open-response questions. The open-response questions require you to spend 20 to 30 minutes each to provide an adequate response. The multiple-choice questions determine 85% of your score, and the open-response questions determine the remaining 15%.

Vocational Technical Literacy Skills Test (91)

This test is broken down as follows, both of which are required if you take it:

- **Reading Subtest:** This subtest includes 60 multiple-choice items.

- **Writing Subtest:** This subtest includes 40 multiple-choice questions and 2 open-response questions. The open-response questions include one summary exercise and one composition exercise. The summary exercise requires you to spend 20 to 30 minutes to provide an adequate response; the composition exercise requires 45 to 60 minutes. The multiple-choice questions determine 55% of your score, and the open-response questions determine the remaining 45%.

Dance Subject Matter Test (46)

This subject matter test includes 55 multiple-choice questions and 2 open-response questions. The open-response questions require you to spend approximately 60 minutes each to provide an adequate response. The multiple-choice questions determine 75% of your score, and the open-response questions determine the remaining 25%.

English as a Second Language Test (54)

This subject matter test includes 100 multiple-choice questions and 4 open-response questions. The open-response questions are all oral, not written. The multiple-choice questions determine 80% of your score, and the open-response questions determine the remaining 20%.

The MTEL website offers practice tests in most of the above subject matters, as well as booklets that give more detailed information on each test. Visit www.mtel.nesinc.com for more information.

What to Expect

The MTEL is offered in morning and afternoon sessions. For a morning session, you'll report to the test center around 7:45 A.M. and finish by 12:30 P.M. Afternoon sessions run from 1:15 to 6:00 P.M. You are allowed to take only one test per session, although tests with two subtests (such as the Communication and Literacy Skills Test) can be done in one session or two at your discretion.

You should be aware that many tests are offered only in the afternoon sessions, while the Communication and Literacy Skills test is available only in morning sessions at the time of this book's publication. Visit www.mtel.nesinc.com for the latest information.

Computer-Based Tests

The Communication and Literacy Skills Test is also offered in a computer-based format, rather than the traditional paper-based method. If you choose to take that test on a computer, you will need to register online at www.mtel.nesinc.com. You will be given an appointment at one of the computer-based testing centers (no less than three days from when you register). You will need to report to the test site 30 minutes before testing begins, and your entire testing session will last 4 hours and 15 minutes (the extra 15 minutes being for a short tutorial and other computer matters). The earliest appointment for computer-based testing is 8:00 A.M.

Registration for the MTEL

Most MTEL tests are offered in paper-based testing format five times a year: two fall sessions, two spring sessions, and one summer session. In addition, there are two extra test sessions specifically for the Communication and Literacy Skills Test only—one in October and one in January, offered only in Boston and Springfield.

Deadlines for registering are approximately six to eight weeks prior to any test date, so plan on registering early! There are late registration options, but they cost more, so regular registration is your best choice. Visit www.mtel.nesinc.com for specific dates and deadlines.

If you choose to take the Communication and Literacy Skills Test in computer-based format, you will be given specific testing days to choose from—and there may be fewer options than with traditional paper-based methods. Again, visit www.mtel.nesinc.com for current testing windows.

You will select one of the following test sites (site number in parentheses) for paper-based testing:

- Boston area (001)
- Greater Boston—northern area (002)
- Greater Boston—southern area (003)
- Central Massachusetts (Worcester County) (004)
- Springfield area (005)
- North Adams area (006)
- Hyannis area (021)
- New Bedford area (022)

Additionally, most MTEL tests are offered at the following out-of-area locations, once in November and once in March, provided that there are enough people enrolled on any given test date:

- Chicago (701)
- New York City (702)
- Los Angeles (703)
- Miami (704)
- Washington, D.C. (706)
- Philadelphia (715)

Computer-based testing (Communication and Literacy Skills Test only) is available through Pearson Professional Centers at the following locations. (Visit www.pearsonvue.com/mtel for further information.)

- Boston
- Boston Back Bay
- Springfield
- Waltham
- Worcester
- Wallingford, CT
- Wethersfield, CT
- Westbrook, ME
- Concord, NH
- Albany, NY
- Warwick, RI

Registration fees and test fees vary greatly from one test to another. Visit www.mtel.nesinc.com for specific, up-to-date information.

The Day of the Test

You should report to your test site early, allowing yourself time to find a comfortable seat and get yourself situated and relaxed. Late arrivals are not given any extra time to make up for time lost, and frequently are not admitted at all. If you arrive late and are not admitted, you will be considered absent and your registration fees will not be reimbursed.

Dress appropriately to the season; test sites might prove chilly in the cold months, and they are specifically *not* air-conditioned in the summer months. Cold-weather layering is a good strategy, wearing a sweater and jacket that you can remove as you warm up.

What to Bring

- your admission ticket
- proper legal identification
- several sharpened #2 pencils

Proper identification is vitally important on the day of the test. You will need *two* forms of identification: a government-issued identifier bearing your name, photograph, and signature (driver's license, passport, etc.), and a second piece of identification that verifies the information (photograph is not necessary). You will also be required to provide a thumbprint at the testing site to verify your identity. If you refuse to provide the thumbprint, you will be considered absent and no refund will be given.

If you do not have the necessary forms of identification, you will be photographed and asked to fill out additional paperwork—and this will reduce the amount of time you have for the test. Your best strategy, therefore, is to have a valid government-issued identification card, such as your driver's license, plus another government document such as a birth certificate, passport, or Social Security card.

Test Site Rules

The following items will not be permitted inside the testing area:

- smoking materials (cigarettes, pipes, etc.)
- visitors (including children and other relatives)
- cell phones
- electronic devices (laptops, PDAs, MP3 players —even watches with calculators or alarms)
- calculators (unless specifically allowed in some tests)
- handwritten or printed materials (notebooks, dictionaries, scratch paper, etc.)
- packages or bags of any kind (including backpacks, briefcases, etc.)
- food and drink (except water in an unlabeled, clear bottle)
- unauthorized aids (slide rules, highlighters, rulers, etc.)

Computer-Based Site Rules

All the preceding rules and stipulations apply to those taking computer-based tests, with the following additions:

- **Report to the site 30 minutes prior to testing.** This is necessary because you will be given a short tutorial on how to use the computer testing system. If you arrive later than this, you may be refused admission.
- **Personal items will be stored in a locker.** This includes wallets, purses, pocketbooks, and watches, as well as the prohibited items in the preceding list.

THE COMMUNICATION AND LITERACY SKILLS (01) TEST

CHAPTER SUMMARY
This chapter focuses specifically on the communication and literacy portion of the MTEL, which consists of two parts: reading and writing. You will learn the details of each part, what types of questions are involved, and how they are scored—and you will gain valuable tips and practice that will help you be well-prepared on test day.

What to Expect on the MTEL Communication and Literacy Skills Test

The MTEL Communication and Literacy Skills Test is broken into two parts, or "subtests": the Reading subtest and the Writing subtest. We will consider each type in depth.

Reading Subtest

The Reading subtest consists of 42 multiple-choice questions that are based on a short passage. Each multiple-choice question offers four possible answers (**a** through **d**), only one of which is correct. These questions are designed to assess your ability to gather information, make inferences, and draw conclusions from a written passage; they are *not* intended to test your specific knowledge on a subject area. For example, you might be given a passage that is an excerpt from a poem. The questions based on that excerpt will address your ability to understand what the author is saying, but they will not expect you to have specific knowledge about the author, poetic forms, and so forth.

The Reading subtest is designed to test six specific areas of skill, and will contain between six and eight questions from each of the following categories:

- meaning of words and phrases
- main idea and supporting details
- outlining, summarizing, and graph interpretation
- writer's purpose and point of view
- relationships among ideas
- critical reasoning

The first three types of questions just listed cover basic factual data that will be contained within a given reading passage, while the remaining three types require you to "read between the lines" of the passage, making inferences and drawing conclusions on your own which might not be directly stated by the author. Let's consider each of these categories in more detail.

Meaning of Words and Phrases

Questions in this category assess your vocabulary and ability to determine from context the meaning of a word or phrase. The best way to prepare for this type of question is to read! The more of a reader you are, the better your vocabulary will become, and the greater mastery you will gain over the English language (and foreign languages, as well, if that is your chosen teaching field).

Of course, no matter how strong your vocabulary skills, you will still need to use the context in which a word is used to determine its meaning. Many words can have more than one use; a word's present meaning is determined by the way that it's being used in the given passage. For instance, the simple word *light* can refer to the energy waves that enable us to see, to a lamp that gives off those energy waves, or to something that doesn't weigh very much. It can also be used as a verb, meaning *to illuminate*, and even in

some forms to mean *make something weigh less*. Consider how *light* is used in these sentences:

- The morning *light* came shining brightly.
- He switched on the *light* as he entered the room.
- This purse feels a bit *light*; did you short-change me?
- The leader's job is to *light* the way for his followers.
- I'll try to *lighten* your load.

Notice how the meaning of *light* is determined by the way that the word is used in each of the previous sentences. It is essentially the same word in each case (with a variant form used in the final sentence), but the meaning is not the same in each case.

Now, this example of using context may seem simplistic; after all, we are all accustomed to recognizing subtle distinctions in words based on the way that they're used in any given sentence. But the principle here is important to remember, because it will enable you to make an educated guess when you encounter a word that is unfamiliar, or when you are asked to define a phrase or *idiomatic expression* with which you are unfamiliar. Idiomatic expressions are simply phrases and metaphors that people commonly use, such as *let the cat out of the bag*, meaning to reveal a secret, or *he has an ace up his sleeve*, meaning that a person has a secret weapon ready to use.

Jane saw that Mark had a new pair of Rollerblades, and she *coveted* the speed they gave him

1. In the sentence above, *coveted* most nearly means
   a. cut short.
   b. envied.
   c. stole.
   d. outperformed.

The answer to this question is choice **b**, *envied*. If you already are familiar with the word *covet*, you will be able to pick out the correct choice quite quickly. But even if *covet* is unfamiliar, you can still make an educated guess at its meaning from the context in which it is used. Mark had something that Jane wanted—new Rollerblades—and she was *envious* of the speed that Mark attained by using them.

Main Idea and Supporting Details

The main idea of a reading passage is its *topic*, the person, thing, or idea that the passage is primarily about. Supporting details include specific facts related to the topic. Here is an example.

> One New York publisher has estimated that 50,000 to 60,000 people in the United States want an anthology that includes the complete works of William Shakespeare. What accounts for this renewed interest in Shakespeare? As scholars point out, the psychological insights that he portrays in both male and female characters are amazing even today.

2. The main idea of this passage is that
  a. modern people don't read Shakespeare.
  b. anthologies make the best textbooks.
  c. Shakespeare's characters are still relevant today.
  d. scholars enjoy Shakespeare's plays.

3. Approximately how many Americans want to read Shakespeare, according to this passage?
  a. 55,000
  b. 63,000
  c. 48,000
  d. not stated

Question 2 addresses the *main idea* of the passage, which has to do with Shakespeare's characters. Choice **c** is the best answer, because the passage focuses specifically on the fact that the characters in Shakespeare's plays portray "psychological insights" that are still relevant today. None of the other choices is directly addressed by the passage.

Question 3 deals with some of the *supporting details* in the passage, specifically the number of people in the United States who want to see Shakespeare included in modern anthologies. You'll notice, of course, that the number 55,000 (choice **a**) is not specifically given in the passage, but the range given (50,000 to 60,000) includes it—whereas the other choices fall outside that range.

Outlining, Summarizing, and Graph Interpretation

An outline is a bare-bones structure listing the order in which certain information is presented in a passage. If you've taken any writing or composition classes, you probably learned the importance of outlining your thoughts and ideas prior to writing an essay. The outline is like the skeleton on which your essay will be created, and some questions in the MTEL will ask you to work backward from a passage, providing a brief outline of its ideas.

> Daffodil bulbs require well-drained soil and a sunny planting location. They should be planted in holes that are 3 to 6 inches deep and there should be 2 to 4 inches between bulbs. The bulb should be placed in the hole, pointed side up, root side down. Once the bulb is planted, water the area thoroughly.

4. Which of the following outlines presents the correct order for planting daffodil bulbs?
  a. plant the bulb, bury the bulb, water the area
  b. water the area thoroughly, plant the bulb, pointed side up, root side down
  c. dig a hole, plant the bulb, water area thoroughly
  d. dig a hole, water the area thoroughly, plant the bulb

One effective way to outline a passage is to use the following as a guide:

   I. Topic: The passage is about _____.
      A. The first major point concerning the topic is _____.
          1. This point is supported or explained by _____.
      B. The second major point concerning the topic is _____.
          1. This point is supported or explained by _____.
      C. The third major point concerning the topic is _____.
          1. This point is supported or explained by _____.
  II. Conclusion: The author draws the conclusion that _____.
      A. The author applies this conclusion to _____.

In the daffodil passage, this outline will be briefer, since the passage does not go into supporting details or draw conclusions—it is a simple how-to description. In this case, your outline might look like this:

   I. Topic: The passage is about how to plant daffodil bulbs.
      A. The first major point concerning the topic is to plant them in holes that are
          1. 3 to 6 inches deep.
          2. 2 to 4 inches apart.
      B. The second major point concerning the topic is to place the bulbs in holes
          1. pointed side up.
          2. root side down.
      C. The third major point concerning the topic is to water the area thoroughly.

Once you have drawn up a short outline of the passage, answering the question becomes very easy. In this example, the correct answer is choice **c**. By scanning the outline, you can quickly see that the correct

order of steps is to dig a hole, then plant the bulb, and finally water the area thoroughly.

When you summarize information, you take a wordy passage and restate its ideas in a short sentence or two. Some questions on the MTEL will ask you to boil down a lengthy passage into a sentence, capturing its main ideas.

> Today's postal service is more efficient than ever. Mail that once took months to move by horse and foot now moves around the country in days or hours by truck, train, and plane. If your letter or package is urgent, the U.S. Postal Service offers Priority Mail and Express Mail services. Priority Mail is guaranteed to go anywhere in the United States in two days or less. Express Mail will get your package there overnight.

5. This paragraph best supports the statement that
   a. more people use the post office for urgent deliveries than any other delivery service.
   b. Express Mail is a good way to send urgent mail.
   c. Priority Mail usually takes two days or less.
   d. mail service today is more effective and dependable.

This question asks you to summarize the main idea of the passage, which is expressed in choice **d**. Remember that even though the details mentioned in other choices may be accurate, the best choice for this type of question will summarize the entire passage, and often touch on the *main idea*.

Graphs and charts are visual representations of facts and figures. Many types are commonly used, such as the pie chart, which presents a circle broken into sections that represent percentages of that circle (looking like a pie with slices cut out). Bar charts feature a series of vertical or horizontal bars of varying lengths, offering a visual demonstration of various numbers—some longer than others. Other types of charts and graphs include spreadsheets, flow charts, *x-y* axis charts, and so forth. The MTEL may present a chart or graph of any of these types and ask you to interpret the basic information that is represented.

6. Use this spreadsheet to answer the following question:

AVERAGE COST PER CUP	
Pete's Café	1.98
Carl's Coffeehouse	2.03
Cup-a-Joe	1.65
Java Express	2.01
Quick Coffee	1.69

Which business listed in the table above charges the least for a cup of coffee?
a. Carl's Coffeehouse
b. Cup-a-Joe
c. Java Express
d. Quick Coffee

The answer is choice **b**, the store called Cup-a-Joe. The first column in the spreadsheet lists the stores' names, and the second lists the cost per cup of coffee—as stated in the chart's title. In this case, you are looking for the smallest number, $1.65.

Sometimes you will be asked to do the reverse of the previous example, suggesting a possible graphic that presents given information in a passage. Here is an example.

Marco Polo was a famous traveler and adventurer who lived in the thirteenth century. Over a period of 24 years, he and his father and uncle traveled from Venice, passed across the Middle East into Asia, and continued all the way to the far eastern coast of China. They spent a good deal of time further exploring China, making their way from north to south as they crossed that vast continent and becoming fast friends with the nation's

emperor, Kublai Khan. Marco later wrote a book entitled *The Travels of Marco Polo*, which became a worldwide best-seller—in an age before the printing press, when books were copied by hand! The explorations of the Polo family inspired many other European adventurers, including Christopher Columbus, so we might safely conclude that Marco Polo played a role in Europe's discovery of North America.

7. Which of the following types of graphics could best be used to present information contained in this passage?
a. a timeline of the thirteenth century
b. a flowchart of the stages of a journey across Asia
c. a circle graph of countries visited by Marco Polo
d. a map of Europe, the Middle East, and Asia

The best answer is choice **d**, a map showing the areas discussed in the passage. The best way to determine this answer is to ask yourself what visual aids you would find helpful while reading the passage. You will quickly see that a map would be very helpful for getting a visual feel of the great distance covered by Marco Polo, while a timeline of thirteenth century events would not prove helpful at all, since the passage focuses only on Marco Polo's travels and does not address any other events of the thirteenth century.

Writer's Purpose and Point of View

The remaining three types of reading multiple-choice questions are intended to have you "read between the lines" of a given passage, forcing you to find answers that are not directly presented in the text. The first of these types will ask you to determine the *writer's purpose* and *point of view*. Specifically, the test questions are intended to assess your ability to:

- identify a writer's stated or implied purpose for writing
- identify the audience for a given piece of writing

- identify why a writer has included specific information or examples
- identify the likely response of an audience to a writer's choice of words or phrases
- interpret content, word choice, and phrasing to determine a writer's opinion or point of view

The writer's purpose refers to the reason that the author wrote the given passage, what he or she hoped to accomplish. For example, an author might want to convince the reader to hold a certain opinion, or might want to present a series of facts and statistics. Perhaps the author hopes to make the reader laugh, or to move the reader with sympathy for the conditions faced by the poor. Here is an example, Mark Twain's description of a coyote from his book *Roughing It*.

> He is always poor, out of luck and friendless. The meanest creatures despise him, and even the fleas would desert him for a [bicycle]. He is so spiritless and cowardly that even while his exposed teeth are pretending a threat, the rest of his face is apologizing for it. And he is so homely!—so scrawny, and ribby, and coarse-haired, and pitiful. When he sees you he lifts his lip and lets a flash of his teeth out, and then turns a little out of the course he was pursuing, depresses his head a bit, and strikes a long, soft-footed trot through the sage-brush, glancing over his shoulder at you, from time to time, till he is about out of easy pistol range, and then he stops and takes a deliberate survey of you; he will trot fifty yards and stop again—another fifty and stop again; and finally the gray of his gliding body blends with the gray of the sage-brush, and he disappears. All this is when you make no demonstration against him; but if you do, he develops a livelier interest in his journey, and instantly electrifies his heels and puts such a deal of real estate between himself and your weapon, that by the time you have raised the

hammer you see that you need a minié rifle, and by the time you have got him in line you need a rifled cannon, and by the time you have "drawn a bead" on him you see well enough that nothing but an unusually long-winded streak of lightning could reach him where he is now.

8. The author's purpose in this passage is to
   a. teach about coyotes.
   b. write a history of westward expansion in America.
   c. amuse his readers.
   d. urge his readers to protect endangered species.

The best answer is choice **c**, to amuse his readers. Twain is deliberately exaggerating the behavior of coyotes, and his extreme descriptions, such as the idea that fleas would abandon the coyote in exchange for a bicycle, are intended to raise a laugh. But Twain does not openly state that he wants his readers to laugh; it is up to you to recognize that fact through the tone and wording that he uses in the passage.

That process is similar when discerning an author's point of view or opinion on the given topic. When you read the newspaper or listen to news reports on television, for example, the reporter will generally not openly state his or her opinion on the events that are being described—but if you pay attention to the tone, word choices, details given (and not given), and so forth, you can frequently read between the lines to determine the reporter's opinion on the topic. The same skills are used in recognizing an author's point of view on the MTEL.

> The film *Lawrence of Arabia* may seem somewhat dated by modern special effects standards, but it remains a high-water mark in the annals of filmmaking. Since we're on the subject of CGI and other computer-generated special effects, *Lawrence* has practically none for

the simple reason that it was filmed using real people who really performed the action. The long, slow scenes of camels walking in the desert may seem dull to the modern animation-jaded viewer, but those willing to pay attention to the underlying themes will be well rewarded by what the movie is saying.

9. Which of the following statements best expresses the author's point of view in the passage?

   a. The author believes that *Lawrence of Arabia* is one of the best films ever made.

   b. The author feels that *Lawrence of Arabia* is outdated by modern standards.

   c. The author does not approve of modern computerized special effects.

   d. The author prefers films with lots of action, rather than slowly developed characterizations.

The best answer is choice **a**, that *Lawrence* is one of the best films ever made. The author does not come out and make that statement openly, but you can interpret his enthusiasm from the tone and wording of the passage. The author also states that the film is "a high-water mark in the annals of filmmaking," meaning that it set a high standard that other films have not surpassed. The author does mention modern special effects, but he does not make any value judgment on them, saying that they are good or bad—he merely states that *Lawrence of Arabia* did not use any CGI. Therefore, choice **c** is not the best answer.

Relationships among Ideas

Questions of this type are designed to assess your ability to

- identify cause-and-effect relationships.
- identify the order of events or steps described in written material.

- analyze relationships between similar ideas or ideas in opposition.
- draw conclusions from information stated or implied within a passage.

Frequently, you will be asked to read a passage that contains numerous details, facts, or figures, and you will be asked to show how those facts and figures relate to one another. Specifically, you might be called on to explain how details in a passage support the author's main point. Activities such as this require that you be able to understand the *relationships among ideas*, explaining how one bit of the passage interrelates with another bit.

This is a step beyond finding the main idea and supporting details that we discussed previously. You will be asked to do more than merely identify certain details from the passage; you will need to understand *why* those details were included and *what* they are intended to accomplish. Here is an example.

1. The school's homework policies need to be re-evaluated in light of our recent standing in the national testing averages. **2.** It is true that our students have gained more free time under our present policies, time that they can invest into other activities such as band and athletics. **3.** Nor can it safely be argued that testing scores would improve dramatically if we enforced excessive loads of unnecessary work just for the sake of adding to their study time. **4.** But we must also recognize that our present policies of light load homework are not helping the students gain the level of knowledge and skill required to excel on the national level. **5.** The fact is, higher scores can only come from more diligent effort—and that effort requires stricter policies and higher expectations, taking the risk of increasing what we demand of our students.

10. Which sentence in this passage best supports the author's assertion that "the school's homework policies need to be re-evaluated"?
  a. Sentence 2
  b. Sentence 3
  c. Sentence 4
  d. Sentence 5

The best choice in this question is **d**, sentence 5. Sentences 2 and 3 actually contradict the author's assertion, if taken out of context. Sentence 4 does reiterate the author's assertion, but it does not develop *why* his assertion is true or *what* the effects would be of increased homework. Only sentence 5 answers those *why* and *what* questions.

Critical Reasoning

The process of using critical reasoning is closely associated with the ability to determine an author's point of view, discussed previously. This type of question will ask you to

- identify the assumptions underlying a writer's argument.
- assess the relevance of facts, examples, or data to a writer's argument.
- distinguish between statements of fact and expressions of opinion.
- assess a writer's objectivity or bias.

We can break down this type of question into three categories: *evaluation, inference,* and *generalization.*

Evaluation

Evaluation questions ask you to evaluate the strengths and weaknesses of the argument presented in a passage. Evaluation questions will ask you to judge whether something is fact or opinion, or whether the evidence presented supports the message of the passage. Here are some examples of evaluation questions.

- In order to evaluate the validity of the author's claim regarding Jackson Pollock, it would be most helpful to know which of the following?
- Which of the following is NOT mentioned in the passage as a weakness in the new law?
- Which of the following numbered sentences of the passage expresses a fact rather than an opinion?

Inference

This type of question asks you to make an inference (draw a logical conclusion) based on the content of the passage. Inference questions will ask you to determine an author's underlying assumptions or attitude toward the subject of the passage. Here are some examples.

- Which of the following is an unstated assumption made by the author of the passage?
- It can be inferred from the passage that the art of Picasso and Matisse differ in all the following ways EXCEPT. . . .
- This passage suggests that Greek tragedies are still so powerful because. . . .
- The author would be least likely to agree with which of the following statements?

Generalization

Generalization questions require you to apply the ideas of a passage to new situations, recognize similar situations, and draw conclusions about the content of the passage.

- Which of the following conclusions can you make based on the passage?
- Given the information in the passage, what appeared to be an important post–World War II trend in the United States?

Following are some sample questions using *critical reasoning.*

The town council met Wednesday night to discuss the recent vandalism at the park. Police have stated that the vandalism is caused by several youths in town who are angry that the park closes at sunset. Several parents spoke out, however, to say that the problems are being caused by transient workers who have no place to sleep. The mayor disagreed, and suggested that the vandalism is being done by students from the rival high school in the next town.

Since the next Council meeting won't take place until the 3rd of next month, police have been instructed to increase security on the park at night. Town council members also asked the school board to implement stronger methods of policing at high school athletic events to ensure that students do not bring cans of spray paint or other tools of vandalism.

11. Which of the following statements provides the best evaluation of the author's objectivity in the passage?
  a. The emphasis on the police suggests that the author favors a strong disciplinary hand in the matter.
  b. The author has presented a straightforward, unbiased account of the town council meeting.
  c. The author presents a bias against the town council for their lack of decision making.
  d. The account is somewhat subjective, with a slight bias toward the outspoken parents.

This question asks you to assess the writer's objectivity or bias. The author has made an even-handed presentation of the facts of the meeting, giving equal representation to all sides of the argument. The absence of "loaded language," use of words or phrases that subtly manipulate the reader's opinion, underscores the absence of bias, so choice **b** is correct.

In 1440, a German named Johannes Gutenberg created a new invention that revolutionized Western society—the printing press. In modern times, most of us take printing for granted, being able to create printed documents with the push of a button and the click of a mouse, but 600 years ago no such technology existed. Books were produced by hand, people working long hours to write out each page using pens made from feathers. The closest thing to a printing press was the art of xylography, which involved engraving an entire page of text into a wooden block, which was then covered with ink and pressed against paper.

Gutenberg invented something called moveable type, which consisted of individual letters made of lead that could be placed together to form words and sentences. His press allowed a printer to set those lead letters together to produce an entire page of text, which was then inked and printed onto paper. Books could be reproduced on a large scale very quickly, which allowed printers to disseminate ideas around the world without much effort and expense.

12. Which of the following facts best supports the author's contention that the printing press "revolutionized Western society"?
  a. 600 years ago no such technology existed.
  b. The closest thing to a printing press was the art of xylography.
  c. Books allowed printers to disseminate ideas around the world without much effort and expense.
  d. In modern times, most of us take printing for granted, being able to create printed documents with the push of a button and the click of a mouse.

This question asks you to assess the relevance of facts, examples, or data to a writer's argument. It points to various pieces of information contained in the passage and asks you to determine which piece of information is critical to the author's basic argument: that the printing press revolutionized Western society. Each of the choices presented is included in the text, but only choice **c** explains *why* the printing press was revolutionary.

Writing Subtest

The writing subtest consists of several sections, divided as follows:

QUESTION TYPE	NUMBER	TIME	PERCENT OF SCORE
Multiple choice	35	–	25
Short answer	7	–	25
Open response: summary	1	20–30 minutes	15
Open response: composition	1	45–60 minutes	35

Multiple Choice

The multiple choice questions consist of the following types:

- establish and maintain a main idea
- sentence construction, grammar, and usage
- spelling, capitalization, and punctuation

Main Idea

The main idea of a passage is the same thing that we discussed at the beginning of this chapter. It consists of

- identifying effective thesis statements and topic sentences.
- identifying information, statements, or details that detract from the development of a main idea.

- identifying ineffective repetition and redundancy.
- reorganizing sentences or paragraphs to achieve a logical sequence of ideas.
- identifying effective transitions from one paragraph to another.

Construction, Grammar, and Usage

This type of multiple choice question asks you to identify common errors in grammar and word use. Specifically, these questions ask you to

- identify sentence fragments and run-on sentences (comma splices, fused sentences).
- identify verbs in the wrong tense or form, incorrect shifts in tense or person, lack of subject-verb agreement, and wrong or missing verb endings.
- identify vague pronoun references, lack of agreement between pronouns and antecedents, and incorrect shifts in pronoun person and number.
- identify misplaced or dangling modifiers.
- identify wrong or missing prepositions.
- identify incorrect use of relative pronouns (that, which, who).
- identify imprecise or inappropriate words and phrases.
- identify common errors in the use of homonyms (accept/except, affect/effect, its/it's, their/there/they're, to/too/two, weather/whether, who's/whose, your/you're).

Spelling, Capitalization, and Punctuation

These multiple choice questions ask you to

- identify common spelling errors.
- identify common errors in standard capitalization.
- identify missing commas after an introductory phrase or in a compound sentence.
- identify missing or misplaced apostrophes.

(1) The stories about King Arthur are an enduring legend, in Western literature. (2) Most people are familiar with the Round Table and famous characters such as Merlin, Sir Lancelot, Guinevere, and King Arthur himself. (3) The stories dates back to the Middle Ages, with Sir Thomas Malory's famous classic, *Le Morte D'Arthur* (*The Death of Arthur*). (4) The legend is so enjoyable that writers even today use it to create new works of fiction. (5) But many people are not aware that there was a real King Arthur, a real Merlin, and even a real castle of Camelot! (6) The actual details of these historical facts and personalities are very sketchy, but historical documents record a man named Arthur who led an army against Anglo-Saxon invasions during the sixth century. (7) A man named *Merlinus Ambrosius* was instrumental in establishing a lasting British independence, and he was probably the prototype of Merlin. (8) Perhaps someday archeology will unveil more history about this legendary topic.

13. Which change is needed in the passage to correct an error in subject-verb agreement?
  a. Sentence 1: change "are" to "is"
  b. Sentence 3: change "dates" to "date"
  c. Sentence 5: change "was" to "is"
  d. Sentence 7: change "establishing" to "establish"

14. What change is needed in the passage to correct an error in punctuation?
  a. Sentence 1: remove the comma after "legend"
  b. Sentence 4: insert a comma after "enjoyable"
  c. Sentence 6: remove the comma after "sketchy"
  d. Sentence 8: insert a comma after "legendary"

The answer to question 13 is choice **b**. The verb *dates* is singular, while the subject *stories* is plural, so it should read "the stories *date* back." The answer to question 14 is choice **a**, because the comma after *legend* interrupts a unified clause. The actual phrase is *a legend in Western literature*, but the comma sets off *Western literature* into its own clause, which is not correct.

Short Answer: Revising Sentences Containing Errors

This type of question is a composite of all the preceding multiple-choice types. In these questions, however, you must do more than simply identify an error and choose from a list of possible answers; you must actually write a sentence that *corrects* the error. You will be asked to:

- correct errors related to sentence construction.
- correct common errors related to grammar and usage.
- correct common errors related to spelling, capitalization, and punctuation.

15. The following sentence contains two errors (e.g., in construction, grammar, usage, spelling, capitalization, punctuation). Rewrite the text so that the errors are addressed and the original meaning is maintained.

Each of the choices on the menu are attractive, but I should first consider the affect on my health.

_____

_____

_____

The errors in the sentence for question 15 are subject-verb agreement and spelling. The word *each* is always singular, even if the subject seems to be plural—in this case, *each of the choices* may sound plural, but *each* makes it singular just the same, so it should be *is attractive. Affect* should be *effect*. Here is a possible sentence that you might have written to correct it: *Each of the choices on the menu is attractive, but I should consider the effect on my health.*

Here are some of the errors that you will likely encounter on this portion of the MTEL:

- sentence fragments
- run-on sentences
- verbs in the wrong tense or form
- lack of subject-verb agreement
- wrong or missing verb endings
- lack of agreement between pronouns and antecedents
- mixing a singular subject with plural references ("When a person eats, they should chew quietly.")
- misplaced or dangling modifiers
- wrong or missing prepositions
- incorrect use of relative pronouns (that, which, who)
- imprecise or inappropriate words and phrases
- common errors in the use of homonyms (accept/except, affect/effect, its/it's, their/there/they're, to/too/two, weather/whether, who's/whose, your/you're)
- common spelling errors
- common errors in standard capitalization
- missing commas after an introductory phrase and missing commas in a compound sentence
- missing or misplaced apostrophes

Open-Response Questions

The open-response portion of the MTEL is vastly different from the multiple choice section, because it asks you to write a short essay in your own words. This can seem very intimidating to most test takers, since most of us tend to be somewhat shy of committing ourselves in written form for a panel of experts

to critique. We tend to ask ourselves: "Do I know enough to expound at length on this topic?" "Can I express my ideas clearly and convincingly?" "Do I even *have* any ideas worth expressing?"

But do not let yourself be intimidated! Remember that thousands of others have taken this test and passed, so you can, too. It is also important to remember that the questions are not testing your knowledge on esoteric subjects; they are merely testing your ability to organize and express your thoughts—and anybody can do that.

The open response questions are of two types: one summary question and one composition question. The summary portion of the test will give you a passage to read and ask you to:

- Summarize the main ideas, key arguments, and significant supporting details presented in an extended passage.
- Demonstrate effective paragraph and sentence construction.
- Demonstrate command of standard English conventions of grammar and usage, without making common errors.
- Demonstrate command of standard English conventions of spelling, capitalization, and punctuation, without making common errors.

The composition question asks you to:

- Take a position on an issue, proposition, or statement related to education and defend that position.
- Maintain a central theme or main idea through the effective use of a thesis statement, topic sentences, and transitions.
- Develop a well-organized argument using sound reasoning and relevant supporting information and examples.
- Demonstrate effective paragraph and sentence structure and employ vocabulary appropriate for the audience and the purpose of the writing task.

- Use precise and appropriate words and phrases.
- Demonstrate command of standard English conventions of grammar and usage, without making common errors.
- Demonstrate command of standard English conventions of spelling, capitalization, and punctuation, without making common errors.

Open Response: Summary

The summary question will be similar to others in which you've been asked to read a passage and answer questions, but this time you will not be given multiple choices for your answer. Instead, you will write your own short answer, summarizing the information provided in the passage. The purpose of this exercise is primarily to determine whether you can express yourself clearly and effectively; it is not a test to determine your knowledge in any particular field.

The only way to improve a skill—any skill—is by practice, and writing is certainly no exception. If you feel weak in this area, pick up a copy of *501 Grammar and Writing Questions* or *501 Writing Prompts*, both from LearningExpress. The more you practice, the better you'll do—and effective writing is a skill that will benefit you for the rest of your life.

16. Use the following passage to prepare a summary of 100 to 150 words.

The coconut is an unusual food for many reasons. It is technically a seed, produced by the coconut palm tree, and as such is one of the largest edible seeds produced by any plant. Its unusual contents also make it unique in the seed world—the interior consists of both "meat" and "water." The meat is the white pith with which we are all familiar, as it is used extensively for cooking and flavorings; the coconut water is a white liquid that is very sweet and thirst-quenching.

Portuguese explorers gave the nut its name in the 15th century, referring to it as *coco*, meaning "ghost" in their language. The three dimples and the hairy texture reminded them of a ghost's face, and the tree has retained that name ever since.

The coconut has many varied uses. It is used to make margarine as well as various cooking oils, and these cooking oils are used by fast-food restaurants around the world to make such diet staples as French fries. The coconut fluid is a favorite drink in hot climates, providing a cool and refreshing beverage right off the tree. This water is also used by manufacturers of various sports drinks because of its isotonic electrolyte properties. Even the shell itself has many uses, including cattle food and fertilizer.

Yet the coconut is also useful in many ways that have nothing to do with food. Coconut oil is used for cosmetics and medicines, and can even be used in place of diesel fuel. Dried coconut shells are used in many countries as a tool, such as a buffer for shining wood floors. The shells are also used for shirt buttons, and are commonly found on Hawaiian clothing. They are even used for musical instruments and bird houses.

And all these are only some of the uses found for the coconut fruit. The coconut palm tree, which produces the nut, also produces countless useful items. It's no wonder that the coconut palm has been called "the tree of life."

_____

_____

_____

_____

_____

On the MTEL, your summary response will be assessed based on the following criteria:

- **Fidelity:** how accurately you summarize the information presented in the passage. A strong summary will state the passage's main idea clearly, and will summarize each of the supporting points.
- **Conciseness:** a measurement of how much you've written. An answer can actually be too concise, not long enough to incorporate the important information included in the passage. It can also be too long, of course, but that is a less common problem. When writing your summary,

do a quick word count and aim for approximately 125 words.

- **Expression:** how well you have communicated your information. A strong summary response will avoid vague generalizations and will stick closely to the facts and information contained in the passage.
- **Grammar and conventions:** good spelling, punctuation, and word use.

Have a friend or colleague read through your summary exercise and grade it in each of the above areas, using the following grading rubric. These are the same criteria that will be used to grade your MTEL test.

SCORE	ASSESSMENT CRITERIA
1	**Inadequately formed response:** fails to convey the main idea and details of the original passage; might consist of opinions or details not contained in the passage; not concise, either including or excluding all the information from the original; serious errors in sentence structure, word choice, usage, or mechanics
2	**Partially formed response:** addresses only some of the main points and supporting details of the original passage; includes or excludes too much of the original material; some errors in sentence structure, word choice, usage, or mechanics
3	**Adequately formed response:** conveys most of the main ideas and details of the original passage, and is generally accurate and clear; might be too long or too short, but in general conveys most of the information from the original; some minor errors in sentence structure, word choice, usage, or mechanics
4	**Well-formed response:** clearly and accurately conveys all the main ideas and details of the original passage; does not introduce opinions or details not contained in the original; response is concise while still adequately covering the material contained in the passage; sentence structure, word choice, usage, and mechanics are precise and effective

Sample Essay with Score of 1

Cocount unusual food for many reasons. Anyways, their a seed. And there chewy and dry, so I don't like them much. But I did like them when I was in Hawii once cause I climb a tree and pick one and threw it at my friend for fun. The outside was hairy and sort of creepy but my friend laughed. Some candy use coconuts for flavor and it's ok but it takes too long to eat cause it's all chewy and like that. They grow on trees.

Sample Essay with Score of 4

Coconuts are unusual in many ways. For one thing, they are actually seeds, not fruit, and are the largest edible seed in the world. Yet food is only one of the many ways that coconuts are used; they are also used to make cosmetics, medicines, and even diesel fuel. And of course, they are used for many types of food, including margarine, cooking oil, and even cattle food. One interesting fact is that it is called a "nut" when it's really a seed. The word "coconut" actually comes from the Portuguese word for "ghost" because early explorers could see a sort of ghostlike face in the shell of the coconut. It is also interesting that this "ghost nut" should grow on a tree that is referred to as "the tree of life." Yet the coconut palm tree produces so many good things that it fully deserves its nickname.

The first sample received a score of 1 for many reasons. First, there are numerous words that are misspelled, such as "coconut" and "Hawaii." Wrong forms of words (homonyms, words that sound the same) are used frequently, such as "their" instead of "they're." The writer also does not summarize anything in the passage about coconuts, but goes off on her own tangents concerning a trip to Hawaii. Finally, the writer expresses her own opinions about coconuts, which is not part of summarizing information in a passage.

The second sample received a score of 4 because it avoided common errors in spelling, punctuation, and grammar, and it effectively presented a good summary of the coconut passage. The writer avoided interjecting his own opinions, only discussing the facts contained in the passage. Furthermore, the writer discussed most of the major points contained in the passage—and this is the essence of a good summary. He did not get bogged down on the minor details and he managed to discuss the major points briefly.

Open Response: Composition

The final item on your MTEL will be a written composition of 300 to 600 words. You will be given a passage or two to read, then a specific assignment for how you should respond to the text. For example, you may be given two passages that present an opinion on a topic, one in favor of an idea and the other opposed. Your assignment would then be to write an essay taking a stand on that topic.

Your written composition will be evaluated on the following criteria:

- **appropriateness:** how well your essay addresses the assigned topic, and whether the language and style are suited to the audience and assignment
- **mechanical conventions:** good spelling, punctuation, and grammar
- **usage:** whether you use words correctly, and whether your wording is appropriate for the assignment
- **sentence structure:** how well you craft your sentences, avoiding awkward wording and common grammatical errors
- **focus and unity:** whether you have stuck closely to the assignment without wandering off-topic, and how fully you have expressed an opinion
- **organization:** the clarity of your writing, how clearly you have expressed your ideas, and whether your presentation of supporting details follows a logical sequence
- **development:** whether your response includes statements of appropriate depth, specificity, and accuracy

As you can see, the MTEL scorers are not interested in what opinion you express or how much you know about the assigned topic; they are interested solely in how well you express your thoughts in written form, and how well you stick to the assigned topic. Here is an example of a composition question.

COMPOSITION EXERCISE

Read the passages about academic discipline; then follow the instructions for writing your composition.

Strong discipline is necessary to the academic environment.	Strong discipline is not necessary to the academic environment.
Any grouping of children or adolescents will bring with it an inherent tendency toward chaos, and chaos is the enemy of education. A well-ordered classroom is vital to teaching any subject, and that order can only be attained through a consistent enforcement of rules and consequences. This does not mean that a teacher must inflict draconian punishments or arbitrary rules, but it does mean that an effective educator must be willing to establish meaningful policies and to enforce those policies on a consistent, unbiased basis. Where there is no discipline, there will be no learning.	People of all ages respond to kindness more readily than to fear, and fear is never conducive to education. The educator who afflicts students with arbitrary rules and regulations, enforcing those rules with anger and threats, will lose the trust of the students very quickly. And strong trust is what is vital to learning, not strong discipline. A teacher who treats his or her students with respect and generosity will achieve lasting results.

Your purpose is to write a persuasive composition, to be read by a classroom instructor, in which you take a position on whether discipline is or is not necessary to the academic environment. Be sure to defend your position with logical arguments and appropriate examples.

Have a friend or colleague read through your composition exercise and grade it in each of the previously stated areas, using the following grading rubric. The table shows the same criteria that will be used to grade your MTEL test.

SCORE	ASSESSMENT CRITERIA
1	**Inadequately formed response:** language and style not appropriate for audience; numerous errors in spelling, punctuation, or grammar; imprecise word choices; main idea of the response or passage is not clearly identified.
2	**Partially formed response:** partially addresses the assignment, but fails to fully summarize the passage; frequent errors in spelling, punctuation, or grammar; imprecise word choices; some attempt at summary is evident; poorly organized.
3	**Adequately formed response:** addresses the assignment adequately and generally demonstrates appropriate language and style for the audience; some errors in spelling, punctuation, or grammar; minor errors in word choices; main idea is reasonably clear, although there could be room for some improvement.
4	**Well-formed response:** addresses the assignment fully and demonstrates appropriate language and style for the audience throughout; demonstrates mastery of spelling, punctuation, and grammar; word choices are careful and precise; sentence structure is clear and free of errors; states a main idea and develops it fully; organized and supported well.

THE LEARNINGEXPRESS TEST PREPARATION SYSTEM

CHAPTER SUMMARY

Taking the MTEL can be tough. They demand a lot of preparation if you want to achieve top scores. Your future depends on your passing the exams. The LearningExpress Test Preparation System, developed exclusively for LearningExpress by leading test experts, gives you the discipline and attitude you need to be successful.

Taking the Massachusetts Tests for Educator Licensure is not easy, and neither is getting ready for them. Your future career as a teacher depends on your getting passing scores, but there are all sorts of pitfalls that can keep you from doing your best on your exams. Here are some of the obstacles that can stand in the way of your success:

- being unfamiliar with the format of the exams
- being paralyzed by test anxiety
- leaving your preparation until the last minute
- not preparing at all!
- not knowing vital test-taking skills: how to pace yourself through the exams, how to use the process of elimination, and when to guess
- not being in tip-top mental and physical shape

- messing up on test day by arriving late at the test site, having to work on an empty stomach, or shivering through the exam because the room is cold

What's the common denominator in all these test-taking pitfalls? One word: control. Who's in control, you or the exam?

Here's some good news: The LearningExpress Test Preparation System puts you in control. In nine easy-to-follow steps, you will learn everything you need to know to make sure that you are in charge of your preparation and your performance on the ex-

ams. Other test takers may let the test get the better of them; other test takers may be unprepared or out of shape, but not you. You will have taken all the steps you need to take to get high scores on the MTEL.

Here's how the LearningExpress Test Preparation System works: Nine easy steps lead you through everything you need to know and do to get ready to master your exams. Each of the steps includes both reading about the step and one or more activities. It's important that you do the activities along with the reading, or you won't be getting the full benefit of the system. Each step tells you approximately how much time that step will take you to complete.

Step 1: Get Information	50 minutes
Step 2: Conquer Test Anxiety	20 minutes
Step 3: Make a Plan	30 minutes
Step 4: Learn to Manage Your Time	10 minutes
Step 5: Learn to Use the Process of Elimination	20 minutes
Step 6: Know When to Guess	20 minutes
Step 7: Reach Your Peak Performance Zone	10 minutes
Step 8: Get Your Act Together	10 minutes
Step 9: Do It!	10 minutes
Total	**3 hours**

We estimate that working through the entire system will take you approximately three hours, though it's perfectly okay if you work faster or slower. If you take an afternoon or evening, you can work through the whole LearningExpress Test Preparation System in one sitting. Otherwise, you can break it up, and do just one or two steps a day for the next several days. It's up to you—remember, you are in control.

Step 1: Get Information

Time to complete: 50 minutes
Activity: Read Chapters 4–6

Knowledge is power. The first step in the LearningExpress Test Preparation System is finding out everything you can about the tests that comprise the MTEL. Once you have your information, the next steps in the LearningExpress Test Preparation System will show you what to do about it.

Part A: Straight Talk about the MTEL

Why do you have to take these rigorous exams, anyway? It's simply an attempt to be sure you have the knowledge and skills necessary for a teacher.

It's important for you to remember that your scores on the MTEL do not determine how smart you are or even whether you will make a good teacher. There are all kinds of things exams like this can't test, like whether you have the drive, determination, and dedication to be a teacher. Those kinds of things are hard to evaluate, while tests are easy to evaluate.

This is not to say that the exams aren't important! The knowledge tested on the exams is knowledge you will need to do your job. And your ability to enter the profession you've trained for depends on your passing these exams. And that's why you are here—using the LearningExpress Test Preparation System to achieve control over the exams.

Part B: What's on the Test

If you haven't already done so, stop here and read Chapters 4–6 of this book, which give you an overview of the exams. Then, go to the official MTEL website, www.mtel.nesinc.com, and read the most up-to-date information about your exams directly from the test developers.

Step 2: Conquer Test Anxiety

Time to complete: 20 minutes
Activity: Take the Test Anxiety Quiz

Having complete information about the exams is the first step in getting control of them. Next, you have to overcome one of the biggest obstacles to test success: test anxiety. Test anxiety not only impairs your performance on an exam, but also keeps you from preparing! In Step 2, you will learn stress management techniques that will help you succeed on your exams. Learn these strategies now, and practice them as you work through the exams in this book, so they will be second nature to you by exam day.

Combating Test Anxiety

The first thing you need to know is that a little test anxiety is a good thing. Everyone gets nervous before a big exam—and if that nervousness motivates you to prepare thoroughly, so much the better. It's said that Sir Laurence Olivier, one of the foremost British actors of the last century, felt ill before every performance. His stage fright didn't impair his performance; in fact, it probably gave him a little extra edge—just the kind of edge you need to do well, whether on a stage or in an examination room.

On page 36 is the Test Stress Quiz. Stop and answer the questions to find out whether your level of test anxiety is something you should worry about.

You only need to worry about test anxiety if it is extreme enough to impair your performance. The following questionnaire will provide a diagnosis of your level of test anxiety. In the blank before each statement, write the number that most accurately describes your experience.

0 = Never   1 = Once or twice   2 = Sometimes   3 = Often

_____ I have gotten so nervous before an exam that I simply put down the books and didn't study for it.

_____ I have experienced disabling physical symptoms such as vomiting and severe headaches because I was nervous about an exam.

_____ I have simply not showed up for an exam because I was afraid to take it.

_____ I have experienced dizziness and disorientation while taking an exam.

_____ I have had trouble filling in the little circles because my hands were shaking too hard.

_____ I have failed an exam because I was too nervous to complete it.

_____ **Total: Add up the numbers in the blanks.**

Your Test Stress Score

Here are the steps you should take, depending on your score:

- **Below 3:** Your level of test anxiety is nothing to worry about; it's probably just enough to give you that little extra edge.
- **Between 3 and 6:** Your test anxiety may be enough to impair your performance, and you should practice the stress management techniques listed in this section to try to bring your test anxiety down to manageable levels.
- **Above 6:** Your level of test anxiety is a serious concern. In addition to practicing the stress management techniques listed in this section, you may want to seek additional personal help. Call your community college and ask for the academic counselor. Tell the counselor that you have a level of test anxiety that sometimes keeps you from being able to take an exam. The counselor may be willing to help you or may suggest someone else you should talk to.

Stress Management before the Test

If you feel your level of anxiety getting the best of you in the weeks before a test, here is what you need to do to bring the level down again.

- **Get prepared.** There's nothing like knowing what to expect and being prepared for it to put you in control of test anxiety. That's why you are reading this book. Use it faithfully, and remind yourself that you are better prepared than most of the people taking the test.

- **Practice self-confidence.** A positive attitude is a great way to combat test anxiety. This is no time to be humble or shy. Stand in front of the mirror and say to your reflection, "I am prepared. I am full of self-confidence. I am going to ace this test. I know I can do it." Record it onto an MP3 player and play it back once a day. If you hear it often enough, you will believe it.

- **Fight negative messages.** Every time someone starts telling you how hard the exam is or how it's almost impossible to get a high score, start saying your self-confidence messages. Don't listen to the negative messages. Turn on your MP3 player and listen to your self-confidence messages.

- **Visualize.** Imagine yourself reporting for duty on your first day as a teacher or in your teacher training program. Visualizing success can help make it happen—and it reminds you of why you are doing all this work in preparing for the exam.
- **Exercise.** Physical activity helps calm your body down and focus your mind. Besides, being in good physical shape can actually help you do well on the exam. Go for a run, lift weights, go swimming—and do it regularly.

Stress Management on Test Day

There are several ways you can bring down your level of test anxiety on test day. They will work best if you practice them in the weeks before the test, so you know which ones work best for you.

- **Practice deep breathing.** Take a deep breath while you count to five. Hold it for a count of one, then let it out on a count of five. Repeat several times.
- **Move your body.** Try rolling your head in a circle. Rotate your shoulders. Shake your hands from the wrist. Many people find these movements very relaxing.
- **Visualize again.** Think of the place where you are most relaxed: lying on the beach in the sun, walking through the park, or whatever. Now, close your eyes and imagine you are actually there. If you practice in advance, you will find that you only need a few seconds of this exercise to experience a significant increase in your sense of well-being.

When anxiety threatens to overwhelm you right there during the exam, there are still things you can do to manage the stress level.

- **Repeat your self-confidence messages.** You should have them memorized by now. Say them quietly to yourself, and believe them!
- **Visualize one more time.** This time, visualize yourself moving smoothly and quickly through the test answering every question right and finishing just before time is up. Like most visualization techniques, this one works best if you have practiced it ahead of time.
- **Find an easy question.** Find an easy question, and answer it. Getting even one question finished gets you into the test-taking groove.
- **Take a mental break.** Everyone loses concentration once in a while during a long test. It's normal, so you shouldn't worry about it. Instead, accept what has happened. Say to yourself, "Hey, I lost it there for a minute. My brain is taking a break." Put down your pencil, close your eyes, and do some deep breathing for a few seconds. Then you will be ready to go back to work.

Try these techniques ahead of time, and see if they work for you.

Step 3: Make a Plan

Time to complete: 30 minutes
Activity: Construct a study plan

Maybe the most important thing you can do to get control of yourself and your exam is to make a study plan. Too many people fail to prepare simply because they fail to plan. Spending hours on the day before the exam poring over sample test questions not only raises your level of test anxiety, it also is simply no substitute for careful preparation and practice over time.

Don't fall into the cram trap. Take control of your preparation time by mapping out a study schedule. On the following pages are two sample schedules, based on the amount of time you have before you take your exams. If you are the kind of person who needs deadlines and assignments to motivate you for a project, here they are. If you are the kind of person who doesn't like to follow other people's plans, you can use the suggested schedules here to construct your own.

Even more important than making a plan is making a commitment. You have to set aside some time every day for study and practice. Try for at least 20 minutes a day. Twenty minutes daily will do you much more good than two hours on Saturday.

Don't put off your study until the day before an exam. Start now. A few minutes a day, with half an hour or more on weekends, can make a big difference in your score.

Schedule A: The 30-Day Plan

If you have at least a month before you take the Communication and Literacy Skills Test, you have plenty of time to prepare—as long as you don't waste it! If you have less than a month, turn to Schedule B.

TIME	PREPARATION
Days 1–4	Skim over any study materials you may have. Make a note of (1) areas you expect to be emphasized on the exam, and (2) areas you don't feel confident in. On Day 4, concentrate on those areas.
Day 5	Take the diagnostic test in Chapter 6.
Day 6	Score the practice test. Identify two areas that you will concentrate your studies on.
Days 7–10	Study one of the areas you identified as your weak point. Don't forget, for preparation there is a Reading Skills Review in Chapter 7, and a Writing Skills Review in Chapter 8. Review one of these chapters in detail to improve your score on the next practice test.
Days 11–14	Study the other area you identified as your weak point.
Day 15	Take the first practice test in Chapter 9.
Day 16	Score the first practice test. Identify another area to concentrate your studies on.
Days 17–21	Study the one area you identified for review.
Day 22	Take the second practice extestam in Chapter 10.
Day 23	Score the second practice exam. Identify another area to concentrate on and note your progress in all areas from the diagnostic test.
Days 24–25	Study the final area you identified for review.
Days 26–29	Take an overview of all your study materials, consolidating your strengths and improving on your weaknesses.
Day before the exam	Relax. Do something unrelated to the exam and go to bed at a reasonable hour.

Schedule B: The Ten-Day Plan

If you have two weeks or less before you take the Communication and Literacy Skills Test, use this ten-day schedule to help you make the most of your time.

TIME	PREPARATION
Day 1	Take the diagnostic exam in this book and score it using the answer key at the end. Note which topics you need to review most.
Day 2	Review one area that gave you trouble on the diagnostic test. Use the Reading Skills Review in Chapter 7, and the Writing Skills Review in Chapter 8. Review one of these chapters in detail to improve your score on the next practice test.
Day 3	Review another area that gave you trouble on your diagnostic test.
Day 4	Take the first practice test in Chapter 9 and score it.
Day 5	If your score on the first practice test doesn't show improvement on the two areas you studied, review them. If you did improve in those areas, choose a new weak area to study today.
Day 6	Take the second practice test in Chapter 10. Note whether you improved in the third weak area, and what other areas you should concentrate your studies on.
Days 7–8	Continue to use the review chapters to improve some skills and reinforce others.
Day 9	Use your last study days to brush up on any areas that are still giving you trouble. Use the resources in this book and from your classes.
Day before the exam	Relax. Do something unrelated to the exam and go to bed at a reasonable hour.

Step 4: Learn to Manage Your Time

Time to complete: 10 minutes to read, many hours of practice!

Activity: Practice these strategies as you take the sample tests in this book

Steps 4, 5, and 6 of the LearningExpress Test Preparation System put you in charge of your exam by showing you test-taking strategies that work. Practice these strategies as you take the sample tests in this book, and then you will be ready to use them on test day.

First, you will take control of your time on the exams. It's a terrible feeling to know there are only five minutes left when you are only three-quarters of the way through a test. Here are some tips to keep that from happening to you.

- **Follow directions.** Read the directions carefully and ask questions before the exam begins if there's anything you don't understand.
- **Pace yourself.** Use your watch or the clock in the testing room to keep track of the time you have left.
- **Keep moving.** Don't waste time on one question. If you don't know the answer, skip the question and move on. You can always go back to it later.
- **Don't rush.** Although you should keep moving, rushing won't help. Try to keep calm and work methodically and quickly.

Step 5: Learn to Use the Process of Elimination

Time to complete: 20 minutes
Activity: Complete the worksheet on
Using the Process of Elimination

After time management, your next most important tool for taking control of your exam is using the process of elimination wisely. It's standard test-taking wisdom that you should always read all the answer choices before choosing your answer. This helps you find the right answer by eliminating wrong answer choices. And, sure enough, that standard wisdom applies to your exam, too.

You should always use the process of elimination on tough questions, even if the right answer jumps out at you. Sometimes the answer that jumps out isn't right after all. You should always proceed through the choices in order. You can start with choice **a** and eliminate any choices that are clearly incorrect.

If you are taking the test on paper, like the practice exams in this book, it's good to have a system for marking good, bad, and maybe answers. We're recommending this one:

X = bad
✔ = good
? = maybe

If you don't like these marks, devise your own system. Just make sure you do it long before test day—while you're working through the practice exams in this book—so you won't have to worry about it just before the exam.

Even when you think you are absolutely clueless about a question, you can often use the process of elimination to get rid of one answer choice. If so, you are better prepared to make an educated guess, as you will see in Step 6. More often, the process of elimination allows you to get down to only two possibly right answers. Then you are in a strong position to guess. And sometimes, even though you don't know the right answer, you find it simply by getting rid of the wrong ones.

Try using your powers of elimination on the questions in the worksheet Using the Process of Elimination on page 41–42. The questions aren't about teaching; they're just designed to show you how the process of elimination works. The answer explanations for this worksheet show one possible way you might use the process to arrive at the right answer.

The process of elimination is your tool for the next step, which is knowing when to guess.

Use the process of elimination to answer the following questions.

1. Ilsa is as old as Meghan will be in five years. The difference between Ed's age and Meghan's age is twice the difference between Ilsa's age and Meghan's age. Ed is 29.

How old is Ilsa?

a. 4
b. 10
c. 19
d. 24

2. "All drivers of commercial vehicles must carry a valid commercial driver's license whenever operating a commercial vehicle."

According to this sentence, which of the following people need NOT carry a commercial driver's license?

a. a truck driver idling his engine while waiting to be directed to a loading dock
b. a bus operator backing her bus out of the way of another bus in the bus lot
c. a taxi driver driving his personal car to the grocery store
d. a limousine driver taking the limousine to her home after dropping off her last passenger of the evening

3. Smoking tobacco has been linked to

a. increased risk of stroke and heart attack.
b. all forms of respiratory disease.
c. increasing mortality rates over the past ten years.
d. juvenile delinquency.

4. Which of the following words is spelled correctly?

a. incorrigible
b. outragous
c. domestickated
d. understandible

Answers

Here are the answers, as well as some suggestions as to how you might have used the process of elimination to find them.

1. d. You should have eliminated choice **a** right off the bat. Ilsa can't be four years old if Meghan is going to be Ilsa's age in five years. The best way to eliminate other answer choices is to try plugging them in to the information given in the problem. For instance, for choice **b**, if Ilsa is 10, then Meghan must be 5. The difference between their ages is 5. The difference between Ed's age, 29, and Meghan's age, 5, is 24. Is 24 two times 5? No. Then choice **b** is wrong.

You could eliminate choice **c** in the same way and be left with choice **d**.

2. c. Note the word NOT in the question, and go through the answers one by one. Is the truck driver in choice **a**, "operating a commercial vehicle"? Yes, idling counts as "operating," so he needs to have a commercial driver's license. Likewise, the bus operator in choice **b** is operating a commercial vehicle; the question doesn't say the operator has to be on the street. The limo driver in choice **d** is operating a passenger in it. However, the driver in choice **c** is *not* operating a commercial vehicle, but his own private car.

3. a. You could eliminate choice **b** simply because of the presence of the word *all*. Such absolutes hardly ever appear in correct answer choices. Choice **c** looks attractive until you think a little about what you know—aren't *fewer* people smoking these days, rather than more? So how could smoking be responsible for a higher mortality rate? (If you didn't know that *mortality* rate means the rate at which people die, you might keep this choice as a possibility, but you would still be able to eliminate two answers and have only two to choose from.) And choice **d** is *plain silly*, so you could eliminate that one, too. You are left with the correct choice, **a**.

4. a. How you used the process of elimination here depends on which words you recognized as being spelled incorrectly. If you knew that the correct spellings were *outrageous, domesticated,* and *understandable,* then you were home free. You probably knew that at least one of those words was wrong!

Step 6: Know When to Guess

Time to complete: 20 minutes
Activity: Complete the worksheet on Your Guessing Ability

Armed with the process of elimination, you are ready to take control of one of the big questions in test taking: Should I guess? The first and main answer is: Yes. Some exams have what's called a "guessing penalty," in which a fraction of your wrong answers is subtracted from your right answers, but the MTEL does NOT work like that. The number of questions you answer correctly yields your raw score. So you have nothing to lose and everything to gain by guessing.

The following are ten really hard questions. You are not supposed to know the answers. Rather, this is an assessment of your ability to guess when you don't have a clue. Read each question carefully, as if you were expected to answer it. If you have any knowledge of the subject, use that knowledge to help you eliminate wrong answer choices.

1. September 7 is Independence Day in
   a. India.
   b. Costa Rica.
   c. Brazil.
   d. Australia.

2. Which of the following is the formula for determining the momentum of an object?
   a. $p = MV$
   b. $F = ma$
   c. $P = IV$
   d. $E = mc^2$

3. Because of the expansion of the universe, the stars and other celestial bodies are all moving away from each other. This phenomenon is known as
   a. Newton's first law.
   b. the big bang.
   c. gravitational collapse.
   d. Hubble flow.

4. American author Gertrude Stein was born in
   a. 1713.
   b. 1830.
   c. 1874.
   d. 1901.

5. Which of the following is NOT one of the Five Classics attributed to Confucius?
   a. *I Ching*
   b. *Book of Holiness*
   c. *Spring and Autumn Annals*
   d. *Book of History*

6. The religious and philosophical doctrine that holds that the universe is constantly in a struggle between good and evil is known as
   a. Pelagianism.
   b. Manichaeanism.
   c. neo-Hegelianism.
   d. Epicureanism.

7. The third Chief Justice of the U.S. Supreme Court was
   a. John Blair.
   b. William Cushing.
   c. James Wilson.
   d. John Jay.

8. Which of the following is the poisonous portion of a daffodil?
   a. the bulb
   b. the leaves
   c. the stem
   d. the flowers

9. The winner of the Masters golf tournament in 1953 was
   a. Sam Snead.
   b. Cary Middlecoff.
   c. Arnold Palmer.
   d. Ben Hogan.

10. The state with the highest per capita personal income in 1980 was
   a. Alaska.
   b. Connecticut.
   c. New York.
   d. Texas.

Answers

Check your answers against the following correct answers.

1. c.
2. a.
3. d.
4. c.
5. b.
6. b.
7. b.
8. a.
9. d.
10. a.

How Did You Do?

You may have simply gotten lucky and actually known the answer to one or two questions. In addition, your guessing was probably more successful if you were able to use the process of elimination on any of the questions. Maybe you didn't know who the third Chief Justice was (question 7), but you knew that John Jay was the first. In that case, you would have eliminated choice **d** and, therefore, improved your odds of guessing right from one in four to one in three.

According to probability, you should get two-and-a-half answers correct, so getting either two or three right would be average. If you got four or more right, you may be a really terrific guesser. If you got one or none right, you may be a really bad guesser.

Keep in mind, though, that this is only a small sample. You should continue to keep track of your guessing ability as you work through the sample questions in this book. Circle the numbers of questions you guess on as you make your guess; or, if you don't have time while you take the practice tests, go back afterward and try to remember which questions you guessed at.

Remember, on a test with four answer choices, your chance of guessing correctly is one in four. So keep a separate "guessing" score for each exam. How many questions did you guess on? How many did you get right? If the number you got right is at least one-fourth of the number of questions you guessed on, you are at least an average guesser—maybe better—and you should always go ahead and guess on the real exam. If the number you got right is significantly lower than one-fourth of the number you guessed on, you would be safe in guessing anyway, but maybe you would feel more comfortable if you guessed only selectively, when you can eliminate a wrong answer or at least have a good feeling about one of the answer choices.

Remember, even if you are a play-it-safe person with lousy intuition, you are still safe guessing every time.

Step 7: Reach Your Peak Performance Zone

Time to complete: 10 minutes to read; weeks to complete!
Activity: Complete the Physical Preparation Checklist

To get ready for a challenge like a big exam, you have to take control of your physical, as well as your mental, state. Exercise, proper diet, and rest will ensure that your body works with, rather than against, your mind on test day, as well as during your preparation.

Exercise

If you don't already have a regular exercise program going, the time during which you are preparing for an exam is actually an excellent time to start one. And if you are already keeping fit—or trying to get that way—don't let the pressure of preparing for an exam fool you into quitting now. Exercise helps reduce stress by pumping wonderful good-feeling hormones called endorphins into your system. It also increases the oxygen supply throughout your body, including your brain, so you will be at peak performance on test day.

A half hour of vigorous activity—enough to raise a sweat—every day should be your aim. If you are really pressed for time, every other day is Okay. Choose an activity you like and get out there and do it. Jogging with a friend always makes the time go faster, or take a radio.

But don't overdo it. You don't want to exhaust yourself. Moderation is the key.

Diet

First of all, cut out the junk. Go easy on caffeine and nicotine, and eliminate alcohol and any other drugs from your system at least two weeks before the exam.

What your body needs for peak performance is simply a balanced diet. Eat plenty of fruits and vegetables, along with protein and carbohydrates. Foods that are high in lecithin (an amino acid), such as fish and beans, are especially good "brain foods."

The night before the exam, you might "carbo-load" the way athletes do before a contest. Eat a big plate of spaghetti, rice and beans, or whatever your favorite carbohydrate is.

Rest

You probably know how much sleep you need every night to be at your best, even if you don't always get it. Make sure you do get that much sleep, though, for at least a week before the exam. Moderation is important here, too. Extra sleep will just make you groggy.

If you are not a morning person and your exam will be given in the morning, you should reset your internal clock so that your body doesn't think you are taking an exam at 3:00 A.M. You have to start this process well before the exam. The way it works is to get up half an hour earlier each morning, and then go to bed half an hour earlier that night. Don't try it the other way around; you will just toss and turn if you go to bed early without having gotten up early. The next morning, get up another half an hour earlier, and so on. How long you will have to do this depends on how late you are used to getting up. Use the Physical Preparation Checklist on the next page to make sure you are in top form.

Step 8: Get Your Act Together

Time to complete: 10 minutes to read; time to complete will vary
Activity: Complete the Final Preparations worksheet

You are in control of your mind and body; you are in charge of test anxiety, your preparation, and your test-taking strategies. Now it's time to take charge of external factors, like the testing site and the materials you need to take the exam.

Find Out Where the Exam Is and Make a Trial Run

Do you know how to get to the testing site? Do you know how long it will take to get there? If not, make a trial run, preferably on the same day of the week at the same time of day. Make note on the Final Preparations worksheet of the amount of time it will take you to get to the exam site. Plan on arriving 30 to 45 minutes early so you can get the lay of the land, use the bathroom, and calm down. Then figure out how early you will have to get up that morning, and make

PHYSICAL PREPARATION CHECKLIST

For the week before the exam, write down what physical exercise you engaged in and for how long and what you ate for each meal. Remember, you are trying for at least half an hour of exercise every other day (preferably every day) and a balanced diet that's light on junk food.

Exam minus 7 days

Exercise: _____ for _____ minutes
Breakfast: _____
Lunch: _____
Dinner: _____
Snacks: _____

Exam minus 6 days

Exercise: _____ for _____ minutes
Breakfast: _____
Lunch: _____
Dinner: _____
Snacks: _____

Exam minus 5 days

Exercise: _____ for _____ minutes
Breakfast: _____
Lunch: _____
Dinner: _____
Snacks: _____

Exam minus 4 days

Exercise: _____ for _____ minutes
Breakfast: _____
Lunch: _____
Dinner: _____
Snacks: _____

Exam minus 3 days

Exercise: _____ for _____ minutes
Breakfast: _____
Lunch: _____
Dinner: _____
Snacks: _____

Exam minus 2 days

Exercise: _____ for _____ minutes
Breakfast: _____
Lunch: _____
Dinner: _____
Snacks: _____

Exam minus 1 day

Exercise: _____ for _____ minutes
Breakfast: _____
Lunch: _____
Dinner: _____
Snacks: _____

---

sure you get up that early every day for a week before the exam.

Gather Your Materials

The night before the exam, lay out the clothes you will wear and the materials you have to bring with you to the exam. Plan on dressing in layers; you won't have any control over the temperature of the examination room. Have a sweater or jacket you can take off if it's warm. Use the checklist on the Final Preparations worksheet to help you pull together what you will need.

Don't Skip Breakfast

Even if you don't usually eat breakfast, do so on exam morning. A cup of coffee doesn't count. Don't eat doughnuts or other sweet foods, either. A sugar high will leave you with a sugar low in the middle of the exam. A mix of protein and carbohydrates is best: Cereal with milk or eggs with toast will do your body a world of good.

FINAL PREPARATIONS

Getting to the Exam Site

Location of exam site: _____

Date: _____

Departure time: _____

Do I know how to get to the exam site?   Yes _____   No _____   (If no, make a trial run.)

Time it will take to get to exam site _____

Things to Lay Out the Night Before

Clothes I will wear   _____

Sweater/jacket   _____

Watch   _____

Photo ID   _____

Four #2 pencils   _____

Step 9: Do It!

**Time to complete: 10 minutes, plus test-taking time
Activity: Ace the Literacy and Communication
    Skills Test!**

Fast forward to exam day. You are ready. You made a study plan and followed through. You practiced your test-taking strategies while working through this book. You are in control of your physical, mental, and emotional state. You know when and where to show up and what to bring with you. In other words, you are better prepared than most of the other people taking the exam. You are psyched.

Just one more thing. When you have finished the exam, you will have earned a reward. Plan a celebration. Call up your friends and plan a party, or have a nice dinner for two—whatever your heart desires. Give yourself something to look forward to.

And then do it. Go into the exam, full of confidence, armed with test-taking strategies you have practiced until they're second nature. You are in control of yourself, your environment, and your performance on the exam. You are ready to succeed. So do it. Go in there and ace the exam. And look forward to your future career as a teacher!

COMMUNICATION AND LITERACY SKILLS DIAGNOSTIC TEST

CHAPTER SUMMARY
This is the first of the three practice Massachusetts Tests for Educator Licensure (MTEL) Communication and Literacy Skills Tests in this book based on the format and content of the official MTEL. The Communication and Literacy Skills portion of the MTEL consists of two subtests: reading and writing. Both sections contain multiple-choice items testing various skills. The writing section also contains short-answer items and two open-response exercises.

This diagnostic pretest will help you gauge your strengths and weaknesses on the Communication and Literacy Skills Test. It will also help you focus your preparation and review. There will be a four-hour time limit when you the take the official exam. As you take this pretest, however, do not worry too much about timing. Just take the test in a relaxed manner to find out which areas you are skilled in and which areas will need extra work.

You'll find an answer fill-in sheet for the multiple-choice questions on the following page. You will be writing your answers to the short-answer items on blank lines provided following each question. Lined pages are provided for your answers to the open-response questions following each such item. After you finish taking both subtests, you should review the answer explanations found beginning on page 83.

Reading Subtest

	a	b	c	d
1.	a	b	c	d
2.	a	b	c	d
3.	a	b	c	d
4.	a	b	c	d
5.	a	b	c	d
6.	a	b	c	d
7.	a	b	c	d
8.	a	b	c	d
9.	a	b	c	d
10.	a	b	c	d
11.	a	b	c	d
12.	a	b	c	d
13.	a	b	c	d
14.	a	b	c	d

	a	b	c	d
15.	a	b	c	d
16.	a	b	c	d
17.	a	b	c	d
18.	a	b	c	d
19.	a	b	c	d
20.	a	b	c	d
21.	a	b	c	d
22.	a	b	c	d
23.	a	b	c	d
24.	a	b	c	d
25.	a	b	c	d
26.	a	b	c	d
27.	a	b	c	d
28.	a	b	c	d

	a	b	c	d
29.	a	b	c	d
30.	a	b	c	d
31.	a	b	c	d
32.	a	b	c	d
33.	a	b	c	d
34.	a	b	c	d
35.	a	b	c	d
36.	a	b	c	d
37.	a	b	c	d
38.	a	b	c	d
39.	a	b	c	d
40.	a	b	c	d
41.	a	b	c	d
42.	a	b	c	d

Writing Subtest

	a	b	c	d
1.	a	b	c	d
2.	a	b	c	d
3.	a	b	c	d
4.	a	b	c	d
5.	a	b	c	d
6.	a	b	c	d
7.	a	b	c	d
8.	a	b	c	d
9.	a	b	c	d
10.	a	b	c	d
11.	a	b	c	d
12.	a	b	c	d

	a	b	c	d
13.	a	b	c	d
14.	a	b	c	d
15.	a	b	c	d
16.	a	b	c	d
17.	a	b	c	d
18.	a	b	c	d
19.	a	b	c	d
20.	a	b	c	d
21.	a	b	c	d
22.	a	b	c	d
23.	a	b	c	d
24.	a	b	c	d

	a	b	c	d
25.	a	b	c	d
26.	a	b	c	d
27.	a	b	c	d
28.	a	b	c	d
29.	a	b	c	d
30.	a	b	c	d
31.	a	b	c	d
32.	a	b	c	d
33.	a	b	c	d
34.	a	b	c	d
35.	a	b	c	d

Reading Subtest

Directions: Read each of the following selections and then answer the corresponding questions. Each question has only one correct answer.

> **Read the passage, then answer the six questions that follow.**

Milton Hershey

1 Milton Hershey was born near the small village of Derry Church, Pennsylvania, in 1857. It was a humble beginning that did not foretell his later popularity. Milton only attended school through the fourth grade; at that point, he was apprenticed to a printer in a nearby town. Fortunately for all chocolate lovers, Milton did not excel as a printer. After a while, he left the printing business and was apprenticed to a Lancaster, Pennsylvania candy maker. It was apparent he had found his calling in life, and at the age of 18, he opened his own candy store in Philadelphia. In spite of his talents as a candy maker, the shop failed after six years.

2 It may come as a surprise to current Milton Hershey fans, but his first candy success came with the manufacture of caramel. After the failure of his Philadelphia store, Milton headed for Denver, where he learned the art of making caramels. There he took a job with a local manufacturer who made the finest caramels in the United States by using fresh milk in his recipe. Milton saw that this made the caramels especially tasty. After a time in Denver, Milton once again attempted to open his own candy-making businesses, in Chicago, New Orleans, and New York City. Finally, in 1886, he went to Lancaster, Pennsylvania, where he raised the money necessary to try again. This company—the Lancaster Caramel Company—established Milton's reputation as a master candy maker.

3 In 1893, Milton attended the Chicago International Exposition, where he saw a display of German chocolate-making implements. Captivated by the equipment, he purchased it for his Lancaster candy factory and began producing chocolate, which he used for coating his caramels. By the next year, production had grown to include cocoa, sweet chocolate, and baking chocolate. The Hershey Chocolate company was born in 1894 as a <u>subsidiary</u> of the Lancaster Caramel Company. Six years later, Milton sold the caramel company, but retained the rights, and the equipment, to make chocolate. He believed that a large market of chocolate consumers was waiting for someone to produce reasonably priced candy. He was right.

4 Milton Hershey returned to the village where he had been born, in the heart of dairy country, and opened his chocolate manufacturing plant. With access to all the fresh milk he needed, he began producing the finest milk chocolate. The plant that opened in a small Pennsylvania village in 1905 is today the largest chocolate factory in the world. The confections created at this facility are favorites around the world.

5 The area where the factory is located is now known as Hershey, Pennsylvania. Within the first decades of its existence, the town of Hershey thrived, as did the chocolate business. A bank, a school, churches, a department store, even a park and a trolley system all appeared in short order; the town soon even had a zoo. Today, a visit to the area reveals the Hershey Medical Center, Milton Hershey School, and Hershey's Chocolate World—a theme park where visitors are greeted by a giant Reese's Peanut Butter Cup. All these things—and a huge number of

happy chocolate lovers—were made possible because a caramel maker visited the Chicago Exposition of 1893!

_____

1. In which of the following statements from Paragraph 2 of the passage does the author most clearly express an opinion rather than a fact?
   a. It may come as a surprise to current Milton Hershey fans, but his first candy success came with the manufacture of caramel.
   b. After the failure of his Philadelphia store, Milton headed for Denver, where he learned the art of making caramels.
   c. There he took a job with a local manufacturer who made the finest caramels in the United States by using fresh milk in his recipe.
   d. After a time in Denver, Milton once again attempted to open his own candy-making businesses, in Chicago, New Orleans, and New York City.

2. Information presented in the passage supports which of the following conclusions?
   a. Chocolate is extremely popular in every single country in the world.
   b. Reese's Peanut Butter Cups are manufactured by the Hershey Chocolate Company.
   c. Chocolate had never been manufactured in the United States before Milton Hershey did it.
   d. Hershey makes more money from Hershey's Chocolate World than from the sale of chocolate.

3. Which of the following words is closest in meaning to subsidiary as it is used in the third paragraph of the passage?
   a. a company owned entirely by one person
   b. a company founded to support another company
   c. a company that is not incorporated
   d. a company controlled by another company

4. The author's main purpose in this passage is to
   a. recount the founding of the Hershey Chocolate Company.
   b. describe the process of manufacturing chocolate.
   c. compare the popularity of chocolate to other candies.
   d. explain how apprentices find and perform their jobs.

5. According to information presented in the passage, Milton Hershey sold his caramel company in
   a. 1894.
   b. 1900.
   c. 1904.
   d. 1905.

6. Information presented in the passage supports which of the following conclusions?
   a. The exposition in Chicago is held once every three years.
   b. The theme of the exposition of 1893 was "Food from Around the World."
   c. The exposition contained displays from a variety of countries.
   d. The site of the exposition is now a branch of the Hershey Chocolate Company.

Read the passage, then answer the six questions that follow.

Angioplasty

1 Arteries of the heart blocked by plaque can reduce the flow of blood to the heart, possibly resulting in heart attack or death. Plaque is actually fat and cholesterol that accumulates on the inside of the arteries. The arteries of the heart are small and can be blocked by such accumulations. There is a medical procedure that creates more space in the blocked artery by inserting and inflating a tiny balloon into the blood vessel. It is called coronary balloon angioplasty. *Angioplasty* means "blood vessel repair." When the balloon is inflated, it compresses the plaque against the wall of the artery, creating more space and improving the flow of blood.

2 Many doctors choose this technique, because it is less <u>invasive</u> than bypass surgery. Yes, both involve entering the body cavity, but in bypass surgery the chest must be opened, the ribs must be cut, and the section of diseased artery must be removed and replaced. To replace it, the patient's body is opened, once again, to acquire a healthy section of artery. Usually, this blood vessel is removed from an artery located in the calf of the leg. This means the patient now has two painful incisions that must heal at the same time. There is far more risk in such bypass surgery than in angioplasty, which involves threading a thin tube, called a catheter, into the circulatory system and working it into the damaged artery.

3 Angioplasty may take between 30 minutes and 3 hours to complete. It begins with a distinctive dye that is injected into the bloodstream. A thin catheter is then inserted into the femoral artery of the leg, near the groin. The doctor monitors the path of the dye using X-rays. He or she moves the tube through the heart and into the plaque-filled artery. He or she inflates the balloon, creating more space, deflates the balloon, and removes the tube. It is important to note that the plaque has not been removed; it has just been compressed against the sides of the artery. Sometimes, a *stent* may be implanted, a tiny tube of stainless steel that is expandable when necessary. Its function is to keep the artery open.

4 There is good news and there is bad news. The good news is that the statistics compiled are superb. Ninety percent of all angioplasty procedures are successful. The risk of dying during an operation of this type is less than 2%. The risk of heart attack is also small: 3 to 5%. Yet heart surgeons do not take any risk lightly; therefore, a team of surgeons stands ready to perform bypass surgery if needed. The length of hospitalization is only three days. The bad news is twofold. First, this procedure treats the condition but does not eradicate the cause. In 20% of the cases, there is a recurrence of plaque. Second, angioplasty is not recommended for all patients. The surgeons must consider the patient's age, physical history, how severe the blockage is, and, finally, the degree of damage to the artery before they make their determination.

7. Which of the following lists best outlines the main topics addressed in the passage?

   a. ▪ Plaque is fat and cholesterol.

      ▪ Bypass surgery involves entering the chest cavity.

      ▪ Angioplasty may take 30 minutes to complete.

      ▪ Ninety percent of all angioplasty procedures are successful.

   b. ▪ Angioplasty repairs blocked arteries.

      ▪ Angioplasty is not as risky as bypass surgery.

      ▪ Angioplasty is performed with a balloon.

      ▪ Angioplasty is often successful, but is not for everyone.

   c. ▪ *Angioplasty* means "blood vessel repair."

      ▪ The blocked blood vessel is removed during bypass surgery.

      ▪ A stent can be used to keep the artery open.

      ▪ The patient's age may prevent him or her from having an angioplasty.

   d. ▪ Angioplasty is an alternative to bypass surgery.

      ▪ Angioplasty involves entering the body cavity.

      ▪ Angioplasty involves threading a catheter into the circulatory system.

      ▪ Angioplasty is used to repair a damaged artery.

8. According to information presented in the passage, when coronary arteries are blocked by plaque, one of the results could be

   a. a stroke.

   b. a heart attack.

   c. hospitalization.

   d. femoral artery deterioration.

9. Which of the following is closest in meaning to <u>invasive</u> as it is used in the second paragraph of the passage?

   a. entering the body cavity

   b. causing infection

   c. resulting in hospitalization

   d. requiring a specialist's opinion

10. According to information presented in the passage, the angioplasty procedure begins with

   a. a thin catheter being inserted into the femoral artery.

   b. a balloon being inflated in the heart.

   c. a special dye being injected into the bloodstream.

   d. a healthy artery being removed from the calf.

11. Information presented in the passage supports which of the following conclusions?

   a. A healthy artery is often removed to await possible bypass surgery.

   b. Patients cannot accept the idea that a tiny balloon will cure them.

   c. Three to five percent of the patients refuse to undergo this procedure.

   d. Surgeons do not take even a 2% chance of death lightly.

12. Which of the following statements from the passages expresses a fact?

   a. The plaque that has caused the problem is not removed during angioplasty.

   b. The risk of dying during an angioplasty procedure is 3 to 5%.

   c. Angioplasty is a separate procedure from inflating a balloon into a blocked artery.

   d. The statistics related to angioplasty procedures are superb.

Read the passage, then answer the six questions that follow.

Monopoly

1   In 1904, the U.S. Patent Office granted a patent for a board game called The Landlord's Game, which was invented by a Virginia Quaker named Lizzie Magie. Magie was a follower of Henry George, who started a tax movement that supported the theory that the renting of land and real estate produced an unearned increase in land values that profited a few individuals (landlords) rather than the majority of the people (tenants). George proposed a single federal tax based on land ownership; he believed this tax would weaken the ability to form monopolies, encourage equal opportunity, and narrow the gap between rich and poor.

2   Lizzie Magie wanted to spread the word about George's proposal, making it more understandable to a majority of people who were basically unfamiliar with economics. As a result, she invented a board game that would serve as a teaching device. The Landlord's Game was intended to explain the evils of monopolies, showing that they repressed the possibility for equal opportunity. Her instructions read in part: "The object of this game is not only to afford amusement to players, but to illustrate to them how, under the present or prevailing system of land tenure, the landlord has an advantage over other enterprisers, and also how the single tax would discourage speculation."

3   The board for the game was painted with forty spaces around its perimeter, including four railroads, two utilities, twenty-two rental properties, and a jail. There were other squares directing players to go to jail, pay a luxury tax, and park. All properties were available for rent, rather than purchase. Magie's invention became very popular, spreading through word of mouth, and altering slightly as it did. Since it was not manufactured by Magie, the boards and game pieces were homemade. Rules were explained and transmuted from one group of friends to another. There is evidence to suggest that The Landlord's Game was played at Princeton University, Harvard University, and the University of Pennsylvania.

4   In 1924, Magie approached George Parker (president of Parker Brothers) to see if he was interested in purchasing the rights to her game. Parker turned her down, saying that it was too political. The game increased in popularity, migrating north to New York state, west to Michigan, and as far south as Texas. By the early 1930s, it reached Charles Darrow in Philadelphia. In 1935, claiming to be the inventor, Darrow got a patent for the game, and approached Parker Brothers. This time, the company loved it, swallowed Darrow's prevarication, and not only purchased his patent, but paid him royalties for every game sold. The game quickly became Parker Brothers' bestseller, and made the company, and Darrow, millions of dollars.

5   When Parker Brothers found out that Darrow was not the true inventor of the game, the company wanted to protect its rights to the successful game, so they went back to Lizzie Magie, now Mrs. Elizabeth Magie Phillips of Clarendon, Virginia. She agreed to a payment of $500 for her patent, with no royalties, so she could stay true to the original intent of her game's invention. She therefore required in return that Parker

Brothers manufacture and market The Landlord's Game in addition to Monopoly. However, only a few hundred games were ever produced. Monopoly went on to become the world's best-selling board game, with an objective that is the exact opposite of the one Magie intended: "The idea of the game is to buy and rent or sell property so profitably that one becomes the wealthiest player and eventually monopolist. The game is one of shrewd and amusing trading and excitement."

_____

13. Which of the following is closest in meaning to repressed the possibility for equal opportunity as it is used in the second paragraph of the passage?
   a. Monopolies led to people being forced into servitude.
   b. Monopolies were responsible for the single tax problems.
   c. Monopolies made it impossible for poorer people to follow Henry George.
   d. Monopolies were responsible for Magie's $500 payment and Darrow's millions.

14. According to information presented in the passage, a difference between the objective of The Landlord's Game and that of Monopoly is:
   a. In The Landlord's Game, you can only rent the properties, but in Monopoly you may buy them.
   b. The Landlord's Game illustrates the inequality of the landlord/tenant system, while Monopoly encourages players to become landlords and become wealthy at the expense of others.
   c. The Landlord's Game teaches the problems of capitalism and Monopoly encourages equal opportunity.
   d. The Landlord's Game explains the theories of George to Quakers, and Monopoly explains the theories of Darrow.

15. Which of the following is closest in meaning to swallowed Darrow's prevarication as it is used in the fourth paragraph of the passage?
   a. ate his lunch
   b. believed his lie
   c. understood his problem
   d. drank his champagne

16. Which of the following is closest in meaning to transmuted as it is used in the third paragraph of the passage?
   a. went through changes
   b. took on a different appearance
   c. relied on another for vital information
   d. had difficulty playing by the rules

17. According to information presented in the fourth paragraph of the passage, the author implies that:
   a. Parker Brothers bought the game from Charles Darrow.
   b. it is not difficult to get a patent for an idea you didn't invent.
   c. Monopoly made Parker Brothers and Darrow millions of dollars.
   d. Lizzie Magie tried to sell her game to George Parker.

18. According to information presented in the passage, Mrs. Phillips sold her patent to Parker Brothers so
   a. a large company would market her game and spread the word about Henry George's single tax theory.
   b. she could make a lot more money by having it sold by such a large company.
   c. The Landlord's Game could compete with Monopoly.
   d. the truth would be told about Charles Darrow.

Read the passage, then answer
the six questions that follow.

Diabetes

1 There are two types of diabetes, *insulin-dependent* and *non-insulin-dependent*. Between 90 and 95% of the estimated 13 to 14 million people in the United States with diabetes have non-insulin-dependent, or Type II, diabetes. Because this form of diabetes usually begins in adults over the age of 40 and is most common after the age of 55, it used to be called adult-onset diabetes. Its symptoms often develop gradually and are hard to identify at first; therefore, nearly half of all people with diabetes do not know they have it. For instance, someone who has developed Type II diabetes may feel tired or ill without knowing why. This can be particularly dangerous because untreated diabetes can cause damage to the heart, blood vessels, eyes, kidneys, and nerves. While the causes, short-term effects, and treatments of the two types of diabetes differ, both types can cause the same long-term health problems.

2 Most importantly, both types affect the body's ability to use digested food for energy. Diabetes does not interfere with digestion, but it does prevent the body from using an important product of digestion, *glucose* (commonly known as sugar), for energy. After a meal, the normal digestive system breaks some food down into glucose. The blood carries the glucose or sugar through-out the body, causing blood glucose levels to rise. In response to this rise, the hormone insulin is released into the bloodstream and signals the body tissues to metabolize or burn the glucose for fuel, which causes blood glucose levels to return to normal. The

glucose that the body does not use right away is stored in the liver, muscle, or fat.

3 In both types of diabetes, however, this normal process malfunctions. A gland called the *pancreas*, found just behind the stomach, makes *insulin*. In people with insulin-dependent diabetes, the pancreas does not produce insulin at all. This condition usually begins in childhood and is known as Type I (formerly called juvenile-onset) diabetes. These patients must have daily insulin injections to survive. People with non-insulin-dependent diabetes usually produce some insulin in their pancreas, but their bodies' tissues do not respond well to the insulin signal and, therefore, do not metabolize the glucose properly, a condition known as insulin resistance.

4 Insulin resistance is an important factor in non-insulin-dependent diabetes, and scientists are searching for the causes of insulin resistance. They have identified two possibilities. The first is that there could be a defect in the insulin receptors on cells. Like an appliance that needs to be plugged into an electrical outlet, insulin has to bind to a receptor in order to function. Several things can go wrong with receptors. For example, there may not be enough receptors to which insulin may bind, or a defect in the receptors may prevent insulin from binding. The second possible cause of insulin resistance is that, although insulin may bind to the receptors, the cells do not read the signal to metabolize the glucose. Scientists continue to study these cells to see why this might happen.

5 A number of diseases are currently incurable. There's no cure for diabetes yet. However, there are ways to alleviate its symptoms. In 1986, a National Institutes of Health panel of experts recommended that

the best treatment for non-insulin-dependent diabetes is a diet that helps one maintain a normal weight and pays particular attention to a proper balance of the different food groups. Many experts, including those in the American Diabetes Association, recommend that 50 to 60% of daily calories come from carbohydrates, 12 to 20% from protein, and no more than 30% from fat. Foods that are rich in carbohydrates, like breads, cereals, fruits, and vegetables, break down into glucose during digestion, causing blood glucose to rise. Additionally, studies have shown that cooked foods raise blood glucose higher than raw, unpeeled foods. A doctor or nutritionist should always be consulted for more of this kind of information and for help in planning a diet to <u>offset</u> the effects of this form of diabetes.

---

19. Which of the following statements best summarizes the main points of the passage?
  a. Type I and Type II diabetes are best treated by maintaining a high-protein diet.
  b. Type II diabetes is a distinct condition that can be managed by maintaining a healthy diet.
  c. Type I diabetes is a condition most harmful when the patient is not taking daily insulin injections.
  d. Adults who suspect they may have Type II diabetes should always adopt a high-carbohydrate diet.

20. Based on the information in the passage, which of the following best describes people with Type I diabetes?
  a. They do not need to be treated with injections of insulin.
  b. They comprise the majority of people with diabetes.
  c. Their pancreases do not produce insulin.
  d. They are usually diagnosed as adults.

21. Which of the following words is closest in meaning to <u>offset</u> as it is used in the fifth paragraph of the passage?
  a. counteract
  b. cure
  c. soothe
  d. erase

22. Which of the following statements from Paragraph 5 is least relevant?
  a. A number of diseases are currently incurable.
  b. There's no cure for diabetes yet.
  c. Foods that are rich in carbohydrates, like breads, cereals, fruits, and vegetables, break down into glucose during digestion, causing blood glucose to rise.
  d. Additionally, studies have shown that cooked foods raise blood glucose higher than raw, unpeeled foods.

23. According to information presented in the passage, the number of people in the United States with insulin-dependent diabetes is:
  a. 1 to 2 million
  b. 13 to 14 million
  c. 40 to 55 million
  d. 90 to 95 million

24. Which of the following lists best outlines the main topics addressed in the third paragraph of the passage?

a. Insulin resistance is an important factor in non-insulin-dependent diabetes.

- A defect in the insulin receptors on cells may be a cause of insulin resistance.
- The inability of cells to read the insulin signal may also cause insulin resistance.

b. The pancreas is found just behind the stomach.

- People with non-insulin-dependent diabetes produce insulin.
- Type I diabetes was once called juvenile-onset diabetes.

c. There are two types of diabetes, insulin-dependent and non-insulin-dependent.

- Both types of diabetes affect the body's ability to use digested food for energy.
- There is no cure for diabetes yet, but there are ways to alleviate its symptoms.

d. The pancreas does not produce insulin in people with insulin-dependent diabetes.

- People with insulin-dependent diabetes need daily insulin injections.
- People with non-insulin-dependent diabetes do not metabolize the glucose properly.

> **Read the passage, then answer the six questions that follow.**

The Civil Rights Movement

1 The post–World War II era marked a period of <u>unprecedented</u> energy against the second-class citizenship accorded to African Americans in many parts of the nation. Resistance to racial segregation and discrimination with strategies like civil disobedience, nonviolent resistance, marches, protests, boycotts, freedom rides, and rallies received national attention as newspaper, radio, and television reporters and cameramen documented the struggle to end racial inequality.

2 When Rosa Parks refused to give up her seat to a white person in Montgomery, Alabama, and was arrested in December 1955, she set off a train of events that generated a momentum the civil rights movement had never before experienced. Local civil rights leaders were hoping for such an opportunity to test the city's segregation laws. Deciding to boycott the buses, the African American community soon formed a new organization to supervise the boycott, the Montgomery Improvement Association (MIA). The young pastor of the Dexter Avenue Baptist Church, Reverend Martin Luther King, Jr., was chosen as the first MIA leader. The boycott, more successful than anyone hoped, led to a 1956 Supreme Court decision banning segregated buses.

3 In 1960, four black freshmen from North Carolina Agricultural and Technical College in Greensboro strolled into the F.W. Woolworth store and quietly sat down at the lunch counter. They were not served, but they stayed until closing time. The next

morning, they came with 25 more students. Two weeks later, similar demonstrations had spread to several cities; within a year similar peaceful demonstrations took place in over a hundred cities in the North and the South. At Shaw University in Raleigh, North Carolina, the students formed their own organization, the Student Non-Violent Coordinating Committee (SNCC, pronounced "Snick"). The students' bravery in the face of verbal and physical abuse led to integration in many stores even before the passage of the Civil Rights Act of 1964.

4 The August 28, 1963, March on Washington riveted the nation's attention. Rather than the anticipated hundred thousand marchers, more than twice that number appeared, astonishing even its organizers. Blacks and whites, side by side, called on President John F. Kennedy and Congress to provide equal access to public facilities, quality education, adequate employment, and decent housing for African Americans. During the assembly at the Lincoln Memorial, the young preacher who had led the successful Montgomery, Alabama, bus boycott, Reverend Dr. Martin Luther King, Jr., delivered a stirring message with the refrain "I Have a Dream."

5 There were also continuing efforts to legally challenge segregation through the courts. Success crowned these efforts: The Brown decision in 1954, the Civil Rights Act of 1964, and the Voting Rights Act in 1965 helped bring about the demise of the entangling web of legislation that bound blacks to second-class citizenship. One hundred years after the Civil War, blacks and their white allies still pursued the battle for equal rights in every area of American life. While there is more to achieve in ending discrimination, major milestones in civil rights laws are on the books for the purpose of regulating equal access to public accommodations; equal justice before the law; and equal employment, housing opportunities, and most important of all, education. African Americans have had newfound openings in many fields of learning and in the arts. The black struggle for civil rights also inspired other liberation and rights movements, including those of Native Americans, Latinos, and women, and African Americans have lent their support to liberation struggles in Africa.

---

25. The author's main purpose for citing Rosa Parks's refusal to relinquish her bus seat is to
   a. demonstrate the accidental nature of political change.
   b. show a conventional response to a common situation.
   c. describe a seminal event that influenced a larger movement.
   d. portray an outcome instead of a cause.

26. Which of the following words is the best meaning of <u>unprecedented</u> as it is used in the first paragraph of the passage?
   a. exhausting
   b. disruptive
   c. frightening
   d. extraordinary

27. According to information presented in the passage, where were four black students refused service in 1960, leading to a series of peaceful demonstrations?
   a. a bus in Montgomery, Alabama
   b. North Carolina Agricultural and Technical College
   c. an F.W. Woolworth store
   d. Shaw University in Raleigh, North Carolina

28. Which of the following summaries best captures the most important ideas in the passage?

   a. More than two hundred thousand people marched on Washington, D.C., on August 28, 1963, a protest that riveted the nation's attention and even astonished its organizers.

   b. The Civil Rights Movement was advanced by the efforts of several people throughout the 1950s and 1960s, including Rosa Parks, four students in Greensboro, and Dr. Martin Luther King, Jr.

   c. Reverend Dr. Martin Luther King, Jr., the preacher who had led the successful Montgomery boycott, delivered his stirring "I Have a Dream" speech during an assembly at the Lincoln Memorial.

   d. Students at Shaw University in Raleigh, North Carolina, formed an organization called the Student Non-Violent Coordinating Committee that led to integration in many stores before the Civil Rights Act was passed.

29. In which of the following statements from Paragraph 5 of the passage does the author most clearly express an opinion rather than a fact?

   a. Equal opportunities in education are more important than equal opportunities in employment.

   b. The Brown decision, the Civil Rights Act, and the Voting Rights Act were all successfully passed.

   c. The black struggle for civil rights also inspired other liberation and rights movements.

   d. African Americans have lent their support to the liberation struggles of people in Africa.

30. Which of the following summaries best captures the most important ideas in the second paragraph of the passage?

   a. When Rosa Parks was arrested for refusing to give up her seat to a white person in Montgomery, Alabama, the African American community organized a boycott of the buses, which led to a 1956 Supreme Court decision banning segregated buses.

   b. Reverend Martin Luther King, Jr., a young pastor of the Dexter Avenue Baptist Church, was chosen as the first leader of the Montgomery Improvement Association (MIA).

   c. In December 1955, a woman named Rosa Parks was arrested for refusing to give up her seat to a white person on a bus in Montgomery, Alabama, which was a violation of her civil rights.

   d. The Brown decision, the Civil Rights Act, and the Voting Rights Act helped bring free blacks from second-class citizenship one hundred years after the Civil War, and inspired blacks and their white allies to continue a fight for civil rights that continues today.

Read the passage, then answer
the six questions that follow.

A Collision of Cultures

1 When Thomas Jefferson sent Lewis and Clark into the West, he patterned their mission on the methods of Enlightenment science: to observe, collect, document, and classify. Such strategies were already in place for the epic voyages made by explorers like Cook and Vancouver. Like their contemporaries, Lewis and Clark were more than representatives of European rationalism. They also represented a rising American empire, one built on aggressive territorial expansion and commercial gain.

2 But there was another view of the West: that of the native inhabitants of the land. Their understandings of landscapes, peoples, and resources formed both a contrast and counterpoint to those of Jefferson's travelers. One of Lewis and Clark's missions was to open diplomatic relations between the United States and the Native American nations of the West. As Jefferson told Lewis, "it will now be proper you should inform those through whose country you will pass . . . that henceforth we become their fathers and friends." Meriwether Lewis was born to Lt. William Lewis and Lucy Meriwether Lewis in Albemarle County, Virginia, on August 18, 1774. When Euro-Americans and Native Americans met, they used ancient diplomatic protocols that included formal language, ceremonial gifts, and displays of military power. But behind these symbols and rituals there were often very different ways of understanding power and authority. Such differences sometimes made communication across the cultural divide difficult and caused confusion and misunderstanding.

3 An important organizing principle in Euro-American society was hierarchy. Both soldiers and civilians had complex gradations of rank to define who gave orders and who obeyed. While kinship was important in the Euro-American world, it was even more fundamental in tribal societies. Everyone's power and place depended on a complex network of real and symbolic relationships. When the two groups met—whether for trade or diplomacy—each tried to reshape the other in its own image. Lewis and Clark sought to impose their own notions of hierarchy on Native Americans by "making chiefs" with medals, printed certificates, and gifts. Native people tried to impose the obligations of kinship on the visitors by means of adoption ceremonies, shared names, and ritual gifts.

4 The American republic began to issue peace medals during the first Washington administration, continuing a tradition established by the European nations. Lewis and Clark brought at least 89 medals in five sizes in order to designate five "ranks" of chief. In the eyes of Americans, Native Americans who accepted such medals were also acknowledging American sovereignty as "children" of a new "great father." And in a moment of imperial bravado, Lewis hung a peace medal around the neck of a Piegan Blackfoot warrior killed by the expedition in late July 1806. As Lewis later explained, he used a peace medal as a way to let the Blackfeet know "who we were."

5 In tribal society, kinship was like a legal system—people depended on relatives to protect them from crime, war, and misfortune. People with no kin were outside

of society and its rules. To adopt Lewis and Clark into tribal society, the Plains Indians used their most beautiful ritual: a pipe ceremony. Smoking and sharing the pipe was at the heart of much Native American diplomacy. With the pipe the captains accepted sacred obligations to share wealth, aid in war, and avenge injustice. At the end of the ceremony, the pipe was presented to them so they would never forget their obligations.

6 Gift giving was an essential part of diplomacy. To Native Americans, gifts proved the giver's sincerity and honored the tribe. To Lewis and Clark, some gifts advertised the technological superiority and others encouraged the Native Americans to adopt an agrarian lifestyle. Like salesmen handing out free samples, Lewis and Clark packed bales of manufactured goods to open diplomatic relations with Native American tribes. Jefferson advised Lewis to give out corn mills to introduce the Native Americans to mechanized agriculture as part of his plan to "civilize and instruct" them. Clark believed the mills were "verry Thankfully recived," but by the next year the Mandan had demolished theirs to use the metal for weapons.

31. Which of the following lists best outlines the main topics addressed in the passage?
a. Thomas Jefferson patterned Lewis and Clark's mission on the methods of Enlightenment science.
   - The methods of Enlightenment science had already been set in place during the epic voyages made by explorers like Cook and Vancouver.
   - Lewis and Clark were both representatives of European rationalism and the rising American empire.
      - The American empire was built on aggressive territorial expansion and commercial gain.
b. Native American understandings of landscapes and resources contrasted those of Lewis and Clark.
   - Soldiers and civilians in Euro-American society had complex gradations of rank to define who gave orders and who obeyed.
   - Lewis hung a peace medal around the neck of a Piegan Blackfoot warrior killed by the expedition in July 1806.
   - Lewis and Clark were very similar to salesmen handing out free samples to Native Americans.
c. Lewis and Clark's mission was to open diplomatic relations between the United States and Native American nations.
   - Euro-Americans and Native Americans used ancient diplomatic protocols that were actually intended to establish roles of power and authority.
   - The American republic issued peace medals to Native Americans to assert its power over Native Americans.
   - Native Americans gave gifts to prove their sincerity and honor their tribe, which contrasted with the republic's reasons for giving gifts.
d. Kinship was more important and fundamental in tribal societies than in the Euro-American world.
   - Lewis and Clark brought medals in five sizes in order to designate five "ranks" of chief.
   - To Native Americans, pipe smoking symbolized sacred obligations to share wealth, aid in war, and avenge injustice.
   - Clark believed the Mandan people were very thankful for the corn mills he gave to them.

32. According to information presented in the passage, Lewis's reason for placing a medal on a Piegan Blackfoot warrior was to
   a. apologize for the warrior's death during the expedition.
   b. honor the dead Blackfoot warrior and his tribe.
   c. designate the rank of the dead Blackfoot warrior.
   d. show the Blackfeet who the Americans were.

33. The author's main purpose for writing this passage is to
   a. prove that Lewis and Clark were more interested in power than trade.
   b. describe Lewis and Clark's meetings with Native American tribes.
   c. show the path that Lewis and Clark followed throughout the West.
   d. explain why Lewis and Clark presented Native Americans with medals.

34. Which of the following statements from the passage expresses an opinion rather than a fact?
   a. To adopt Lewis and Clark into tribal society, the Plains Indians used their most beautiful ritual: a pipe ceremony.
   b. Smoking and sharing the pipe was at the heart of much Native American diplomacy.
   c. With the pipe, the captains accepted sacred obligations to share wealth, aid in war, and avenge injustice.
   d. At the end of the ceremony, the pipe was presented to them so they would never forget their obligations.

35. Which of the following statements from Paragraph 2 is least relevant?
   a. Meriwether Lewis was born to Lt. William Lewis and Lucy Meriwether Lewis in Albemarle County, Virginia, on August 18, 1774.
   b. Their understandings of landscapes, peoples, and resources formed both a contrast and counterpoint to those of Jefferson's travelers.
   c. One of Lewis and Clark's missions was to open diplomatic relations between the United States and the Native American nations of the West.
   d. Such differences sometimes made communication across the cultural divide difficult and open to confusion and misunderstanding.

36. The author's main purpose for explaining that the Mandan people demolished the corn mills given to them by white people to use the metal for weapons is to
   a. suggest that the white people were not very good at manufacturing corn mills.
   b. illustrate the differences of ideals between the Mandan and white cultures.
   c. prove that the Mandan did not have any use for corn.
   d. show that the Mandan were powerful and could easily demolish corn mills.

Maintaining Privacy in a High-Tech Society

1 A recent *New York Times* "House and Home" article featured the story of a man who lives in a glass house. Every wall in his home is transparent; he has no walls to hide behind, not even in the bathroom. Of course, he lives in an isolated area, so he doesn't exactly have neighbors peering in and watching his every move. But he has chosen to live without any physical privacy in a home that allows every action to be seen. He has created his own *panopticon* of sorts, a place in which everything is in full view of others.

2 The term *panopticon* was coined by Jeremy Bentham in the late eighteenth century when he was describing an idea about how prisons should be designed. The prisoner's cells would be placed in a circle with a guard tower in the middle. All walls facing the center of the circle would be glass. In that way, every prisoner's cell would be in full view of the guards. The prisoners could do nothing unobserved, but the prisoners would not be able to see the guard tower. They would know they were being watched—or rather, they would know that they *could be* being watched—but because they could not see the observer, they would never know when the guard was actually monitoring their actions.

3 It is common knowledge that people behave differently when they know they are being watched. We act differently when we know someone is looking; we act differently when we think someone else *might be* be looking. In these situations, we are less likely to be ourselves; instead, we will act the way we think we should act when we are being observed by others.

4 In our wired society, many people view the panopticon as a metaphor for the future. Only one industrial building was ever built using the open panopticon structure: the Round Mill constructed in 1811 in Belper, Derbyshire, England. But in many ways, the panopticon is already here. Surveillance cameras are everywhere, and we often don't even know our actions are being recorded. In fact, the surveillance camera industry is enormous, and these cameras keep getting smaller and smaller to make surveillance easier and more ubiquitous. In addition, we leave a record of everything we do online; our cyber whereabouts can be tracked and that information used for various purposes. Every time we use a credit card, make a major purchase, answer a survey, apply for a loan, or join a mailing list, our actions are observed and recorded. And most of us have no idea just how much information about us has been recorded and how much data is available to various sources. The scale of information gathering and the scale of exchange have both expanded so rapidly in the last decade that there are now millions of electronic profiles of individuals existing in cyberspace, profiles that are bought and sold, traded, and often used for important decisions, such as whether to grant someone a loan. However, that information is essentially beyond our control. We can do little to stop the information gathering and exchange and can only hope to be able to control the damage if something goes wrong.

5 Something went wrong recently for me. Someone obtained my Social Security

number, address, work number and address, and a few other vital pieces of data. That person then applied for a credit account in my name. The application was approved, and I soon received a bill for nearly $5,000 worth of computer-related purchases.

6 Fraud, of course, is a different issue, but this kind of fraud couldn't happen—or at least, couldn't happen with such ease and frequency—in a world of paper-based records. With so much information floating about in cyberspace, and so much technology that can record and observe, our privacy has been deeply compromised.

7 I find it truly amazing that someone would want to live in a transparent house at any time, but especially in an age when individual privacy is becoming increasingly difficult to maintain and defend against those who argue that information must be gathered for the social good. Or perhaps this man's house is an attempt to call our attention to the fact that the panopticon is already here, and that we are all just as exposed as he is.

Federal Trade Commission Identity Theft Overview (2009)

37. According to information presented in the passage, the author was a victim of what form of identity theft?
   a. government fraud
   b. bank fraud
   c. loan fraud
   d. credit card fraud

38. The author's main purpose for describing a personal experience with identity theft is to
   a. show that identity theft is not as serious a problem as the media suggests.
   b. show how angry he is about having his privacy invaded.
   c. show an example of how private information can be misused.
   d. show that there are some major flaws in the panopticon.

39. The author's main purpose for writing this passage is to
   a. suggest that most of us will be victims of identity theft.
   b. show how common identity theft is in today's society.
   c. prove that living in a glass house will lead to identity theft.
   d. explain in detail how thieves commit identity theft.

40. This passage was most likely written for an audience of
   a. people who live in glass houses.
   b. people who commit identity theft.
   c. people who use the Internet.
   d. victims of identity theft.

41. Which of the following statements from Paragraph 4 is least relevant?

a. Only one industrial building was ever built using the open panopticon structure: the Round Mill constructed in 1811 in Belper, Derbyshire, England.

b. In fact, the surveillance camera industry is enormous, and these cameras keep getting smaller and smaller to make surveillance easier and more ubiquitous.

c. Every time we use a credit card, make a major purchase, answer a survey, apply for a loan, or join a mailing list, our actions are observed and recorded.

d. We can do little to stop the information gathering and exchange and can only hope to be able to control the damage if something goes wrong.

42. Information presented in the chart best supports which of the following conclusions?

a. Credit card fraud is more profitable than employment fraud.

b. Government fraud is a more common problem than utilities fraud.

c. Employment fraud will likely rise over the next three years.

d. Bank fraud tends to be committed using paperwork rather than online data.

Writing Subtest

Multiple-Choice Questions

Directions: Read each of the following passages and then choose the one best answer for each of the multiple choice questions that follow. Each of these passages has numbered parts that are referred to in the associated questions.

> **Read the passage, then answer the six questions that follow.**

(1) In her lecture "Keeping Your Heart Healthy," Dr. Miranda Woodhouse challenged Americans to join her in the fight to reduce the risks of heart disease. (2) Her plan includes four basic strategies meant to increase public awareness and prevent heart disease. (3) Eating a healthy diet that contains nine full servings of fruits and vegetables each day can help lower cholesterol levels. (4) More fruits and vegetables means less dairy and meat, which, in turn, means less cholesterol-boosting saturated fat. (5) Do not smoke. (6) Cigarette smoking increases the risk of heart disease and when it is combined with other factors, the risk is even greater. (7) Smoking increases blood pressure, increases the tendency for blood to clot, decreases good cholesterol, and decreases tolerance for exercise. (8) Be aware of your blood pressure and cholesterol levels at all times. (9) Because their are often no symptoms, many people don't even know that they have high blood pressure. (10) This is extremely dangerous, since uncontrolled high blood pressure can lead to heart attack, kidney failure, and stroke. (11) Finally, relax and be happy. (12) Studies show that being constantly angry and depressed can increase your risk of heart disease, so take a deep breath, smile, and focus

on the positive things in life. (13) Always be sure to drink plenty of clean water to keep your kidneys working properly.

_____

1. Which of the following numbered parts contains a nonstandard sentence?
   a. sentence 2
   b. sentence 3
   c. sentence 6
   d. sentence 10

2. Which of the following sentences, if added between Sentence 2 and Sentence 3, provides the best transition between the sentences?
   a. The following is a brief outline of each of the four strategies.
   b. Extending the life of American citizens will make our country's life expectancy rates the highest in the world.
   c. While the guidelines will help those who are free of heart disease, they will not help those who have already experienced a heart attack.
   d. Getting people to stop smoking is the most important element of Dr. Woodhouse's program.

3. Which change is needed in the passage?
   a. Sentence 2: Change "includes" to "is inclusive of."
   b. Sentence 3: Change "Eating" to "To eat."
   c. Sentence 9: Change "their" to "there."
   d. Sentence 12: Change "show" to "shown."

4. Which part of the passage draws attention away from its main idea?
   a. sentence 1
   b. sentence 4
   c. sentence 5
   d. sentence 13

Read the passage, then answer the six questions that follow.

(1) Theodore Roosevelt were born with <u>asthma</u> and poor eyesight. (2) Yet this sickly child later won fame as a political leader, Rough Rider, and hero of the common people. (3) To <u>conquer</u> his handicaps, Teddy trained in a gym and became a lightweight boxer at Harvard. (4) Out west, he hunted buffalo and ran a cattle ranch. (5) Back east, he became a civil service reformer and police <u>commisioner</u>. (6) He became President McKinley's assistant navy secretary during the Spanish-American War and worked to improve the state of civil service in the United States. (7) Also, he led a charge of cavalry Rough Riders up San Juan Hill in Cuba. (8) After Roosevelt <u>achieved</u> fame, they became Governor of New York and went on to become the Vice-President.

5. Which part of the passage contains a redundant expression of ideas or information?
   a. sentence 1
   b. sentence 3
   c. sentence 6
   d. sentence 8

6. Which change is needed in the passage?
   a. Sentence 1: Change "were" to "will be."
   b. Sentence 1: Change "were" to "are."
   c. Sentence 1: Change "were" to "is."
   d. Sentence 1: Change "were" to "was."

It's as easy as...

1) Go to **virginwines.com/3049006**

2) **Now use your $100** towards your choice of 12-bottle introductory cases — smooth reds, fresh whites or a delicious mix of both.

3) We will also send you **3 FREE bottles of award-winning Malbec** worth $56.97.

+

The smarter way to buy wine

There's no catch. When you buy this case we'll offer you a specially selected case of wine every 3 months. It's entirely up to you whether you take it. This is our Explorers Club, a way of helping you to find new wines without the hassle.

Oh, and if you don't like a wine, let us know and we'll give you your money back!

Claim your $100 at **virginwines.com/3049006**   Or, call us at **866-426-0336** Quote 3049006

7. Which part of the passage should be revised to correct an error in pronoun-antecedent agreement?

a. sentence 3
b. sentence 4
c. sentence 5
d. sentence 8

8. Which underlined word in the passage is spelled incorrectly?

a. asthma
b. conquer
c. commisioner
d. achieved

> **Read the passage, then answer the six questions that follow.**
> (Note: An error in paragraph organization has been purposely included in the passage.)

(1) The Chunnel, or underwater tunnel that runs underneath the English Channel between England and France, is one of the most remarkable feats of architecture ever created. (2) The incredible notion of connecting those two powerful countries, which had been separated for more than 12,000 years, had been tossed around for more than two centuries. (3) Everyone from engineers to architects to politicians had come up with a plan or a blueprint. (4) The Chunnel is considered to be one of the true wonders of the modern world for its size and complexity and the fact that it succeeded although plagued by dilemmas, such as budget <u>catastrofees</u> and safety nightmares.

(5) Although frequently ignored, squashed, and thrown out, the idea just would not die. (6) The idea for a connection between France and England was first mentioned at the end of the eighteenth century. (7) It continued to pop up again and again for over 200 years. (8) Power and trade between the two european countries was on the rise. (9) A century ago, the 20-plus miles that separated them made trade not only slow, but also quite dangerous. (10) Under the best weather conditions, the trip from one coastline the other took six to eight hours, and frequently, <u>vicious</u> storms delayed ships for days—even weeks. (11) Frustration on both ends grew as shipments fell behind schedule and workers arrived at the docks too seasick to load or unload their cargo. (12) Even later, when ferries and airplanes came along to make the trip faster and safer, passengers still had to put up with paying high transportation fees, standing in crowded airports, and other <u>inconveniences</u>.

(13) For decades, the debate had raged over the best way to link these two countries. (14) Ideas ranged from sunken tubes to iron bridges. (15) Which could be easiest and safest—a bridge, a tunnel, or some combination of the two? (16) Every single plan posed some kind of unique problems. (17) A bridge over 20 miles long was a nightmare to try to support. (18) Experts argued that it would cause problems with the many ships that needed to pass through the Channel. (19) Even the best of lighthouses, foghorns, and other <u>precautions</u> might not be enough to warn a ship that the bridge was ahead.

9. Which part of the passage is missing a preposition?

a. sentence 10
b. sentence 12
c. sentence 14
d. sentence 18

10. Which part of the passage contains an error in capitalization?
a. sentence 1
b. sentence 7
c. sentence 8
d. sentence 11

11. Which of the following changes would make the sequence of ideas in the paragraph clearer?
a. Delete sentence 4.
b. Reverse the orders of sentence 5 and sentence 6.
c. Delete sentence 13.
d. Reverse the orders of sentence 13 and sentence 14.

12. Which underlined word in the passage is spelled incorrectly?
a. catastrofees
b. vicious
c. inconveniences
d. precautions

> Read the passage, then answer the four questions that follow.

Year-Round School versus Regular School Schedule

(1) Both year-round school and regular school schedules are found throughout the United States. (2) With year-round school schedules, students attend classes for nine weeks, and then have three week of vacation. (3) This continues all year long. (4) The regular school schedule requires students to attend classes from September to June, with a three-month summer vacation at the end of the year. (5) This schedule began because farmers needed their children at home to help with crops during the summer. (6) Today, most people work in businesses and offices. (7) Office jobs often involve a good deal of computer work, filing, and phone calls. (8) Year-round school is easier for parents who work in businesses and dont have the summer to be with their children. (9) The regular school schedule is great for kids. (10) Who like to have a long summer vacation. (11) While some educational systems have changed them schedules to keep up with their population, others still use the old agrarian calendar. (12) Both systems have disadvantages and advantages, which is why different schools use different systems.

---

13. Which part of the passage draws attention away from the main idea?
a. sentence 1
b. sentence 4
c. sentence 5
d. sentence 7

14. Which part of the passage contains a fragment?
a. sentence 3
b. sentence 8
c. sentence 10
d. sentence 12

15. Which part of the passage is missing an apostrophe?
a. sentence 2
b. sentence 4
c. sentence 5
d. sentence 8

16. Which change is needed in the passage?
a. Sentence 1: Change "are" to "is."
b. Sentence 5: Change "This" to "those."
c. Sentence 8: Change "who" to "whose."
d. Sentence 11: Change "them" to "their."

Read the passage, then answer the four questions that follow.
(Note: An error in paragraph organization has been purposely included in the passage.)

(1) Police officers must read suspects their Miranda rights upon taking them into custody. (2) Miranda rights are the rights of a criminal suspect taken into police custody. (3) Before being interrogated, suspects must know that they have the right to remain silent to avoid incriminating themselves. (4) When a suspect who is merely being questioned incriminates himself, he might later claim to have been in custody and seek to have the case dismissed on the grounds of not having been apprised of his Miranda rights. (5) In such cases, a judge must make a determination as to whether a reasonable person would have believed himself to have been in custody, based on certain criteria. (6) Officers must be aware of these criteria and take care not to give suspects grounds for later claiming they believed themselves to be in custody. (7) The judge must asertain whether the suspect was questioned in a threatening manner (threatening could mean that the suspect was seated while both officers remained standing) and whether the suspect was aware that he or she was free to leave at any time. (8) The judge must make this determination because the suspect might claim to have been in custody without having been read his Miranda rights, and the case would have to be dismissed. (9) When a suspect of a serious crime is arrested, he is usually handcuffed and held in a police station or jail.

17. Which of the following changes would make the sequence of ideas in the paragraph clearer?
a. Place sentence 7 after sentence 1.
b. Reverse sentences 1 and 3.
c. Reverse the order of sentences 6 and 7.
d. Delete sentence 4.

18. Which part of the passage contains an error in spelling?
a. sentence 2
b. sentence 7
c. sentence 8
d. sentence 9

19. Which part of the passage contains a redundant expression of ideas or information?
a. sentence 3
b. sentence 4
c. sentence 7
d. sentence 8

20. Which part of the passage draws attention away from the main idea?
a. sentence 4
b. sentence 7
c. sentence 8
d. sentence 9

> **Read the passage, then answer the four questions that follow.**

(1) Ecosystems include physical and chemical components, such as soils, water, and nutrients that support the organisms living there. (2) These organisms may range from large animals to microscopic bacteria. (3) Ecosystems also can be thought of as the interactions among all organisms in a given habitat; for instance, one species may serve as food for another. (4) People are part of the ecosystems where they live and work. (5) Environmental groups are forming in many communities. (6) Human activities can harm or destroy local ecosystems unless actions, such as land development for housing or businesses, are carefully planned too conserve and sustain the ecology of the area. (7) An important part of ecosystem management involves finding ways to protect and enhance economic and social well-being while protecting local ecosystems.

_____

21. Which of the following changes would make the sequence of ideas in the paragraph clearer?
   a. Delete sentence 1.
   b. Delete sentence 5.
   c. Delete sentence 6.
   d. Delete sentence 7.

22. Which sentence, if added before part 1 of the passage, would be the most effective topic sentence of the paragraph?
   a. The rain forest is one of the most complex and diverse ecosystems on the planet.
   b. Arthur Roy Clapham, the British botanist who coined the term _ecosystem_ in 1930, was a respected scientist, teacher, and writer.
   c. An ecosystem is a group of animals and plants living in a specific region and interacting with one another and with their physical environment.
   d. Some ecosystems might suffer due to the actions of humans if proper measures are not taken to conserve the ecology of a specific area.

23. Which part of the passage contains an error in spelling?
   a. sentence 1
   b. sentence 2
   c. sentence 3
   d. sentence 4

24. Which part of the passage contains a homonym error?
   a. sentence 3
   b. sentence 4
   c. sentence 5
   d. sentence 6

(1) It is clear that the United States is a nation that needs to eat healthier and slim down. (2) One of the most important steps in the right direction would be for school cafeterias to provide healthy, low-fat options for students. (3) Such a move would help the nation to lose weight.

(4) School cafeterias, in an effort to provide food that is appetizing to young people, too often mimic fast-food menus, serving items such as burgers and fries, pizza, hot dogs, and fried chicken. (5) While these foods do provide some nutritional value, they are relatively high in fat. (6) According to nutritionist Elizabeth Warner many of the lunch selections currently offered by school cafeterias could be made healthier with a few simple and inexpensive substitutions.

(7) "Veggie burgers offered alongside beef burgers would be a positive addition, says Warner. (8) "A salad bar would also serve the purpose of providing a healthy and satisfying meal. (9) And tasty grilled chicken sandwiches would be a far better option than fried chicken. (10) Additionally, the beverage case should be stocked with containers of low-fat milk."

25. Which of the following changes is needed in the third paragraph?
    a. Sentence 7: Insert quotation marks after "addition."
    b. Sentence 8: Delete the quotation marks before "A."
    c. Sentence 9: Change "than" to "then."
    d. Sentence 10: Insert a comma after "case."

26. Which of the following changes would make the sequence of ideas in the third paragraph clearer?
    a. Reverse the order of sentence 8 and sentence 10.
    b. Delete sentence 7.
    c. Combine sentences 8 and 9 into one sentence.
    d. Make sentences 6 the first sentence of the third paragraph.

27. Which part of the passage contains a redundant expression of ideas or information?
    a. sentence 3
    b. sentence 4
    c. sentence 5
    d. sentence 6

28. Which part of the passage is missing a comma?
    a. sentence 5
    b. sentence 6
    c. sentence 7
    d. sentence 8

Read the passage, then answer the four questions that follow.
(Note: An error in paragraph organization has been purposely included in the passage.)

(1) Everglades National Park is the largest remaining subtropical wilderness in the continental United States. (2) Its home to abundant wildlife, including alligators, crocodiles, manatees, and Florida panthers. (3) The climate of the Everglades is mild and pleasant from December through April although rare cold fronts may create near freezing conditions. (4) Summers are hot and humid. (5) Afternoon thunderstorms are common, and mosquitoes are abundant. (6) In summer, the temperatures often soars to around 90° and the humidity climbs to over 90%. (7) If you visit the Everglades, wear comfortable sportswear in winter; loose-fitting, long-sleeved shirts and pants, and insect repellent are recommended in the summer.

(8) Walking and canoe trails, boat tours, and tram tours are excellent for viewing wildlife, including alligators and a multitude of tropical and temperate birds. (9) Camping, whether in the back country or at established campgrounds, offers the opportunity to enjoy what the park offers firsthand. (10) Year-round, ranger-led activities may help you to enjoy your visit even more; such activities are offered throughout the park in all seasons.

29. Which part of the passage contains a punctuation error?
   a. sentence 2
   b. sentence 3
   c. sentence 5
   d. sentence 10

30. Which part of the passage contains a redundant expression of ideas or information?
   a. sentence 4
   b. sentence 7
   c. sentence 9
   d. sentence 10

31. Which part of the passage is missing an apostrophe?
   a. sentence 2
   b. sentence 5
   c. sentence 8
   d. sentence 10

32. Which of the following changes would make the sequence of ideas in the paragraph clearer?
   a. Reverse the order of sentence 5 and sentence 6.
   b. Delete sentence 3.
   c. Reverse the order of sentence 8 and sentence 9.
   d. Delete sentence 9.

> **Read the passage, then answer the three questions that follow.**

(1) Being able to type good is no longer a requirement limited to secretaries and novelists; thanks to the computer, anyone who wants to enter the working world needs to be <u>accustomed</u> to a keyboard. (2) Just knowing your way around a keyboard does not mean that you can use one efficeintly, though; while you may have progressed beyond the hunt-and-peck method, you may never have learned to type quickly and accurately. (3) Doing so is a skill that will not only ensure that you pass a typing <u>proficiency</u> exam, but one that is essential if you want to advance your career in any number of fields. (4) This chapter <u>assures</u> that you are familiar enough with a standard keyboard to be able to use it without looking at the keys, which is the first step in learning to type, and that you are aware of the proper <u>fingering</u>. (5) The following information will help you increase your speed and accuracy and to do our best when being tested on timed writing passages.

_____

33. Which part of the passage contains a nonstandard use of a modifier?
   a. sentence 1
   b. sentence 2
   c. sentence 3
   d. sentence 5

34. Which underlined word in the passage is misused in its context?
   a. assures
   b. proficiency
   c. fingering
   d. accustomed

35. Which part of the passage contains an error in spelling?
   a. sentence 1
   b. sentence 2
   c. sentence 3
   d. sentence 4

Short-Answer Questions

Directions: Each of the following seven sentences contains two errors in construction, grammar, usage, spelling, capitalization, or punctuation. Rewrite each sentence so these errors are revised but the original meaning remains, without introducing any new errors.

36. According to the reporter, there is multiple political reasons behind the unexpected riot going on downtown those afternoon.

_____

_____

_____

37. On the stage the magician created an allusion that shocked the entire audience into total silence, which was followed by thundering applause.

_____

_____

_____

38. Although various fans seen the winning shot clearly, the referee still would not change his initial ruling, and the player was instant put on the bench.

_____

_____

_____

39. When Sal visited the Washington monument, he asked his aunt Ernestine to photograph him in front of it.

_____

_____

_____

40. Patricia turned on the television, so she decided to read the book she took out of the library instead, but none of the show's interested her.

_____

_____

_____

41. When a few drops of rain quickly grew into a terrential downpour the bus driver made sure to switch on the windshield wipers quickly.

_____

_____

_____

42. The Captain peered through his telescope, and saw a small ship riding the ocean waves far in the distance.

_____

_____

_____

Writing Summary Exercise

Directions: Use the following passage to prepare a summary of 100 to 150 words.

For centuries, time was measured by the position of the sun, with the use of sundials. Noon was recognized when the sun was the highest in the sky, and cities would set their clocks by this apparent solar time, even though some cities would often be on a slightly different time. Daylight saving time (DST), sometimes called "summer time," was instituted to make better use of daylight. Thus, clocks are set forward one hour in the spring to move an hour of daylight from the morning to the evening and then set back one hour in the fall to return to normal daylight.

Benjamin Franklin first conceived the idea of daylight saving during his tenure as an American delegate in Paris in 1784 and wrote about it extensively in his essay, "An Economical Project." It is said that Franklin awoke early one morning and was surprised to see the sunlight at such an hour. Always the economist, Franklin believed the practice of moving the time could save on the use of candlelight, as candles were expensive at the time.

In England, builder William Willett (1857–1915) became a strong supporter for daylight saving time upon noticing blinds of many houses were closed on an early sunny morning. Willett believed everyone, including himself, would appreciate longer hours of light in the evenings. In 1909, Sir Robert Pearce introduced a bill in the House of Commons to make it obligatory to adjust the clocks. A bill was drafted and introduced into Parliament several times but met with great opposition, mostly from farmers. Eventually, in 1925, it was decided that summer time should begin on the day following the third Saturday in April and close after the first Saturday in October.

The U.S. Congress passed the Standard Time Act of 1918 to establish standard time and preserve and set daylight saving time across the continent. This act also devised five time zones throughout the United States: Eastern, Central, Mountain, Pacific, and Alaska. The first time zone was set on "the mean astronomical time of the seventy-fifth degree of longitude west from Greenwich (England)." In 1919, this act was repealed.

President Roosevelt established year-round daylight saving time (also called war time) from 1942–1945. However, after this period, each state adopted its own DST, which proved to be disconcerting to television and radio broadcasting and transportation. In 1966, President Lyndon Johnson created the Department of Transportation and signed the Uniform Time Act. As a result, the Department of Transportation was given the responsibility for the time laws. During the oil embargo and energy crisis of the 1970s, President Richard Nixon extended DST through the Daylight Saving Time Energy Act of 1973 to conserve energy further. This law was modified in 1986, and daylight saving time was reset to begin on the first Sunday in April (to "spring ahead") and end on the last Sunday in October (to "fall back"). Most recently, daylight saving standards were altered yet again; as of 2007, daylight saving time would begin on the second Sunday of March and end on the first Sunday in November. This change was established by Congress as part of the Energy Policy Act of 2005.

Writing Summary

_____

_____

_____

_____

_____

_____

_____

_____

_____

_____

_____

_____

_____

Composition Exercise

Directions: Read the passages below about school uniforms; then follow the instructions for writing your composition.

Mandatory School Uniforms Are Appropriate in Our School

Contemporary schools forge far too casual environments for contemporary students. While individual freedom is important, we must not forget that schools are places where serious work is accomplished, and serious attitudes are imperative for performing such work. School uniforms help instill a sense of seriousness in students and help remind them that they are at school to work, not socialize.

Mandatory School Uniforms Are Not Appropriate in Our School

Developing a sense of individuality is an integral part of any young person's emotional growth. One way young people express their individuality is through the clothing they choose to wear. By forcing them to all dress the same by mandating a school uniform policy, we may be impeding their emotional development and violating their personal freedom.

Your purpose is to write a persuasive composition, to be read by a classroom instructor, in which you take a position on whether or not student uniforms should be mandatory in your school. Be sure to defend your position with logical arguments and appropriate examples.

Composition

_____

_____

_____

_____

_____

_____

_____

_____

_____

_____

Reading Subtest Answers

1. c. The assertion that the manufacturer "made the finest caramels in the United States" is a personal opinion of the author rather than an inarguable fact. Another person may feel that another manufacturer made finer caramels. The other answer choices all express facts.

2. b. This is an inference question. The writer indicates that visitors to Hershey's Chocolate World are greeted by a giant Reese's Peanut Butter Cup, so it is logical to assume that these are manufactured by Hershey. Although the writer mentions the popularity of chocolate internationally, you cannot assume that it is popular in every country (choice **a**), nor is there any indication that Milton Hershey was the first person to manufacture chocolate in the United States (choice **c**). Choice **d** is not discussed in the passage at all.

3. d. This question tests your ability to use context clues to determine the intended meaning of a word. In paragraph 3, the passage says *The Hershey Chocolate company was born in 1894 as a subsidiary of the Lancaster Caramel Company*. This indicates that a subsidiary is one controlled by another company, choice **d**. Although it may be true that Milton Hershey owned each company in its entirety (choice **a**), that is not clear from the material. There is also no indication that the chocolate company was created to support the caramel company (choice **b**). Finally, the passage contains no discussion of whether any of Hershey's companies were incorporated (choice **c**).

4. a. Choice **a** is the best choice because it is the most complete statement of the material. Choices **c** and **d** focus on small details of the passage; choice **b** is not discussed in the passage.

5. b. Paragraph 3 states that Hershey sold the caramel company six years after the founding of the chocolate company. The chocolate company was founded in 1894; the correct choice is **b**.

6. c. The Chicago International Exposition was where Hershey saw a demonstration of German chocolate-making techniques, which indicates, along with the word *international* in its title, that the exposition contained displays from a variety of countries, choice **c**. None of the other choices can be inferred from the information in the passage.

7. b. This answer is the most accurate outline of the passage. Choices **a** and **c** do not focus on the main idea of each paragraph. Choice **d** is limited to the information in paragraph 2, and therefore is not a good outline of the main topics in the passage as a whole.

8. b. This answer is explicitly stated in the first sentence of the selection. Choices **a** and **d** are not mentioned as a result of plaque-laden arteries. Choice **c** is too general to be the best answer.

9. a. The first and second sentences of paragraph 2 state how both procedures, angioplasty and bypass surgery, are invasive because *both involve entering the body cavity*. None of the other choices are supported or implied as a definition for invasive.

10. c. The procedure is detailed in paragraph 3. It begins with injecting a special dye. Choices **a** and **b** follow later in the procedure, whereas choice **d** deals with bypass surgery rather than the angioplasty procedure.

11. d. This answer can be found in paragraph 4. A team of surgeons stands ready to perform bypass surgery even though the risk factor of death is only 2%. Choice **a** is not supported in the passage. Choices **b** and **c** are incorrect because the passage does not discuss patient reaction at all.

12. a. This choice is supported in the last sentence of paragraph 3. Choice **b** is incorrect: The risk factor is 2%. Choice **c** is a complete misunderstanding of the text. Inflating a balloon into a blocked artery is coronary balloon angioplasty. Choice **d** expresses an opinion, not a fact.

13. b. Look back to paragraph 1, where George's single tax proposal (the idea The Landlord's Game was meant to teach) is described as aiming to *weaken the ability to form monopolies, encourage equal opportunity, and narrow the gap between rich and poor.*

14. b. Paragraph 2 explains the first part of the question, while paragraph 5 contains the answer to the second. Choice **c** is incorrect because encouraging equal opportunity is not an objective of Monopoly. Don't be distracted by choices **a** and **d**, which contain true statements that are not the objectives of the games. Note also that evolution was a theory of Charles Darwin, not Charles Darrow.

15. b. Paragraph 4 explains that Darrow fraudulently claimed to be the game's inventor (he was introduced to it before he got a patent as its inventor). Parker Brothers bought his patent believing that it was genuine, meaning that they believed Darrow's falsehood.

16. a. The answer is in Paragraph 3. Having the game and its rules spread by word of mouth means it will *alter slightly* from one person to another.

17. b. To *imply* means to hint at, rather than to state outright. The other choices are all directly stated in the paragraph, while **b** is implied.

18. a. Paragraph 5 states she sold the game to remain true to her original intent, which was to spread the word about George's single tax theory.

19. b. Type II, or non-insulin-dependent, diabetes is the main subject of the passage, which distinguishes Type II from Type I and goes on to stress the importance of diet.

20. c. Type I diabetes is the insulin-dependent form of this condition. The minority of diabetics are afflicted with this form. They are diagnosed as children and must take daily injections of insulin to compensate for what their pancreases do not produce.

21. a. The final paragraph says that there is no cure for diabetes, so choices **b** and **d** are incorrect. Choice **c** is a possibility, but consider the sound of the word *soothe*. It does not fit with the objective tone of the passage nearly as well as the word *counteract*.

22. a. This passage is focused solely on diabetes, not on an assortment of diseases, so whether many diseases are currently incurable is irrelevant. Choice **b** essentially restates this sentence, while maintaining a focus on diabetes, so it is relevant. Choices **c** and **d** are also relevant to the passage.

23. a. Paragraph 1 states that there are between 13 and 14 million people in the United States with diabetes. According to the passage, 90 to 95% of these people have non-insulin-dependent, or Type II, diabetes. Therefore, the remaining 5 to 10% of people have insulin-dependent diabetes. The only answer choice that reflects realistically reflects this population is choice **a**, because it is the only choice that is less than 13 to 14 million.

24. d. This answer choice summarizes the third paragraph sufficiently. Choice **a** summarizes the fourth paragraph. Choice **b** does not focus on the most important details in the third paragraph and choice **c** repeats details scattered throughout the entire passage.

25. c. The passage states that Rosa Parks's actions and arrest *set off a train of events that generated a momentum the civil rights movement had never before experienced* (paragraph 2).

26. d. The amount of energy people put into challenging the second-class citizenship treatment received by African Americans following World War II was stronger than it had ever been before, which means it was out of the ordinary or extraordinary. Therefore, *extraordinary* means the same thing as *unprecedented* as it is used in this context. While the fight for equality may have been *exhausting*, as well as *disruptive* and *frightening* to those who cling to the ideas of racial segregation and discrimination, none of these words has the same meaning as *unprecedented*.

27. c. This answer can be found in paragraph 3. The four men were refused service at the lunch counter in an F.W. Woolworth store. Choice **b** is incorrect because the four students attended North Carolina Agricultural and Technical College, but it is not where they were refused service. Choices **a** and **d** refer to other incidents that helped fuel the civil rights movement.

28. b. Choice **b** adequately addresses all the major ideas in the passage. Choices **a**, **c**, and **d** only refer to individual details without covering the passage as a whole.

29. a. Choice **a** is an opinion rather than a fact because not everyone will agree that equal opportunities in education are more important than equal opportunities in employment.

30. a. Choice **a** sums up all the major ideas in paragraph 2 of the passage. Choices **b** and **c** refer to specific details in paragraph 2 without summarizing the paragraph as a whole. Choice **d** summarizes paragraph 5.

31. c. Choice **c** adequately outlines the most important ideas throughout the entire passage. Choice **a** only outlines the first paragraph. Choices **b** and **d** collect random details scattered throughout the passage.

32. d. Paragraph 4 states that Lewis later said that he used a peace medal as a way to let the Blackfeet know "who we were." Although the paragraph also says that medals were ways to *designate five "ranks" of chief*, this is not the reason Clark gave, so choice **c** is incorrect.

33. b. The author mainly wrote this passage to describe Lewis and Clark's mission to meet with various Native American tribes. While Lewis and Clark often had ulterior motives for meeting with these tribes, the writer is not mainly concerned with proving this, so choice **a** is incorrect. The writer never describes the path they took throughout the West, which eliminates choice **c**. Choice **d** only describes one detail in the passage without addressing the passage as a whole.

34. a. Since everyone might not agree that the pipe ceremony was the Plains Indians' most beautiful ritual, this statement is an opinion rather than an indisputable fact. The other answer choices are all inarguable facts.

35. a. Details about Lewis's birth and parents are not relevant to paragraph focused on Lewis and Clark's mission and methods. Choices **b**, **c**, and **d** all help develop the topic.

36. b. The purpose of this detail is to show that the white people thought it was important to use machines to manufacture corn, while the Mandan people felt it more necessary to produce weapons for their survival, which illustrates a difference in ideals. That the Mandan were capable of demolishing the mills does not necessarily suggest the white people made inferiors mills, so choice **a** is incorrect. There is no evidence to suggest that the Mandan had no use for corn; they just didn't necessarily need machines to process it, so choice **c** is incorrect.

37. d. In the fifth paragraph, the author writes: *Someone obtained my Social Security number, address, work number and address, and a few other vital pieces of data. That person then applied for a credit account in my name.*

38. c. The paragraph describing the author's experience with identity theft immediately follows the sentence: *We can do little to stop the information gathering and exchange and can only hope to be able to control the damage if something goes wrong* (paragraph 4) and serves as an example of something *going wrong*—the misuse of private information.

39. b. The author describes various forms of identity theft and shows how modern technology is used to commit the crime. Still, the author never suggests that everyone will be victims of this crime, so choice **a** is incorrect, nor does the author write that the man who lives in the glass house will be a victim of such a crime, so choice **c** is incorrect, as well.

40. c. Because this passage largely describes how technology, and specifically Internet use, has led to a rise in identity theft, it was mainly written to inform those who use the Internet frequently.

41. a. A mill built using panopticon structure has nothing to do with the prevalence of surveillance and technological identity theft in contemporary society, which is the main theme of paragraph 4.

42. a. Considering that more people have committed credit card fraud than employment fraud, one can conclude that credit card fraud is a more profitable crime. According to the chart, utilities fraud is more common than government fraud, so choice **b** is incorrect. There is no information on the chart to support choices **c** and **d**.

Writing Subtest Answers

Multiple Choice

1. c. Sentence 6 contains a sentence fragment; the sentence is a dependent clause. Choices **a**, **b**, and **d** all refer to standard sentences.

2. a. The main purpose of this paragraph is to outline Dr. Miranda Woodhouse's plan to reduce the risks of heart disease, and choice **a** focuses the reader's attention on the four strategies that Dr. Woodhouse proposes as part of this plan. Choice **b** focuses on the life expectancy rates of American citizens, and while lowering heart disease may boost life expectancy rates, this paragraph does not deal with that at all. It focuses exclusively on Dr. Woodhouse's plan for preventing heart disease. Choice **c** contains seemingly contradictory information, which is in no way implied or stated in the paragraph. Choice **d** makes an argumentative claim about one part of Dr. Woodhouse's plan, which is out of place in a paragraph that seeks only to outline the basic strategies.

3. c. The possessive pronoun *their* is used erroneously in sentence 9. *There* is the word that should be used.

4. d. The passage is mainly about taking measures to maintain a healthy heart, while sentence 13 focuses on the kidneys. Choice **a** is the topic sentence, so it is extremely necessary to the passage. Choices **b** and **c** are on topic because they mention ways to maintain heart health.

5. c. Sentence 5 states that Roosevelt became a *civil service reformer* back east. Choice **c** repeats this information, substituting the word *improve* for the synonym *reform*. Choices **a**, **b**, and **d** all express information that is not needlessly repeated elsewhere in the passage.

6. d. The verb needs to be singular to agree with the singular subject of the sentence, *Theodore Roosevelt*. Choices **a**, **b**, and **c** are incorrect because they introduce a shift in tense.

7. d. There is a lack of agreement between the singular *Roosevelt* and the plural pronoun *they*, which should be changed to *he*. Sentence 3 contains proper agreement between Teddy and the pronoun *his*. Sentences 4 and 5 both contain pronouns, but neither contains antecedents.

8. c. The word <u>commisioner</u> should be spelled *commissioner*. Choices **a**, **b**, and **d** are all spelled correctly.

9. a. Sentence 10 is missing the preposition *to*, which should link *one coastline* and *the other*. Therefore the sentence should read, *Under the best weather conditions, the trip from one coastline to the other took six to eight hours, and frequently, vicious storms delayed ships for days—even weeks.*

10. c. The word *european* is a proper adjective and should be capitalized. The other choices are capitalized correctly.

11. b. Sentence 6 introduces the idea of connecting France and England, which is the topic of the paragraph, therefore this topic sentence should introduce the paragraph. Sentence 5 develops on that sentence and should therefore be placed after sentence 6. Part 4 serves a necessary transitional function by setting up ideas that will be introduced throughout the rest of the passage, and therefore should not be deleted, so choice **a** is incorrect. Choice **c** is incorrect because sentence 13 serves a valuable function as the topic sentence of paragraph 3. As such, it belongs at the beginning of the paragraph and should not be moved, as is suggested by the incorrect choice **d**.

12. a. The word *catastrophes* is misspelled in sentence 4 of the passage. Choices **b**, **c**, and **d** are spelled correctly.

13. d. The jobs that some people perform in offices have nothing to do with the paragraph's main idea, which is the difference between year-round and regular school schedules.

14. c. Sentence 9 lacks a subject, so it is a fragment. Although it is short, sentence 3 is a complete sentence.

15. d. The word *don't* in sentence 8 is a contraction of the words *do* and *not*. Contractions always need apostrophes to join the two words that comprise them. Choices **a**, **b**, and **c** do not require apostrophes for that or any other reason.

16. d. The schedules belong to the educational systems, so the possessive form *their* is needed in sentence 11.

17. c. The information in sentence 7 continues the description of what judges must ascertain about such cases, which began in sentence 5. Skipping to the responsibilities of officers and back to judges is confusing. Choices **a** and **b** are incorrect because they introduce examples before the passage states what the examples are supposed to show.

18. b. The word *ascertain* is misspelled in sentence 7.

19. c. Part 8 is redundant because it repeats information from sentence 4.

20. d. The procedure of handcuffing and jailing suspects of serious crimes has nothing to with Miranda rights, which is the main idea of this passage.

21. b. The topic of the paragraph is about the ecology of an area; it does not specifically address environmental organizations.

22. c. This sentence sets up the main idea of the passage very well. The passage focuses on ecosystems in general without specifically describing rain forests, so choice **a** is incorrect. Choice **b** is incorrect because the passage is about ecosystems, not the person who coined the term *ecosystem*. Choice **d** basically just rewords information in sentence 6.

23. a. The word *nutrients* is misspelled in sentence 1.

24. d. The word *too* means *also*, which does not make sense in the context of sentence 6. The correct spelling of the word when used to express an aim or purpose, as it is in sentence 6, should be spelled *to*.

25. a. End quotation marks must be inserted before the tag phrase, *says Warner*. Choice **b** is incorrect because the quotation marks are necessary to begin the quotation again after the tag phrase. It is essential to the meaning of the sentence. Choice **c** is incorrect because *than* is a conjunction used to compare things and is the word that should be used here. Choice **d** is incorrect because *the beverage case* is not a clause that should be set off with commas.

26. d. Sentence 6 acts as a topic sentence for the ideas and quotations in the third paragraph. Combining sentence 6 with paragraph 3 makes the subject of the third paragraph clearer to the reader and brings information on the main topic together in the same place. Choice **a** would not really make any major difference in the paragraph and doesn't do anything to help focus attention on the main idea. Choice **b** would make the main idea less, not more, clear. Choice **c** would just make for a much longer sentence without adding any emphasis to the main idea.

27. a. Sentence 3 needlessly combines information already introduced in sentences 1 and 2, therefore it is redundant. Choices **b**, **c**, and **d** all introduce new information that helps develop the main idea of the passage.

28. b. Sentence 6 needs a comma to offset the introductory phrase *According to nutritionist Elizabeth Warner* from the rest of the sentence. Therefore, a comma should be placed between *Warner* and *many*.

29. b. Sentence 3 is a compound sentence and requires a comma to separate its two halves. A comma should be placed between the words *December* and *although*. Choice **a** correctly uses commas to separate items in a list. Choice **b** correctly uses a comma to separate the two halves of a compound sentence. Choice **d** correctly uses a comma to separate the two hyphenated words that modify the word *activities*.

30. d. The expressions *year-round* and *in all seasons* repeat the same idea. Choices **a**, **b**, and **c** are incorrect because none of these sentences contain unnecessary repetition. Part 4 may seem to, at first; however, the words *hot* and *humid* are described in more interesting and specific terms in the second part of the sentence.

31. a. The word *Its* is the possessive form of *It*, which does not make sense in this context. The word is used to mean *It is*, so it requires an apostrophe and should be written *It's*.

32. a. Sentence 6 discusses the heat in the Everglades, which would follow the statement *Summers are hot and humid* in sentence sentence 9 would remove information that helps develop the passage, so choice **b** and choice **d** are incorrect. Choice **c** is incorrect because reversing the order of sentence 8 and sentence 9 would not make the passage clearer.

33. a. In part 1, the adjective *good* is misused as an adverb; it needs to be replaced by the adverb *well*.

34. a. In sentence 4, the verb *assure*, to make certain, is nonsensical in the context; it should be replaced by the verb *assume*, to suppose or take for granted. Choices **b**, **c**, and **d** are incorrect because all these words are used properly in their context.

35. b. The word *efficiently* is misspelled in sentence 2. All the words in choices **a**, **c**, and **d** are spelled correctly.

Short Answer

36. This sentence should read, *According to the reporter, there are multiple political reasons behind the unexpected riot going on downtown this afternoon.* In this question, the subject of the sentence (*reasons*) follows the verb (*is*). Plural subjects need plural verbs. Instead of *is*, the verb should be *are* in order to have subject-verb agreement. For this same reason, the adjective *those* should be changed to *this* since *afternoon* is singular.

37. This sentence should read, *On the stage, the magician created an illusion that shocked the entire audience into total silence, which was followed by thundering applause.* At first glance, this sentence may seem correct. The first error is in using the wrong word. It should not be *allusion*, which means to allude to something. It should be *illusion*. Furthermore, the introductory phrase *On the stage* needs to be separated from the rest of the sentence with a comma.

38. This sentence should read, *Although various fans saw the winning shot clearly, the referee still would not change his initial ruling and the player was instantly put on the bench.* The first error in this question is testing your understanding of the past participle. In this example, the verb (*seen*) is a past participle and requires a helping verb (*have* or *be*). The way to correct the sentence is to change *seen* to *saw*. The second error tests your understanding of usage. Since *instant* modifies the verb *put*, it should be written in the adverb form as *instantly*, rather than the adjective form.

39. This sentence should read, *When Sal visited the Washington Monument, he asked his Aunt Ernestine to photograph him in front of it.* It contains two capitalization errors. The first is the failure to capitalize *Monument*, which is one half of the proper name *Washington Monument*. The second is the failure to capitalize *Aunt*, which should be capitalized in this context because it is used as a title.

40. This sentence should read, *Patricia turned on the television, but none of the shows interested her, so she decided to read the book she took out of the library instead.* The first error is a mistake in construction. The phrase *but none of the shows interested her* continues the idea presented in the opening statement, *Patricia turned on the television,* so it should be moved to follow that phrase in the sentence. The second error is a punctuation mistake. The word *show's* is possessive, although it is used as the plural form of *show.* Therefore, the apostrophe should be deleted.

41. This sentence should read, *When a few drops of rain quickly grew into a torrential downpour, the bus driver made sure to switch on the windshield wipers quickly.* The first error is a spelling error; *terrential* should read *torrential.* The second error is a missing comma, which should be used to separate the introductory phrase *When a few drops of rain quickly grew into a torrential downpour* from the rest of the sentence.

42. This sentence should read, *The captain peered through his telescope and saw a small ship riding the ocean waves far in the distance.* Because the word captain is not used as a title in this sentence, it should not be capitalized. The comma is also used incorrectly, since *saw a small ship riding the ocean waves far in the distance* is not an independent clause with its own subject. Therefore, the comma should be deleted.

Sample Strong Response for Writing Summary Exercise

Daylight saving time (DST) is a practice implemented to make better use of sunlight and save energy. The idea was first conceived in 1784 by Benjamin Franklin, who believed the practice would help save money on expensive candles. The builder William Willett helped promote the idea in England by focusing on how DST would extend sunlight hours through the evenings. The idea was controversial, especially among farmers, but British Parliament passed a bill instating DST in 1925. The U.S. Congress had passed its own such bill in 1918, which also devised the concept of time zones. DST standards have changed a good deal through the years, from President Roosevelt's year-round daylight saving time schedule of the early 1940s, to the state-by-state DST schedule that followed, to President Nixon's extension of DST in 1973 to conserve energy during an energy crisis, to acts that further modified it in 1986 and 2007.

Sample Strong Response for Composition Exercise

Imagine a school auditorium full of alert children, all dressed neatly in blue and white uniforms. Imagine these same children happily running out to play in their blue shorts and white oxford shirts, playing tag and flying on swings. Whether to dress public school children alike has been the subject of much controversy in recent decades. Opponents suggest that requiring uniforms will stifle children's ability to choose, squash necessary individuality, and infringe on the rights of children and families. Although there is some justification for these arguments, the benefits of uniforms far outweigh the disadvantages. Adopting a uniform policy will benefit parents, children, and the school staff.

A uniform policy will benefit parents. Uniforms save parents money. Parents will not have to provide their children with a different matched set of clothes for each day, so fewer school clothes will be needed. Children will have already agreed on what clothes their parents will need to buy, so there will be fewer arguments on this often touchy subject.

Not only are parents happy to see a uniform policy in place, but their children benefit, as well. If you were from a low-income home, wouldn't you feel badly if you were not dressed as well as your peers?

Children who dress differently may be alienated from cliques at school and left to feel like outsiders. Dressing in uniforms helps children feel an increased sense of belonging that enables them to be more relaxed and quieter in school.

Adopting a uniform policy will lighten the burden of parents. It will promote cheerfulness and seriousness in children. So what are we waiting for? We need to talk to our school boards and give our children all the tools we can that will enhance their growth and development.

Scoring Your Subtests

Your scores on the Reading and Writing subtests of the official MTEL Communication and Literacy Skills Test will be scaled scores representing all subareas of each subtest, including all multiple-choice questions, short-answer questions, and open-response assignments. The scaled score for both the Reading and Writing subtest is a conversion of the number of raw points earned on the test to a score in the range of 100 to 300. A scaled score of 240 represents the qualifying, or passing, score for each subtest. You can use the charts on the following pages to find approximate MTEL scores for your performance on this diagnostic

and to help guide your studies with the two review chapters in this book, as well as outside resources. Remember, these are only practice tests and the scores you receive here are only an approximation of what your official scores might be.

Find Your Reading Subtest Score

To find your approximate MTEL score for the practice reading subtest, you must first figure out how many raw subtest points you earned. Each question answered correctly on this subtest is worth one point, for a maximum of 42 points. Use Table 6.1 to add up your points; giving yourself a "1" for each correct answer, and a "0" for each incorrect answer.

You can also use Table 6.1 to help diagnose your strengths and weaknesses to better focus your studies. The rows in the "Objective" column include the MTEL Reading Subtest objectives that correspond to each question in this practice test. After you have filled in the table, note any particular objective or objectives in which you could use more practice, and then turn to **Chapter 7: Reading Skills Review** and use the review resources there to help strengthen your skills in that area.

TABLE 6.1 READING SUBTEST SCORING AND REVIEW CHART

QUESTION NUMBER	CORRECT ANSWER	POINTS Correct Answer = 1 Point Incorrect Answer = 0 Points	OBJECTIVE
1.	c		0005 Use critical reasoning skills to evaluate written material.
2.	b		0004 Analyze the relationships among ideas in written material.
3.	d		0001 Determine the meaning of words and phrases in the context in which they occur.
4.	a		0003 Identify a writer's purpose, point of view, and intended meaning.
5.	b		0002 Understand the main idea and supporting details in written material.
6.	c		0004 Analyze the relationships among ideas in written material.
7.	b		0006 Apply skills for outlining and summarizing written materials and interpreting information presented in graphic form.
8.	b		0002 Understand the main idea and supporting details in written material.
9.	a		0001 Determine the meaning of words and phrases in the context in which they occur.
10.	c		0004 Analyze the relationships among ideas in written material.
11.	d		0004 Analyze the relationships among ideas in written material.
12.	a		0005 Use critical reasoning skills to evaluate written material.
13.	b		0001 Determine the meaning of words and phrases in the context in which they occur.
14.	b		0004 Analyze the relationships among ideas in written material.
15.	b		0001 Determine the meaning of words and phrases in the context in which they occur.
16.	a		0001 Determine the meaning of words and phrases in the context in which they occur.
17.	b		0004 Analyze the relationships among ideas in written material.
18.	a		0002 Understand the main idea and supporting details in written material.
19.	b		0006 Apply skills for outlining and summarizing written materials and interpreting information presented in graphic form.

TABLE 6.1 READING SUBTEST SCORING AND REVIEW CHART (continued)

QUESTION NUMBER	CORRECT ANSWER	POINTS Correct Answer = 1 Point Incorrect Answer = 0 Points	OBJECTIVE
20.	c		0004 Analyze the relationships among ideas in written material.
21.	a		0001 Determine the meaning of words and phrases in the context in which they occur.
22.	a		0005 Use critical reasoning skills to evaluate written material.
23.	a		0002 Understand the main idea and supporting details in written material.
24.	d		0006 Apply skills for outlining and summarizing written materials and interpreting information presented in graphic form.
25.	c		0003 Identify a writer's purpose, point of view, and intended meaning.
26.	d		0001 Determine the meaning of words and phrases in the context in which they occur.
27.	c		0002 Understand the main idea and supporting details in written material.
28.	b		0006 Apply skills for outlining and summarizing written materials and interpreting information presented in graphic form.
29.	a		0005 Use critical reasoning skills to evaluate written material.
30.	a		0006 Apply skills for outlining and summarizing written materials and interpreting information presented in graphic form.
31.	c		0006 Apply skills for outlining and summarizing written materials and interpreting information presented in graphic form.
32.	d		0002 Understand the main idea and supporting details in written material.
33.	b		0003 Identify a writer's purpose, point of view, and intended meaning.
34.	a		0005 Use critical reasoning skills to evaluate written material.
35.	a		0005 Use critical reasoning skills to evaluate written material.
36.	b		0003 Identify a writer's purpose, point of view, and intended meaning.
37.	d		0002 Understand the main idea and supporting details in written material.
38.	c		0003 Identify a writer's purpose, point of view, and intended meaning.

(continued)

TABLE 6.1 READING SUBTEST SCORING AND REVIEW CHART (continued)

QUESTION NUMBER	CORRECT ANSWER	POINTS Correct Answer = 1 Point Incorrect Answer = 0 Points	OBJECTIVE
39.	b		0003 Identify a writer's purpose, point of view, and intended meaning.
40.	c		0003 Identify a writer's purpose, point of view, and intended meaning.
41.	a		0005 Use critical reasoning skills to evaluate written material.
42.	a		0006 Apply skills for outlining and summarizing written materials and interpreting information presented in graphic form.
Total Reading Subtest Points:			

Now, find the number of reading subtest points you earned in the left-hand column of Table 6.2. The corresponding number in the right-hand column is your approximate MTEL score.

TABLE 6.2 READING SUBTEST SCORE CONVERSION CHART

POINTS	APPROXIMATE MTEL READING SCORE
0–14	100
15–16	101
17–18	116
19–20	131
21–22	146
23–24	161
25–26	176
27–28	191
29–30	206
31–32	221
33–34	236
35–36	251
37–38	266
39–40	281
41–42	296

Find Your Writing Subtest Score

There are a number of steps to finding your total approximate MTEL score for a practice writing subtest. The first step is to total the number of raw points you earned for your responses to the multiple-choice and short-answer questions. Like the reading subtest, each multiple-choice question answered correctly on this subtest is worth one point. Use Table 6.3 to add up those multiple-choice points. In Table 6.3, you'll also find each question's related objective to help focus your studying using **Chapter 8: Writing Skills Review**.

TABLE 6.3	WRITING SUBTEST MULTIPLE-CHOICE QUESTIONS SCORING AND REVIEW CHART		
QUESTION NUMBER	**CORRECT ANSWER**	**POINTS** Correct Answer = 1 Point Incorrect Answer = 0 Points	**OBJECTIVE**
1.	c		0008 Recognize common errors of sentence construction, grammar, and usage.
2.	a		0007 Understand methods for establishing and maintaining a central theme or main idea.
3.	c		0008 Recognize common errors of sentence construction, grammar, and usage.
4.	d		0007 Understand methods for establishing and maintaining a central theme or main idea.
5.	c		0007 Understand methods for establishing and maintaining a central theme or main idea.
6.	d		0008 Recognize common errors of sentence construction, grammar, and usage.
7.	d		0008 Recognize common errors of sentence construction, grammar, and usage.
8.	c		0009 Recognize common errors of spelling, capitalization, and punctuation.
9.	a		0008 Recognize common errors of sentence construction, grammar, and usage.
10.	c		0009 Recognize common errors of spelling, capitalization, and punctuation.
11.	b		0007 Understand methods for establishing and maintaining a central theme or main idea.
12.	a		0009 Recognize common errors of spelling, capitalization, and punctuation.
13.	d		0007 Understand methods for establishing and maintaining a central theme or main idea.
14.	c		0008 Recognize common errors of sentence construction, grammar, and usage.
15.	d		0009 Recognize common errors of spelling, capitalization, and punctuation.
16.	d		0008 Recognize common errors of sentence construction, grammar, and usage.

(continued)

QUESTION NUMBER	CORRECT ANSWER	POINTS Correct Answer = 1 Point Incorrect Answer = 0 Points	OBJECTIVE
17.	c		0007 Understand methods for establishing and maintaining a central theme or main idea.
18.	b		0009 Recognize common errors of spelling, capitalization, and punctuation.
19.	c		0007 Understand methods for establishing and maintaining a central theme or main idea.
20.	d		0007 Understand methods for establishing and maintaining a central theme or main idea.
21.	b		0007 Understand methods for establishing and maintaining a central theme or main idea.
22.	c		0007 Understand methods for establishing and maintaining a central theme or main idea.
23.	a		0009 Recognize common errors of spelling, capitalization, and punctuation.
24.	d		0008 Recognize common errors of sentence construction, grammar, and usage.
25.	a		0009 Recognize common errors of spelling, capitalization, and punctuation.
26.	d		0007 Understand methods for establishing and maintaining a central theme or main idea.
27.	a		0007 Understand methods for establishing and maintaining a central theme or main idea.
28.	b		0009 Recognize common errors of spelling, capitalization, and punctuation.
29.	b		0009 Recognize common errors of spelling, capitalization, and punctuation.
30.	d		0007 Understand methods for establishing and maintaining a central theme or main idea.
31.	a		0007 Understand methods for establishing and maintaining a central theme or main idea.
32.	a		0007 Understand methods for establishing and maintaining a central theme or main idea.
33.	a		0008 Recognize common errors of sentence construction, grammar, and usage.
34.	a		0008 Recognize common errors of sentence construction, grammar, and usage.
35.	b		0009 Recognize common errors of spelling, capitalization, and punctuation.

TABLE 6.3 WRITING SUBTEST MULTIPLE-CHOICE QUESTIONS SCORING AND REVIEW CHART (continued)

Multiple-Choice Points Subtotal: _____

The short-answer questions in the writing subtest are worth zero, one, or two points, depending on the success of your response. Use the answer explanations and the following key to figure out how many points you earned for each of your short-answer questions:

SCORING KEY FOR WRITING SUBTEST SHORT-ANSWER QUESTIONS	
POINTS EARNED	**DESCRIPTION**
2	**Fully Correct:** ■ You successfully corrected both errors in the question and did not introduce any new ones.
1	**Partially Correct:** ■ You properly corrected only ONE of the two errors in the question. You did not introduce any new errors. ■ You successfully corrected both errors in the question, but introduced a new one.
0	**Incorrect:** ■ You did not correct either of the errors in the question. ■ You properly corrected ONE of the two errors in the question, but introduced one or more new errors.

Next, use Table 6.4 to add up the number of short answer points you earned on this subtest.

TABLE 6.4	WRITING SUBTEST SHORT-ANSWER QUESTIONS SCORING AND REVIEW CHART	
QUESTION NUMBER	**SHORT-ANSWER POINTS** Fully Correct = 2 Points Partially Correct = 1 Point Incorrect = 0 Points	**OBJECTIVE**
36. 37.		0010 Demonstrate the ability to analyze and revise sentences containing common errors of sentence construction, grammar, usage, spelling, capitalization, and punctuation.
38. 39. 40. 41. 42.		
Short-Answer Points Subtotal:		

Add up the multiple-choice and short-answer point subtotals from Table 6.2 and Table 6.3:

_____ + _____ = [   ]

Table 6.3 Subtotal   Table 6.4 Subtotal   Total

Next, take that total number and use it in Table 6.5 to find the approximate MTEL score for the multiple choice and short response section of this practice writing subtest.

Once you have assigned your two open responses a score between 0 and 4, use Table 6.6 to find your approximate score for the open response section of the writing subtest.

TABLE 6.5 WRITING SUBTEST MULTIPLE-CHOICE AND SHORT-ANSWER SCORE CONVERSION CHART	
MULTIPLE CHOICE + SHORT ANSWER POINTS	APPROXIMATE MTEL SCORE
0–10	50
11–13	59
14–16	68
17–19	77
20–22	86
23–25	95
26–28	104
29–31	113
32–34	122
35–37	131
38–40	140
41–42	150

Write your approximate MTEL score for this section here: [   ]

MTEL Score for Section 1

The next step is to score your Summary and Composition responses. Of course, you can do this yourself, but it is highly recommended that you ask a professional friend or colleague familiar with the official MTEL writing rubrics to do it for you to get the most accurate gauge of your work. The MTEL writing rubrics you should use to help score your two open responses are available on NES's official website on pages 48 through 51 of the document found here: www.mtel.nesinc.com/PDFs/MA_FLD201_Writing_PRACTICE_TEST.pdf.

TABLE 6.6 WRITING SUBTEST OPEN-RESPONSE SCORE CONVERSION CHART		
SUMMARY RESPONSE POINTS	COMPOSITION RESPONSE POINTS	APPROXIMATE MTEL SCORE
1	1	83
1	2	99
1	3	114
1	4	130
2	1	90
2	2	106
2	3	121
2	4	137
3	1	97
3	2	112
3	3	128
3	4	143
4	1	103
4	2	119
4	3	134
4	4	150

Write your approximate MTEL score for this section here: [   ]

MTEL Score for Section 2

Finally, to find your overall approximate MTEL writing subtest score, add up your MTEL scores from both sections:

[   ] + [   ] = [   ]

Section 1 MTEL Score   Section 2 MTEL Score   Overall Writing Subtest Score

READING SKILLS REVIEW

CHAPTER SUMMARY

Strong reading comprehension skills are important to have in life, in your teaching career, and most pressing to you right now, on the Reading subtest of the Communication and Literacy Skills Test. This chapter covers, by objective, the essential reading and reading comprehension strategies for needed for MTEL success. You will learn to become an active reader, to understand the difference between the main idea and supporting ideas, and to recognize information that is implied, but not stated, in a passage.

Types of Questions

All the questions on the Reading subtest are passage-based and multiple choice. Some questions focus on *what* information is presented in a passage, others deal with *how* information is presented. The questions fall into two basic categories: *literal comprehension* and *critical and inferential comprehension*.

Literal Comprehension

Literal comprehension questions measure your ability to understand the literal content of a passage. You might be asked to identify the main purpose of a passage, locate a fact or detail, describe how the passage is organized, or define how a word is used in a passage.

There are four types of literal comprehension questions:

1. **Main Idea.** For this question type, you need to be able to identify the main idea of the passage or a specific paragraph in the passage.
   Examples
   - The views expressed in this selection are most consistent with _____.
   - The passage is primarily concerned with _____.
   - Which of the following best describes a central aspect of Mel's daily ritual?

2. **Supporting Idea.** This question type asks you to summarize a supporting idea in the passage. You will need to be able to locate specific information in the passage, such as a fact, figure, or name.
   Examples
   - According to the charts, how many people in the United States have Type II diabetes?
   - The passage states that a lunar eclipse occurs when _____.
   - Which of the following is NOT mentioned as one of the reasons for the Cuban Missile Crisis?
   - Use the following information to answer the questions that follow.

3. **Organization.** In this type of question, you will be asked to recognize how a reading passage is organized. Organization questions may ask you to identify how a passage uses transitions and key phrases or how ideas within a passage relate to each other.
   Examples
   - Which of the following best describes the theme of the passage?
   - This passage is most likely taken from a (newspaper column, textbook, etc.)?
   - The phrase "the contrast in meaning and tone" refers to the contrast between _____.
   - Why is the word *indescribably* used in sentence 4?

4. **Vocabulary.** This question type asks you to determine the meaning of a word.
   Examples
   - Which of the following words, if substituted for the word *indelible* in the passage, would introduce the LEAST change in the meaning of the sentence?
   - The word *protest* in the passage could best be replaced by _____.
   - Which of the following is the best meaning of the word *experience* as it is used in the passage?

Critical and Inferential Comprehension

Whereas literal comprehension questions are straightforward, critical and inferential comprehension questions ask you to read between the lines of a text. These questions are about what is *implied* in the passage or statement. They ask you to identify the author's assumptions and attitudes and evaluate the weaknesses and strengths of the author's argument or logic. Critical and inferential comprehension questions include three types:

1. **Evaluation.** This question type asks you to evaluate the strengths and weaknesses of the argument presented in a passage. Evaluation questions will ask you to judge whether something is fact or opinion, or whether the evidence presented supports the message of the passage.
   Examples
   - In order to evaluate the validity of the author's claim regarding Jackson Pollock, it would be most helpful to know which of the following?
   - Which of the following is NOT mentioned in the passage as a weakness in the new law?

- Which of the following numbered sentences of the passage expresses a fact rather than an opinion?
- Use the reproduction to answer the following questions.

2. **Inferences.** This type of question asks you to make an inference (draw a logical conclusion) based on the content of the passage. Inference questions may ask you to determine an author's underlying assumptions or attitude toward the subject of the passage.

   Examples

   - Which of the following is an unstated assumption made by the author of the passage?
   - It can be inferred from the passage that the art of Picasso and Matisse differ in all the following ways EXCEPT _____.
   - The author would be LEAST likely to agree with which of the following statements?

3. **Generalizations.** This question type requires you to apply the ideas of a passage to new situations, recognize similar situations, and draw conclusions about the content of the passage. Many of the questions found on the Assessment of Teaching Skills—Written (ATS-W) are generalization questions.

   Examples

   - Which of the following conclusions about rainfall is best supported by information in the graphs?
   - Which of the following conclusions can you make based on the passage?
   - Given the information in the passage, what appeared to be an important post–World War II trend in the United States?
   - Which of the following would be considered primary sources?
   - Which of these strategies——?

Now that you have a better idea of what to expect on the exams, you can begin to review some reading comprehension skills and test-taking strategies. By honing these skills, you will be better equipped to understand reading passages and to do your best on the exams.

Reading Skill Builders

Reading may seem like a passive activity—after all, you are sitting, looking at words on a page. However, to improve your reading comprehension you need to read *actively*, meaning that you need to interact with the text. Incorporate these active-reading techniques into your study plan for the Communication and Literacy Skills Test. Each time you read a magazine, newspaper, or book, sharpen your reading comprehension skills using these strategies:

- **Skim ahead.** Scan the text *before* you read. Look at how the text is organized: How is it broken into sections? In what order are the topics presented? Note key words and ideas that are highlighted in boldface type or in bulleted lists.
- **Jump back.** Review the text after you read. By looking at summaries, headings, and highlighted information, you increase your ability to remember information and make connections between ideas.
- **Look up new words.** Keep a dictionary on hand as you read. Look up unfamiliar words and list them with their definitions in a notebook or make flash cards. To help you remember new words, connect them to something in your life or reading. Make a point of using new words in your writing and conversation. By increasing your vocabulary, you build your reading comprehension.
- **Highlight key ideas.** As you read, highlight or underline key terms, main ideas, or concepts that are new to you. Be selective—if you highlight too much of the text, nothing will stand out for you on the page. (If you don't own the book, use a notebook to jot down information.)
- **Take notes.** Note taking can help you remember material, even if you never look at your notes

again. That's because it's a muscle activity, and using your muscles can actually aid your memory. Record your questions, observations, and opinions as you read. Write down the main idea of the passage, the author's point of view, and whether you agree with the author.

- **Make connections.** When you connect two ideas, you improve your chances of remembering the material. For example, if you are reading about a current presidential race, you may note how it is similar to or different from past elections. How have circumstances changed? You may also connect the topic to your own experience: How did you feel about the past election versus the current race?

Test-Taking Tips

Now that you have reviewed the components that will help you understand and analyze what you read, you are ready to consider some specific test-taking strategies. The following techniques will help you read the passages quickly and effectively and answer the multiple-choice questions strategically so that you can boost your score.

Reading passages for a test is different than reading at home. For one thing, you have a time limit. The time you spend reading each passage detracts from the time you have to answer questions. Here are some basic guidelines for keeping you moving through the test in a time-efficient way:

- **Spend no more than two minutes on a question.** Circle difficult questions and return to them if you have time.
- **Skim and answer short passages quickly.** Short passages have only one or two questions, so you should move through them with speed. Give yourself a bit more time for long passages that are followed by more than two questions.

- **Guess, if necessary.** The MTEL does not penalize for wrong answers. Make sure to answer each question, even if you think you might return to it later.
- **Circle, underline, and make notes.** You can write in your test booklet, so be sure to mark up the passage as you read. Scribble down quick notes that will help you answer the questions.
- **Target the first part of the passage.** The first third of many reading passages is packed with essential information. Often you can answer main idea questions based on the information at the start of a passage. Likewise, for longer passages of 200 words, you will often find what each paragraph is about in its first two sentences.
- **Locate details, but don't learn them.** Detail-heavy portions of passages can be dense and difficult to read. Don't spend precious time rereading and absorbing details—just make sure you know where to find them in the passage. That way you can locate a detail if a question asks about it.

Eliminating Wrong Answers

Test makers use "distracters" in test questions that can confuse you into choosing an incorrect answer. Familiarizing yourself with some of the common distraction techniques that test makers use will increase your chances of eliminating wrong answers and selecting the right answer.

- **The choice that does too little.** This distracter type often follows main idea questions. The answer choice makes a true statement, but it is too narrow, too specific to be a main idea of the passage. It zeros in on select elements or supporting ideas of a passage instead of expressing a main idea.

- **The choice that does too much.** This distracter also relates to main idea questions. Unlike the type discussed previously, this answer choice goes too far, or beyond the scope of the passage. It may be a true statement, but it cannot be supported by what the author expresses in the text.
- **The close, but not close enough, choice.** This type of answer is very close to the correct answer, but is wrong in some detail.
- **The off-topic choice.** Test takers often find this answer choice the easiest to spot and eliminate. It may have nothing at all to do with the passage itself.
- **The irrelevant choice.** This option uses language found in the text—elements, ideas, phrases, words—but does not answer the question correctly. These distracters are tricky because test designers "bait" them with a good deal of information from the passage.
- **The contradictory choice.** This answer may in fact be opposite or nearly opposite to the correct answer. If two of the answer choices seem contrary to each other, there is a good chance that one of these choices will be correct.
- **The choice that is too broad.** This distracter relates to supporting detail questions. Although it may be a true statement, it is too general and does not address the specifics the question is looking for.

Look Out for Absolutes

Reading comprehension questions that use words that represent absolutes should alert you to the likely presence of clever distracters among the answer choices. Two or more answers may be close contenders—they may reflect language from the passage and be true in general principle, but not true in *all* circumstances. Beware of these commonly used absolutes in reading questions:

best
most closely
always
all
primarily
most nearly
never
none

Types of Readers

How you approach a reading passage may show what kind of reader you are. Each of the following approaches has some merit. When you practice reading passages as part of your study plan, experiment with some of these different styles to see what works best for you.

- The **concentrator** reads the passage thoroughly before looking at the questions. By concentrating on the passage, you can locate answers quickly if you don't already know them.
- The **skimmer** skims the passage before looking at the questions. Once you understand how the passage is arranged, you can go back and find the answers.
- The **cautious reader** reads the questions and answer choices first. Because you know what questions to expect, you can be on the lookout as you read the passage.
- The **game player** reads the questions first and answers them by guessing. By guessing the answers, you become familiar with the questions and can recognize the answers when you read the passage.
- The **educated guesser** reads the questions first, but not the answers. When you find the answer in the passage, you can quickly look among the answer choices for the right one.
- The **efficiency expert** reads the questions first, looking for key words that indicate where an

answer is located. By doing this, you can skim the passage for answers instead of reading the whole passage.

Five-Step Approach to Answering Reading Subtest Questions

If you feel daunted by the task of quickly reading and understanding dense passages, here is a quick approach that you can use. Feel free to adapt it to your style or change the order of the steps, but try to incorporate each of the five steps somewhere in your process.

Step 1—Preview

To get an idea of the content and organization of a passage, begin by skimming it. With practice, you will quickly discern topic sentences and key adjectives. Often, the first two sentences in a paragraph are topic sentences—they will tell you what a paragraph is about. If the passage is several paragraphs long, read the first and last sentence of each paragraph. You can't depend 100% on this technique, though; use your judgment to determine if a sentence is truly a topic sentence.

Step 2—Skim the Questions

Quickly take in the question or questions that follow a passage, marking important words and phrases. Don't bother reading the multiple-choice answers. You simply want to gather clues about what to look for when you read.

Step 3—Read Actively

Although you do not want to memorize or analyze the passage, you do need to read it. Keep your pencil handy to mark the passage as you read, looking for information that applies to the questions you skimmed. Circle or underline topic sentences, main ideas, or phrases that reveal the author's point of view. Check important names, dates, or difficult words. Mark transitions and phrases, such as *however, on the other hand, most importantly, but,* or *except* that help you to follow the author's direction or the organization of the passage.

As you read, ask yourself some of the following questions:

- What is the main theme or idea in the passage?
- What is the author's purpose or goal?
- How do ideas in the passage relate to the main idea?
- What is the tone or mood of the passage? Informative? Critical? Playful?
- How is the passage structured?

Step 4—Review the Passage

After actively reading the passage, take a few seconds to look over the main idea, the topic sentences, or other elements you have marked. Ask yourself what you have just read. Your goal is not to understand the passage thoroughly, but rather to get the gist of it. Quickly summarize it in your own words.

Don't get hung up on difficult phrasing or technical elements in the passage that you might not even need to know. Instead of focusing on absorbing specific details, just know the location of details in the passage. Remember, you can refer back to the passage several times while answering the questions. Focus on the general direction, main ideas, organization, purpose, and point of view of the passage, rather than learning details.

Step 5—Answer the Questions

Now it's time to answer the questions. Base your answers only on what is stated and implied in the passage. Some answer choices will try to trick you with information that is beyond the scope of the passage. Read *all* multiple choice answers before rushing to choose one. Eliminate and mark off as many choices as possible. If you eliminate all the answer choices but two, reach your decision quickly between the remaining two.

Objective 0001: Determine the Meaning of Words and Phrases in the Context in Which They Occur

For example:

- Identify the meaning of commonly used words.
- Determine the meaning of a word with multiple meanings.
- Determine the meaning of an uncommon word or phrase.
- Identify synonyms or antonyms for words used in a given passage.
- Determine the meaning of figurative language.

If you encounter an unfamiliar word when you are reading, you may likely grab a dictionary and look it up. During the Communication and Literacy Skills Test, however, you can't use a dictionary. You *can* use a number of strategies to figure out what a word means. When you aren't sure what a word means, check its context. Context is defined as the surroundings, circumstances, environment, or background of an event. Looking at the context in which an unfamiliar word appears may be an easy way to determine the word's meaning.

Identify the Meaning of Commonly Used Words

Here's an example of how it works. What's the meaning of the underlined word in the following sentence?

Sherlock Holmes <u>deciphered</u> the mystery of the crook's identity by puzzling out the clues left behind at the scene of the crime.
  a. wrote
  b. forgot
  c. photographed
  d. discovered

If you weren't sure of the meaning of *deciphered*, you could have figured it out by using other words in the sentence. The words *puzzling out* help to choose the right word. Knowing that Sherlock Holmes was trying to solve a crime helps to eliminate words like *forgot*, *photographed*, and *wrote*. The correct answer is **d**; *deciphered* means discovered.

Vocabulary questions measure your word power, but they also evaluate an essential reading comprehension skill, which is the ability to determine the meaning of a word from its **context**. The sentences that surround the word offer important clues about its meaning. For example, see if you can figure out the meaning of the word *incessant* from this context:

The incessant demands of the job are too much for me. The responsibilities are endless!

The word *incessant* most nearly means
  a. inaccessible.
  b. difficult.
  c. unceasing.
  d. compatible.

The best choice is **c**. The sentence, *The responsibilities are endless*, restates the phrase in the first sentence, *incessant demands*. This restatement, or elaboration, suggests the meaning of *incessant*: continuing or following without interruption.

Determine the Meaning of a Word with Multiple Meanings

As you know, many words have two or more meanings. These words are called **homonyms**, from the Greek for "same name." For example, the word *fly* is a *noun* that means "a small insect."

A pesky *fly* kept buzzing by my ear!

But *fly* can also be a *verb*.

My brother likes to design and *fly* paper airplanes.

You can tell from the word's context which use the author intends.

Here are some common words that have more than one meaning:

WORD	MEANING 1	MEANING 2
bark	growl	tree covering
bat	animal	wooden stick
bowl	dish	a sport
can	able to	container
kind	nice	type
light	lamp	not heavy
mean	unkind	suggest
play	have fun	a drama
roll	revolve	a very small loaf of bread
story	tale	one floor of a building
watch	look at	timepiece

Read the selection, and then answer the questions that follow. The answers appear after the exercise.

(1) Have you ever thought about how important a bridge is? After all, without bridges, how would people get across rivers and wide gorges? Bridges are an essential part of our transportation system for moving people and goods.

(2) The first bridges were simply trees that fell or were placed across water or canyons. The wood was strong enough to bear the weight of a person or two at a time, but not strong enough for carrying heavy loads. People made bridges by stretching rope cables across an open area. In China and other places, rope bridges are still used. They're strong enough to hold people and pack animals with light loads.

(3) Later, people built arch bridges by wedging together large blocks of stone to form a half circle. Arch bridges are among the strongest and longest lasting: Some built more than 1,500 years ago are still being used. Even today, people build arch bridges, but usually from concrete, wood, or steel.

(2) Another kind of bridge is the cantilever. It has two independent steel or concrete beams, one extending toward the center of a river from each bank. A third beam is lifted up to connect the beams. Canada's Quebec Bridge is one of the world's longest, spanning 1,800 feet (549 m) across the St. Lawrence River.

(5) A suspension bridge spans even more space with its roadway hanging from steel cables supported by massive towers. Each cable can hold thousands of pounds of weight. Probably the most familiar suspension bridge is California's Golden Gate, with a main span of 4,200 feet (1,280 m). When completed in 1937, it was the world's longest, but in 1964, New York's Verrazano Narrows Bridge beat that with a span of 4,260 feet (1,298 m). Then, in 1981, England's Humber Bridge beat that with a span of 4,626 feet (1,410 m). And since 1998, Japan's Akashi-Kaikyo Bridge has held the record, with a span of 6,529 feet (1,991 m). Will that record be beaten? Stay tuned!

1. What is the meaning of the word *bridge* as used in the article?
   a. the upper bony part of the nose
   b. the part of a ship where the captain works
   c. a card game
   d. pathway structure over a river or valley

2. Which is NOT a meaning of *bear* as used in the story?
   a. hold
   b. carry
   c. furry mammal
   d. support

3. What is the meaning of the word *beam* as used in the article?
   a. a long piece of heavy wood or metal used in construction
   b. the width of a ship at its widest part
   c. a ray of light
   d. a smile

4. Which of the following words from the last paragraph is a multiple meaning word?
   a. familiar
   b. record
   c. steel
   d. since

5. The meaning of *still* as used in the article is
   a. quiet.
   b. unmoving.
   c. calm.
   d. even now.

6. What is the meaning of the word *light* as used in the second paragraph?
   a. beam
   b. bright
   c. not heavy
   d. pale

Answers

1. d
2. c
3. a
4. b
5. d
6. c

Determine the Meaning of an Uncommon Word or Phrase

When authors use words they know will be unfamiliar to their readers, they sometimes slip in other words or phrases to help readers figure out the unknowns. Authors may define the word, give examples of similar things, or restate the idea to make it clearer. And authors may put the clues in the text itself or in nearby pictures. Readers use these context clues to make good guesses about what unfamiliar words mean.

Add a Definition

He played the *harpsichord*, a pianolike musical instrument.

The largest group is *arthropods*, like spiders, insects, and lobsters.

Restate to Clarify

She ran to the *escarpment*. Could she climb down the steep hill in time to escape?

Sometimes an author just wants readers to understand the context of a word, not necessarily the exact meaning.

Dan was surprised that he hadn't won the election. "That's *implausible!*" he whined.

Dan whines, so he's not *happily* surprised! *Implausible* means *unbelievable.*

Read the selection, and then answer the questions that follow.

(1) What causes myopia? You probably know that we see because light bounces off objects and into our eyes. In a normal eye, the light rays go through the lens and focus on the retina, the sensory membrane or sheet that lines the eye, to create images. In myopic eyes, the light focuses in front of the retina instead of directly on it. So nearsighted people can usually see really well up close, but they squint to try to see things far away.

(2) Often, nearsightedness is suspected if a child has trouble seeing the chalkboard or whiteboard in school. Then a vision test is set up to diagnose perception. In other words, a doctor checks how well the person can read various sized letters at various distances.

(3) Early diagnosis is important because nearsightedness can be ameliorated with corrective visual devices, like glasses and contact lenses. These devices can't cure myopia, but they help a nearsighted person see distant objects more clearly. The lens of the glasses or contacts refocuses the light before it reaches the eye so it hits the retina where it should.

(4) Doctors can also do surgery to help some people who have myopia. Adults with myopia, whose glasses or contact lens prescription hasn't changed for at least a year, may be able to have a laser procedure that can clear up their problem.

(5) Nearsightedness affects men and women equally. People with a family history of myopia are more likely to develop it. And there's no way to prevent it. At one time people actually believed that reading too much or watching too much TV caused nearsightedness. Those activities can make your eyes tired, but they can't cause myopia.

1. What kind of context clue does the author use for *myopia*?
   a. a restatement to clarify
   b. a definition
   c. a homonym
   d. examples of other eye problems

2. What is the retina?
   a. a ray of light
   b. a lens
   c. a membrane, or lining
   d. a light shaft

3. What is the meaning of *diagnose*?
   a. detect
   b. identify
   c. analyze
   d. all the above

4. Which is most likely the meaning of *ameliorated*?
   a. worsened
   b. improved
   c. continued
   d. renewed

5. For which does the author give two or more examples as context clues?
   a. kinds of membranes in the body
   b. lenses in cameras
   c. corrective visual devices
   d. types of eye conditions

6. If you didn't know the meaning of *surgery*, which nearby word would be a clue?
   a. doctors
   b. myopia
   c. glasses
   d. problem

Answers

1. b
2. c
3. d
4. b
5. c
6. a

Identify Synonyms or Antonyms for Words Used in a Given Passage

When you come across a word you don't know, you can often figure out its meaning by thinking of a synonym or antonym for it. To review:

A **synonym** means the same, or almost the same, as the unknown word.

> I felt so *ungainly*, tripping over my own feet as we headed to the dance floor!

Can you think of a word to replace *ungainly* that would still describe someone who trips? How about *clumsy*, *awkward*, or *gawky*? They all have about the same meaning, but doesn't it sound more embarrassing to be *ungainly* than *clumsy*? By using *ungainly*, the author tells you more about the person's feelings.

An **antonym** means the opposite of the unknown word. For example, *graceful* is an antonym of *ungainly*.

Also, *or*, and *like* often signal a synonym in the text near an unknown word. *But* or *unlike* often signal an antonym. Use the synonym or antonym to help you figure out the unknown word.

> Gigi thought she'd be calm once the test was over, but now she was *angst-ridden* about the results.

The word *but* in the example signals an antonym. Gigi thought she'd be calm, but she's the opposite. So *angst-ridden* must mean anxious or worried. Here are just a few words with their synonyms and antonyms. Note how a synonym may mean the same but give a different feeling to the original word.

WORD	SYNONYM	ANTONYM
afraid	petrified	valiant
ask	interrogate	retort
begin	commence	terminate
correct	accurate	erroneous
friend	cohort	antagonist
laugh	chortle	snivel
naughty	mischievous	compliant
noisy	boisterous	tranquil
repair	renovate	demolish
small	minuscule	gargantuan
true	authentic	bogus

Read the selection, and then answer the questions that follow.

One day, a *vagrant* knocked on a farmhouse door. The farmer's wife peered out at the weary *drifter*. "I can't let you in," she said, "for my husband is not at home. And besides, I have no *sustenance* to offer because my husband is bringing groceries back from town."

"Then, Madam, you can share some of my pebble pottage!" the man replied, and he pulled from his pocket what looked like an ordinary stone. "Pebble pottage?" asked the woman, suddenly interested in the ragged man.

"Oh, yes, it is delicious," he said with a smile. "If I had a pot of water and a fire, I could demonstrate how this stone can magically make the best soup you've ever tasted!"

The woman was curious, so she opened the door and the *wayfarer* came inside. Soon a pot of water was boiling away. He dropped in the stone, then tasted the watery broth. "It needs a pinch of salt, and a dash of pepper," he said. "You wouldn't have any, would you? And perhaps a tiny bit of butter?"

"Yes, I have them," said the woman, and she ran to get the requested *components*.

When she returned, he added the salt, pepper, and butter to the broth and tasted it again. "Yum. Much better!" he said. "But vegetables would add even more flavor! Are there none in your cellar or garden?"

"Oh, there must be a few," she said, eager to taste the magic soup. So she ran to the garden and returned with some potatoes, carrots, and beans.

These were added and the *vagabond* tasted the mixture again. "The magic stone has not failed me!" he whispered *surreptitiously*. "It is almost ready. All it needs is a bit of meat."

The woman found some leftover chicken in the refrigerator and added it to the pot, saying, "Magic stone, do your thing!"

Before long, a wonderful aroma filled the kitchen, *portending* that the soup was done. The woman filled a bowl for the man and one for herself. And there was enough left for her husband to have a bowlful when he returned.

"Thank you so much for letting me use your pot and fire," the stranger said as he prepared to leave. He *extracted* his stone from the bottom of the pot, washed it off, and put it back into his pocket.

"Oh, you are welcome. Do come again," said the woman.

"Indeed I will," replied the hobo. "Now, because of your kindness, I want to leave you a gift." He fished into his other pocket and brought out a tiny pebble. "Here," he said with a smile, "is your very own magic pebble. It is not yet fully matured so it can only make enough soup for one. Use it well."

Then he left and disappeared into the woods. The farmer's wife never saw him again, but she did enjoy a small cup of magic pebble pottage from time to time!

---

1. Which synonym was NOT used to describe the stranger?
   a. hobo
   b. vagrant
   c. wayfarer
   d. bum

2. An antonym for the word *extricated* is
   a. rescued.
   b. inserted.
   c. took out.
   d. removed.

3. Which is a synonym for *portending*?
   a. suggesting
   b. signifying
   c. indicating
   d. all the above

4. Which is NOT an antonym for *surreptitiously*?
   a. sneakily
   b. furtively
   c. openly
   d. secretly

Answers

1. d
2. b
3. d
4. c

Determine the Meaning of Figurative Language

As you know, authors use words to help readers create images in their minds. Most words are literal—they mean what they say. Sometimes, though, authors use more creative, or figurative, language, like idioms, personification, and hyperbole.

An **idiom** is a group of words that doesn't mean exactly what it says.

> "That homework we had last night was a piece of cake!" Bill said.

Does Bill mean that the teacher handed out cake for the class to eat as homework? No, of course not. "A piece of cake" means the task was easy. Look for content clues to help you figure out the meanings of idioms.

Idiom Examples

She feels *down in the dumps*. She feels sad, unhappy, discouraged.
When I told them, they were *all ears*! They paid attention and listened.
Don't be such *a couch potato*! Don't be lazy, inactive.
Don't *let the cat out of the bag*! Don't tell the secret.
Wow, that was *a close shave*! A narrow escape; almost got caught.
She has a *chip on her shoulder*! Is resentful, holds a grudge.

Personification gives human qualities to animals or objects.

> "I cannot see in this tall grass, Moon," cried the tiger. So Moon smiled down while Wind puffed her cheeks and blew the grass aside.

In this example, the tiger has the human ability to speak, the moon can smile, and the wind has cheeks

and a mouth. Readers relate to the actions because they share the qualities. Personification adds interest to some stories, especially fables and myths that teach lessons about life and human behavior.

Hyperbole is the use of exaggeration to make a point.

> "This suitcase weighs a ton!" Ray grumbled. "No wonder my back hurts!"

Does the suitcase really weigh a ton? Not likely, since a ton is 2,000 pounds. But the author wants to make the point that the suitcase is really heavy.

Read the selection, and then answer the questions that follow.

PAUL BUNYAN AND THE BIG JAM
A Legend Retold

Folks say that one spring, the lumberjacks up North had cut down so many trees that there was the biggest logjam ever seen. There must have been a zillion logs crammed together 200 feet high by the bend of the river! The loggers chopped, sawed, and tugged at the wood, but they couldn't budge that jam one inch. That's when the call went out to get Paul Bunyan, the greatest logger who ever lived.

It was raining cats and dogs as Paul and his faithful Blue Ox, Babe, arrived. Suddenly the rain stopped and Paul led Babe to the front of the huge log pile. "You stay here," Paul said. "Okay," Babe replied with a nod of her head. Then Paul took a slingshot and fired bits of feathers at Babe, who thought she was being attacked by pesky flies. Babe began to swish her big old tail back and forth. It stirred up the river so much that the water turned and flowed upstream, taking the logs with it! The giant jam was broken! When Paul called Babe out of the water, the logs turned again and began to float back downstream to the mill!

1. The idiom *raining cats and dogs* means
   a. toy puppies and kittens fell from the sky.
   b. it was raining very hard.
   c. the message was sent quickly.
   d. people were talking very fast.

2. The author uses personification by
   a. making the river water go upstream.
   b. saying the loggers called for Paul Bunyan.
   c. having Paul talk to Babe.
   d. having Babe talk to Paul.

3. Which is an example of hyperbole?
   a. swish her big old tail
   b. couldn't budge that jam one inch
   c. there must have been a zillion logs
   d. attacked by pesky flies

Answers

1. b
2. d
3. c

Authors also use the figurative language of **similes** and **metaphors** to add interest to their writing.

A **simile** compares two things by using the words *like* or *as*. A simile may help you visualize the character and understand his or her motives in a story.

> I was so embarrassed that my face was as red as a beet!

Here are few more similes. What do they help you visualize?

> You and I are as alike as two peas in a pod!
> She is as quiet as a mouse.
> His sadness was as unending as the waves crashing on shore.

> I know I can trust him; he's as honest as the day is long.
> I can't get her to do anything; she's as stubborn as a mule!

A **metaphor** compares two things without using *like* or *as*. The text states that one thing is, or has the characteristics of, another.

> The dog's eyes were searchlights, looking for any sign of kindness.

Is the author tying to get you to picture a dog with huge searchlights for eyes?

No, the author wants you to visualize a poor dog staring intently, looking for kindness from a stranger.

Here are a few more metaphors. What do you visualize with each?

> Night is a curtain that eventually falls.
> The quarterback is a well-maintained machine.
> She is a beacon of light, guiding us home.
> Strength and honor are his uniform.
> Silence is an invited guest, allowing me time to think.

Here are three very short four-line rhymes that contain similes and metaphors. Read each, and then answer the questions that follow.

> The breeze is a messenger,
> As sweet as roses in bloom,
> That fills all the corners
> Of my lonely room.

> The sky is a blanket
> Bejeweled with diamonds so bright
> That twinkle and sparkle
> Like fireflies at night.

The street is a river
On which traffic can flow
Where cars scurry like fish
And swish to and fro.

_____

1. In the first rhyme, the author uses a simile to compare a
   a. fish to the scent of a rose.
   b. breeze to the sweet smell of roses.
   c. messenger to a lonely room.
   d. lonely room to a windstorm.

2. Which of these is NOT a metaphor?
   a. The breeze is a messenger.
   b. The sky is a blanket.
   c. Like fireflies at night.
   d. The street is a river.

3. How does the author use a simile in the last rhyme?
   a. to compare the street to a river
   b. to compare cars to fish
   c. to compare stars to fireflies
   d. to compare roses to traffic

Answers

1. b
2. c
3. b

0002: Understand the Main Idea and Supporting Details in Written Material

For example:

- Identify the explicit main idea of a paragraph or passage.
- Identify the implied main idea of a paragraph or passage.

- Identify ideas, information, data, and details that support, illustrate, or elaborate the main idea of a paragraph or passage.

When tests ask you to find the main idea of a passage, they are asking you to determine an overall feeling or thought that a writer wants to convey about the subject. To find the main idea, think about a **general statement** that brings together all the ideas in a paragraph or passage. The main idea is the most important thing the author wants readers to know. Other facts in the selection are details that support, or tell more about, the main idea. This section reviews the differences.

Identify the Explicit Main Idea of a Paragraph or Passage

Sometimes the main idea is stated directly, as in the following paragraph:

Grass is one of Earth's most useful plants. Most people think of it as the stuff that grows in the yard and needs to be mowed, but there are thousands of different kinds. Wheat, rice, and other grains are grasses that help people and animals exist.

The main idea is stated: Grass is a useful plant.

But sometimes you have to find the main idea yourself. To do that, use information from the text to figure it out. Look out for statements that are too specific—a main idea must be broad enough to contain all the concepts presented in a passage.

Try the following example:

In 1483, Italian artist Leonardo da Vinci sketched a flying machine. He was also a scientist and fascinated by movement. His sketch showed a screwlike wing made of stiff linen. He never got it off the ground, but a real helicopter like it flew almost 500 years later!

The main idea is that Leonardo da Vinci designed the first helicopter more than 500 years ago. That's what the author most wants you to remember.

Do you always find main ideas in the first sentence of the passage? The answer is no; although a first sentence may contain the main idea, an author may decide to build up to the main point. In that case, you may find the main idea in the last sentence of an introductory paragraph, or even in the last paragraph of the passage.

Read the following paragraph and answer the practice question that follows:

Experts say that if you feel drowsy during the day, even during boring activities, you haven't had enough sleep. If you routinely fall asleep within five minutes of lying down, you probably have severe sleep deprivation, possibly even a sleep disorder. Microsleep, or a very brief episode of sleep in an otherwise awake person, is another mark of sleep deprivation. In many cases, people are not aware that they are experiencing microsleeps. The widespread practice of "burning the candle at both ends" in Western industrialized societies has created so much sleep deprivation that what is really abnormal sleepiness is now almost the norm.

Source: National Institute of Neurological Disorders and Stroke, National Institutes of Health, www.ninds.nih.gov.

What is the main point of this passage?
- **a.** If you fall asleep within five minutes every time you lie down, you are sleep deprived.
- **b.** If you experience enough microsleeps, you can attain the sleep you need to function.
- **c.** Sleep deprivation is a pervasive problem in the United States and other Western nations.
- **d.** If trends in sleep deprivation continue, our society will experience grave consequences.

Answer

Choice **a** is a true statement, but too specific to be a main idea. Choice **b** is a false statement and choice **d** is a speculative statement that is not implied in the passage. Only choice **c** represents a general or "umbrella" statement that covers all the information in the paragraph.

Notice that in that sample passage, the author does not present the main idea in the first sentence, but rather builds up to the main point, which is expressed in the last sentence of the paragraph.

Subject versus Main Idea

Test takers often confuse the main idea of a passage with its main topic. The topic is the **subject**—what the passage is about. The main idea is what the author wants to express *about* the subject.

To see the difference, read the following passage carefully.

Today's postal service is more efficient and reliable than ever before. Mail that used to take months to move by horse and foot now moves around the country in days or hours by truck, train, and plane. First-class mail usually moves from New York City to Los Angeles in three days or less. If your letter or package is urgent, the U.S. Postal Service offers Priority Mail and Express Mail services. Priority Mail is guaranteed to go anywhere in the United States in two to three days or less. Express Mail will get your package there overnight.

You might be asked on a standardized test, "What is the main idea of this passage?" This passage is *about* the post office—but the post office is not the main idea of the passage. The post office is merely the *subject* of the passage (*who* or *what* the passage is about). The main idea must say something *about* this subject.

The main idea of a passage is

- an assertion about the subject. An assertion is a statement that requires evidence (proof) to be accepted as true.
- the general idea that controls or holds together the paragraph or passage. The other sentences and ideas in the passage will all relate to that main idea and serve as evidence that the assertion is true. You might think of the main idea as a net that is cast over the other sentences. The main idea must be general enough to hold these ideas together.

Read the passage again and look for the idea that makes an assertion about the postal service *and* holds together or controls the whole paragraph. Then answer the following question:

Which of the following sentences best summarizes the main idea of the passage?
   a. Express Mail is a good way to send urgent mail.
   b. Mail service today is more effective and dependable than it was in the past.
   c. First-class mail usually takes three days or less.

Because choice **a** is specific—it tells us *only* about Express Mail—it cannot be the main idea. It does not encompass the rest of the sentences in the paragraph—it doesn't cover Priority Mail or first-class mail. Choice **c** is also very specific. It tells us only about first class mail, so it, too, cannot be the main idea. But choice **b**—"Mail service today is more effective and dependable than it was in the past"—*is* general enough to encompass the whole passage. And the rest of the sentences *support* the idea that this sentence asserts: Each sentence offers proof that the postal service today is indeed more efficient and reliable. Thus, the writer aims to tell us about the efficiency and reliability of today's postal service.

If you are having trouble identifying the main ideas in a story, try asking yourself these questions:

- What unifying concept is the author striving to communicate?
- Is there a moral or lesson that the author is trying to teach?
- Are there any reoccurring symbols or imagery that the author is using to communicate a deeper meaning?

Identify the Implied Main Idea

Writers can use implication to convey meaning rather than directly stating their ideas. This is especially true in literature, where readers generally prefer suggestion to direct statements. Instead of providing a topic sentence that expresses their main idea, many writers simply omit that sentence and instead provide a series of clues through structure and language to get their ideas across. Finding an implied main idea is much like finding a stated main idea.

How to Find an Implied Main Idea

Finding an implied main idea requires you to use your observations to make an inference that, like a topic sentence, encompasses the whole passage. It might take a little detective work, but you can make observations that will enable you to find main ideas even when they're not explicitly stated.

For the first example of finding an implied main idea, let's look at a statement from a parking garage manager in response to recent thefts:

Radios have been stolen from four cars in our parking garage this month. Each time, the thieves have managed to get past the parking garage security with radios in hand, even though they do not have parking garage identification cards, which people must show as they enter and exit the garage. Yet each time, the security officers say they have seen nothing unusual.

———————————

There is no topic sentence in this paragraph, but you should be able to determine the main idea of this statement from the facts provided and from the tone. What does the statement suggest?

1. Which of the following best summarizes the statement's main idea?
   a. There are too many thefts in the garage.
   b. There are not enough security guards.
   c. There is something wrong with the security in the parking garage.
   d. There are too many security guards

Answer

The correct answer is choice **c**, "There is something wrong with the security in the parking garage." How can you tell that this is the main idea? For one thing, it's the only one of the three choices general enough to serve as a "net" for the paragraph; choice **a** is implied only in the first sentence; and choice **b** isn't mentioned at all. In addition, each sentence on its own suggests that security in the parking garage has not been working properly. Furthermore, the word *yet* indicates that there is a conflict between the events that have taken place and the duties of the security officers.

Now examine the following statement that a neighbor wrote about Mr. Miller, who owned one of the cars that was vandalized in the parking garage:

> Well, Mr. Miller's a pretty carefree person. I've borrowed his car on several occasions, and a few times, I've found the doors unlocked when I arrived at the garage. He often forgets things, too, like exactly where he parked the car on a particular day or where he put his keys. One time, I found him wandering around the garage looking for his keys, which he thought he had dropped on the way to the car, and it turned out the car door was unlocked anyway. Sometimes, I wonder how he remembers his address, let alone to take care of his car.

———————————

2. What is Mr. Miller's neighbor suggesting?
   a. Mr. Miller forgets everything.
   b. Mr. Miller may have left his car door unlocked the day the radio was stolen.
   c. Mr. Miller is too carefree for his own good.
   d. Mr. Miller is the vandal.

Answer

You can attack the question this way: Which of these four statements do the sentences in the neighbor's statement support? Try a process of elimination. Do all the sentences support choice **a**? If not, cross **a** out. Do all the sentences support choice **b**, that his car door may have been unlocked the day the radio was stolen? How can you tell? Because this is the only idea that all of the sentences in the neighbor's statement support. You know that Mr. Miller often doesn't lock his car doors; you also know that he often forgets things. The combination makes it likely that Mr. Miller left his car door unlocked on the day his car radio was stolen.

Good writers *show* you instead of *telling* you by using symbolism, metaphor, and other literary devices that help illustrate meaning. When working to find the main idea in a text, it's important to use your knowledge, logical thinking skills, and your own ideas to infer what symbols and other clues signify. Before concluding what the main idea is, be sure you can support your theories based on information presented in the text.

Now look at a paragraph in which the *language* the writer uses is what enables you to determine meaning. Here is a description of Coach Lerner, a college basketball coach, written by one of his players. Read the paragraph carefully and see whether you can determine the implied main idea of the paragraph.

> Coach Lerner, my basketball coach, is six feet ten inches tall with a voice that booms like a foghorn and the haircut of a drill sergeant. Every morning, he marches onto the basketball court at precisely 8:00 and dominates the gymnasium for the next three hours. He barks orders at us the entire time and expects that we will respond like troops on a battlefield. And if we fail to obey his commands, he makes us spend another 45 minutes under his rule.

3. Which of the following best expresses the implied message of the passage?
   a. Playing on Coach Lerner's team is difficult.
   b. Playing on Coach Lerner's team is like being under the command of an army general.
   c. Coach Lerner is a terrible basketball coach.
   d. Coach Lerner was a famous basketball player in his day.

Answer

The correct answer is choice **b**, "Playing on Coach Lerner's team is like being under the command of an army general." There are many clues in the language of this paragraph that lead you to this inference. First, you probably noticed that Coach Lerner's voice "booms like a foghorn." This comparison (called a *simile*) suggests that Coach Lerner wants his voice to be heard and obeyed. Second, the description of Coach Lerner's haircut is a critical part of the way the author establishes the tone of this paragraph. To say that he has "the haircut of a drill sergeant" (also a *simile*) makes us think of a military leader whose job it is to train soldiers. A writer wouldn't use this comparison unless he or she wanted to emphasize military-like discipline. The author tells us that Coach Lerner "marches onto the basketball court," "barks orders," and expects his players to re-

spond like "troops on a battlefield." The author is trying to paint a picture of Coach Lerner that will bring to mind a military leader.

Thus, though choices **a** and **c** may be true—it *might* be difficult to play for Coach Lerner and he *might* be a terrible basketball coach—choice **b** is the only idea that all the sentences in the paragraph support. Of course, this person's description of Coach Lerner is very subjective, since it uses the first-person point of view.

Identify Ideas, Information, Data, and Details That Support, Illustrate, or Elaborate the Main Idea

Some of the literal comprehension questions on the Communication and Literacy Skills Test will ask you to identify a paraphrase or rewording of supporting details. How can you distinguish a main idea from a supporting idea? Unlike main ideas, supporting ideas present facts or **specific information**. They often answer the questions *what? where? when? why?* or *how?*

How can you locate a supporting detail in a passage that is 200 words long? One thing you don't have to do is memorize the passage. This test does not require that you have perfect recall. Instead, it measures your ability to read carefully and know where to look for specific information. Here are some tips for finding supporting details.

- **Look for language clues.** Writers often use transitional words or phrases to signal that they are introducing a fact or supporting idea. As you read, keep your eyes open for these common phrases:

for example	furthermore
for instance	some other
in particular	specifically
in addition	such as

- **Focus on key words from the question.** Questions often contain two or three important words that signal what information to look for in the passage. For example, a question following a passage about the American car industry reads, "The passage states that hybrid automobiles work best if. . . ." The key words are *hybrid automobiles* and *best*. They tell you to look for a sentence that contains the phrase *hybrid automobiles* and describes an optimal situation. Instead of rereading the passage, *skim* through the paragraphs looking for the key word. Keep in mind that the passage may use a slightly different wording than the key word. As you scan, look for words that address the same idea.

- **Pay attention to the structure of the passage.** Take note of how the passage is organized as you read. Does the author begin with or build to the main point? Is information presented chronologically? Where does the author offer evidence to back up the main point? Understanding how a passage is structured can help you locate the information you need.

Read the following paragraph, focusing on its main idea and the details that support the main idea. Then, answer the practice questions that follow. Answers and explanations follow the exercise.

(1) The history of microbiology begins with a Dutch haberdasher named Antoni van Leeuwenhoek, a man of no formal scientific education. (2) In the late 1600s, Leeuwenhoek, inspired by the magnifying lenses used by drapers to examine cloth, assembled some of the first microscopes. (3) He developed a technique for grinding and polishing tiny, convex lenses, some of which could magnify an object up to 270 times. (4) After scraping some plaque from between his teeth and examining it under a lens, Leeuwenhoek found tiny squirming creatures, which he called "animalcules." (5) His observations, which he reported to the Royal Society of London, are among the first descriptions of living bacteria.

---

1. What inspired Leeuwenhoek's invention of the microscope?
   a. his training in science
   b. the great microbiologists of his era
   c. the lenses used by the practitioners of his profession
   d. the desire to observe bacteria

2. In which sentence does the author give Leeuwenhoek's description of living bacteria?
   a. sentence 2
   b. sentence 3
   c. sentence 4
   d. sentence 5

Answers

1. c. The first paragraph provides the supporting detail to answer this question. Leeuwenhoek, a haberdasher, was "inspired by the magnifying lenses used by drapers to examine cloth." One of the key words from the question—*inspired*—leads you to the location of the detail in the passage. Choice **a** is refuted by a detail presented in the line "a man of no formal scientific education." Choice **b** is untrue, because the first sentence of the passage states that "the history of microbiology begins" with Leeuwenhoek. Choice **d** is also incorrect, because Leeuwenhoek did not know *what* he would discover under his microscope.

2. c. You can find Leeuwenhoek's description of bacteria in sentence 4: "tiny squirming creatures, which he called 'animalcules.'" You may have been tricked into selecting choice **d**, because of its repetition of the phrase "description of living bacteria," from sentence 4. Be sure to always refer back to the passage when answering a question—do not rely on your memory. Choice **d** is incorrect, because it does not refer to Leeuwenhoek's own description, but rather the significance of his observation. This question highlights the importance of taking note of where crucial details are located in a passage. Again, do not try to memorize or learn facts or details, but have an idea about where to find them.

Read this selection, and then answer the questions that follow.

There are many different kinds of mice. Some are good swimmers; others like to swing from trees by their tails. And one kind, the white-footed mouse, is not only a good swimmer and tree climber, but it's also quite musical!

This minute, furry creature's body is about 8 inches (20 cm) long, with a tail of another 3 inches (7.5 cm). It weighs only about 0.8 ounces (23 g). It's been around North America for a long time; scientists have found 40-million-year-old fossils of the tiny creature's ancestors.

Some people call the white-footed mouse the "wood mouse" because it lives in so many wooded areas throughout North America. Other people call the white-footed mouse the "deer mouse." One reason is that its fur is the same colors as a deer's—soft brown on its back; white on its underside. Another reason is that the mice carry deer ticks that spread Lyme disease.

The whitefoot makes its nest almost anywhere. It likes a home that is warm and dry, like a hollow tree or empty bird's nest. But most of the time the whitefoot runs along the ground looking for food. It eats seeds, nuts, leaves, bark, and insects. It sleeps by day and looks for food at night—its long whiskers and big ears help it find its way in the dark.

Does the whitefoot really make music? In a way, it does because it often makes a humming sound. And it taps its little paws very fast on a dead leaf or hollow log to make a buzzing, drumming sound. Scientists aren't sure why the mouse is a drummer; it just is!

So, the next time you're in the woods, walk quietly. There might be a white-footed mouse nearby, and you wouldn't want to interrupt a mouse in the middle of its song, would you?

———————————

1. What is the main idea of this selection?
   a. Deer are brown and white.
   b. The white-footed mouse taps its paws in a drumming sound.
   c. The woods of North America are full of mice.
   d. Scientists study the habits of mice.

2. Which is a supporting detail for that main idea?
   a. The white-footed mouse is also known as the wood mouse.
   b. The deer mouse may carry ticks that transmit a disease.
   c. The mouse taps on a dead leaf or hollow log.
   d. The white-footed mouse isn't very big.

3. Which would make the best substitute title for this selection?
   a. "How to Build a Better Mousetrap"
   b. "Concert in the Woods"
   c. "Caution: Lyme Disease Ahead!"
   d. "All about Rodents"

4. What is the main idea of paragraph 2?
   a. The white-footed mouse lives in Canada.
   b. The white-footed mouse is also called the wood or deer mouse.
   c. The white-footed mouse hums.
   d. The white-footed mouse is very small.

5. Which detail in paragraph 2 is interesting, but not needed to find the main idea of that paragraph?
   a. Its tail is 3 inches (7.5 cm) long.
   b. Scientists found 40-million-year-old fossils of its ancestors.
   c. It weighs 0.8 ounces (23 g).
   d. Its body is about 8 inches (20 cm) long.

Answers

1. b
2. c
3. b
4. d
5. b

0003: Identify a Writer's Purpose, Point of View, and Intended Meaning

For example:

- Identify a writer's stated or implied purpose for writing.
- Identify the audience for a given piece of writing.

- Identify why a writer has included specific information or examples.
- Identify the likely response of an audience to a writer's choice of words or phrases.
- Interpret content, word choice, and phrasing to determine a writer's opinion or point of view.

In some passages, the author's ideas and purpose are very clear. But what happens when they're not? Even then, you'll find plenty of clues about the author's meaning if you read carefully. This section reviews some of the clues to an author's intentions.

Identify a Writer's Stated or Implied Purpose for Writing

An author's purpose is why he or she wrote something. It might be to:

- inform readers
  Every president except George Washington has lived in the White House. However, Washington did help design the building.
- teach readers how to do something
  To do a waltz jump, take off from the outside edge of one skate, make a half turn, and land on the outside edge of the other blade.
- entertain or amuse readers
  The cat leaped just as Pam came in with a bowl of milk. Pam went down and the milk went up—and then down, on her head!
- persuade readers to do something
  Good citizens donate old clothes to charity. It may be hard to give up a favorite outgrown sweater, but we have needy people in our community. Why not let your old sweater keep another kid warm this winter instead of hanging it in the back of your closet?

Sometimes an author has more than one purpose, such as wanting to inform readers but be entertaining at the same time. To identify an author's purpose, ask yourself questions like: Did I find out something new? Did I learn how to do something? How did this make me feel: happy, sad, scared, or excited? Did the author try to get me to do something or think a certain way?

Read the selection, and then answer the questions that follow.

Ripples of Energy

A wave is any movement that carries energy. Some waves carry energy through water. Others carry energy through gases, like air, or solid materials. If you drop a rock into a pool of water, a wave, or ripple of energy, skims across the pool's surface. In the same way, an underwater earthquake can release energy into ocean water. Then it carries a giant wave, or tsunami, across the surface until it hits land.

If you hear a clap of thunder, sound waves (or vibrations) have carried the crashing *boom* to your ears. Sound waves speed through the air at about 1,100 feet (335 meters) per second.

Light also travels through the air in waves. These waves travel at more than 186,000 miles (300 million meters) per second—so the light waves from a flash of lightning reach your eyes before that clap of thunder reaches your ears.

Electrons travel in waves, too. They move back and forth in a solid wire, sending waves of electricity so you can turn on a light during the storm.

___

1. What is the author's most important purpose for writing the selection?
   a. to persuade readers to throw rocks into the water
   b. to entertain readers with the legend of Wally Wave
   c. to teach readers how to use a surfboard to ride waves
   d. to inform readers about different kinds of waves

2. Which question could best help someone figure out this author's purpose?
   a. Did the author give me information?
   b. Did I learn how to make an electric light?
   c. Did the selection make me feel sad or scared?
   d. Did the author want me to make waves?

3. Which might also have been an author's purpose for this selection?
   a. to teach readers why people wave at one another
   b. to inform readers about gravity and magnetic pull
   c. to persuade readers to study more about tsunamis
   d. to entertain readers with a little humor

Answers

1. d
2. a
3. c

On many reading tests, extended passages may be followed by questions that test a variety of your skills. Read "Prometheus" carefully and answer the question that follows. Then continue to the next sections for more questions based on the same passage. Answers appear after each question.

Prometheus

Without a doubt, one of the most interesting mythological characters is the Greek god Prometheus. A complex character with an undying love for the human beings he created, Prometheus embodies a rich combination of often contradictory characteristics, including loyalty and defiance, trickery and trustworthiness. He shows resilience and resolve in his actions, yet weakness in his fondness for humankind.

To reward Prometheus (whose name means "forethought") and his brother Epimetheus ("afterthought") for helping him defeat the Titans, Zeus, the great ruler of Olympian gods, gave the brothers the task of creating mortals to populate the land around Mount Olympus. Prometheus asked Epimetheus to give the creatures their various characteristics, such as cunning, swiftness, and flight. By the time he got to man, however, there was nothing left to give. So Prometheus decided to make man in his image: He stood man upright like the gods and became the benefactor and protector of mankind.

Although Prometheus was particularly fond of his creation, Zeus didn't care for mankind and didn't want men to have the divine gift of knowledge. But Prometheus took pity on mortal men and gave them knowledge of the arts and sciences, including the healing arts and agriculture.

Always seeking the best for his creation, one day Prometheus decided to trick Zeus into giving the best meat of an ox to men. He cut up the ox and hid the bones in layers of fat; then he hid the meat and innards inside the hide. When Prometheus presented the piles to Zeus, Zeus chose the pile that looked like fat and meat. He was enraged to find that it was nothing but bones.

To punish Prometheus for his deceit and his fondness for humans, Zeus forbade men fire—a symbol of creative power, life force, and divine knowledge. But Prometheus would not let his children be denied this greatest of gifts. He took a hollow reed, stole fire from Mount Olympus, and gave it to man. With this gift of fire came divine power, creativity, ingenuity, and culture in the land of mortals.

Zeus punished man for Prometheus's transgression by sending the first woman, Pandora, to Earth. Pandora brought with her a "gift" from Zeus: a jar* filled with evils of every kind. Prometheus knew Zeus to be vengeful and warned Epimetheus not to accept any gifts from Zeus, but Epimetheus was too taken with Pandora's beauty and allowed her to stay. Eventually Pandora opened the jar she'd been forbidden to open, releasing all manner of evils, including Treachery, Sorrow, Villainy, Misfortune, and Plague. Zeus had slipped Hope in among the evils, but Hope was at the very bottom of the jar, and Pandora closed the lid before she could escape.

Prometheus drew Zeus's greatest wrath when he refused to tell Zeus which of Zeus's sons would kill him and take over the throne. Believing he could torture Prometheus into revealing the secret, Zeus bound Prometheus to a rock where every day an eagle would come to tear at his flesh and eat his liver, which would regenerate each night. But Prometheus refused to reveal his knowledge of the future to Zeus and maintained his silence. Eventually, Prometheus was released by Heracles (also known as Hercules), the last mortal son of Zeus and the strongest of all mortals. Soon afterward, Prometheus received immortality from a dying centaur, to take his place forever among the great gods of Olympus.

*Pandora's container is commonly mistranslated "box" from the Greek word for "jar."

The author's primary purpose in this passage is to
   a. demonstrate the vengeful nature of Zeus.
   b. show how much Prometheus cared for humans.
   c. create in readers an interest in mythology.
   d. relate the story of Prometheus.

Answer

d. The passage relates the key episodes in the life of Prometheus. This is the only idea broad enough and relevant enough to be the main idea, or primary purpose, of the passage.

Identify the Audience for a Given Piece of Writing

Writers must consider their audiences because there is a relationship between the writing and the reader. An article in a school newspaper is meant for students and teachers, so it might casually mention people or locations that all the readers will recognize. If that same article were published in a national newspaper, though, it would need more details and explanation to help the new audience understand it. The audience might know a lot about the topic or nothing at all. Each member of the audience will require a slightly different use of style, tone, and word choice.

The content and style of "Prometheus" suggest that the intended audience
- **a.** are experts on Greek mythology.
- **b.** are religious officials.
- **c.** is a general lay audience.
- **d.** are family members and friends.

Answer

c. The style is neither formal nor informal but an easygoing in-between to make the material easily understood and interesting to a lay audience. In addition, the passage does not take for granted that the reader knows basic information about mythology. For example, the author states that Zeus was the *great ruler of Olympian gods*.

Identify Why a Writer Has Included Specific Information or Examples

A skillful author carefully selects each detail to include for a reason.

1. By noting that Zeus included Hope in Pandora's jar, the author suggests that
   - **a.** Zeus really did love humans as much as Prometheus did.
   - **b.** while Zeus was a vengeful god, he was not completely lacking in sympathy for humans.
   - **c.** Zeus was just playing a trick on humans.
   - **d.** Zeus was trying to make amends with Prometheus.

2. This passage suggests that Zeus disliked humans because
   - **a.** Prometheus spent too much time with them.
   - **b.** Prometheus cared for humans more than he did for Zeus.
   - **c.** humans could not be trusted.
   - **d.** humans did not respect Zeus.

3. The details included reveal that Zeus became angry at Prometheus for all the following EXCEPT
   - **a.** creating man.
   - **b.** giving man fire.
   - **c.** being excessively fond of humans.
   - **d.** refusing to reveal which of his sons would kill him.

Answers

1. b. The author drew attention to the inclusion of Hope in the jar to show that Zeus had some pity on mankind and did not wish them to live in utter despair.

2. b. Prometheus's actions show that he cared for humans more than he cared for Zeus. He gave man knowledge of the arts and sciences although Zeus wanted men to be kept in ignorance (paragraph 3); he tricked Zeus into giving mankind the best meat from an ox (paragraph 4); and he stole fire from Mt. Olympus to give mortals the fire that Zeus had denied them (paragraph 5).

3. a. The author tells us that Zeus had given Prometheus and his brother the task of creating beings as a reward for their help in defeating the Titans.

Identify the Likely Response of an Audience to a Writer's Choice of Words or Phrases

When choosing words and phrases, an author selects words most likely to convey meaning to his or her audience. We have established that "Prometheus" was written for a general lay audience. Consider how that audience is likely to respond to the essay.

1. Based on the author's descriptions, readers are likely to consider the most appealing character in the story to be
   a. Zeus
   b. Prometheus
   c. Pandora
   d. Hope

2. From the author's use of the phrases *loyalty and defiance, trickery and trustworthiness, resilience and resolve in his actions yet weakness*, the audience is likely to judge that Prometheus is
   a. consistent and steadfast.
   b. quiet and scholarly.
   c. a bold warrior.
   d. a complicated personality.

3. The audience is most likely to respond to the essay about Prometheus as
   a. an exciting action-adventure tale.
   b. an accurate recounting of historical facts.
   c. an entertaining myth about the origins of humans.
   d. a scholarly report on human origins.

Answers

1. b. Prometheus is consistently described as loving and helpful to humans. There is no evidence that any other character is especially likeable.

2. d. Prometheus is presented as an inconsistent personality except in his love for humans.

3. c. The author identifies the story as a myth in the first paragraph.

Interpret Content, Word Choice, and Phrasing to Determine a Writer's Opinion or Point of View

Even when the information in a passage is clear, a writer doesn't always state the main idea or offer a conclusion. The reader must infer the writer's meaning. Often, the best clues to meaning come from the specific words a writer chooses to describe people, places, and things. By looking closely at word choice, you will find clues that can help you better understand the text.

Word choice includes these forms:

- particular words or phrases a writer uses
- the way words are arranged in a sentence
- repetition of words or phrases
- inclusion of particular details

Consider how word choice affects the following two sentences:

a. Lesson preparation benefits a teacher's performance in the classroom.
b. Lesson preparation improves a teacher's performance in the classroom.

The only difference between the two sentences is that sentence **a** uses *benefits*, and sentence **b** uses *improves*. Both sentences state that lesson preparation has a positive influence on a teacher's performance in the classroom. However, sentence **a** is stronger because of word choice: *to benefit* means to be useful or advantageous, whereas *to improve* means to enhance in value. The writer of sentence **b** believes that preparation is not only useful, it actually increases a teacher's effectiveness. The writer doesn't have to spell this out for you, because the word choice makes the position clear.

For example, answer the following questions based on the passage about Prometheus:

1. In the first paragraph, the author selects words and phrases to communicate that Prometheus
  a. is disrespectful of authority.
  b. is the mythological creator of humans.
  c. has many admirable characteristics.
  d. is a fascinating character because of his complexity.

2. The author considers the relationship between Prometheus and humans to be like that of
  a. parent and child.
  b. close friends.
  c. master and servants.
  d. reluctant allies.

Answers

1. d. In the second sentence, the author states that Prometheus is a *complex character*, and in this and the following sentence, the author lists several specific examples of the *rich combination of often contradictory characteristics* of Prometheus.
2. a. Prometheus helped create mortals and then became their *benefactor and protector*. The author considers him most like a *parent* to humans.

Point of View

Another strategy that writers use to convey their meaning to readers is through **point of view**. Point of view is the person or perspective through which the writer channels the information and ideas. It determines *who* is speaking to the reader. Depending on the writer's intentions, he or she may present a **subjective** point of view (a perspective based on thoughts, feelings, and experiences), or an **objective** one (one that discounts the writer's personal feelings and attempts to offer an unbiased view). Understanding the point of view of a passage will help you answer questions that ask you to identify an author's assumptions or attitude. Here are three approaches to point of view.

First-person point of view expresses the writer's personal feelings and experiences directly to the reader using these pronouns: *I, me, mine; we, our, us*. The first person creates a sense of intimacy between the reader and writer because it expresses a *subjective* point of view. This excerpt from Kate Simon's 1982 memoir, *Bronx Primitive*, provides an example of first-person perspective.

> Instead of a city of silver rivers and golden bridges, America turned out to be Uncle David's flat on Avenue C in which my father

had first lived when he came to America. We walked up several flights of dark stairs and knocked on a door pasted over with glazed patterned paper of connecting rectangles and circles in blue and red and green, whose lines I liked to trace with my eye while the others talked.

Second-person point of view is another personal perspective in which the writer speaks directly to the reader, addressing the reader as *you*. Writers use the second person to give directions or to make the reader feel directly involved with the argument or action of their message. The following excerpt uses the second person.

Next week you will begin reading what most critics label the first science fiction novel: Mary Shelley's *Frankenstein*. Understanding what makes this novel a work of science fiction can help you understand why it has so much power.

Third-person point of view expresses an impersonal point of view by presenting the perspective of an outsider (a "third person") who is not directly involved with the action. Writers use the third person to establish distance from the reader and present a seemingly *objective* point of view. The third person uses these pronouns: *he, him, his*; *she, her, hers*; *it, its*; and *they, them, theirs*. The following is an example of the third-person perspective.

The Sami are an indigenous people living in the northern parts of Norway, Sweden, Finland, and Russia's Kola peninsula. Originally, the Sami religion was animistic; that is, for them, nature and natural objects had a conscious life, a spirit.

Read the following passage from Frank McCourt's 1996 memoir *Angela's Ashes* to answer the practice questions. Consider the writer's choice of words and point of view and how they affect the message presented in the text.

We go to school through lanes and back streets so that we won't meet the respectable boys who go to the Christian Brothers' School or the rich ones who go to the Jesuit school, Crescent College. The Christian Brothers' boys wear tweed jackets, warm woolen sweaters, shirts, ties, and shiny new boots. We know they're the ones who will get jobs in the civil service and help the people who run the world. The Crescent College boys wear blazers and school scarves tossed around their necks and over their shoulders to show they're cock o' the walk. They have long hair which falls across their foreheads and over their eyes so that they can toss their quaffs like Englishmen. We know they're the ones who will go to university, take over the family business, run the government, run the world. We'll be the messenger boys on bicycles who deliver their groceries or we'll go to England to work on the building sites. Our sisters will mind their children and scrub their floors unless they go off to England, too. We know that. We're ashamed of the way we look and if boys from the rich schools pass remarks we'll get into a fight and wind up with bloody noses or torn clothes. Our masters will have no patience with us and our fights because their sons go to the rich schools and, "Ye have no right to raise your hands to a better class of people so ye don't."

---

1. The *we* the author uses throughout the passage refers to
a. his family.
b. the poor children in his neighborhood.
c. the children who attend rich schools.
d. the author and his father.

2. The passage suggests that the author goes to school
   a. in shabby clothing.
   b. in a taxicab.
   c. in warm sweaters and shorts.
   d. on a bicycle.

3. The word *pass* as used in the passage means
   a. to move ahead of.
   b. to go by without stopping.
   c. to be approved or adopted.
   d. to utter.

4. The author quotes his schoolmasters saying, "Ye have no right to raise your hands to a better class of people so ye don't" in order to
   a. demonstrate how strict his schoolmasters were.
   b. contrast his school to the Christian Brothers' School and Crescent College.
   c. show how his teachers reinforced class lines.
   d. prove that the author thought his teacher was mean.

Answers

1. b. The author is talking about school, so the reference must be to school-aged children. In addition, the passage contrasts *we* with the *respectable boys* and the *rich ones*, so *we* are neither wealthy nor respected.
2. a. The author and his classmates *go to school through lanes and back streets* to avoid the students who go to school dressed in warm and *respectable* clothing. He also states that they are *ashamed of the way we look*, implying that they are poorly dressed.
3. d. The boys would get into fights if the rich boys were to utter derogatory words or *pass remarks.*

4. c. While the quote here does show how the author's schoolmasters talked, it has a more important function: to show that his schoolmasters reinforced the class system by telling the author and his classmates to stay in their place and not challenge the existing class structure.

0004: Analyze the Relationships among Ideas in Written Material

For example:

- Identify cause-and-effect relationships.
- Identify the order of events or steps described in written material.
- Analyze relationships between similar ideas or ideas in opposition.
- Draw conclusions from information stated or implied within a passage.

Authors can organize their ideas, arguments, or plots in a variety of ways, and you may be asked to recognize and evaluate these organizational patterns on the Reading subtest. For example, you may be asked to identify the relationships among ideas and to draw conclusions from a passage. This section reviews relationships and the ideas they express.

Identify Cause-and-Effect Relationships

Cause and effect arranges ideas to explain why an event took place (cause) and what happened as a result (effect). Sometimes one cause has several effects, or an effect may have several causes. For example, a historian writing about World War I might investigate several causes of the war (assassination of the heir to the Austro-Hungarian throne, European conflicts over territory and economic power), and describe the various effects of the war (ten million soldiers killed, weakened European powers, enormous financial debt).

Key words offer clues that a writer is describing cause and effect. Pay attention to these words as you read:

Words Indicating Cause
because
created by
since
caused by

Words Indicating Effect
therefore
so
hence
consequently
as a result

A writer might also describe a **contributing** cause, which is a factor that *helps* to make something happen but can't make that thing happen by itself. On the opposite end of the spectrum is a **sufficient** cause, which is a factor that, by itself, is strong enough to make the event happen.

Here's an example of a short chain of cause and effect. Read the passage carefully, noting the key words that indicate cause and effect.

Yesterday my mother told me I was grounded for life. I was supposed to pick up my sister from her playdate at Ellie's house at 4:00, but I was playing Judo Master-Extreme at Charlie's house, and I'd actually made it to the fourth level for the first time. So I decided to keep playing. I figured Rosie would enjoy the extra playtime. But Ellie's mom had an appointment and couldn't leave until someone picked up Rosie. She had to call my mom, who had to leave an important meeting to get Rosie.

Like most events, the narrator's trouble wasn't caused by just *one* thing. Instead, it was caused by a *series* of actions and reactions—a chain of cause and effect. This particular chain began when the narrator reached the fourth level in Judo Master. That's cause number one. Because of that, he decided to keep playing instead of picking up his sister as he was supposed to do.

Cause 1: He reached the fourth level.
Effect 1: He decided not to get Rosie on time.

There are three other sets of causes and effects in the preceding passage. Fill them in following cause 2.

Cause 2: He decided not to get Rosie on time.
Effect 2: _____

Cause 3: _____
Effect 3: _____

Cause 4: _____
Effect 4: _____

Answers

Effect 2: Ellie's mom couldn't leave for her appointment.

Cause 3: Ellie's mom couldn't leave for her appointment.
Effect 3: She called Rosie's mom.

Cause 4: She called Rosie's mom.
Effect 4: Rosie's mom had to leave a big meeting.

Implied Cause and Effect

Often an author will offer an opinion about the cause or effect of an event. In that case, readers must judge the validity of the author's analysis. Are the author's ideas logical? Do the ideas support the conclusions?

Read the following excerpt and answer the practice question.

> When Rosa Parks refused to give up her seat to a white person in Montgomery, Alabama, and was arrested in December 1955, she set off a chain of events that generated a momentum the civil rights movement had never before experienced. Local civil rights leaders were hoping for such an opportunity to test the city's segregation laws. Deciding to boycott the buses, the African American community soon formed a new organization to supervise the boycott, the Montgomery Improvement Association (MIA). The young pastor of the Dexter Avenue Baptist Church, Reverend Martin Luther King, Jr., was chosen as the first MIA leader. The boycott, more successful than anyone hoped, led to a 1956 Supreme Court decision banning segregated buses.
>
> *Source:* Excerpt from the Library of Congress, "The African American Odyssey: A Quest for Full Citizenship."

The author implies that the action and arrest of Rosa Parks directly resulted in

  a. the 1956 Supreme Court decision banning segregated buses.
  b. Martin Luther King, Jr.'s ascendancy as a civil rights leader.
  c. the formation of the civil rights movement in Montgomery, Alabama.
  d. the bus boycott in Montgomery, Alabama.

Answer

The answer is choice **d**. According to the passage, Rosa Parks's action directly inspired local civil rights leaders to institute the Montgomery bus boycott. Although Rosa Parks's action may have been a *contributing* fac-tor to King's emergence as a civil rights leader (choice **b**) and the Supreme Court's later decision to ban segregated buses (choice **a**), it was not the *direct* cause of these events, according to the passage. Choice **c** is incorrect because the passage makes clear that a local civil rights movement already existed and was not the result of Rosa Parks's refusal to give up her bus seat.

Identify the Order of Events or Steps Described in Written Material

One of the basic organizing principles is time, and many writers organize their ideas chronologically. The content of a passage could also be presented in order of importance, starting with either the most important or the least important point.

Chronological Order

When writers tell a story in the order in which things occurred, they are using chronological order. Transitional words and phrases connect the ideas and events within the text.

There are many ways writers signal time order in a chronological passage. An author might simply state *first*, *second*, *third*, or use other transitional words and phrases, such as these:

afterward
eventually
later
suddenly
as soon as
finally
meanwhile
then
at last
next
when
before
after

immediately
now
while
during
in the meantime
soon

Here is a paragraph with all the transitional words and phrases removed. Read it carefully. Then, choose from the list of transitions that follows to fill in the blanks and create a smooth, readable paragraph. Check your work against the example answer that follows the exercise.

It was just one of those days. _____, I woke up half an hour late. _____, _____ rushing to get ready, I realized that the shirt I was wearing had a big stain on it. _____ I quickly changed, grabbed a granola bar and banana for breakfast, and raced out the door. _____, I was standing at the bus stop wondering where my bus could be. _____ I remembered that I was supposed to set my clock back an hour for the end of daylight saving time. _____ I realized I wasn't late—I was a whole hour early!

a few minutes later
suddenly
after
that's when
first
then
so

Answer

Here's the paragraph with the transitions in place. Your answers may vary slightly:

It was just one of those days. <u>First</u>, I woke up half an hour late. <u>Then, after</u> rushing to get ready, I realized that the shirt I was wearing had a big stain on it. <u>So</u> I quickly changed, grabbed a granola bar and banana for breakfast, and raced out the door. <u>A few minutes later</u>, I was standing at the bus stop wondering where my bus could be. <u>Suddenly</u> I remembered that I was supposed to set my clock back an hour for the end of daylight saving time. <u>That's when</u> I realized I wasn't late—I was a whole hour early!

Lists and Transitions

One of the most obvious sequencing clues is a numbered list, as in a recipe. Writers may sometimes use the transitions *first*, *second*, *third*, and so on instead of numbers. In addition, writers can show the sequence of events with carryover clues that show a relationship between two events. For example, the instruction "Drizzle the melted chocolate over the cake" must come after "Melt the chocolate in a double boiler."

A jam recipe includes instructions for sterilizing the jam jars. These steps are listed below in random order. Place them in the proper order by numbering them from 1 through 7.

_____ Boil gently and uncovered for 15 minutes.
_____ Place washed jars in a pan with a rack and cover with hot water.
_____ Wash inspected jars in hot, soapy water.
_____ Let jars stand in the hot water until 5 minutes before you are ready to fill with jam.
_____ Examine the tops and edges of jars and discard any with chips or cracks, because they will prevent an airtight seal.
_____ Remove pan from heat but keep jars in the hot water. Cover.
_____ Heat water in pan to boiling.

Answers

The correct order is as follows. The sequencing clues are underlined.

1. Examine the tops and edges of jars and discard any with chips or cracks, because they will prevent an airtight seal.
2. Wash inspected jars in hot, soapy water.
3. Place washed jars in a pan with a rack and cover with hot water.
4. Heat water in pan to boiling.
5. Boil gently and uncovered for 15 minutes.
6. Remove pan from heat but keep jars in the hot water. Cover.
7. Let jars stand in the hot water until 5 minutes before you are ready to fill with jam.

Order of Importance

Another common organizational pattern is **order of importance**. With this pattern, writers use *rank* instead of time as their organizing principle. That is, the first idea a writer describes isn't what *happened* first; it's the idea that's most or least *important*.

Here's a list of the most common transitions writers apply when using the order of importance organizational pattern.

> above all
> first and foremost
> first, second, third
> last but not least
> more importantly
> moreover
> most importantly

Most Important to Least Important

Organizing ideas from most important to least important puts the most essential information *first*. A newspaper article is a good example. News reports generally don't follow chronological order; instead, they begin with the most important information. Writers give us the *who, what, when, where,* and *why* information about the event.

Here's an example from a school newspaper article.

Chess Team Wins First Championship!
Yesterday, the Oakville High Chess Team won its first state championship in an exciting victory over Winslow High. The team, led by captain Vassil Matic, was losing four matches to three when Magdalena Lukas, a sophomore, won a decisive game against Winslow High captain Julian Mille. Matic then won the tiebreaker to defeat Winslow and bring home the trophy.

This was only the second time the team qualified for the state championship. Two years ago, the team made it to the state championship for the first time but was eliminated during the first round of competitions. The chess team was formed in 1994 by former students Ainsley Pace, Mark Waters, and Shane Trombull. Mr. Trombull is now an advisor for the team.

Notice how this article begins with the most important information: the chess team's victory. Chronologically, this was the *last* event in the series of events described in the article, but here it comes first because it is most important. Next, the article describes the decisive moments in the match—the second most important information. Finally, the article offers some history of the chess club. This information may be interesting, but in terms of the event, it isn't all that important.

Here is a passage about safety on the Internet. Read it carefully, then answer the questions that follow.

Net Safety
Though it may seem like cyberspace is a pretty safe place, in reality, the Internet poses some

very real dangers for teens. To be safe when you're online, follow these guidelines. First and foremost, protect your privacy. Never give your real last name, address, or telephone number to anyone. Second, never agree to meet with someone you've talked with on the Internet without asking permission from your parents first. Third, remember that people are not always what they seem. Someone who is very nice to you online could turn out to be someone eager to hurt you in person. Finally, trust your instincts. If someone uses bad language or mentions things that make you uncomfortable, don't respond; log off instead. If you come across a site where the content makes you uncomfortable, exit it as quickly as possible.

1. According to this passage, what's the most important thing you can do to be safe on the Internet?

   _____

2. What is the second most important thing?

   _____

3. What is the third most important thing?

   _____

4. What is the fourth most important thing?

   _____

Answers

1. Protect your privacy: Don't give out your name, address, or phone number.
2. Never agree to meet someone you met online without your parents' permission.

3. Remember that people are not always what they seem.
4. Trust your instincts.

Least Important to Most Important

Sometimes instead of *starting* with the most important idea, writers prefer to *end* with the most important idea. This takes advantage of the snowball effect, the buildup or force that a writer gets from starting with what's least important and moving toward what's most important. With this order, writers can also create suspense, since the reader has to wait for the final and most important idea.

Writers often use the least-to-most-important structure when they are presenting an argument. That's because this kind of structure is more convincing. In an argument, you need to build your case piece by piece and win your readers over point by point. If your less important points make sense to the reader, then your more important points will come off stronger. Writers often save the best for last because that's where the best has the most impact.

Look at the following student essay, for example. Notice how the writer builds her case, piece by piece, saving her strongest and most important point for last. As you read, identify her main idea and note the order of her supporting points. What transitions does she use?

Make Us Volunteers!

There's been a proposal to add a new requirement to the eighth grade curriculum: 10 hours of volunteer work each quarter. Some will argue that this is forced volunteerism, and therefore not volunteerism at all. But I think that's beside the point. What matters is that students will benefit enormously from such a program.

For one thing, volunteer work is a confidence booster. When you help someone else—when you make someone else feel good—it makes you feel better about yourself. Students will go through the year knowing that they are helping others and making a difference in their community. They will know that they have the power to make people's lives better.

More importantly, volunteering will help students become more compassionate and tolerant. They will see that there are all kinds of people in the world with all kinds of problems. But underneath those problems, they're still people just like you and me.

The most important benefit of this program is that it will teach students that they have a responsibility to other people. We have a duty to help others whenever we can. Students will learn that other people are counting on them to meet very real and important needs. They will learn that when they fail to fulfill their responsibilities, they may hurt other human beings. They will learn that when they make a commitment, it is important to honor it.

Answers

This writer states her main idea in the last sentence of the first paragraph—that "students will benefit enormously from such a program." Her supporting ideas are listed from least important to most important.

- Volunteering will boost students' confidence.
- Volunteering will help students become more compassionate and tolerant.
- Volunteering will teach students that they have a responsibility to others.

The transitions are our biggest clues to this structure. Here are the transitions in the order in which they're used:

- for one thing
- more importantly
- the most important benefit

This structure works well for this argument. The first point is difficult to disagree with; we all know how good it feels to help someone else. The second point is a little more controversial. Some readers might be hesitant about working with people they feel are different. The third point is the one the author thinks is most important, and it's also perhaps the most controversial.

Some people would argue that we are not duty bound to help others. But this point is easier to accept if we've already accepted the writer's previous two points.

Identifying the Order

Read the following passage and answer the questions that follows.

Too much sun can be deadly. First of all, too much sun can dry your skin, which in turn reduces its elasticity and speeds up the aging process. Second, too much sun can burn unprotected skin and cause permanent discoloration and damage to the dermis (the second layer of skin). Most important, long-term exposure of unprotected skin can result in skin cancer.

_____

1. According to the passage, what is the most important reason to avoid too much sun?
   a. It can dry skin.
   b. It can speed up the aging process.
   c. It can burn skin.
   d. It can cause skin cancer.

2. Which organizational pattern does this paragraph use?
   a. chronological
   b. order of importance from least to most important
   c. order of importance from most to least important
   d. none of the above

Answers

1. **d.** The beginning of the fourth sentence tells us that this is the most important effect.
2. **b.** This paragraph lists three effects of too much sun from least to most important.

Analyze Relationships between Similar Ideas or Ideas in Opposition

Writers use the comparison and contrast structure to show how two things are alike and how they are different. Look for topic sentences that show the writer's focus (main idea). Watch for transitions, too, that signal comparison or contrast.

Transitions

One of the keys to a good comparison and contrast is strong transitions. It's important to let readers know when you're comparing and when you're contrasting. As a reader, it's important to watch for these transitions.

Words and Phrases That Show Similarity
and
just as
also
like
both
likewise
in a like manner
similarly
in the same way

Words and Phrases That Show Difference
but
on the other hand
conversely
unlike
however
while
in contrast
yet
on the contrary

Whenever an author is comparing and contrasting two or more items, he or she is doing it for a reason. There's something the author wants to point out by putting these two items side by side for analysis. This reason or point is the main idea, which is often stated in a topic sentence.

The following passage is a comparison and contrast of *Star Wars* and *Crouching Tiger, Hidden Dragon*. Read the passage carefully, noting how each paragraph provides support for the overall main idea. Then answer the questions about the passage and check your work with the answers that follow the exercise.

The Best of the Best
Two of the best films ever made are *Star Wars* and *Crouching Tiger, Hidden Dragon*. I've seen both movies at least a dozen times. While I always will be a loyal *Star Wars* fan, I do have to say that *Crouching Tiger* is an even better film.

Both films feature warriors with special powers. In *Star Wars*, Luke Skywalker, a Jedi knight, has "the force"—a special energy that he can channel to help him overcome evil. Similarly, in *Crouching Tiger*, Li Mu Bai, Yu Shu Lien, and Jen all have special powers that they've developed through rigorous martial arts training. But the characters in *Star Wars* rely heavily on automatic weapons. The warriors in *Crouching Tiger*, in contrast, do all their fighting with old-fashioned weapons such as swords and the most old-fashioned weapon of all—their bodies. What they're able to do with their bodies is much more impressive than anything Luke Skywalker can do with his light saber.

More importantly, *Crouching Tiger* gives equal treatment to both sexes. In *Star Wars*, although Princess Leia can (and does) fight, she still relies mostly on the men to fight and save her. In *Crouching Tiger*, however, the female warriors are every bit as strong as the male warriors and do all the fighting on their own. Shu Lien, Jen, and another woman, Jade Fox, actually do most of the fighting in the movie and defeat many men throughout the film.

The best thing about *Crouching Tiger*, though, is the story of Jen. While *Star Wars* is a great story about good forces against evil forces, *Crouching Tiger* is a great story about a personal rebellion that all young people can relate to. Jen rebels against the society that is going to force her to marry. Who wants to be told whom to love? She rejects being forced into this relationship and runs off. She doesn't know how to handle her strength, though, and is so independent that she even rejects the chance to be Mu Bai's student. Under his guidance, Jen could have become an even greater warrior. But Jen is too independent, and she unintentionally helps to bring about Mu Bai's death and her own. Jen's story shows us that we have a right to determine the course of our lives, but that we also need the guidance of our elders.

_____

1. What is the similarity discussed in paragraph 3?

_____

2. What is the difference discussed in paragraph 3?

_____

3. What is the similarity discussed in paragraph 4?

_____

4. What is the difference discussed in paragraph 4?

_____

5. Underline the transition words and phrases used in the following paragraph:

Both films feature warriors with special powers. In *Star Wars*, Luke Skywalker, a Jedi knight, has "the force"—a special energy that he can

channel to help him overcome evil. Similarly, in *Crouching Tiger*, Li Mu Bai, Yu Shu Lien, and Jen all have special powers that they've developed through rigorous martial arts training. But the characters in *Star Wars* rely heavily on automatic weapons. The warriors in *Crouching Tiger*, in contrast, do all their fighting with old-fashioned weapons such as swords and the most old-fashioned weapon of all—their bodies. What they're able to do with their bodies is much more impressive than anything Luke Skywalker can do with his light saber.

Answers

1. In both movies, the female characters can and do fight.
2. In *Crouching Tiger*, the women don't rely on men at all—they fight for themselves.
3. They're both great stories.
4. They're different kinds of stories. In *Crouching Tiger*, the story is one all young people can relate to.
5. <u>Both</u> films feature warriors with special powers. In *Star Wars*, Luke Skywalker, a Jedi knight, has "the force"—a special energy that he can channel to help him overcome evil. <u>Similarly</u>, in *Crouching Tiger*, Li Mu Bai, Yu Shu Lien, and Jen all have special powers that they've developed through rigorous martial arts training. <u>But</u> the characters in *Star Wars* rely heavily on automatic weapons. The warriors in *Crouching Tiger*, <u>in contrast</u>, do all their fighting with old-fashioned weapons such as swords and the most old-fashioned weapon of all—their bodies. What they're able to do with their bodies is much more impressive than anything Luke Skywalker can do with his light saber.

Note that comparison and contrast passages are usually organized one of two ways: the **point-by-point** or **block** technique. You may need to recognize the relationships between similar or opposite ideas in both types of structure.

A point-by-point structure first states the main idea, then supports this idea point by point. The writer makes a point about A, then counters it with a similar point about B.

I'm the oldest of five kids. Yesterday, my youngest sister said she wished she was the oldest. Ha! Let me tell you, being the youngest is better any day. For one thing, the oldest has tons of responsibility. What about the youngest? None. My sis simply has to be there. She doesn't have to do chores, watch the other kids, or help make dinner. For another, the oldest has to "break in" the parents. Since I was the first, my parents had to learn how to be parents—and if they made mistakes, well, I was the one who suffered. Lucky Emily has parents who've already been through this four times. Unlike me, she has parents who are already well trained.

The block technique, on the other hand, discusses all the characteristics of A and *then* discusses all the characteristics of B. We get a block of text about one item that's being compared and then get a block of text about the other item.

I'm the oldest of five kids. Yesterday, my youngest sister said she wished she was the oldest. Ha! Let me tell you, being the youngest is better any day. For one thing, the oldest has tons of responsibility. I always have to do chores, watch the other kids, and help make dinner. For another, the oldest has to "break in" the parents. Since I was the first, my parents had to learn how to be parents—and if they made mistakes, well, I was the one who suffered. What about the youngest? What kind of responsibility does my sister have? None. My sis simply has to be there. Lucky Emily also has parents who've already been through this four

times. Unlike me, she has parents who are already well trained.

Draw Conclusions from Information Stated or Implied within a Passage

You may be asked to draw a conclusion from reading a passage—a decision based on facts and inferences. Drawing a conclusion is kind of like solving a mystery. You put together clues, or facts, from the text and all the inferences you made as you read it. Then you decide what's true.

Read the selection, and then answer the questions that follow.

Mom was busy in the kitchen when my brother Marco and I got home from school Friday. "Did you remember your grandmother's coming today?" she asked.

"Sure, Mom," we laughed. "Didn't you notice we cleaned our rooms?"

Mom smiled. "Thanks. I know I shouldn't be nervous, but my mother hasn't been here in almost six years! As I was growing up, her house always looked perfect. So I want everything to be, well—"

"Perfect," I said with a smile. "What else can we do to help before she gets here?"

Mom looked around. "You two could set the table. Use the good china—and be very careful with the glasses. Grandma gave those to your dad and me before you were born!"

As Mom prepared a sumptuous meal, Marco and I set the table. We carefully put a plate, glass, and silverware at each place. I taught Marco how to line up the forks on the left side of each plate and the knives and spoons on the right. In the center of the table, we placed a set of tall white candles. Then we stepped back and looked at our work. It seemed something was missing. "What's missing?" I asked Marco.

"Napkins?" he asked. "And I don't think Mom would want us to use paper ones!"

We both laughed. Marco opened a drawer and took out the nice cloth napkins Mom saved for special occasions. The soft white squares were folded in the middle, and we placed one on each plate. "Do you think that looks good enough?" I mumbled.

"No," Marco whispered. "Let's make them look fancier. Remember that restaurant we went to last year? Their napkins were folded to look like crowns! Now that was elegant!"

I nodded and unfolded the cloth napkin in front of me. "Look," I said, pointing to the creases in the cloth, "these lines make triangle shapes. That gives me a great idea! Let's do origami—that'll make the napkins unique."

Marco looked confused, so I explained, "Origami's a kind of folding art. People usually use paper, but you can use cloth. You make boats, birds, or flowers just by folding. No glue, tape, or staples are needed."

Mom overheard us. "I know how to make an origami bird and flower," she said. She quickly folded a napkin, then unfolded it to show us how the shapes fit together.

Just then, Dad came home from work and showed us how to make a crown and a boat. "Okay," he said, "in 20 minutes your grandma will walk through that door. Better get these napkins folded once and for all!"

We did. We placed a different origami napkin on each plate. Now, the table looked elegant! And just in time.

Grandma arrived by taxi and shared hugs all around. She gave us gifts from a bag labeled ORLY AIRPORT—PARIS. Then, as we walked into the dining room, she said, "Oh, my, who fixed these fabulous folded napkins? I've never seen anything so perfect!"

We all smiled, happy that Grandma thought Mom's home was perfect, too!

1. You can draw a conclusion that Marco is younger than the narrator because
   a. he wants to make the napkins look elegant.
   b. the narrator and he come home from school together.
   c. the narrator teaches him how to set a table and explains what origami is.
   d. he opens the drawer to get out the napkins.

2. Why might you conclude that Grandma lives in France?
   a. She came in a taxi.
   b. She had a bag labeled PARIS.
   c. She had not visited in six years.
   d. Both b and c.

3. What conclusion can you draw about an everyday meal at Marco's house?
   a. His dad never cooks.
   b. The family never has time to eat together.
   c. His mother is not a very good cook.
   d. The family uses paper napkins.

4. From the story, what can you conclude about the narrator and Marco?
   a. They usually don't keep their rooms clean.
   b. They very seldom go to bed on time!
   c. Spaghetti is their favorite food.
   d. They were named after their father's grandparents.

Answers

1. c
2. d
3. d
4. a

0005: Use Critical Reasoning Skills to Evaluate Written Material

For example:

- Identify the assumptions underlying a writer's argument.
- Assess the relevance of facts, examples, or data to a writer's argument.
- Distinguish between statements of fact and expressions of opinion.
- Assess a writer's objectivity or bias.

On the Reading subtest you may be asked to evaluate what you read in terms of reliability, evidence, and hidden agendas. You will need to differentiate between fact and opinion, identify an assumption that the author has made but has not stated explicitly, or identify the opinion or bias the author reveals by what is or is not included in the passage. This section reviews some of the important issues to keep in mind.

Identify the Assumptions Underlying a Writer's Argument

In a poorly thought out passage, the author may simply take for granted that certain ideas are true. Then the reader is faced with information or reasoning that is based on assumptions rather than evidence. You can learn to spot such flaws in passages you read, and avoid them in your own essays.

For example, the following was found on an Internet chat room about the rising costs of healthcare. As you read, see if you can spot the underlying assumptions that make this a flawed argument.

Today, doctors in large cities make more money than doctors in small towns or rural areas. Just because a doctor's office is in a fancy building or at a fancy address, he or she can charge patients more. Of course, some medical schools cost more than others, but basically all doctors spend a lot of money and a long time in school. There's no proof that graduates of more expensive schools practice in big cities and graduates of less expensive schools practice in small towns. Whether a patient goes to a doctor in a big city or small town, healthcare should cost the same.

Assumptions: This author never provides evidence to support the general statement on which the argument is based: "... doctors in large cities make more money than doctors in small towns or rural areas." The author just makes that statement without presenting any hard evidence or qualifying it.

The passage is also based on the assumption that the care that doctors give should cost the same amount no matter where the doctors live, and no matter how their living or business costs might differ.

The underlying assumption of the final sentence is that doctors determine the cost of healthcare. Certainly, doctors are involved in deciding how much money they charge for their time and services; however, the term *healthcare* means more than doctor visits. It includes having tests done, getting X-rays, purchasing medicine, staying in the hospital, and many other services. In today's healthcare web, full of HMOs, expensive insurance, and malpractice lawsuits, much more is involved in the cost of healthcare than where a doctor lives or how much that doctor owes in student loans.

For practice in spotting underlying assumptions, read these two paragraphs excerpted from an article about contemporary Moscow, Russia, and answer the question that follows.

Recognizing that new building represents progress, and progress is necessary for the growth of the nation, new building is flourishing in Moscow. However, the Department of Preservation of Historical Monuments is ensuring that building is done in a manner that respects the past. There are approximately 160 active archeological sites currently in Moscow; 5,000 buildings have been designated as protected locations.

Archaeologists working in Manege Square uncovered the commercial life of eight centuries. By excavating five meters deep, archaeologists provided a picture of the evolution of commercial Moscow. Among the finds: wooden street pavement from the time of Ivan the Terrible (sixteenth century), a wide cobblestone road from the era of Peter the Great (early eighteenth century), street paving from the reign of Catherine the Great (mid- to late eighteenth century), and a wealthy merchant's estate (nineteenth century). Smaller finds—a belt and buckle, a gold chain, shoes, locks, and a horse harness—provide rich details about the lives of Muscovites of the past. The citizens of the present are determined that history will not repeat itself, and that the past will be uncovered and celebrated rather than shrouded and forgotten. As a result of this respectful approach to modernization, Moscow, a city with more and more modern structures appearing all the time, remains largely distinguished by Byzantine cathedrals, fifteenth- and sixteenth-century stone buildings, and the ostentatious estates of the eighteenth and nineteenth centuries.

———————

Which of the following assumptions most influenced the views expressed by the writer in this passage?
  a. Progress and preservation are equally important principles of urban planning.
  b. Generally speaking, Muscovites are more interested in building new structures than in saving old ones.
  c. Architectural history has little meaning to people struggling to form a new government.
  d. Archaeologists and bureaucrats generally do not work well together.

Answer

  a. In reporting on present-day Moscow, the writer speaks approvingly of both progress and preservation. In the first paragraph, *new building* is assumed to be connected with necessary progress. The author also assumes that respecting the past is important. See especially the middle of the second paragraph: *The citizens of the present are determined that . . . the past will be uncovered and celebrated rather than shrouded and forgotten.*

Assess the Relevance of Facts, Examples, or Data to a Writer's Argument

An author's conclusions must be based on the evidence supplied by the passage. Statements that are not supported by relevant evidence are assumptions or opinions, or may be false information. Statements that have nothing to do with an argument distract from the main idea, and they weaken an argument.

Details included in a passage need to supply relevant information. For example, read the following statement from an essay in progress.

According to the respected American historian Frederick Jackson Turner, America's western frontier finally closed in the year 1890.

Which of the following facts from the 1890 census could be included in the essay as evidence for Jackson's statement?
  a. In 1890, 35% of Americans lived in cities.
  b. In 1890, there was no longer any single large area in the West without settlers.
  c. In 1890, the population of Los Angeles reached 50,000.
  d. In 1890, Chicago had become the second largest city in the United States.

Answer

The frontier referred to the hypothetical boundary between settled areas of the United States and open territory that had not yet been settled by people. With no single area in the West without settlers in 1890, the frontier, in effect, no longer existed. Therefore, choice **b** supplies the most relevant information. Choice **c**, which refers to the population of Los Angeles, might at first seem relevant; however, it is not legitimate to draw conclusions about a vast region based on the population of a single city within that region. None of the other choices supports Jackson's conclusion.

Details that are not relevant distract from the author's message. Read the following and note which statement has no place in this paragraph.

An ecosystem is a group of animals and plants living in a specific region and interacting with one another and with their physical environment. Ecosystems also can be thought of as the interacting among all organisms in a given habitat; for instance, one species may serve as food for another. People are part of the ecosystems where they live and work. Environmental groups are forming in many communities. Human activities can harm or destroy local ecosystems unless actions such as land development for housing or businesses are carefully planned to conserve and sustain the ecology of the area. An important part of ecosystem management involves finding ways to protect and enhance economic and social well-being while protecting local ecosystems.

Which of the following is the least relevant to the main idea of the paragraph?
a. An ecosystem is a group of animals and plants living in a specific region and interacting with one another and with their physical environment.
b. Environmental groups are forming in many communities.
c. Human activities can harm or destroy local ecosystems unless actions such as land development for housing or businesses are carefully planned to conserve and sustain the ecology of the area.
d. An important part of ecosystem management involves finding ways to protect and enhance economic and social well-being while protecting local ecosystems.

Answer

b. The topic of the paragraph is about the ecology of an area; it does not specifically address environmental organizations. Although other parts of the essay might discuss organizations, here the sentence distracts from the message of the paragraph.

Some arguments use irrelevant information in a form known as a **red herring**. A red herring is a fallacy that looks like this:

1. There is discussion of issue A.
2. There is introduction of issue B (irrelevant to issue A, but pretending to be relevant).
3. Issue A is forgotten and issue B becomes the focal point.

Nuclear power is a necessity, even though it has the potential to be dangerous. You know what is really dangerous, though? Bathtubs. More people die in accidents in their bathtubs every year than you can imagine.

Issue A: Nuclear power is a necessity, even though it has the potential to be dangerous. Issue B: Bathtubs are really dangerous. Issue B is not relevant to issue A, but we hear more about issue B, and issue A is forgotten.

What is the red herring in the following argument?

It is a great idea to eliminate free checking from our bank services. There is a lot of support for it. You know, if the bank does not meet its profit goals, we could be out of a job.

Answer

The red herring is the last line, "if the bank does not meet its profit goals, we could be out of a job." The argument is supposed to be about the elimination of free checking. Instead, the speaker goes off track by inserting the uncomfortable idea of job losses.

Distinguish between Statements of Fact and Expressions of Opinion

On the Reading subtest you may be required to distinguish between fact and opinion, and to decide whether the supporting details, or evidence, effectively back up the author's main point.

To separate fact from opinion, consider these differences:

- A **fact** is a statement that can be verified by a reliable source.
- An **opinion** is a statement about the beliefs or feelings of a person or group.

When determining whether a statement is factual, consider whether a source gives researched, accurate information. The following is an example of a factual statement—it can be supported by the national census.

The U.S. population is growing older—in fact, adults over age 65 are the fastest-growing segment of today's population.

Opinions, on the other hand, reflect judgments that may or may not be true. Opinions include speculation or predictions of the future that cannot be proven at the present time. The following statement represents an opinion—it offers a belief about the future. Others may disagree with the prediction.

Many believe that the population boom among elderly Americans will create a future healthcare crisis.

Language clues can alert you to a statement that reflects an opinion. Look for these common words that introduce opinions:

likely
should/could
say
possibly
think
charge
probably
believe
attest

People can, and often do, have opinions on just about anything. But some opinions are more reasonable than others. A *reasonable* opinion is one that is supported by relevant facts. That's what most nonfiction writing is all about. Writers make a claim about their subject, and that claim is often an opinion. Then they offer facts to support that opinion.

A writer can use different types of evidence to build an argument, but some forms of proof are more reliable than others. When you read, look for the forms of evidence listed below and consider how accurate each might be.

- observations
- experiments
- interviews
- personal experience
- surveys and questionnaires
- expert opinions

Read the following passage and answer the questions that follow.

Age of Enlightenment

The Enlightenment describes a period in Europe and America during the eighteenth century in which philosophers celebrated rational thought, science, and technological progress. The scientific developments of the sixteenth and seventeenth centuries acted as a precursor to the Enlightenment. Galileo Galilei, Nicolaus Copernicus, and Isaac Newton contributed new ideas about astronomy and physics that challenged the conventional understanding of the physical world. Later, the philosophy of John Locke influenced attitudes about the role of the individual in society and challenged the notion that knowledge is inborn. The works of the French philosopher Jean Jacques Rousseau shaped political and educational theory, as did the ideas of Immanuel Kant in Germany, David Hume in England, and Benjamin Franklin and Thomas Jefferson in the American colonies.

1. Which of the following statements about the Enlightenment is an opinion?
   a. The proponents of the Enlightenment believed in rationality.
   b. The Enlightenment philosophers challenged formerly held beliefs.
   c. The Enlightenment was an international movement.
   d. John Locke contributed the most to the Enlightenment philosophy.

2. Based on the passage, which of the following opinions is most likely true?
   a. Scientific discoveries in the previous century contributed to the beginning of the Enlightenment.
   b. Feudalism was the underlying cause of the Enlightenment.
   c. The French Revolution almost prevented the Enlightenment from taking place.
   d. The Crusades eventually resulted in the Enlightenment.

3. Which is a fact from the passage?
   a. Galileo, Copernicus, and Newton had some disagreements about the nature of the physical world.
   b. Benjamin Franklin and Thomas Jefferson brought Enlightenment ideas from the American colonies to Europe.
   c. The Enlightenment occurred during the eighteenth century in Europe and America.
   d. John Locke's theories must have influenced attitudes about the role of the individual in society.

Answers

1. d. *John Locke contributed the most to the Enlightenment philosophy* is a statement of opinion. Scholars could, and do, argue about who contributed the most to the Enlightenment, also known as the Age of Reason, or who is considered the most influential writer or thinker of the time.

2. a. Although the proponents of the Enlightenment were reacting against the influences of the Middle Ages—feudalism, the Crusades, and the Roman Catholic Church—the most likely factors that contributed positively to the Age of Enlightenment were the scientific discoveries of the sixteenth and seventeenth centuries.

3. c. The time period and locations of the Enlightenment are given in the passage and that information can be verified. The other statements are opinions, are false, or are not covered in the passage.

Assess a Writer's Objectivity or Bias

Bias refers to a preference that makes one prejudiced. Newspaper and television reporters, for example, are expected to be objective—to deliver the facts without offering an opinion. However, you should never assume a lack of bias. As a skeptical reader, be aware of its existence and keep an eye out for it. The more you agree with an author or a subject, the more you should consider whether it is biased.

Sometimes a writer's beliefs unknowingly affect how he or she writes about a topic. In other cases, a writer deliberately attempts to shape the reader's reaction and position. For example, a writer may present only one perspective about a subject or include only facts that support his or her point of view.

Certain words are sometimes used to communicate or reinforce bias, a person's individual opinion or interpretation of something. Biased words often illustrate the writer's emotions, and can also trigger emotions in a reader. Biased words are not rooted in fact. Instead, they convey judgment and personal belief.

Here are some words that demonstrate bias:

best
favorite
horrible
awful
strange
smart
stupid
mailman (words like this one are gender-biased, as they pertain only to the male sex)

Sometimes a writer's beliefs unknowingly affect how he or she writes about a topic. In other cases, a writer deliberately attempts to shape the reader's reaction and position. For example, a writer may present only one perspective about a subject or include only facts that support his or her point of view.

Bias can lead the author to make a purely emotional argument, leaving out logical reasons, information, or anything that might counter the argument. Consider the following paragraph:

> Hunting should be abolished! For one thing, hunting is not a "sport," as so many people like to call it. For another, poor, defenseless animals have just as much right to live as people do. What right do hunters have to take an animal's life just for sport? None! Further, most hunters don't even use the animals for food. They should be ashamed of such cruelty!

Even though you may find this argument convincing, there's no real logic in this passage. This writer relies solely on emotional appeals to convince you that hunting should be abolished.

Let's take a closer look to see how this works. In the first paragraph, the writer begins by claiming that hunting "is not a 'sport.' " But she does not explain why it's not a sport. Instead, she tries to make us feel outraged because poor, defenseless animals are being killed. She hasn't offered any logical reasons for why it should be abolished.

Next, the writer claims that animals have "just as much right to live as people do." But she doesn't explain why. Instead, she asks a question that really just restates her claim. She also uses the words "poor" and "defenseless" to describe animals. Here, her goal is to make us feel pity for the animals and anger toward the hunters.

The rest of the paragraph deals with the issue of hunters not eating the animals they kill. Again, the language the writer uses is designed to make us angry with hunters, to make us feel as if the hunters are heartless, horrible people. Unfortunately, she never offers a *logical* reason to abolish hunting.

Another clue, by the way, that this argument is too emotional is the number of exclamation points. You can see that the writer feels very passionately about her subject by how often she uses exclamation points. Being passionate about a subject is not in itself a bad thing; but when we're too emotional, sometimes we forget to back up those emotions with logic.

Keep in mind that an **explanation** is not necessarily evidence for an argument. For example, an advertiser who wants you to buy a product often gives irrelevant information such as "our dish detergent is much better than Brand X, because it smells like lemons." Critical thinking skills help you to understand that weak or unsubstantiated explanations are no substitute for scarce or missing evidence, whether in a passage you're reading or an essay you're writing.

For example, list two things wrong with the following survey.

A politician sent out a questionnaire to 1,000 of his supporters. It began with an introduction about how different people used their tax refund checks to support local charities. Then

he asked them, "Do you believe tax refunds to hard-working Americans should stop, and that your taxes should be increased to burdensome levels again?"

Answers

Correct answers should include at least two of the following:

- The population surveyed was not random—the questionnaire was only sent to the politician's supporters.
- The introduction was biased—it shows people how beneficial tax refunds are.
- The question was biased—"hard-working" and "burdensome" indicate the author's subjective intent.

Stereotypes are oversimplified opinions or prejudiced attitudes about a group of people. Biases and stereotypes should not be used to make decisions. Here is an example of stereotyping.

A study is done of a doctor's painkiller prescription writing habits. It is found that 75% of the prescriptions are written for male patients, even though his practice is 50% male and 50% female. When asked about this discrepancy, he reveals, "My female patients have a lower pain threshold. They should tolerate pain better, and stop relying on drugs." This doctor believes the stereotype that women are the "weaker sex." He thinks women tend toward hypochondria, and therefore their complaints of pain are not as valid as men's. The stereotype prevents him from making logical decisions, and from adequately caring for half of his practice.

1. Which of the following statements is an example of bias?
   a. He belongs to Greenpeace. I don't want to go out with him again because my uncle's law firm is fighting them in court.
   b. I will take it to her office myself; the people in the mailroom are all lazy.
   c. My favorite store is selling boots at 20% off this week. I bet Sara will buy some.
   d. I like the egg rolls better than the dumplings.

2. Which of the following statements is an example of stereotyping?
   a. He belongs to Greenpeace. I don't want to go out with him again because my uncle's law firm is fighting them in court.
   b. I will take it to her office myself; the people in the mailroom are all lazy.
   c. My favorite store is selling boots at 20% off this week. I bet Sara will buy some.
   d. I like the egg rolls better than the dumplings.

Answers

1. a. The first statement involves bias. The speaker takes her uncle's side against the environmental group.
2. b. The second statement declares a stereotype (all mailroom workers are lazy). The third statement is a fact, followed by a prediction. The fourth statement is also not an example of bias or stereotyping. Although it is an opinion, it is based on the fact that the speaker has tried both, and prefers one over the other. This type of opinion does not prevent the speaker from thinking objectively about anyone or anything.

0006: Apply Skills for Outlining and Summarizing Written Materials and Interpreting Information Presented in Graphic Form

For example:

- Identify an effective outline or graphic representation of information presented in a paragraph or passage.
- Identify an effective summary of information presented in a paragraph or passage.
- Interpret information presented in graphs, tables, charts, or diagrams.
- Draw conclusions based on information presented in graphs, tables, charts, or diagrams.
- Select the graphic form best suited to the presentation of information contained in a paragraph or passage.

After we read longer works such as books and articles, we often remember only a few of the most interesting points. Taking good notes is a valuable skill for both readers and writers. Making summaries and outlines are two good ways to record and keep track of all the significant information you read about. In cases where authors choose to convey information in pictures, graphs, or diagrams, you'll need to interpret them quickly. This section will help you develop skills for using these special forms.

Identify an Effective Outline or Graphic Representation of Information Presented in a Paragraph or Passage

An **outline** shows the main idea and supporting details in a list. Outlines can be used to take notes on fiction passages, but they are best for readings that contain lots of facts and information.

Outlines usually are formatted like this one:

Surfing
I. history
    A. Polynesian culture
    B. Captain Cook's travel notes
    C. modern surfing
II. equipment
    A. surfboards
        1. longboards
        2. funboards
        3. shortboards
    B. wetsuits
    C. board wax

Note that the topic appears at the top; if you are taking notes from a book or article, include the author's name or the book title as well. This sample outline uses three **levels** to list the two main topics and several smaller details. The main ideas should be the first level in your outline. Usually the first level of the outline uses Roman numerals (I, II, III, IV, V, and so on). The second level uses capital letters, and the third level uses Arabic numbers. These levels help you show how the details are related.

A good way to begin an outline is to locate the main topics of the passage. Read this article about cuttlefish and choose the best outline from the choices that follow.

Cuttlefish are intriguing little animals. The cuttlefish resembles a rather large squid and is, like the octopus, a member of the order of cephalopods. Although they are not considered the most highly evolved of the cephalopods, they are extremely intelligent. While observing them, it is hard to tell who is doing the observing, you or the cuttlefish, especially since the eye of the cuttlefish is similar in structure to the human eye. Cuttlefish are also highly mobile and fast creatures. They come equipped with a small jet located just below the tentacles that can expel water to help them move. Ribbons of flexible fins on each side of the body allow cuttlefish to hover, move, stop, and start.

The cuttlefish is sometimes referred to as the "chameleon of the sea" because it can change its skin color and pattern instantaneously. Masters of camouflage, they can blend into any environment for protection, but they are also capable of the most imaginative displays of iridescent, brilliant color and intricate designs, which scientists believe they use for communication and for mating displays. However, judging from the riot of ornaments and hues cuttlefish produce, it is hard not to believe they paint themselves so beautifully just for the sheer joy of it. At the very least, cuttlefish conversation must be the most sparkling in all the sea.

Which of the following best outlines the main topics addressed in the passage?
    a. I. explanation of why cuttlefish are intriguing
        II. communication skills of cuttlefish
    b. I. classification and difficulties of observing cuttlefish
        II. scientific explanation of modes of cuttlefish communication
    c. I. explanation of the cuttlefish's method of locomotion
        II. description of color displays in mating behavior
    d. I. general classification and characteristics of cuttlefish
        II. uses and beauty of the cuttlefish's ability to change color

Answer

d. Choice **d** covers the most important ideas in the two paragraphs. All the other choices choose minor details from the paragraphs as the main subjects.

At times, you may want to draw a quick sketch to remind you of some important detail in a passage. Or you might be asked on a test to choose the best of several images to go with a text. Like an outline, a **graphic** must represent important information correctly. Read this passage and select the **diagram** that follows that could be used to accompany this text.

The sun is at the center of our solar system; Earth orbits around the sun, and the moon orbits around Earth. When these three moving bodies line up in a certain way, some locations on Earth experience an eerie darkness. That's because the moon is blocking light from the sun. We call this event a solar eclipse. During a solar eclipse, the moon passes between Earth and the sun, fully or partially hiding the sun from some areas on Earth.

Carefully examine the graphics that follow (not drawn to scale). Note that some actually have the orbits of Earth, the moon, or the sun wrong. Based on the passage, which of the following diagrams best represents the position of the sun, Earth, and the moon during a solar eclipse?

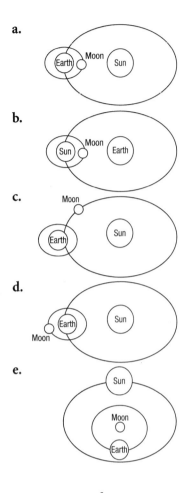

Answer

a. The diagram in choice **a** corresponds to the correct arrangement of Earth, the moon, and the sun during a solar eclipse. The moon is located between Earth and the sun, blocking Earth's view of the sun. It also corresponds to the correct orbits, with the moon orbiting around Earth, and Earth around the sun. Choice **b** is incorrect because it shows the sun orbiting around Earth, and the moon around the sun. Choice **c** is incorrect because Earth, the moon, and the sun are not aligned as they should be during an eclipse, and the moon is not orbiting around Earth. Choice **d** shows correct orbits, but the moon is not blocking the sun from Earth's view. Choice **e** is incorrect because it shows Earth and the sun orbiting around the moon.

Identify an Effective Summary of Information Presented in a Paragraph or Passage

Unlike an outline, a summary uses complete sentences to briefly explain the main ideas of a passage. It does not include all the supporting details.

Here are three summaries of a story about Xerxes' attack on the Greeks. Read each version, then answer the questions that follow.

a. In 484 BCE, the Persian king Xerxes attacked the Greeks.

b. In 484 BCE, the Phoenicians joined Persia in a war against the Greeks. Their warships and sailing expertise helped King Xerxes fight the Greek navy.

c. In 484 BCE, the Persian king Xerxes asked the Phoenicians to help him make war on the Greeks. The Phoenicians contributed 300 warships and helped build a bridge of ships across the Hellespont. Xerxes' army crossed on the bridge to reach the mainland. There they began to attack the Greek cities.

1. Which summary provides only the main idea?

2. Which summary provides the most supporting details? Do these details seem necessary in a summary?

3. Which summary do you think is most effective? Why?

Answers

1. a. This summary presents the topic and the main idea, but no supporting details.

2. c. The third summary presents numerous details, but the number of ships, the location of the ships, and the sequence of events are probably more information than we need.

3. b. The second summary is most effective because it includes the main idea and some supporting details without being too specific.

The answer choices for summary questions are sometimes rather long, making the question more difficult. Realize, however, that the test makers had to make three of the choices wrong in some way. Your task is to discover the errors. These seven steps will help you answer questions about summaries:

1. Read or skim the passage, noting or underlining main ideas as they flow from one to the other.

2. Look for phrases that restate the main ideas you underlined.

3. Eliminate answers that contain phrases that contradict ideas in the passage.

4. Eliminate answers that are off topic or only deal with part of the passage.

5. Eliminate answers that state one or more ideas that the author has not mentioned.

6. If you are left with two choices, choose the most complete one.

7. If you have eliminated all the choices, choose the summary that contains the most ideas that actually appear in the passage.

Use the seven steps to answer the question following this passage.

Extended-time programs often feature innovative scheduling, as program staff work to maintain participation and respond to students' and parents' varied schedules and family or employment commitments. Offering students flexibility and some choice regarding when they participate in extended learning may be as simple as offering homework sessions when children need them most—after school and before dinner—as do Kids Crew and the Omaha After-School Study Centers. Or it may mean keeping early and late hours to meet the child care needs of parents who work more than one job or support extended families, as does Yuk Yau Child Development Center. Similarly, the Florida Summer Institute for At-Risk Migrant Students is a residential program so that students' participation does not disrupt their migrant families' travels.

Which of the following paraphrases best summarizes the previous passage?

a. After-school programs should help children finish their homework after school.
b. Kids Crew and other programs meet the needs of children.
c. There are several ways to schedule programs outside school time to meet the needs of students and families.
d. Extended-time programs can be innovative, and Yuk Yau Child Development Center is an example of this.

Answer

Go through the seven steps.

1. The flow goes like this: innovative scheduling, family needs, examples—after school, early and late care, residential.
2. Choices a, c, and d have words and ideas noted in step 1.
3. None of the choices is contrary to the passage. (That tactic is usually used with persuasive passages.)
4. The answers are all on topic, but a and b only deal with part of the paragraph.
5. All the ideas are in the passage.
6. You are left with choices c and d. Choice d only mentions one example and the passage gives three. Choice c does not mention any examples specifically, but is broad enough to include all the examples as well as the main idea of the paragraph. You can conclude that the answer is c, and you don't have to use step 7.

Interpret Information Presented in Graphs, Tables, Charts, or Diagrams

You may be asked to interpret information from a graph, table, chart, or diagram just as you would from a reading passage. Remember that the **title** of a graph, table, chart, or diagram tells you the **main idea** by stating what kind of information is being shown.

A **legend**, also called a key, is a guide to the symbols and colors used in the graph. It tells you what is being measured on the graph. Since some graphs measure more than one set of data, be sure to check the legend to see what's being presented.

Bar graphs, **line graphs**, and **scatter plots** have two axes that form a corner. The **label** tells you what each axis measures.

Look at the following bar graph as an example.

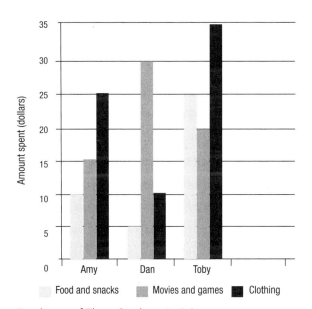

Purchases of Three Students in July

Carefully note the title, the legend, and the type of information shown on each axis, then answer the following questions.

1. According to the graph, how much money did Toby spend on movies and games?
   a. $20
   b. $25
   c. $30
   d. $40

2. Which student spent the most on food and snacks?
   a. Amy
   b. Dan
   c. Toby
   d. Dan and Toby spent an equal amount.

3. What is the total amount that Amy spent?
   a. $45
   b. $50
   c. $65
   d. $75

4. In total, how much did all three students spend on clothing?
   a. $70
   b. $80
   c. $85
   d. $95

5. What did Dan spend most of his money on?
   a. food and snacks
   b. movies and games
   c. clothing
   d. Dan spent an equal amount on clothing and food and snacks.

Answers

1. a
2. c
3. b
4. a
5. b

On a **line graph**, a line connects each point, making it easy to see the up and down trends of the information being tracked.

For example, based on the following line graph, what was the general trend of U.S. immigration between 1950 and 1990?

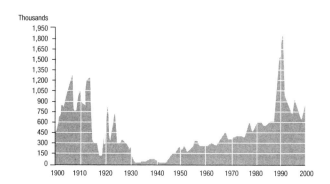

Answer

The trend was increasing. Even though the graph plots small rises and falls in immigration, between 1950 and 1990 the plotted line increases overall.

On a **scatter plot**, a marker (such as a square or circle) represents the point where information on each axis connects. This one shows how many new cars and used cars were sold each month.

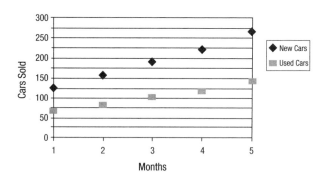

A typical **pie chart** (also called a **pie graph**) looks like a circular pie or pizza divided into sections. These graphs are commonly used to show percentages; the whole pie represents 100 percent of something, so each piece is a fraction of the whole. A pie graph might include a legend, or it might use icons or labels within each slice.

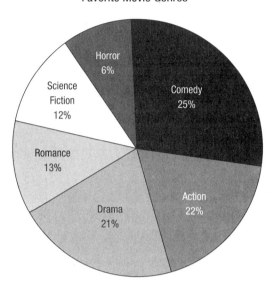

Favorite Movie Genres

Diagrams use shapes to present information. You'll often encounter a **Venn diagram**, made of two or more overlapping circles. It is used to show that two or more sets of data have something in common. Here's a simple Venn diagram that shows you which flowers bloom in each season. You can easily see that if you want to buy fresh flowers in August, you must choose from those listed in the Shared or the Summer areas of the diagram.

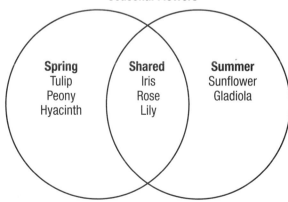

Seasonal Flowers

Draw Conclusions Based on Information Presented in Graphs, Tables, Charts, or Diagrams

On the Reading subtest, you may be asked to analyze the information presented in graphic form to arrive at conclusions. In some cases, the information that leads to a conclusion is very easy to see. For example, take another look at the pie chart about movies and answer the questions that follow.

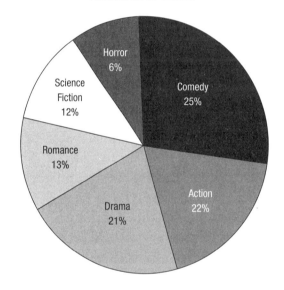

Favorite Movie Genres

1. Do more people like drama or comedy? _____

2. Which two genres are the least popular? _____

3. Which is more popular—action, or romance *and* science fiction? _____

Answers

1. Comedy (26%) is more popular than drama (21%).
2. Horror (6%) and science fiction (12%) are the least popular genres.
3. Romance and science fiction combined (25%) are more popular than action (22%).

In other cases, you'll have to analyze the data more carefully to arrive at a conclusion. Go over this **table**, then answer the question that follows.

	Egypt	Sumer	India	China
Start Date	3000 B.C.	3200 B.C.	2500 B.C.	2100 B.C.
Location	Nile River valley	Euphrates River valley (Iraq)	Indus River valley	Huang Ho River valley
Main Sites	Memphis, Thebes	Ur, Eridu	Harappa, Mohenjo-Daro	Zhengzhou, Anyang
Type of Writing	hieroglyphics	cuneiform	Indus writing	Chinese characters
Form of Government	monarchy	monarchy	unknown	monarchy

Earliest Civilizations

Which conclusion is best supported by the information presented in the table?
a. All early civilizations were monarchies.
b. Egypt is the oldest of the world's civilizations.
c. Many of the world's earliest civilizations developed in river valleys.
d. All early civilizations used a type of writing called hieroglyphics.

Answer

c. Choice **a** is incorrect because the chart gives no information about the type of government of the Indian civilization. Choice **b** is incorrect because the civilization of Sumer is the oldest shown in the chart. Choice **d** is also incorrect; only one of the four civilizations mentioned used hieroglyphics. Thus, choice **c** is the best answer.

Time line diagrams present acts from which you can infer more general information. For example, the Neolithic Era saw significant climatic changes that allowed for the beginning of farming in many parts of the world. Based on the time line, answer the questions that follow.

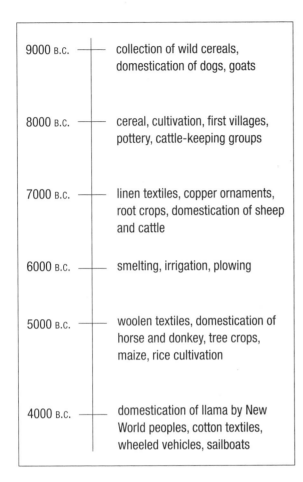

9000 B.C.	collection of wild cereals, domestication of dogs, goats
8000 B.C.	cereal, cultivation, first villages, pottery, cattle-keeping groups
7000 B.C.	linen textiles, copper ornaments, root crops, domestication of sheep and cattle
6000 B.C.	smelting, irrigation, plowing
5000 B.C.	woolen textiles, domestication of horse and donkey, tree crops, maize, rice cultivation
4000 B.C.	domestication of llama by New World peoples, cotton textiles, wheeled vehicles, sailboats

The Rise of Farming in the Neolothic Era

1. How did people's lives change when they began cultivating cereal crops?
   a. They stopped being afraid of wild animals.
   b. They started painting on the walls of caves.
   c. They started using fire to cook their food.
   d. They started settling down in villages.

2. Is it reasonable to conclude that cattle were used for plowing before horses were?
   a. No, because horses were domesticated before cattle were.
   b. No, because cattle were still wild when plowing was introduced.
   c. Yes, because horses were not yet domesticated when plowing was introduced.
   d. Yes, because cattle were more common than horses were.

3. Which statement is NOT a fact presented by the diagram?
   a. The wheel was invented long after people settled down in villages.
   b. Dugout canoes preceded sailboats by thousands of years.
   c. Olive trees and fruit trees were first cultivated around 5000 B.C.
   d. Irrigation was the Neolithic era's most important innovation.

Answers

1. d. According to the time line, the cultivation of cereal crops occurred around 8000 B.C. At that time, the most significant development was the appearance of villages in which people settled. Therefore, choice **e** is the best answer. None of the other choices applies to the appropriate time period. Choice **a** refers to domestication of animals, which had occurred earlier, in 9000 B.C. Wall painting, choice **b**, is never mentioned in the time line; nor is the use of fire for cooking, choice **c**.

2. c. The time line makes it clear that plowing occurred before the domestication of the horse, so it is reasonable to conclude that cattle were used for plowing. Thus, choice **c** is the best answer. The other choices are incorrect because each one is based on a misreading of the information in the time line.

3. d. Choice **d** is the correct answer because it is the only opinion among the five choices. The words *most important* give a clue that the statement is a value judgment, not a fact. All the other answers are facts, not opinions.

Select the Graphic Form Best Suited to the Presentation of Information Contained in a Paragraph or Passage

You may be asked to determine which graphic form would work best to present the information in a certain passage. Familiarize yourself with the possibilities, so you'll be ready for such questions. For example, answer the following.

1. During June, Amy spent the following:

Food $25

Movies $12

Clothing $36

Savings $20

Books $7

What of these types graphics would best show what percentage of the total Amy spent on each item in June?

a. pie chart

b. time line

c. bar graph

d. table

2. Maria and Stanley each have several hobbies. They both like reading, cooking, and hiking. Stanley also enjoys bowling and playing the guitar, though Maria doesn't. Maria likes knitting and kickboxing, neither of which appeals to Stanley. What type of graphic would easily show which of Maria and Stanley's hobbies are the same and which are different?

a. pie chart

b. time line

c. line graph

d. diagram

Answers

1. a. A pie chart is a good choice when you want to show percentages related to single kind of information.

2. d. A Venn diagram would make the overlap of hobbies clear.

CHAPTER

8  WRITING SKILLS REVIEW

CHAPTER SUMMARY

Good writing skills are essential to success on the Writing subtest of the Communication and Literacy Skills Test and critical to success as a teacher. It's important to be able to communicate ideas clearly and accurately in written English. To help you express yourself effectively, this chapter reviews the elements of good writing: basic grammar, capitalization and punctuation, sentence structure, and the preparation of a written essay. Each Objective tested in the Writing subtest is covered.

Multiple-Choice and Short-Answer Questions

On the Writing subtest you'll encounter multiple-choice and short-answer questions that will measure your knowledge of the basics of grammar, sentence construction, and appropriate word choice, as well as your ability to locate and revise errors. You will be asked to analyze the effectiveness of the expression in a passage according to the conventions of edited American English. You may be asked about language usage or sentence correction or to demonstrate your ability to recognize and correct awkward sentence constructions and other grammatical elements.

Open-Response Exercises

Essays can intimidate anyone—even teachers. You know that on the Writing subtest you will be asked to write two open responses, but you don't know your topics beforehand. And you are under pressure: You have limited time to complete both tasks. Even though this sounds nerve-racking, with preparation you will be ready to produce your best writing. The good news is that because the time limit is brief, your open responses don't need to be novels. The Summary Exercise should be no longer than 150 words, and the Composition Exercise should be no longer than 600 words. Furthermore, because you are provided with the passage to summarize and the topic on which to write a composition, you don't need to spend valuable time deciding what to write about.

Let's now review, by test objective, the rules and patterns of English composition, grammar, sentence structure, and word usage, and the writing skills that will appear on the Writing subtest.

Objective 0007: Understand Methods for Establishing and Maintaining a Central Theme or Main Idea

For example:

- Identify effective thesis statements and topic sentences.
- Identify information, statements, or details that detract from the development of a main idea.
- Identify ineffective repetition and redundancy.
- Reorganize sentences or paragraphs to achieve a logical sequence of ideas.
- Identify effective transitions from one paragraph to another.

Identify Effective Thesis Statements and Topic Sentences

Thesis Statements

An effective thesis statement of a passage clearly asserts the main idea of the passage, but it is something more: It is the idea that also holds together or con-

trols the passage. The other sentences and ideas in the passage will all relate to the thesis statement and serve as evidence that the assertion is true. You might think of the thesis statement as a net that is cast over the other sentences. It must be general enough to hold all these ideas together.

Thus an effective thesis statement of a passage must:

- tell the reader what is the subject of the passage
- inform the reader about what the author thinks and feels about the subject
- use clear, active language

Consider the following paragraph.

Today's postal service is more efficient and reliable than ever before. Mail that used to take months to move by horse and foot now moves around the country in days or hours by truck, train, and plane. First-class mail usually moves from New York City to Los Angeles in three days or less. If your letter or package is urgent, the U.S. Postal Service offers Priority Mail and Express Mail services. Priority Mail is guaranteed to go anywhere in the United States in two days or less. Express Mail will get your package there overnight.

1. Which of the following sentences would be the most effective thesis statement for this paragraph?
   a. Express Mail is a good way to send urgent mail.
   b. Mail service today is more effective and dependable.
   c. First-class mail usually takes three days or less.
   d. E-mail is quickly making the USPS obsolete.

Because **a** is specific—it tells us *only* about Express Mail—it cannot be the thesis statement. It does not encompass the rest of the sentences in the paragraph—it doesn't cover Priority Mail or first-class mail. Choice **c** is also very specific. It tells us only about first class mail, so it, too, cannot be the main idea.

But **b**—"Mail service today is more effective and dependable"—*is* general enough to encompass the whole passage. And the sentences **a** and **b** *support* the idea that this sentence asserts: Each sentence offers "proof" that the postal service today is indeed more efficient and reliable. Thus, the writer aims to tell us about the efficiency and reliability of today's postal service.

Topic Sentences

Each paragraph within a passage should include a thesis statement that presents the main idea of the paragraph. This sentence is often referred to as the topic sentence, and is usually the first sentence in the paragraph. However, the topic sentence also can appear in the middle or at the end of a paragraph. A good topic sentence clearly identifies the content of the paragraph.

A strong topic sentence introduces all the ideas contained within the paragraph, and the topic it states must be narrow enough to be completely developed in the paragraph. The topic sentence must also grab the reader's attention. Like a headline in the newspaper, a topic sentence announces the main idea using language that will make the reader want to continue reading. This is also known as a "hook."

Circle the letter of the topic sentence in each of the following paragraphs.

1. **a.** There are two primary approaches to learning a foreign language. **b.** First, there is the textbook approach of understanding the grammar and linguistics while studying vocabulary. **c.** Second, there is immersion in a foreign language, either in a school or in a foreign country where the language is spoken. **d.** Ideally, learning a foreign language involves a combination of both methods.

2. **a.** Did I come to Venice to see the beautiful St. Mark's Basilica? **b.** Am I here to walk across the elegant white stone Bridge of Sighs? **c.** The main reason I am in Venice is to learn to pilot a gondola. **d.** A gondola is the traditional boat taxi of Venice's canals. **e.** It has a low hull and a steel prow and is rowed by a gondolier who wears an old-fashioned striped shirt and steers with a long oar.

3. **a.** He won Rookie of the Year in 1947. **b.** He broke the color barrier in professional baseball. **c.** He excelled despite encountering racist players, managers, and fans and receiving death threats. **d.** Jackie Robinson single-handedly brought equality and civil rights to professional sports.

Answers

1. The topic sentence is **a.** It makes a clear statement of what the paragraph is about,
2. The topic sentence is **c.** In the first two sentences, the author simply questions why he or she is in Venice. The third sentence tells the reader what the paragraph is about.
3. The topic sentence is **d.** The last sentence serves as a kind of punctuation to the entire paragraph, finally telling the reader who accomplished the feats described in other sentences.

Identify Information, Statements, or Details That Detract from the Development of a Main Idea

Each paragraph should support the main idea of a passage, and within a paragraph, each sentence should support the main idea.

The following paragraph is from an essay about Pierre and Marie Curie. Read it and answer the two questions that follow.

(1) First the Curies sifted and ground the pitchblende. (2) Marie boiled it in a big iron pot, stirring for hours with an iron rod. (3) The liquid was thrown away. (4) Pierre would then take what was left and treat it with different chemicals. (5) This helped him separate the elements and know which he wanted to throw away and which he wanted to study. (6) In this way, Marie and Pierre found two mysterious minerals. (7) The first they named polonium in honor of Poland. (8) It is located in eastern Europe. (9) The second one they called radium.

1. Which of the following best describes the purpose of the paragraph?
   a. to explain the process of separating different minerals
   b. to prove how the Curies discovered uranium
   c. to show how Pierre met and married Marie Curie
   d. to discuss what things can be made with radium

2. Which of the following sentences from the passage should be deleted because it does not support the main idea?
   a. sentence 1
   b. sentence 4
   c. sentence 6
   d. sentence 8

Answers

1. a. This content question asks you to figure out the main idea of a particular paragraph. In this case, the paragraph is focused on a very detailed and specific process of separating different materials, not on how the Curies met, the discovery of uranium, what can be made with radium, or how to find pitchblende.

2. e. This content question asks you to remove the unnecessary sentence. Choices a, b, and c are all relevant to each other. Choice d, however, contains unnecessary extra information that distracts the reader's attention from the main idea.

Identify Ineffective Repetition and Redundancy

You may be asked to identify redundant or wordy language within a passage. Look for repetition of ideas and statements that merely say the same thing in different words. To eliminate unnecessary repetition or wordiness in sentences, look for words that add no new information.

For example:

Redundant: Due to the fact that the circumstances of the case were sensitive in nature, the proceedings were kept confidential.
Correct: Because the circumstances of the case were sensitive, the proceedings were kept confidential.

Redundant: Charles returned back to his room at 10 A.M. in the morning.
Correct: Charles returned to his room at 10 A.M.

Redundant: They met at 4 P.M. in the afternoon.
Correct: They met at 4 P.M.

Repetition can be found even in short phrases. The list that follows contains dozens of such phrases that can clutter effective writing. Most of them contain a specific word and its more general category. Why state both? The word *memories* can only refer to the past, so you don't need to say *past memories*. We know that blue is a color, so describing something as *blue in color* is repetitive and therefore unnecessary. In most cases, a redundant phrase can be corrected by dropping the category and retaining the specific word.

Some redundant phrases use a modifier that is unneeded, because the specific is implied in the general. For instance, the word *consensus* means general agreement. Therefore, modifying it with the word *general* is repetitive. Similarly, *mathematics* is a field of study, so it does not need to be modified with the word *field*. You can tighten up your writing by eliminating wordiness in phrases such as the following.

Retain only the first word:

any and all
odd in appearance
mathematics field
refer back
cheap quality
close proximity
honest in character
large in size
confused state
often times
reason why
unusual in nature
heavy in weight
extreme in degree
period in time
round in shape

Drop the modifier (first word):

~~past~~ memories
~~terrible~~ tragedy
~~final~~ destination
~~end~~ result
~~general~~ consensus
~~final~~ outcome
~~free~~ gift
~~each~~ individual
~~past~~ history
~~basic~~ fundamentals
~~totally~~ obvious
~~true~~ facts
~~rarely~~ ever
~~important~~ essentials
~~unexpected~~ surprise
~~future~~ plans

Reorganize Sentences or Paragraphs to Achieve a Logical Sequence of Ideas

A well-organized essay or passage will usually adhere to the following formula:

1. **Introduction:** The introduction presents the writer's position or positions to the reader in a thesis statement that effectively and explicitly states the purpose for writing.
2. **Body:** The body should provide specific support for the thesis through examples and/or sound reasoning that reflects the understanding of the focus of the topic.
3. **Conclusion:** An effective conclusion brings closure to a passage and restates the thesis.

Where to put an introduction and conclusion is obvious; however, a pattern, or structure, is needed to effectively organize the ideas in the body of a passage. Writers use one of these common patterns: **chronological order, comparison and contrast, cause and effect,** and **order of importance.**

Chronological Order

Uses time as organizing principle; describes events in the order in which they happened

Effectively used in historical texts, personal narratives, fiction

Order of Importance

Arranges ideas by increasing or decreasing importance instead of by sequence

Effectively used in persuasive essays, newspaper articles

Comparison and Contrast

Places two or more items side by side to show similarities and differences

Effectively used in comparative essays

Cause and Effect

Explains possible reasons why something took place

Effectively used in historical analysis, analysis of current events

Identify Effective Transitions from One Paragraph to Another

The word "transition" means to pass from one thing to another. Transitions between paragraphs help the reader follow your ideas, and they are very important for maintaining coherence in your essay. When revising your writing, examine your transitions between sentences and between paragraphs. If they do not effectively move your ideas along, or are not smooth, use the methods and strategies in this section to improve them.

Here are the ways that transitions order your ideas.

Chronological Order

Chronological order is shown by using such transition words as *first, second, finally, next, then, afterward, later, before, eventually,* and *in the future.* For example:

Before the employees arrive in the morning, the building is empty. It is then that the janitor can clean thoroughly.

Chronological order is a common organizational technique for writers of fiction, as you will see in the next example.

"In consideration of the day and hour of my birth, it was declared by the nurse, and by some sage women in the neighbourhood who had taken a lively interest in me several months before there was any possibility of us becoming personally acquainted, first, that I was destined to be unlucky in life; and secondly, that I was privileged to see ghosts and spirits; both these gifts inevitably attaching, as they believed, to all unlucky infants of either gender, born towards the small hours on a Friday night."

—*David Copperfield*

Spatial Order

Transition words that show spatial order are *beside, in the middle, next to, to the right, on top of, in front of, behind, against,* and *beneath.* Spatial order is helpful when describing a place or the setting of a story. For example:

Against the wall, there is a dresser. *On top* of the dresser is where Brad keeps his spare change.

There is a damp cave *beneath* the house. If you enter the cave, take the fork *to the right*, or, as legend has it, you might disturb the ancient spirits.

Order of Importance

Transition words that show the order of importance are *more*, *less*, *most*, *least*, *most important*, *least important*, and *more importantly*. For example:

> Yesterday was a beautiful, sunny day, but *more importantly*, it was my birthday.

Comparison and Contrast

Transition words that show comparison and contrast are *likewise*, *however*, *similarly*, *in contrast*, *a different kind*, *unlike this*, and *another difference*. For example:

> The book *Of Mice and Men* begins with George and Lennie walking through the woods. *In contrast*, the movie begins with a woman in a red dress running through a field.

> My mother and grandmother both taught preschool. I chose, *however*, to become an engineer.

Cause and Effect

Transition words used to show cause and effect are *therefore*, *as a result of*, *consequently*, *thus*, *one cause*, *one effect*, *another cause*, and *another effect*. For example:

> Security officers guarded the gates of the airport. *As a result*, traffic slowed considerably on the highway.

> The recipe calls for two tablespoons of butter, and, *consequently*, the cookies will be thin and crisp.

Classification

Transition words that show classification are helpful, especially in scientific writing where classification is an important step in understanding the natural world. Transition words include *another group*, *the first type*, *one kind*, *other sorts*, *other types*, and *other kinds*. For example:

> *One type* of tennis player, like John McEnroe, lets his emotions show on the court. *Another type* of player stays calm throughout the match, whether the calls are bothersome or not.

Introducing Examples

Transition words such as *for example*, *one example*, *one kind*, *one type*, *one sort*, and *for instance* are often used to introduce examples in a piece of writing. For example:

> *One example* of a Greek tragedy is *Antigone*.

> Most insects have very short life spans. *For instance*, the fruit fly can expect to complete its life cycle in less than 48 hours.

Introducing Contradictions

When comparing and contrasting in a piece of writing, strong writers often introduce contradictions. They can be very effective tools for persuasion. Transition words that introduce contradictions are *nonetheless*, *however*, *in spite of*, *otherwise*, *instead*, and *on the contrary*. For example:

> The storm continued to toss the ship and managed to snap off the tip of the mast. *In spite of* this, they sailed on, desperate to reach Hawaii.

> Growers have recently marketed prunes as dried plums. *Nonetheless*, most people still refer to them as prunes.

Introducing Conclusions, Summaries, or Generalizations

Wrapping up a passage is a form of transition. Transition words for concluding are *in conclusion, therefore,* and *as a result.* Summaries and generalizations can be effectively introduced using *in summary* or *in general.* For example:

> *Therefore,* Cinco de Mayo is celebrated differently in the United States than in Mexico.

> *In general,* the phenomenon of the Bermuda Triangle is believed to be coincidental.

To practice using transitions, revise these sentences by following the directions in parentheses. Write the new sentences on the lines. Suggested answers follow.

1. It rained all morning. We went to the park. (Begin the second sentence with a transition word that introduces **contradiction**.)

_____

2. The company wants to hire experienced employees. Those people with no experience need not apply. (Combine these sentences using a **cause and effect** transition word.)

_____

3. Sylvia greeted all her guests at the door. She seated them at the dinner table. (Combine these sentences using a transition word that shows **chronological order**.)

_____

4. Bob Marley used Sly and Robbie for a rhythm section. Peter Tosh recorded with Sly and Robbie on at least one of his records. (Begin the second sentence with a transition word that shows **comparison and contrast**.)

_____

5. We kept adding water to the paint. It was too thin to use. (Begin the second sentence with a transition word used for **concluding**.)

_____

Suggested Answers

Exercise 1
Remember, these are suggested answers. Other transition words could work if the paragraph makes sense with them.

1. It rained all morning. In spite of this, we went to the park.
2. The company wants to hire experienced employees, therefore, those people with no experience need not apply.
3. Sylvia greeted all her guests at the door, then she seated them at the dinner table.
4. Bob Marley used Sly and Robbie for a rhythm section. Likewise, Peter Tosh recorded with Sly and Robbie on at least one of his records.
5. We kept adding water to the paint. As a result, it was too thin to use.

Here's one way to check your transitions between paragraphs. Place a box around the last sentence of a paragraph and the first sentence of the next paragraph. Identify the relationship that connects the two ideas. If the relationship is clear and the transition is smooth, then there is no need to revise. If the relationship is not clear and there is not a smooth transition, sentences within the paragraphs may need to be rearranged, the paragraphs may need to be better organized, or the transition between the paragraphs may need to be revised.

Objective 0008: Recognize Common Errors of Sentence Construction, Grammar, and Usage

For example:

- Identify sentence fragments and run-on sentences (comma splices, fused sentences).
- Identify verbs in the wrong tense or form, incorrect shifts in tense or person, lack of subject-verb agreement, and wrong or missing verb endings.
- Identify vague pronoun references, lack of agreement between pronouns and antecedents, and incorrect shifts in pronoun person and number.
- Identify misplaced or dangling modifiers.
- Identify wrong or missing prepositions.
- Identify incorrect use of relative pronouns (that, which, who).
- Identify imprecise or inappropriate words and phrases.
- Identify common errors in the use of homonyms (accept/except, affect/effect, its/it's, their/there/they're, to/too/two, weather/whether, who's/whose, your/you're).

When you speak, you may leave your sentences unfinished or run your sentences together. Written expression makes a more permanent impression than speech. In writing, the parts of sentences must have a clear relationship to each other to make sense. Sentence fragments, run-on sentences, misplaced modifiers, and dangling modifiers are structural problems that obscure meaning in writing.

The incorrect use of parts of speech or confusing use of words and phrases can also make ideas unclear. This section helps you recognize and correct the most persistent errors in sentence construction and gives you tips on some of the most common grammar and usage problems.

Identify Sentence Fragments and Run-on Sentences (Comma Splices, Fused Sentences)

All inventory at reduced prices! Spectacular savings for you! Although pithy and popular with advertisers, sentence fragments are incomplete. In most cases, they don't communicate ideas accurately. To be complete, a sentence needs more than capitalization and punctuation—it needs both a subject and the proper form of a verb.

Sentence Fragments

One common fragment error is the use of the *-ing* form of a verb without a helping verb.

> *Incorrect:* Emily sitting on the sofa, wondering what to do next.
> *Correct:* Emily was sitting on the sofa, wondering what to do next.

Another common type of sentence fragment is a **subordinate clause** that is used to stand alone. To review, clauses are groups of words that have a subject and a verb. An **independent clause** expresses a complete thought and can stand alone. Even though a subordinate clause has a subject and a verb, it does not express a complete thought and cannot stand alone. It needs an independent clause to support it.

To identify a sentence fragment or subordinate clause, look for the following joining words, called **subordinating conjunctions**. A clause that has a subordinating conjunction needs an independent clause to complete an idea.

> after
> although
> as, as if
> because
> before
> if
> once
> since
> that
> though
> unless
> until
> when
> where
> while

Examples

The Canadian goose that built a nest in the pond outside our building.

As if the storm never happened, as if no damage was done.

In the first example, removing the connector *that* would make a complete sentence. The second example consists of two subordinate clauses. An independent clause needs to be added to make logical sense: *As if the storm never happened, as if no damage was done, Esme remained blithely optimistic.*

Locate the sentence fragment in the following example.

> <u>One participant</u> in the civil rights movement
>   A
>
> <u>explained</u> that <u>in the heated atmosphere</u> of
>   B   C
>
> the 1960s, <u>sit-in protests effective enough</u> to draw
>   D
>
> the attention of the nation.

The sentence fragment is found in part D. In this question, the independent clause has a subject (*one participant*) and a verb (*explained*). However, the subordinate clause, beginning with the connector *that*, needs a verb to make sense. Adding the verb *were* completes the thought and fixes the fragment: *that in the heated atmosphere of the 1960s, sit-in protests were effective enough to draw the attention of the nation.*

Run-on Sentences

"Planning ahead and studying for a test builds confidence do you know what I mean?" In speech, you may run your sentences together, but if you do so in writing, you will confuse your reader. In a run-on sentence, two independent clauses run together as one sentence without being separated by punctuation.

There are four ways to correct a run-on sentence. Study how each fix listed here changes the following run-on sentence.

We stopped for lunch we were starving.

1. **Add a period.** This separates the run-on sentence and makes two simple sentences. We stopped for lunch. We were starving.
2. **Add a semicolon.**
   We stopped for lunch; we were starving.
3. **Use a comma and a coordinating conjunction** (*and, but, or, for, nor, yet, so*) to connect the two clauses.
   We were starving, **so** we stopped for lunch.

4. **Use a subordinating conjunction.** By doing this, you turn one of the independent clauses into a subordinate clause.

Because we were starving, we stopped for lunch.

Be sure to look out for another common form of run-on sentence, the **comma splice.** A comma splice incorrectly uses a comma to separate two independent clauses. For example:

> *Incorrect:* Jacob bought the groceries, Lucy cooked dinner.

You can repair a comma splice in two ways: add a conjunction after the comma or replace the comma with a semicolon.

> *Correct:* Jacob bought the groceries, and Lucy cooked dinner.

OR

> Jacob bought the groceries; Lucy cooked dinner.

Select the choice that corrects the run-on in the following sentence.

Citizen Kane, Orson Welles's first full-length film, is considered an American classic, however it did not manage to garner the 1941 Academy Award for best picture.

  a. is considered an American classic, however it did not manage

  b. is considered an American classic. However, it did not manage

  c. is considered an American classic however it did not manage

  d. is considered an American classic however. It did not manage

  e. is considered an American classic because it did not manage

Choice **b** is correct. This original sentence is a run-on because the word *however* is used as if it were a conjunction. The words *however, therefore,* and *then* are not conjunctions, but rather a special kind of adverb that expresses a relationship between two clauses. Called **conjunctive adverbs,** these words cannot join two independent clauses the way a conjunction does. To repair this kind of run-on or comma splice, you can make two sentences (the way that choice **b** does). Another option for fixing the original sentence is to separate the two main clauses with a semicolon and set the adverb off from the rest of the clause with a comma.

Note that you can move the adverb around in its clause without changing the meaning of the sentence.

- *Citizen Kane,* Orson Welles's first full-length film, is considered an American classic; however, it did not manage to garner the 1941 Academy Award for best picture.
- *Citizen Kane,* Orson Welles's first full-length film, is considered an American classic; it did not manage, however, to garner the 1941 Academy Award for best picture.

Identify Verbs in the Wrong Tense or Form, Incorrect Shifts in Tense or Person, Lack of Subject-Verb Agreement, and Wrong or Missing Verb Endings

A verb is the action word of a sentence. The three basic verb tenses—present, past, and future—let you know when something happens, happened, or will happen. Some of these common verb trouble spots often appear on the Writing subtest.

Shifting Verb Tense. Verb tense should be consistent. If a sentence describes an event in the past, its verbs should all be in the past tense.

Incorrect: When Kate visited Japan, she sees many Shinto temples.

Correct: When Kate visited Japan, she saw many Shinto temples.

Past Tense for Present Conditions. It's incorrect to describe a present condition in the past tense.

Incorrect: My sister met her husband in a cafe. He was very tall.

Correct: My sister met her husband in a cafe. He is very tall.

Incomplete Verbs. Test makers may trick you by including the *-ing* form, or progressive form, of a verb without a helping verb (*is, has, has been, was, had, had been,* etc.). Make sure that verbs are complete and make sense in the sentence.

Incorrect: The major newspapers covering the story throughout the year because of the controversy.

Correct: The major newspapers have been covering the story throughout the year because of the controversy.

Subjunctive Mood. The subjunctive mood of verbs expresses something that is imagined, wished for, or contrary to fact. The subjunctive of *was* is *were.*

Incorrect: If I was a movie star, I would buy a fleet of Rolls Royces.

Correct: If I were a movie star, I would buy a fleet of Rolls Royces.

Find the usage error in the following sentence.

<u>Unhappy</u> about the lack <u>of</u> parking at the old
　　A　　　　　　　　B
stadium, season ticket holders <u>considering</u>
　　　　　　　　　　　　　　　C
<u>boycotting</u> next week's game.
　　D

The error is in part C. *Considering* needs a helping verb to be complete and to make sense in this sentence. The clause should read *season ticket holders are considering boycotting next week's game.*

Subject-Verb Agreement

They goes together, or *they go together?* You probably don't even have to think about which subject goes with which verb in this clause—your ear easily discerns that the second version is correct. Subject-verb agreement is when the subject of a clause matches the verb *in number.* Singular nouns take singular verbs; plural nouns take plural verbs. However, some instances of subject-verb agreement are tricky. Look out for the following three problem areas on the writing test.

1. **Phrases Following the Subject.** Pay close attention to the subject of the sentence. Do not be misled by phrases that may follow the subject. These phrases may confuse you into selecting a verb that does not agree with the subject.

Find the usage error in this sentence:

Betty Friedan's 1963 book, <u>an exposé</u> of
　　　　　　　　　　　　　　A
domesticity <u>that challenged</u> long-held American
　　　　　　　　B
attitudes, <u>remain</u> an <u>important contribution</u> to
　　　　　　C　　　　　　　D
feminism.

The error is in part C. The singular subject, *book,* needs a singular verb, *remains.* Don't be confused by the plural noun *attitudes,* which is part of a phrase that follows the subject.

2. **Subjects Following the Verb.** Be sure to locate the subject of the sentence. The MTEL test makers may use subjects that come after the verb to confuse you. Sentence constructions that begin with *there is* or *there are* signal that the subject comes after the verb.

Which answer gives the correct replacement phrase for the following sentence?

> Although the Australian government protects the Great Barrier Reef, there is environmental factors that continue to threaten the world's largest coral reef ecosystem.
> **a.** there is environmental factors that continue to threaten
> **b.** environmental factors that continue to threaten
> **c.** there are environmental factors that continue to threaten
> **d.** there are environmental factors that continued to threaten

The answer is **c**. The plural subject *factors* requires a plural form of the verb, *are*. The verb *continue* is in the correct tense in the original sentence, so choice **d** is incorrect. The deletion of *there are* in choice **b** does not make sense in the sentence, and leaving the word *that* is grammatically incorrect.

3. **Special Singular Nouns.** Some words that end in *s*, like *measles*, *news*, *checkers*, *economics*, *sports*, and *politics*, are often singular despite their plural form, because we think of them as one thing. Keep a watch out for collective nouns—nouns that refer to a number of people or things that form a single unit. These words, such as *audience*, *stuff*, *crowd*, *government*, *group*, and *orchestra*, need a singular verb.

Find the usage error in this sentence:

> That <u>rowdy</u> group of drama students <u>were</u>
>   A   B
> labeled "the anarchists," <u>because</u> they took
>   C
> over the university president's office <u>in a protest</u>
>   D
> against the dress code.

The error is in part B. The collective noun, *group*, is the singular subject of the sentence. Notice how the position of the prepositional phrase *of drama students* following the subject is misleading.

Identify Vague Pronoun References, Lack of Agreement between Pronouns and Antecedents, and Incorrect Shifts in Pronoun Person and Number

Pronouns are words that take the place of a noun or another pronoun, called an **antecedent**. The relationships between pronouns and their antecedents must be clear and correct. This section points out some common pronoun errors.

Vague Pronoun Reference

When a pronoun can refer to more than one antecedent in a sentence, it is called an unclear, or ambiguous, reference. An ambiguous pronoun reference also occurs when there is no apparent antecedent. Look carefully for this common error in the test questions—a sentence may read smoothly, but may still contain an unclear reference.

Look at the following sentence. Which underlined part contains a vague pronoun reference?

A regular feature in American newspapers <u>since</u>
                                          A

the early nineteenth century, <u>they</u> use
                               B

satirical humor to <u>visually</u> comment <u>on</u> a
                    C   D

current event.

The error is in part B. Who or what uses satirical humor? You don't know how to answer, because the pronoun *they* does not have a clear antecedent. If you replace *they* with *political cartoons*, the sentence makes sense.

Pronoun Agreement and Incorrect Shifts in Pronoun Person and Number

Just as subjects and verbs must agree in number, pronouns and their antecedents must match *in number*. If an antecedent is singular, the pronoun must be singular. If an antecedent is plural, the pronoun must be plural.

Pronouns also need to match their antecedent in case. **Case** refers to a word's grammatical relationship to other words in a sentence. A pronoun that takes the place of the subject of a sentence should be in the nominative case (*I, you, we, he, she, it, they*), whereas a pronoun that refers to the object in a sentence should be in the objective case (*me, us, you, him, her, it, them*). Here are some examples:

Matteo is funny, but *he* can also be very serious. (subject)
Bernadette hired Will, and she also fired *him*. (object)

In most cases, you will automatically recognize errors in pronoun agreement. The phrase *Me worked on the project with him* is clearly incorrect. However, some instances of pronoun agreement can be tricky.

Review these common pronoun problems:

- **Indefinite pronouns** like *each, everyone, anybody, no one, one, either,* are singular.
  Each of the boys presented *his* science project.
- **Two or more nouns joined by *and*** use a plural pronoun.
  Andy Warhol and Roy Lichtenstein engaged popular culture in *their* art.
- **Two or more singular nouns joined by *or*** use a singular pronoun.
  Francis or Andrew will loan you *his* book.
- **He or she?** In speech, people often use the pronoun *they* to refer to a single person of unknown gender. However, this is incorrect—a singular antecedent requires a singular pronoun.

A person has the right to do whatever he or she wants.

Try this practice sentence correction question:

A child who is eager to please will often follow everything that their parents say.
  a. everything that their parents say.
  b. everything which their parents say.
  c. everything that his or her parents say.
  d. most everything that their parents say.
  e. everything that their parents said.

Choice **c** is the correct answer. The antecedent, *a child*, is singular. Even though you don't know the gender of the child, the possessive pronoun should be *his* or *her* in order to agree in number.

The following table lists some pronouns that are commonly confused with verb contractions or other words. Watch for these errors in multiple-choice questions.

Confusing Word	Quick Definition
its	belonging to it
it's	it is
your	belonging to you
you're	you are
their	belonging to them
they're	they are
there	describes where an action takes place
whose	belonging to whom
who's	who is or who has
who	refers to people
that	refers to things
which	introduces clauses that are not essential to the information in the sentence, unless they refer to people. In that case, use who.

Identify Misplaced or Dangling Modifiers

Modifiers are words, phrases, or clauses that describe nouns, pronouns, and verbs. A misused modifier can confuse the meaning of a sentence.

Misplaced Modifiers

In a sentence, modifiers must be placed as closely as possible to the words they describe. If they are mis-placed, a sentence may say something other than what was intended.

Misplaced Modifier: My uncle told me about feeding cows in the kitchen. (*Why are there cows in the kitchen?*)

Correct: In the kitchen, my uncle told me about feeding cows.

Misplaced Modifier: A huge python followed the man that was slithering slowly through the grass. (*Why was the man slithering through the grass?*)

Correct: Slithering through the grass, a huge python followed the man.

OR

A huge python that was slithering slowly through the grass followed the man.

Dangling Modifiers

Phrases located at the beginning of a sentence and set off by a comma, that mistakenly modify the wrong noun or pronoun, are dangling modifiers. To be cor-rect, modifying phrases at the beginning of a sentence should describe the noun or pronoun (the subject of the sentence) that directly follows the comma.

Dangling Modifier: Broken and beyond repair, Grandma threw the serving dish away. (*Why was Grandma broken?*)

Correct: Broken and beyond repair, the serving dish was thrown away by Grandma.

OR

Grandma threw away the serving dish that was broken and beyond repair.

Choose the answer that best corrects the following sentence:

Subsidized by the federal government, <u>students can get help financing their post-secondary education through the Federal Work-Study Program.</u>

a. students can get help financing their post-secondary education through the Federal Work-Study Program.

b. since students finance their post-secondary education through the Federal Work-Study Program.

c. to students who need help financing their post-secondary education.

d. the Federal Work-Study Program helps students finance their post-secondary education.

The correct answer is **d**. In the original sentence, the modifying phrase incorrectly describes the subject *students*. Choices **b** and **c** are subordinate clauses, and, therefore, incorrect. Only choice **d** answers the question "What is subsidized by the federal government?" in a way that makes sense.

Identify Wrong or Missing Prepositions

Prepositions are connecting words that link a noun or pronoun to another word in a sentence. They are often used to show a relationship of space or time. For example:

The box *on* your desk is your birthday present.
The holiday that follows immediately *after* your birthday is Valentine's Day.

The first sentence uses the preposition *on* to describe the spatial relationship between the *box* and the *desk*. The second sentence uses the preposition *after* to describe the time relationship between *holiday* and *birthday*. *On your desk* and *after your birthday* are prepositional phrases.

Here is a list of common prepositions.

aboard	in
about	inside
above	into
after	like
among	of
around	off
at	on
before	outside
behind	over
below	to
beneath	under
beside	until
between	up
by	upon
except	with
for	within
from	

Wrong Prepositions

The three most common problems with prepositions are using prepositions unnecessarily, using the wrong preposition in a standard combination, and confusing *between* and *among*.

1. **Using prepositions unnecessarily.** When two or more prepositions are used together, chances are at least one is unnecessary.

2. **Using the wrong preposition in a standard combination.** Certain words must always be followed by specific prepositions. These necessary prepositions are always used in combina-

tion with their respective supported words. Here is a list of several required prepositional pairings:

account for   interested in
argue about   angry with
differ from   correspond with
independent of   identical to
agree upon   speak with
compare to

Using *different than* instead of *different from* is a common error. In general, *different from* is preferred in standard English.

When comparing two nouns or pronouns always use *different from*.

Algebra is *different from* mathematics.
When it comes to teaching styles, hers is *different from* his.

Different than is acceptable only when you are are comparing a noun to a clause.

George's presentation was very *different than* we had anticipated.
The beach is *different than* it was the last time we came here.

A sentence can usually be recast to avoid *different than* altogether.

George's presentation was very *different from* the speech we had anticipated.

3. **Confusing *between* and *among*.** The third common mistake with prepositions involves the use of *between* and *among*. *Between* is used when talking about two things. *Among* is used when talking about more than two things.

Check your use of these tricky prepositions:

Poor form: I cleaned *up under* the kitchen cabinets.
Good form: I cleaned *under* the kitchen cabinets.

Poor form: She likes all sports *except for* soccer.
Good form: She likes all sports *except* soccer.

Poor form: They looked *outside of* the house for the lost cat.
Good form: They looked *outside* the house for the lost cat.

Poor form: The professor had to decide *between* giving a test, a quiz, or assigning a paper on *Hamlet*.
Good form: The professor had to decide *between* giving a quiz, or continuing our discussion of *Hamlet*.

Poor form: The work was divided *among* Luis and Joti.
Good form: The work was divided evenly *among* Chester, Luis, and Joti.

Of all the rules governing prepositions, none is more famous than *Never end a sentence with a preposition!* While this rule holds true for many situations, it is not an absolute. It is perfectly acceptable to end a sentence with a preposition, especially if it makes a sentence flow better. For example, in popular speech, it sounds much more natural to say "That's all I can think of" than "That's all of which I can think." The best technique for deciding to keep or remove prepositions at the end of sentences is to use your ear. What would the statement sound like if you kept—or dropped—the preposition? Does it sound like *you*, or does it sound like a college professor? Prepositions, like large thesaurus words, should not be used in an attempt to add importance or weight to your writing.

Missing Prepositions

Because prepositions are often short words, they are often easy to miss.

Rewrite each sentence, adding the preposition that is missing.

1. Let's not argue that today.

_____

_____

2. The students stayed up late to work their difficult assignments.

_____

_____

3. In hiring new workers, the office manager discriminated older applicants.

_____

_____

Answers

Although more than one preposition might seem to work in a sentence, you should make your choice according to standard usage. For example, forms such as "argue on," "work at," or "discriminated over" would not be correct.

1. Let's not argue *about* that today.
2. The students stayed up late to work *on* their difficult assignments.
3. In hiring new workers, the office manager discriminated *against* older applicants.

Identify Incorrect Use of Relative Pronouns

Relative pronouns refer to nouns that appear earlier in the sentence.

The words *that, which, whichever, who, whoever, whose, whom,* and *whomever* can be used as relative pronouns. For example:

> *whose* mom is so nice
> *which* made him grouchy
> *whichever* comes first

Relative pronouns introduce subordinate clauses that act like adjectives, describing earlier nouns or pronouns. The relative pronoun relates the clause to the rest of the sentence. Even though these **relative clauses** have their own subject and verb, they cannot stand alone as a sentence because they don't express a complete thought. For example:

> I own the boat *that* won the race.
> The man *who* drove it is my best friend, Jack.
> He is someone on *whom* I rely for skill and expertise.
> We have entered the next race, *which* is on Friday.

Who and *whom* refer to a person.

In traditional usage, whom is the form used as an object of a preposition.

> to *whom*, for *whom*, with *whom*
> *who* went, *who* is, the man *who*

Which and *that* refer to things.

Use *that* to signify information that is necessary (restrictive) to the meaning of the sentence. Use *which* to signify information that is discretionary (nonrestrictive). If nonrestrictive information is removed, the meaning of the sentence is not altered.

The computer, *which is old*, has completely stopped working. (nonrestrictive)
Pedestrians may get struck by a car *that they thought had stopped*. (restrictive)

Remember that pronouns can do many different jobs in sentences. Don't confuse relative pronouns with other forms of the same words. In the following sentences, the italicized words are *not* relative pronouns.

That will take him a long time to finish. (*That* is the subject of the sentence.)
Yolanda wrote *that*. (*That* is the direct object of the sentence.)
Who said so? (*Who* is an interrogative pronoun.)

Underline the relative pronouns in the following sentences. Put an X before any sentence that does not include a relative pronoun.

1. That is the most annoying sound that I have ever heard.

2. Who brought that?

3. Those are the boxes of blankets that Mom plans to take to the ASPCA.

4. Is this the channel that you were watching?

Answers

1. That is the most annoying sound <u>that</u> I have ever heard.
2. This sentence does not contain a relative pronoun. Here, *that* is a direct object.
3. Those are the boxes of blankets <u>that</u> Mom plans to take to the SPCA.
4. Is this the channel <u>that</u> you were watching?

Pronouns used as subjects of sentences or objects of verbs are not relative pronouns.

Identify Imprecise or Inappropriate Words and Phrases

Ambiguity and imprecise language prevent ideas from coming across clearly, and overused words may cause a reader to lose interest in being said. Inappropriate connotations and words that convey bias have no place in effective writing. Keep these issues in mind when answering Writing subtest questions.

Avoid Ambiguity
Ambiguous means having two or more possible meanings. Ambiguous language can either be words and phrases that have more than one meaning, or word order that conveys a meaning different from the one intended by the writer:

The quarterback liked to tackle his problems.

This sentence can be read two ways: The quarterback likes to *deal with* his problems, or his problems are his opponents on the field whom he *grabs and knocks down*. This kind of confusion can happen whenever a word has more than one possible meaning. *The quarterback liked to address his problems* is a better sentence, and is unlikely to be misunderstood.

My advisor proofread my essay with the red sports car.

Here, the *word order* of the sentence, not an individual word, causes the confusion. Did the advisor proofread the essay with his car? Because the phrase *with the red sports car* is in the wrong place, the meaning of the sentence is unclear. Try instead: *My advisor with the red sports car proofread my essay.*

Ambiguous: When doing the laundry, the phone rang.
Clear: The phone rang when I was doing the laundry.

Ambiguous: She almost waited an hour for her friend.
Clear: She waited almost an hour for her friend.

Ambiguous: I told her I'd give her a ring tomorrow.
Clear: I told her I'd call her tomorrow.

Ambiguous: A speeding motorist hit a student who was jogging through the park in a blue sedan.
Clear: A speeding motorist in a blue sedan hit a student who was jogging through the park.

Use Precise Language

Precise language helps to communicate meaning effectively while using fewer words. In other words, it makes writing more concise.

Imprecise: Homer managed the project.
Precise: Homer organized the staff and monitored their progress.

Imprecise: This is a good proposal.
Precise: This proposal explains the problem and suggests a solution.

Imprecise: We had a nice time with you.
Precise: We enjoyed eating, chatting, and swimming at your house.

Avoid Overly Informal and Overused Language

Words and phrases that are too formal, too obscure, or overused don't belong in strong writing.

Clichés

Clichés should be avoided not only because they are too informal, but also because they are overused. Strong writing does not rely on stale phrases such as

one step at a time; no news is good news; have a nice day; when life gives you lemons, make lemonade; and *no guts, no glory.*

Slang

Slang is nonstandard English. Its significance is typically far removed from either a word's denotative or connotative meaning, and is particular to certain groups (therefore, it excludes some readers who won't understand it). Examples include *blow off, canned, no sweat,* and *thumbs down* (or *up*). It is also inappropriate and offensive to use slang terms for racial or religious groups.

Buzzwords

Buzzwords are a type of slang. They're words (real or made up) that take the place of simpler, more direct words. They are, at best, pompous, and at worst, confusing. And, like other forms of slang, buzzwords don't belong in your essays. Examples include resultful (*gets results*), suboptimal (*not the best*), guesstimate (*estimate*), requisite (*necessary*), potentiality (*potential*), and facilitate (*help*).

Check for Connotations

What shades of meaning are suggested in a piece of writing? Think beyond the dictionary, or denotative meaning, to what might be implied or inferred. Connotation involves emotions, cultural assumptions, and suggestions. Connotative, or implied, meanings can be positive, negative, or neutral. Some dictionaries offer usage notes that help to explain connotative meanings, but they alone can't be relied on when trying to avoid offensive or incorrect word choices. Keep in mind that using a word without being aware of its implied meaning can annoy your reader or make your message unclear.

For example, what feelings come to mind when you hear the words *plagiarize* or *copy*? *Plagiarize* has negative connotations, while *copy* is a more neutral selection. If you were making travel plans, would you choose to rent a car from an agency whose safety record was described as *adequate*? Although the dictionary definition of the word is "sufficient" or "meeting a requirement," the connotative meaning is negative: "barely satisfactory." Consider all the meanings your words might reveal, and determine whether they belong in your writing.

Positive or Neutral Connotation: natural
Negative Connotation: plain

Positive or Neutral Connotation: individualist
Negative Connotation: eccentric

Positive or Neutral Connotation: look
Negative Connotation: leer

Positive or Neutral Connotation: ethical
Negative Connotation: straitlaced

Positive or Neutral Connotation: clever
Negative Connotation: sly

Eliminate Biased Language

Biased language, which includes negative stereotypes, has no place in strong writing. Your goal is to include rather than to exclude. Understanding the purpose of inclusive language, and using it in your essay, will assure that your message gets across without creating or perpetuating negative social stereotypes. Use the following techniques to help you to replace any possibly offensive words and phrases with inclusive language.

Gender

- Avoid the suffix *-ess*, which has the effect of minimizing the significance of the word to which it is attached (*actor* is preferable to *actress*, *proprietor* to *proprietress*).

- Do not overuse *he* and *him*. Instead, use *his or her*, *their*, and *those*, or alternate between *him* and *her*.
- Degender titles. *Businessman* becomes *businessperson* or *executive*, *chairman* becomes *chair* or *chairperson*, *stewardess* becomes *flight attendant*, *weatherman* becomes *meteorologist*.
- When referring to a couple, don't make assumptions. *Inappropriate*: Mr. Rosenberg and Caryn, Mr. and Mrs. Bill Rosenberg. *Appropriate*: Mr. Rosenberg and Ms. Fetzer
- Use professional, rather than personal, descriptive terms. *Inappropriate*: Robin Benoit, a lovely novelist. *Appropriate*: Robin Benoit, an experienced novelist.
- Avoid making assumptions about traditionally exclusive arenas such as the home and sports. Not all women are homemakers, and not all homemakers are women. The word *housewife* should not be used. Similarly, not all team members are male. *Sportsmanship* should be replaced with *fair play*, and *crewmen* should be *crew members*.

Race

- To avoid stereotyping, leave out any reference to race, unless it is relevant to the subject of your writing.
- Focus on a person's individual, professional characteristics and qualifications, not racial characteristics.

Disability

- Discuss the *person*, not his or her handicap.
- If your writing is specifically focused on disabilities or disease, or you must mention them for another reason, do not use words that imply victimization or create negative stereotypes. Terms such as *victim*, *sufferer*, *poor*, *afflicted*, and *unfortunate* should be omitted.
- Don't use *courageous* to describe a person with a disability unless the context allows the adjective

to be used for all. Someone is not courageous because they are deaf, but they may be because they swam the English Channel.

- Always put the person ahead of the disability, as in *person with impaired hearing*, rather than *hearing-impaired person*.

Identify Common Errors in the Use of Homonyms

A misused word can significantly alter the meaning of a sentence. Here are some commonly confused words and their meanings:

accept	receive, agree to
except	excluding
affect	to influence
effect	result (noun); to bring about (verb)
its	belonging to it
it's	it is
their	belonging to them
there	in that place
they're	they are
to	in the direction of
too	also, excessively
two	the number that comes after one
weather	climate
whether	if
who's	who is
whose	belonging to whom
your	belonging to you
you're	you are

Underline the correct homonym for each sentence.

1. Jo will be here to (accept/except) her award.

2. Do you think (their/there/they're) going to join us?

3. Incorrect answers will (affect/effect) your score.

4. There will be (to, two, too) many people to go in one car.

5. I wonder if (its, it's) too late to change the schedule.

6. Every winner (accept/except) Bob will be present at the ceremony.

7. I'm not sure (weather/whether) tomorrow will be the best day for us to go.

8. Memorize these words to (affect/effect) a rise in your test score.

9. That is (their/there/they're) decision to make.

10. Do you know (who's/whose) going to teach that class?

Answers

1. Jo will be here to (<u>accept</u>/except) her award.
2. Do you think (their/there/<u>they're</u>) going to join us?
3. Incorrect answers will certainly (<u>affect</u>/effect) your score.
4. There will be (to, two, <u>too</u>) many people to go in one car.
5. I wonder if (its, <u>it's</u>) too late to change the schedule.

6. Every winner (accept/<u>except</u>) Bob will be present at the ceremony.
7. I'm not sure (weather/<u>whether</u>) tomorrow will be the best day for us to go.
8. Memorize these words to (affect/<u>effect</u>) a rise in your test score.
9. That is (<u>their</u>/there/they're) decision to make.
10. Do you know (<u>who's</u>/whose) going to teach that class?

Using the wrong homonym is often just a careless mistake, so be sure to check such words when proofreading.

Objective 0009: Recognize Common Errors of Spelling, Capitalization, and Punctuation

For example:

- Identify common spelling errors.
- Identify common errors in standard capitalization.
- Identify missing commas after an introductory phrase and missing commas in a compound sentence.
- Identify missing or misplaced apostrophes.

Some errors are especially easy to miss when you're writing in a hurry. This section reviews common errors that can make your writing appear unprofessional. On the MTEL, you may be asked to recognize and correct these mistakes. Be sure to check for them in your own essays.

Identify Common Spelling Errors

The English language combines words from many different languages, and they don't always look the way they sound. On tests, you will often be asked to spot the misspelled word in a group of words or sentences. Your ability to do this depends largely on your familiarity with English words by sight. You will usually see that the misspelled word "looks wrong." Reviewing the following spelling rules, exceptions to the rules, and examples may help you prepare for these tests.

ie versus ei

When the *ie* combination sounds like long *e* (*ee*), the rule is: *i* before *e* except after *c*.

> *belief, fierce, cashier, fiend, wield, yield, series, chief, achieve, niece, hygiene, relieve*

Exceptions: The *ie* combination does come after *c* when it sounds like *sh* or *sy*.

> *deficient, conscience, omniscient, ancient, society, science*

When the combination of *e* and *i* sounds like *ay*, the rule is: *e* before *i*.

> *neighbor, weigh, eight, feint, freight, reign, sleigh, surveillance, veil, vein, weight, skein*

Exceptions: Sometimes the combination of *e* and *i* sounds like *ee*.

> *either, weird, seizure, sheik, leisure, seize*

Sometimes the combination of *e* and *i* sounds like long *i*.

> *height, sleight, stein, seismology*

Sometimes the combination of *e* and *i* sounds like short *e*.

> *their, heifer, foreign, forfeit*

Vowel Combinations

When two vowels are together, the first one is usually long and the second one is silent.

> *reach, cheapen, conceal, caffeine, paisley, abstain, acquaint, juice, nuisance, buoy*

Exceptions: Sometimes the pair *ai* makes an *eh* sound.

> *Britain, porcelain, fountain, villain, curtain, certain, captain, chieftain*

Sometimes you pronounce both parts of the vowel pair *ia*.

> *civilian, brilliant, alleviate, familiar, genial, congenial, menial, guardian*

Sometimes *ia* is combined with *t* or *c* to make a *sh* sound.

> *artificial, glacial, beneficial, martial, commercial*

Doubling Consonants

Consonants are usually doubled when adding an ending, or suffix, to a word.

When the suffix begins with a vowel (such as *-ed*, *-ing*, *-ance*, *-ence*, or *-ant*) and the word ends with one vowel and one consonant, double the last consonant.

> *Cut* becomes *cutter* or *cutting*.
> *Slip* becomes *slipping* or *slipped*.
> *Quit* becomes *quitter* or *quitting*.

When the final consonant of the word is accented and there is only one consonant in the last syllable, double the final consonant.

> *Commit* becomes *committing* or *committed*.
> *Defer* becomes *deferring* or *deferred*.
> *Prefer* becomes *preferring* or *preferred*.

When the suffix begins with a consonant, keep the final *n* when adding *-ness* and keep the final *l* when adding *-ly*.

> *Mean* becomes *meanness*.
> *Lean* becomes *leanness*.
> *Legal* becomes *legally*.
> *Formal* becomes *formally*.

Exceptions: There are some exceptions to the rules just outlined. Here are just a few examples.

> *Draw* becomes *drawing*.
> *Bus* becomes *buses*.
> *Chagrin* becomes *chagrined*.

Hard and Soft C and G

The letters *c* and *g* can be either soft or hard. A hard *c* sounds like *k*, a soft *c* sounds like *s*. A hard *g* sounds like the *g* in *girl*, a soft *g* sounds like *j*.

The letters *c* and *g* are soft when followed by *e*, *i*, or *y*. Otherwise, they are hard.

> *Soft:* circus, cycle, cell, circle, cyclone, central, giant, gyrate, genius, gipsy, gymnastics, gentle
> *Hard:* case, cousin, corporate, couple, click, crop, go, gab, gobble, glue, grimy, gout

When a word ends in hard *c*, add a *k* before a suffix that begins in *-e*, *-i*, or *-y*.

> *Traffic* becomes *trafficking*.
> *Mimic* becomes *mimicking*.

Exceptions: Very few words keep the soft *c* sound when a suffix beginning with *i* is used: *plasticity, elasticity*.

Final E

Drop the final *e* when adding a suffix that begins with a vowel, such as *-ing*, *-able*, *-ous*, or *-ity*.

Surprise becomes *surprising.*
Leave becomes *leaving.*
Desire becomes *desirable.*
Erase becomes *erasable.*
Grieve becomes *grievous.*
Desire becomes *desirous.*
Opportune becomes *opportunity.*
Scarce becomes *scarcity.*

Exceptions: Keep the final *e* after a soft *c* or soft *g* to keep the soft sound.

Peace becomes *peaceable.*
Advantage becomes *advantageous.*
Outrage becomes *outrageous.*

Keep the final *e* when the pronunciation of the word would be changed if you dropped the *e.*

Guarantee becomes *guaranteeing.*
Snowshoe becomes *snowshoeing.*

Keep the final *e* before endings that begin with consonants, such as *-ment*, *-ness*, *-less*, and *-ful.*

advertisement, enforcement, amusement, politeness, fierceness, appropriateness, wireless, tireless, blameless, disgraceful, tasteful, peaceful

Exceptions: Drop the final *e* when it comes after the letters *u* or *w.*

Argue becomes *argument.*
True becomes *truly.*
Awe becomes *awful.*

Final Y

When adding a suffix, a final *y* is sometimes changed to an *i.*

When you add a suffix to a word ending in *y,* keep the *y* if it follows a vowel.

attorneys, chimneys, monkeys, keys, stayed, delayed, played, relayed, playing, relaying, staying, saying, annoyance, conveyance, employable, playable

Exceptions

Say becomes *said.*
Money becomes *monies.*
Day becomes *daily.*

When you add a suffix to a word ending in *y,* change the *y* to an *i* if it follows a consonant.

Mercy becomes *merciful.*
Pity becomes *pitiful.*
Beauty becomes *beautiful.*

Busy becomes *business.*
Crazy becomes *craziness.*
Lazy becomes *laziness.*

Angry becomes *angrily.*
Busy becomes *busily.*
Healthy becomes *healthily.*

Salary becomes *salaries.*
Busy becomes *busies.*
Flurry becomes *flurries.*

Exceptions: When you add *-ing*, keep the final *y.*

Copy becomes *copying.*
Busy becomes *busying.*
Study becomes *studying.*

-able

If a root word takes the *-ation* suffix, it usually takes *-able.*

demonstration—demonstrable
imagination—imaginable
application—applicable

If a root word is a complete word by itself, it usually takes -*able*.

> *drink—drinkable*
> *read—readable*
> *search—searchable*
> *bear—bearable*

If a word ends in hard *c* or *g*, it uses the suffix -*able*.

> *despicable, navigable, applicable*

-ible

If a word ends in soft *c* or *g*, it takes -*ible*.

> *forcible, invincible, legible, incorrigible*

If a word ends in *ss*, it usually takes -*ible*.

> *repress—repressible*
> *access—accessible*
> *dismiss—dismissible*

If a root word is not a whole word, it usually takes -*ible*.

> *gullible*

If a word takes the -*ion* suffix, it usually takes -*ible*.

> *collection—collectible*
> *vision—visible*
> *division—divisible*

Exception

Predict—prediction becomes *predictable*.

-ary and -ery

Only two common words end in -*ery*: *cemetery* and *stationery* (as in "paper and envelopes for letter writing"). The rest take -*ary*.

> *stationary* (as in "unmoving") *dictionary, military, library, secretary, vocabulary, solitary, secondary, voluntary*

-al and -el

Most words use -*al*. Unfortunately, there is no real rule. These words call for sight memorizing.

> *choral, dismissal, legal, literal, tribal, personal, several, neutral, moral, magical, lyrical, festival cancel, model, kennel, jewel, tunnel, travel, shovel, panel, cruel, towel, channel, hovel*

Prefixes

Usually, when you add a prefix to a root word, the spelling of neither the root nor the prefix changes.

> *misinformed, unprepared, disillusioned infrequent, illegitimate, misspelled, unnerved, dissatisfied*

Silent Vowels

American English makes several vowels silent, but there is no general rule for silent vowels. For example, sometimes a silent *e* on the end of a word makes the vowel before it long, sometimes not. The best way to approach these oddly spelled words is to become familiar with them by sight.

> *carriage, marriage, every, chocolate, miniature, parliament, privilege, sophomore, boundary, towel, vowel, bowel*

Silent Consonants

In addition to silent vowels, the English language uses silent consonants. Like silent vowels, silent consonants do not follow a general rule. The best way to learn these words is by sight.

answer, autumn, calm, debt, ghost, gnarled, gnaw, indict, kneel, knight, know, knowledge, often, subtle, blight, pseudonym, psychology, rhetorical, thorough, through, write

In each of the following questions, find the word that is misspelled. If all of the words are spelled correctly, choose answer **d**. Answers follow the exercise.

1. a. women
   b. people
   c. babys
   d. no mistakes

2. a. anouncement
   b. advisement
   c. description
   d. no mistakes

3. a. omission
   b. aisle
   c. litrature
   d. no mistakes

4. a. informal
   b. servent
   c. comfortable
   d. no mistakes

5. a. vegetable
   b. width
   c. variation
   d. no mistakes

6. a. associacion
   b. unnecessary
   c. illegal
   d. no mistakes

7. a. jockey
   b. equestrian
   c. maneuver
   d. no mistakes

8. a. hindrence
   b. equipped
   c. possessive
   d. no mistakes

9. a. requirement
   b. reverence
   c. resistent
   d. no mistakes

10. a. marshal
   b. martial
   c. tyrenny
   d. no mistakes

For the following sentences, choose the sentence that contains a misspelled word. If there are no mistakes, choose answer **d**.

11. a. We were disatisfied with the results of the experiment.
   b. Our office has a plentiful supply of staples.
   c. Stringent controls were placed on the county's budget.
   d. no mistakes

12. a. Pick up the car on Wednesday.
   b. Let's go shopping on Thursday.
   c. My birthday is on Saturday.
   d. no mistakes

13. a. Check your paper to see if you have any misspellings.
   b. Safety is my primary concern.
   c. We are all individual and unique.
   d. no mistakes

14. a. Mark carved the roast with a razor-sharp knife.
   b. You have been more than charitable.
   c. Which president is buried in this cemetary?
   d. no mistakes

15. a. Smart consumers read food labels.
  b. Your new dress is lovily.
  c. Did you see the lightning?
  d. no mistakes

16. a. Scott was in unaform when he sat for the family portrait.
  b. The tenants' association will hold its meeting tonight.
  c. This is the best value you will find anywhere.
  d. no mistakes

17. a. I am planning to cook two turkeys on Thanksgiving.
  b. Why did you refuse to accept his offer?
  c. The traffic during rush hour today was unbelievable.
  d. no mistakes

18. a. We knew that Ellen was embarassed.
  b. I am teaching my brother to read mathematical symbols.
  c. Neither Joe nor Gary has done any research for the report.
  d. no mistakes

19. a. My mother will soon celebrate her fortieth birthday.
  b. Autumn is my favorite time of year.
  c. My cousin will be skiing in Febuary.
  d. no mistakes

20. a. As treasurer, Jenny has complete financial responsibility.
  b. I have been assured that his illness is not contagious.
  c. The design for the book jacket seemed wierd.
  d. no mistakes

Answers

1. c. babies
2. a. announcement
3. c. literature
4. b. servant
5. d. no mistakes
6. a. association
7. d. no mistakes
8. a. hindrance
9. c. resistant
10. c. tyranny
11. a. dissatisfied
12. d. no mistakes
13. d. no mistakes
14. c. cemetery
15. b. lovely
16. a. uniform
17. d. no mistakes
18. a. embarrassed
19. c. February
20. c. weird

Identify Common Errors in Standard Capitalization

Capitalization is necessary both for specific words and to start sentences and quotations.

Following are six instances when capitalization is needed:

- the first word of the sentence
- proper nouns (names of *specific* people, places, and things)
- the first word of a complete quotation, but not a partial quotation
- the first, last, and any other important words of a title
- languages
- the pronoun *I*, and any contractions made with it

Sometimes knowing when to capitalize a word is tricky. Look for these trouble spots in your writing.

Compass directions, such as *east* or *west*, are not capitalized unless they refer to a specific geographical area.

> The American Civil War was fought between the *North* and the *South*.

Family relationships are not capitalized when they are preceded by a pronoun.

> I met *my mother* for lunch.
> *Uncle Russ* agreed to babysit, so that I could meet *Mother* for lunch.

Seasons and parts of the academic year are not capitalized.

> I'll register for the course this *fall*.

Words modified by proper adjectives are not capitalized, unless they are part of a proper name.

> Jacob recommended the *Italian restaurant* in his neighborhood.

Check your knowledge of these rules with the following sentences. Circle the letters that should be capitalized in each sentence. Make a diagonal mark through the letters that are capitalized, but should not be. Check your work with the correct versions of sentences at the end of the exercise.

1. the instructions were clear. after a careful reading, i could understand them completely.

2. "what do you think you're doing?" my Uncle jack asked.

3. "i'm putting together this gas grill," i answered.

4. the newspaper said our new owner was "An industrial visionary."

5. my new Car is a ford mustang.

6. shakespeare was the most prolific author of the renaissance.

7. the nelsons spent thanksgiving Day with Relatives.

8. andy began work on thursday, april 3.

9. my Friend jon has two Nephews who fought in iraq

10. Additional Security guards will be hired for the white stripes concert.

11. The convention group caught the amtrak train in omaha.

12. Ling applied for admission to the university of Iowa.

13. In canada, some citizens speak french, and others speak english.

14. We followed the colorado river to the border of arizona.

15. Ammar works for apex construction company.

16. Amasu prefers italian dressing on her salad.

17. When I win the lottery, I intend to buy a polynesian island.

18. We were delayed at the canadian border.

19. The great plains are located in the midwest.

20. Cynthia turned West at the stop sign.

21. If my Cousin Kathy comes to the picnic, I know aunt Jan won't.

22. Jacob is an outstanding History student.

23. We went to a sri lankan Restaurant in minneapolis.

Answers

The changes are bolded for you.

1. The instructions were clear. **A**fter a careful reading, **I** could understand them completely.

2. "What do you think you're doing?"my **u**ncle Jack asked.

3. "I'm putting together this gas grill," **I** answered.

4. The newspaper said our new owner was "**an** industrial visionary."

5. **M**y new **c**ar is a Ford Mustang.

6. Shakespeare was the most prolific author of the **R**enaissance.

7. **T**he Nelsons spent Thanksgiving Day with **r**elatives.

8. Andy began work on Thursday**,** April 3.

9. **M**y **f**riend Jon has two **n**ephews who fought in Iraq.

10. Additional **s**ecurity guards will be hired for the **W**hite Stripes concert.

11. The convention group caught the **A**mtrak train in **O**maha.

12. Ling applied for admission to the **U**niversity of Iowa.

13. In Canada**,** some citizens speak French**,** and others speak English.

14. We followed the **C**olorado **R**iver to the border of Arizona.

15. Ammar works for Apex Construction Company.

16. Amasu prefers Italian dressing on her salad.

17. When I win the lottery, I intend to buy a **P**olynesian island.

18. We were delayed at the **C**anadian border.

19. The **G**reat **P**lains are located in the Midwest.

20. Cynthia turned **w**est at the stop sign.

21. If my **c**ousin Kathy comes to the picnic, I know **A**unt Jan won't.

22. Jacob is an outstanding **h**istory student.

23. We went to a **Sri Lankan r**estaurant in Minneapolis.

Identify Missing Commas after an Introductory Phrase and in a Compound Sentence

It's especially easy to overlook the need for commas in these two grammatical situations.

Use a Comma after an Introductory Phrase

A phrase is a group of words that lack either a subject or a predicate. An introductory phrase is a group of words that cannot stand alone, found at the beginning of a sentence. Common introductory phrases include prepositional, participial, and infinitive forms.

> *In early spring*, I notice a change in people's attitudes.
> *Having completed his job*, he went home.
> *To get a seat*, you'd better come early.

After a very short prepositional phrase the comma may be considered optional, but using one is still correct: *By lunchtime*, Aidan had already finished his project.

Use Commas to Separate the Parts of a Compound Sentence

A compound sentence has two or more independent clauses, often joined with a conjunction (*and*, *but, for, or, nor, so, yet*). Place a comma before the conjunction.

> Independent clause: *the children couldn't finish the race*
> Independent clause: *but the adults could easily*
> Compound sentence: *The children couldn't finish the race, but the adults could easily.*

In very short sentences the comma may be considered optional, but using one is still correct: *I walked, but he took a cab.*

Add commas where they are needed in the following sentences. Answers and explanations follow the exercise.

1. Enjoying himself Julio decided to stay at the party.

2. After a long day at work *Mary* decided to relax with a good book.

3. Luke was studying for his midterm exams for two of his hardest classes and he was writing a term paper for his French class.

4. The presentation was over yet the audience continued to ask questions.

5. To finish his report Hiro spent the afternoon in the library.

Answers

1. Enjoying himself, Julio decided to stay at the party. (introductory participial phrase)
2. After a long day at work, *Mary* decided to relax with a good book. (introductory prepositional phrase)
3. Luke was studying for his midterm exams for two of his hardest classes, and he was writing a term paper for his French class. (compound sentence)

4. The presentation was over, yet the audience continued to ask questions. (compound sentence)
5. To finish his report, Hiro spent the afternoon in the library. (introductory infinitive phrase)

Identify Missing or Misplaced Apostrophes

Apostrophes are used in three ways: to show possession, in certain plural forms, and to indicate the omission of letters in contractions.

Review these eight rules so you can easily identify apostrophe errors on tests. When proofreading your own work, check for mistakes in your use of apostrophes.

1. **Add *'s* to form the singular possessive**, even when the noun ends in *s*.
   Mr. Summers's essay convinced me.
2. **Add *'s* to plural words not ending in *s*.**
   The *children's* ability to absorb foreign language is astounding.
   The workshops focus on working *women's* needs.
3. **Add *'* to plural words ending in *s*.**
   The *students'* grades improved each semester.
4. **Add *'s* to indefinite pronouns that show ownership.**
   Everyone's ability level should be considered.
5. **Never use apostrophes with possessive pronouns.**
   This experiment must be *yours*.
6. **Add *'s* to the last word of a compound noun, compound subject, or name of a business or institution.**
   The *president-elect's* speech riveted the audience.
   Gabbie and Michael's wedding is in October.
   The *National Science Teachers Association's* meeting will take place next week.

7. **Use 's to form the plurals of letters, figures, and numbers, as well as expressions of time or money.**
   Mind your *p's* and *q's*.
   The project was the result of a *year's* worth of work.

8. **Use apostrophes to show that letters or words are omitted in contractions.**
   Abby *doesn't* (does not) work today.
   Who's (who is) on first?

In the following sentences, circle the correct word choice. The answers follow the exercise.

1. *Linda's/Lindas* calendar was too small to show all her appointments.

2. *Its/It's a day's/days* drive to the beach

3. The *bus's/buses* always parked in front of the school in the afternoon.

4. Take off *your/you're* boots if *their/they're* muddy.

5. The lion bared *its/it's* huge, sharp teeth.

6. *Central High Schools/Central High School's* schedule was full.

7. *Carlos/Carlos's* mother looked younger than her years.

8. The *puppy's/puppies* were so tiny they could all fit in a shoebox.

9. *Their/They're* studying hard for the exam tomorrow.

10. *Its/It's* a bright sunny day.

Answers

The correct words are bolded.
1. ***Linda's**/Lindas calendar was too small to show all her appointments.*
2. *Its/**It's** a **day's**/days drive to the beach.*
3. The *bus's/**buses*** always parked in front of the school in the afternoon.
4. Take off ***your**/you're* boots if *their/**they're*** muddy.
5. The lion bared ***its**/it's* huge, sharp teeth.
6. *Central High Schools/**Central High School's*** schedule was full.
7. *Carlos/**Carlos's*** mother looked younger than her years.
8. The *puppy's/**puppies*** were so tiny they could all fit in a shoebox.
9. *Their/**They're*** studying hard for the exam tomorrow.
10. *Its/**It's*** a bright sunny day.

0010: Demonstrate the Ability to Analyze and Revise Sentences Containing Common Errors

- Revise sentences to correct errors related to sentence construction.
- Revise sentences to correct common errors related to grammar and usage.
- Revise sentences to correct common errors related to spelling, capitalization, and punctuation.

On the Writing subtest and in your own writing, it is important to recognize and correct errors in sentences. Some mistakes are so common that it's easy to read right over them. If you have trouble spotting errors and revising the sentences in this section, you might want to review rules about sentence construction, grammar and usage, spelling, capitalization, and punctuation in earlier parts of this test preparation book.

Revise Sentences to Correct Errors Related to Sentence Construction

Errors in sentence construction can obscure your meaning. For each sentence, select the best choice for the underlined section.

1. The number of grocery store shoppers that carry a wallet full of coupons with them <u>is growing, approximately 50%</u> of those in line have at least one applicable coupon to apply to their purchases.
   a. is growing, approximately 50%
   b. is growing; approximately 50%
   c. is growing, although approximately 50%
   d. is grown, approximately 50%

2. <u>Because the *Serenity* movie was quite popular in the movie theaters and on home video,</u> there are still no plans to bring back the *Firefly* series, according to former producer Joss Whedon.
   a. Because the *Serenity* movie was quite popular in the movie theaters and on home video,
   b. Although the *Serenity* movie was quite popular in the movie theaters and on home video,
   c. Since the *Serenity* movie was quite popular in the movie theaters and on home video,
   d. However, the *Serenity* movie was quite popular in the movie theaters and on home video,

3. <u>Whenever the telephone rings,</u> everyone in the house knows that it is going to be for Nicole, since she has a social life that is busy enough for at least three people.
   a. Whenever the telephone rings,
   b. The telephone, whenever it rings,
   c. Ringing, whenever the telephone does
   d. Because the telephone rings,

Answers

1. **b.** This is a run-on sentence with two independent clauses joined by a comma. The way to correct the error is to join the clauses with a semicolon as in choice **b.**
2. **b.** The dependent clause in the first half of this sentence does not have the right relationship to the second half. Only the substitution of the word *although* connects the two halves.
3. **a.** The original form is the best.

Revise Sentences to Correct Common Errors Related to Grammar and Usage

Common errors in grammar and usage can ruin the effect of your hard work on your essay. In the following examples, select the best choice for the underlined section.

1. Some teachers think that the option <u>of homeschooling and other educational alternatives have created problems within the public school systems.</u>
   a. of homeschooling and other educational alternatives have created problems within the public school systems.
   b. of homeschooling and other educational alternatives has created problems within the public school systems.
   c. of homeschooling and other educational alternatives is created problems within the public school systems.
   d. of homeschooling and other educational alternatives creating problems within the public school systems.

2. Despite her best efforts, <u>the gourmet meal did not turn out near as glamorous and delicious</u> as Samantha had initially planned.
   a. the gourmet meal did not turn out near as glamorous and delicious
   b. the gourmet meal did not turn out near as glamorously and deliciously
   c. the gourmet meal did not turn out nearly as glamorously and deliciously
   d. the gourmet meal did not turn out nearly as glamorous and delicious

3. When I read through the list of driving rules and regulations, <u>it was amazing how many mistakes you could make without even knowing it.</u>
   a. it was amazing how many mistakes you could make without even knowing it.
   b. it was amazing how many mistakes they could make without even knowing it.
   c. it was amazing how many mistakes I could make without even knowing it.
   d. it was amazing how many mistakes one could make without even knowing it.

Answers

1. **b.** This question tests subject-verb agreement. The subject is *option*, which is singular, so the verb must be singular, too.
2. **d.** The word *near* is modifying *glamorous*, which makes it an adverb. To put *near* in adverb form, you need to add the -*ly* ending. Choice **c** is incorrect because *glamorously* and *deliciously* are adverbs, but should be adjectives, because they describe the meal.
3. **c.** This sentence has a pronoun shift in it. It starts with *I* and then changes to *you*. Choice **c** makes both of the pronouns consistent.

Revise Sentences to Correct Common Errors Related to Spelling, Capitalization, and Punctuation

To sharpen your skills with mechanics and spelling, rewrite each of the following sentences to correct any errors in spelling, capitalization, and punctuation. If there is no error, write no error.

1. "Are you okay," asked Timothy, "Are you sure you don't want to sit down and rest for a while?"

   _____

   _____

2. Everyone except George is prepared to accept the final results of the vote.

_____

_____

3. Marco thought we would need only one bag of Potato Chips for the party, but his judgment was fawlty.

_____

_____

_____

4. Especially on Monday's, the Central high School cafeteria teams with hungry students.

_____

_____

_____

5. Because he was given a local anesthetic Josh was conscience throughout the operation.

_____

_____

_____

6. The Civil Rights movement fought to show everyone that all people are created equal this is a Right set forth in the declaration of Independence.

_____

_____

_____

_____

Answers

The changed parts of each sentence are underlined.

1. "Are you <u>okay?" asked Timothy. "Are</u> you sure you don't want to sit down and rest for a while?"

2. no error

3. Marco thought we would need only one bag of <u>potato chips</u> for the party, but his judgment was <u>faulty</u>.

4. Especially on <u>Mondays</u>, the Central <u>High</u> School cafeteria <u>teems</u> with hungry students.

5. Because he was given a local anesthetic<u>,</u> Josh was <u>conscious</u> throughout the operation.

6. The Civil Rights Movement fought to show everyone that all people are created equal<u>;</u> this is a <u>right</u> set forth in the <u>Declaration</u> of Independence.

0011: Demonstrate the Ability to Prepare an Effective Summary

- Summarize the main ideas, key arguments, and significant supporting details presented in an extended passage.
- Demonstrate effective paragraph and sentence construction.
- Demonstrate command of standard English conventions of grammar and usage, without making common errors.
- Demonstrate command of standard English conventions of spelling, capitalization, and punctuation, without making common errors.

In the Writing Summary exercise you will be asked to demonstrate your writing skills by summarizing a passage and by rewriting paragraphs and sentences. You will need to follow directions carefully, and then recheck your work for correct grammar and punctuation.

Summarize the Main Ideas, Key Arguments, and Significant Supporting Details Presented in an Extended Passage

A **summary** is a retelling of the content in your own words. The summary should briefly paraphrase the main idea and supporting ideas or arguments. The main idea can usually be stated in one sentence, but a summary is often longer.

Read this story carefully, and consider how you would summarize it.

Shiloh swung her leg back and clobbered a clump of dirt. It sailed over the sidewalk and shattered on the grass beyond. "Goal!" she sang. "One point for Shiloh Fanin!" As she continued the long walk home, she kicked at other dirt clumps and even a pile of dry leaves, though they didn't fly far. Fat tears welled in her brown eyes, but she wouldn't let them fall. For weeks she had been practicing her dribbling, long-range kicks, and passing. Every evening after dinner her father had brought out the scuffed soccer ball for an hour of running around the yard, and she had even outrun him a few times. But the hours of practice hadn't done her any good. Today's soccer team tryouts had been dismal. Nearly 30 girls had assembled on the field after school, and many of them were taller, stronger, and more experienced than Shiloh. After they had finished the tryouts, the coach explained that only 15 girls could be chosen, and Shiloh wasn't surprised to be among those sent home. Now she would have to explain to her father that she wasn't good enough to play. As she wandered down the last block to her house, something hit her in the back of the leg. A soccer ball! She spun around and saw Ashley, another girl who hadn't made the team. "Hey, Shiloh," Ashley called. "Would you like to sign

up for the community soccer league with me? You were really good today, and I need a few more girls for our team."

Shiloh smiled. Maybe she could make her father proud after all.

Now look at two possible summaries. Which one seems more effective?

1. Shiloh didn't make the school soccer team. Then a friend asked her to join a different soccer team.

2. Shiloh was hoping to join the school soccer team. Despite hours of practice, she was not chosen for the team. She was upset and disappointed until a friend asked her to join a community soccer team.

Answer

2. The first summary is brief and concise. It tells *who* and *what*. If you were taking notes for yourself, this version might be sufficient to help you remember what the story was about. But the second version gives a bit more information—*how* Shiloh felt about these events and *why* the events were connected. If you wanted to summarize this story for a friend, these details would help explain the mood of the story and the relationship between the events. Thus, the second example is a more complete and effective summary of the story.

Use the following article to practice summarizing. As you read, underline the main ideas. Then write your own summary on the lines that follow the article or use a separate sheet of paper. After you finish, check your summary against the two examples that follow.

Northern Spotted Owl under Threat

Thirty years ago, the Northern spotted owl was one of the most common owls in the Pacific Northwest. But these owls live in old-growth forest, and logging caused much of their habitat to be lost. In 1991, the federal government passed laws to protect the land where the owls live. Now, though, the owls face a new threat— competition with the barred owl. Barred owls are larger and more aggressive, and they scare the spotted owls away from nesting and hunting grounds. Scientists have tried several ways to protect the Northern spotted owl. Some track the owl nests to monitor when their eggs hatch. Some scientists have even tried to reduce the population of barred owls. Environment specialists are working hard to protect this species, but more research is needed. The Northern spotted owl is also threatened by climate change and competition with other birds of prey.

_____

_____

_____

_____

_____

_____

_____

_____

_____

_____

_____

Answer

There are several ways to summarize this article, but your summary should include most of these ideas:

The Northern spotted owl is endangered because of competition with barred owls. The owl is also threatened by climate change and logging in its habitat. Scientists are trying several methods to protect the owl.

Read the following passage from a novel written for teens, then summarize it in 100 to 150 words. (This scene is set in Boston in the mid 1800s. A hackney was a horse-drawn carriage for hire, like today's taxicabs.) After you write your summary, check your work against the weak and strong examples that follow.

A Trip Through the City of Stone

"Where to, Miss?" asked the driver gruffly. He had a jutting forehead, an equally jutting jaw, a disagreeable squint, and an even more disagreeable sneer.

Anna gulped and squeezed her Liberty half dollar tightly. She knew nothing about hackney fares. Did she have enough? She turned to look for the man who had flagged the hackney down for her, but he had already gone back into the theater.

"How much is the fare to 43 Trimble Street?" she asked.

"'S that near the harbor?" asked the driver.

Anna nodded.

"Don't know," growled the driver. "It's a pretty good-sized trip."

Anna could tell that the driver had sensed her ignorance and was testing her to see how much money he could get out of her. But what could she do? Well, she could _try_ haggling—like she sometimes used to do in Papa's store back in Martindale.

"How about ten cents?" she asked.

The driver simply snorted.

"Twenty-five?" she suggested.

"Two bits?" the man huffed. "You're wasting my time, Miss."

It was no good haggling. Anna's ignorance was too great, and so was her frustration. She silently held out the Liberty half dollar to the man.

"It'll have to do," grumbled the man. He snatched the coin out of Anna's hand, turned away from her, and snapped his reins. The hackney lurched forward, then tore along with a speed that startled and almost frightened Anna.

The hackney hurtled on through streets straight and winding, wide and narrow, and Anna watched Boston rush by her dizzied eyes. She remembered Rupert saying that the city was all built out of stone. And indeed it seemed to be—brownstone, limestone, concrete, but most of all, granite.

There were granite churches and granite public buildings designed to look like Greek temples. There were granite monuments, granite houses, and even granite-paved streets. It seemed that Boston was obsessed with stone! Oh, the hackney also passed by some parks and squares with trees, grass, hedges, and bushes. But where were the large and small gardens that could be found everywhere back in Martindale or Goshen?

Since she had been here, Anna had heard that Boston was built largely on swamp land. Whole hills had been leveled to make enough flat dry ground to use.

Perhaps, Anna thought, *that's why people who lived here were desperate to make things solid and permanent.*

Perhaps for Bostonians, earth was too precious to be used in such fleeting work as planting. A flower or even a tree would grow for a time and then surely die, but a granite wall might stand forever.

Source: *Anna's World* (excerpted from Chapter 34, "Choices"), by Wim Coleman and Pat Perrin, ChironBooks, 2009.

Answer

Your summary might emphasize different points, but it should contain all the important information and ideas from the passage. Is your summary closer to the weak example, the strong one, or somewhere in between?

Weak Summary

Anna took a cab to go to Trimble Street. The driver took her Liberty half dollar for the fare. They drove fast through Boston's streets; driving past big buildings and some parks. Anna was frightened at being alone in the cab in the big city.

This summary includes some of the significant details, but does not convey a main idea. The statement *Anna was frightened* is a speculation since it was not indicated in the story. The semicolon in the third sentence is incorrect.

Stronger Summary

A young girl named Anna needed to go to an address in Boston, a city unfamiliar to her. She took a hackney cab, but since she did not know exactly where the street was or what the fare should be, she found that trying to haggle over the fare was useless. She gave the disagreeable driver her only coin, a Liberty half dollar.

The cab raced through the streets of Boston, a city built of granite and other types of stone. They passed large, impressive public buildings, churches, monuments, and houses. They also drove by a few green areas and parks.

Anna knew that Boston had been built on swamps and leveled hills. She wondered whether that was why they had used so much stone in Boston. To her, all that stone indicated that maybe the people who lived there needed something that would last forever.

This summary is smoothly written and contains no errors in grammar and punctuation. From details in the passage, the writer correctly infers that Anna is a young girl and that the city is unfamiliar. This summary also reflects Anna's wondering about the city.

Double check your summary of "A Trip Through the City of Stone" for these very important elements:

- effective paragraph and sentence construction
- correct grammar and usage
- perfect spelling, capitalization, and punctuation.

The following sections review some common errors and offer practice in correcting them.

Demonstrate Effective Paragraph and Sentence Construction

Poorly constructed sentences and paragraphs not only reveal clumsy writing, they can completely obscure your meaning. Rewrite the following sentences and paragraph, correcting any errors. Then check your work against the answers that follow.

1. Although meteorologists continue to get more and more advanced technology and equipment, their weather forecasts wrong about 50% of the time.

   _____

   _____

   _____

   _____

   _____

2. The messenger on the blue 21-speed bicycle with the shiny green pants is on his way to deliver the contract.

   _____

   _____

   _____

   _____

3. The new museum includes submarine tours, planetarium shows, science lab demonstrations, and interactive exhibits, children converge on the place daily.

_____

_____

_____

_____

4. Combine these short, choppy sentences into one smooth sentence.

People followed the author on the street. They want to meet him. They were curious about him.

_____

_____

_____

5. Rewrite the following paragraph, rearranging the sentences so that the main idea and supporting details are in the best order.

A simple sitting yoga pose such as *staff pose*, for example, requires you to tighten and lengthen stomach, back, and arm muscles as you stretch your legs out in front of you and place your hands by your side. More difficult poses, such as *brave warrior*, require you to balance on one leg and hold a pose that strengthens leg, back, and stomach muscles. Although they may seem easy to those who have never practiced, yoga poses require great concentration, and they are surprisingly effective in stretching and strengthening muscles.

_____

_____

_____

Answers

1. This is a sentence fragment because it is missing a verb. Correct: Although meteorologists continue to get more and more advanced technology and equipment, their weather forecasts <u>are</u> wrong about 50% of the time.

2. The way this sentence is written, the bike appears to be wearing the shiny green pants. The sentence needs to be rearranged so that the modifiers clearly describe the messenger, not the bike. Here is one correct way to revise the sentence: The messenger wearing the shiny green pants and riding the blue 21-speed bicycle is on his way to deliver the contract.

3. This is a run-on sentence that needs to be broken into two parts or joined together with the appropriate conjunction. You could make it into two complete sentences. Here are some other solutions.

Use a semicolon: The new museum includes submarine tours, planetarium shows, science lab demonstrations, and interactive exhibits; children converge on the place daily.

Add a conjunction: The new museum includes submarine tours, planetarium shows, science lab demonstrations, and interactive exhibits, and children converge on the place daily. Note that some conjunctions, such as *but*, would obscure the meaning. If you want to use *which*, you must restructure the sentence.

Restructure the sentence to create a clause: The new museum, which children converge on daily, includes submarine tours, planetarium shows, science lab demonstrations, and interactive exhibits.

4. Although there are several ways to combine these sentences, make sure that your choice is not awkward or wordy. Here is one good solution: People followed the author on the street, wanting to meet him as they were curious about him.

5. The last sentence in the paragraph introduces the idea of how yoga poses stretch and strengthen muscles, so it should be placed at the beginning of the paragraph. The second sentence notes a specific example of a pose that stretches and strengthens muscles. The best paragraph structure would be:

Although they may seem easy to those who have never practiced, yoga poses require great concentration, and they are surprisingly effective in stretching and strengthening muscles. A simple sitting pose such as *staff pose*, for example, requires you to tighten and lengthen stomach, back, and arm muscles as you stretch your legs out in front of you and place your hands by your side. More difficult poses, such as *brave warrior*, require you to balance on one leg and hold a pose that strengthens leg, back, and stomach muscles.

Demonstrate Command of Standard English Conventions of Grammar and Usage

Errors in standard English usage will distract from the ideas in your writing and lower your test score. The following sentences test correctness and effectiveness of expression. In choosing answers, follow the requirements of standard written English; in other words, pay attention to grammar, choice of words, and sentence construction.

1. Some of the teachers which were working at the local community college. Discovered they had all attended the same college. Even graduated the very same year.

Combine these fragments into one sentence, adding or subtracting words where necessary and correcting any errors.

_____

_____

_____

2. In large bookstores like Borders and Barnes & Noble, there isn't hardly a single plush chair where no people are sitting, browsing through books or paging through magazines.

Rewrite this sentence to correct any errors.

_____

_____

_____

_____

3. Basketball practice this week was missed because we had a important appointment that we had to keep and to make matters worst my car keys had been either stole or lost, which slowed us down a lot.

Rewrite this sentence to correct any errors.

_____

_____

_____

_____

Answers

1. Standard usage requires the use of *who* rather than *which* when referring to people (teachers). Suggested correction: A number of the teachers who were working at the local community college discovered they had all attended the same college and even graduated the very same year.

2. This sentence contains a double negative. Both *isn't* and *hardly* are negative. Change *isn't* to *is* repairs the problem. Correct: In large bookstores like Borders and Barnes & Noble, there is hardly a single plush chair where no people are sitting, browsing through books or paging through magazines.

3. The opening phrase is written in the passive voice, which is not as direct and clear as the active voice. The word *worst* is the superlative form of *bad*; this sentence is comparing two things, so the comparative form *worse* should be used. The past tense of the irregular verb *steal* is *stolen*, and it requires a helping verb in the correct tense to match the subject. The two independent clauses should be made into two sentences or separated by a semicolon. Make sure that your choice is not awkward or wordy. Here's one way of correcting the problems: We missed basketball practice this week because we had an important appointment that we had to keep. To make matters worse, my car keys had been stolen or lost, which slowed us down a lot.

Demonstrate Command of Standard English Conventions of Spelling, Capitalization, and Punctuation

Rewrite the following sentences, adding, removing, or rearranging words where necessary and correcting any errors.

1. Effective face to face communicasion depends, on the ability to listen well.

_____

_____

2. If you are going to listen to Someone; turn off the television or radio,

_____

_____

3. At the wild west Museum exhibits in several galleries and performances in a new theater all explore Westward expansion.

_____

_____

Answers

1. The words *face-to-face* work together as one adjective to describe a kind of communication, so they must be hyphenated. The correct spelling is *communication*. No comma is necessary between *depends* and *on*. Correct: Effective face-to-face communication depends on the ability to listen well.

2. *Someone* is a pronoun and should not be capitalized. Semicolons can be used between two independent clauses but not between an independent and dependent clause. *If you are going to listen to someone* is a dependent clause and should be followed by a comma. Correct: If you are going to listen to someone, be polite enough to turn off the television or radio.

3. Because it is a general direction (not referring to a specific region), *westward* should not be capitalized. The complete name of the museum should be capitalized. A comma should be used after the opening prepositional phrase. Correct: At the Wild West Museum, exhibits in several galleries and performances in a new theater all explore westward expansion.

0012: Demonstrate the Ability to Prepare a Well-Organized and Focused Piece of Writing for a Given Purpose and Audience, Using Standard English Conventions

- Take a position on an issue, proposition, or statement related to education, and defend that position.
- Maintain a central theme or main idea through the effective use of a thesis statement, topic sentences, and transitions.

- Develop a well-organized argument using sound reasoning and relevant supporting information and/or examples.
- Demonstrate effective paragraph and sentence structure and employ vocabulary appropriate for the audience and the purpose of the writing task.
- Use precise and appropriate words and phrases.
- Demonstrate command of standard English conventions of grammar and usage, without making common errors.
- Demonstrate command of standard English conventions of spelling, capitalization, and punctuation, without making common errors.

The composition exercise is an important part of the Writing subtest. You will be asked to write an essay (200 to 600 words) on a specific issue related to your profession. Your work will be judged on the adequacy, appropriateness, and coherence of your message, and also on grammar, spelling, word usage, and sentence structure. This section reviews some important points and provides a practice writing assignment.

Keep in mind that writing is a *process*, not just a *product*. That process includes planning, drafting, and revising.

Take a Position on an Issue, Proposition, or Statement Related to Education and Defend That Position

You'll be given a **writing prompt** on which to base your essay. For example, here's the writing prompt to use for practicing the composition exercise.

One of the biggest educational trends in recent years is homeschooling. It is growing each year by approximately 15%. More than one million children of all ages are currently being educated at home. Do you think that homeschooling is a valuable educational method?

As you follow each step in this section, base your decisions on that writing prompt. At the end of this chapter, you will be asked to write an essay as a response to the prompt.

Of course, the first step in the planning stage is to decide on the **position** you want to defend. Briefly state your position on the question, "Do you think that homeschooling is a valuable educational method?"

_____

_____

Now you can set the **purpose**, or **goal**, of your essay. The more clearly you can articulate your purpose while you begin work on your essay, the more effective your writing and revising stages will be. What are you trying to tell your audience? Is your goal to _demonstrate_ or _explain_ or _prove_ something about the writing prompt? Do you want to _convince_ your readers of something? Try to find a verb, or verbs, that best describe what you want your essay to do.

Briefly state of the overall goal of the essay you will write on this issue.

_____

_____

Now that you know your goal, you can consider your **supporting details**. Will the specific points and examples you use be based on your observations, studies, reading, or personal experiences? Don't try to list any actual arguments yet, just think about what kinds of materials you might draw on.

List the kinds of defense you plan to use.

_____

_____

_____

Maintain a Central Theme or Main Idea through the Effective Use of a Thesis Statement, Topic Sentences, and Transitions

Your answer to the question in the writing prompt is your **thesis**—your main idea. It is the argument that you are going to make and the idea you need to support. As you know, a thesis does not just repeat or paraphrase the question or the prompt. It does not simply make general statements about the topic or state how _others_ might respond to the question. A good thesis takes a clear, personal position.

Consider the writing prompt, your position on the prompt, and your goal. Write a clear thesis statement that presents the main idea of your essay.

_____

_____

_____

_____

_____

Remember that each paragraph in your essay is also built around a main idea, a mini-thesis presented in the form of a **topic sentence**. A topic sentence introduces the ideas contained within the paragraph.

Linking expressions such as _therefore, consequently_, and _meanwhile_ can be used within a sentence to connect two related clauses and between sentences to connect ideas.

The same transitions—or linking expressions—used to connect sentences can be used to connect paragraphs, and will help clarify the relationship between ideas in paragraphs. Transitions demonstrate the type of order that you are using in your essay.

To refresh your list of transition words and phrases, you might want to review earlier sections of this test preparation book.

Develop a Well-Organized Argument Using Sound Reasoning and Relevant Supporting Information and/or Examples

Early in the writing process, you might want to brainstorm to develop ideas for your essay. Some writers use a cluster diagram or word web to draw out their thoughts. These techniques can help you identify reasons, examples, or specific details to support your thesis. Remember to think freely and then choose the most useful ideas for your composition.

Next, **outline** your ideas for your essay. Outlines help you focus on what's most important by making it easier to review key ideas and see relationships among those ideas. With an outline, you can see how supporting information is related to the main ideas.

As you know, an essay has three parts.

Introduction: Tell your readers what you are going to tell them. (State your thesis.)
Body: Tell them. (Develop your ideas and provide specific support for your thesis.)
Conclusion: Tell them what you have told them. (Restate your thesis.)

Your outline should follow this basic structure, too. The "body" section of your outline should be broken down into the individual supporting ideas for your essay, with supporting evidence or details under each. Outlines can have many layers and variations, but this is the general form:

I. Topic
   A. Main idea
      1. Major supporting idea
         a. Minor supporting idea

Once you have completed an outline, revise and refine it by following these four steps:

1. Look back at your overall goal for your essay. What are you trying to say to your readers?

2. Go over your outline and circle, underline, or highlight your major points or images. Do they all support your goal?
3. Brainstorm words and phrases that will accurately and concisely express those points. Jot them down.
4. Use your word list and your outline to guide your writing. Do not allow yourself to stray from your goal or your major points.

Demonstrate Effective Paragraph and Sentence Structure and Employ Vocabulary Appropriate for the Audience and the Purpose of the Writing Task

Once you have your outline and word list in place, begin drafting your essay. Generally, each major heading (Roman numeral) in your outline will represent the main idea of a paragraph. As you move from point to point, be sure to use effective transitions within sentences and between paragraphs so the piece of writing flows well.

Check back to be sure that each paragraph discusses only one main idea, and that each paragraph supports the main idea of the essay.

As you write, keep in mind that you are communicating with professionals in your field. Your vocabulary and sentence structure should be suitable for a mature and well-educated audience. Your sentences should vary in structure and length.

Use Precise and Appropriate Words and Phrases

One of the best ways to accurately convey your ideas in your essay is to choose the right words. The right word has three essential characteristics:

1. It expresses the idea you wish to convey.
2. It is exact (precise).
3. It is appropriate for the audience and tone.

To refresh your awareness of appropriate words and phrases, you might want to review earlier sections of this test preparation book.

Demonstrate Command of Standard English Conventions of Grammar and Usage

If you're writing hastily, it's all too easy for errors to slip into your work. Double check! Your writing must be completely free of errors in standard English conventions. If you don't feel in complete command of these conventions, you might want to return to earlier sections of this test preparation book for review.

Demonstrate Command of Standard English Conventions of Spelling, Capitalization, and Punctuation

Mistakes in spelling, capitalization, and punctuation make the writer seem sloppy and unprofessional.

Check your work carefully and correct any errors. If you don't feel in complete command of these conventions, you might want to return to earlier sections of this test preparation book for review.

Essay

Now write your essay on the lines provided. Here's that writing prompt again.

One of the biggest educational trends in recent years is homeschooling. It is growing each year by approximately 15%. More than one million children of all ages are currently being educated at home. Do you think that homeschooling is a valuable educational method?

Use your outline, word list, and any other notes to write your essay. After you have completed your composition, checked it, and made any necessary revisions, compare it to the strong and weak examples that follow.

Strong Example

I firmly believe that only informed decisions can be wise decisions. Many of the people who form opinions about homeschooling know little to nothing about it. Instead, they base their perceptions on common myths, inaccurate assumptions, and idle gossip. I am personally a strong advocate of homeschooling, because I have experienced it on a daily basis; I was homeschooled for five years.

When my parents first broached the topic with me, I responded quite negatively. I raised the most common objections: It could not be legal; I would never have anyone to play with; I would be horrendously bored staying home all the time. And certainly my parents could never provide the same high quality education I would get in public school. Despite my vocal and vehement arguments, my parents were determined that homeschooling was the best option for my education. To reach a compromise, we agreed to try it for only a few months and then re-evaluate. I was sure that when that time came, we would mutually agree that it had been a disastrous decision.

Now I can look back at the whole experience and realize how naïve and uneducated I once was about homeschooling. I had fallen prey to the same misconceptions that people continue to believe today. During my five years of homeschooling, I researched the topic, through books, websites, and even regional and national conferences. What I learned—far outside of my daily curriculum—was that homeschooling is one of the best educational options families have today. Instead of being illegal, it was legal in all states. Instead of being lonely and bored at home, I was immersed in classes, workshops, potlucks, meetings, and play dates many times each week. I made multiple new friends and continued to see my public school friends on the weekends. My education was high quality; indeed, I feel I learned more in those five years than I could possibly have learned in school. Best of all, I was al-lowed the time to pursue some of my deepest passions, from drama and theater to foreign languages. I discovered a true love of learning and realized that, as Winston Churchill once said, "I am always ready to learn but I do not always like being taught."

Today, I try to remind myself to never make a hasty judgment about any controversial issue without doing some research. Forming an opinion about something I personally know nothing of is foolhardy. Too often, I suspect later I might have to eat those words.

Scoring evaluation: The writer of this essay has a strong opinion about the issue and makes that clear through the powerful examples he or she uses. The introduction, body, and conclusion are all clearly stated, and there is excellent sentence variety and vocabulary use.

Weak Example

I cannot believe that more than one million kids are being homeschooled today I had no idea the number was so high. I have heard a lot about homeschooling. It is on the news and in the newspaper a lot. Some of the stories say how good these students do, others just say these people are not being watched carefully enough and are committing crimes.

A good education is important. You probably can get it in several ways. That inclues homeschooling. I think that parents have to be very dedicated to their kids. Families spend a lot of time together. I wouldn't mind that part. I don't see very much of my family during the week. We are all going in opposite directions. I miss them.

I think that homeschooling can be a good idea if parents do it right. Research it carefully. Make sure their kids are keeping up in all subjects. Make sure their kids get time to play with friends and do fun stuff, rather than just stay home and study all the time. So, I guess, in conclusion, if done properly, then going to school at home can be a smart idea, in my opinion.

Scoring evaluation: There are some good thoughts here, but they simply are not developed enough. More details and examples are needed to make it longer and give it support. The writer strays from the topic several times into areas that are not pertinent, and there is not much sense of an introduction and body in this example.

COMMUNICATION AND LITERACY SKILLS PRACTICE TEST 1

CHAPTER SUMMARY

Use this practice exam to see how you would do if you were to take the MTEL today, and to see how you've improved in the skills areas identified in the diagnostic test in Chapter 6.

To simulate the test-taking experience, give yourself the time and the space to work. Because you won't be taking the real test in your living room, you might take this one in an unfamiliar location, such as a library. Use a timer or stopwatch to time yourself, allowing ample time for preparing and writing your essay; you'll have four hours to complete your official exam. If you would prefer to take this test for more diagnostic purposes, just take the test in a relaxed manner to find out which areas you are skilled in and which areas will need extra work. After you finish taking your test, you should review the answer explanations found at the end of this test. The answer explanations are followed by information on how to score your exam and diagnose your strengths and weaknesses.

You'll find an answer fill-in sheet for the multiple-choice questions on the following page. You will be writing your answers to the short-answer items on blank lines provided following each question. Lined pages are provided for your answers to the open-response questions following each such item. After you finish taking both subtests, you should review the answer explanations found at the end on page 237.

Reading Subtest

1.	ⓐ ⓑ ⓒ ⓓ	15.	ⓐ ⓑ ⓒ ⓓ	29.	ⓐ ⓑ ⓒ ⓓ
2.	ⓐ ⓑ ⓒ ⓓ	16.	ⓐ ⓑ ⓒ ⓓ	30.	ⓐ ⓑ ⓒ ⓓ
3.	ⓐ ⓑ ⓒ ⓓ	17.	ⓐ ⓑ ⓒ ⓓ	31.	ⓐ ⓑ ⓒ ⓓ
4.	ⓐ ⓑ ⓒ ⓓ	18.	ⓐ ⓑ ⓒ ⓓ	32.	ⓐ ⓑ ⓒ ⓓ
5.	ⓐ ⓑ ⓒ ⓓ	19.	ⓐ ⓑ ⓒ ⓓ	33.	ⓐ ⓑ ⓒ ⓓ
6.	ⓐ ⓑ ⓒ ⓓ	20.	ⓐ ⓑ ⓒ ⓓ	34.	ⓐ ⓑ ⓒ ⓓ
7.	ⓐ ⓑ ⓒ ⓓ	21.	ⓐ ⓑ ⓒ ⓓ	35.	ⓐ ⓑ ⓒ ⓓ
8.	ⓐ ⓑ ⓒ ⓓ	22.	ⓐ ⓑ ⓒ ⓓ	36.	ⓐ ⓑ ⓒ ⓓ
9.	ⓐ ⓑ ⓒ ⓓ	23.	ⓐ ⓑ ⓒ ⓓ	37.	ⓐ ⓑ ⓒ ⓓ
10.	ⓐ ⓑ ⓒ ⓓ	24.	ⓐ ⓑ ⓒ ⓓ	38.	ⓐ ⓑ ⓒ ⓓ
11.	ⓐ ⓑ ⓒ ⓓ	25.	ⓐ ⓑ ⓒ ⓓ	39.	ⓐ ⓑ ⓒ ⓓ
12.	ⓐ ⓑ ⓒ ⓓ	26.	ⓐ ⓑ ⓒ ⓓ	40.	ⓐ ⓑ ⓒ ⓓ
13.	ⓐ ⓑ ⓒ ⓓ	27.	ⓐ ⓑ ⓒ ⓓ	41.	ⓐ ⓑ ⓒ ⓓ
14.	ⓐ ⓑ ⓒ ⓓ	28.	ⓐ ⓑ ⓒ ⓓ	42.	ⓐ ⓑ ⓒ ⓓ

Writing Subtest

1.	ⓐ ⓑ ⓒ ⓓ	13.	ⓐ ⓑ ⓒ ⓓ	25.	ⓐ ⓑ ⓒ ⓓ
2.	ⓐ ⓑ ⓒ ⓓ	14.	ⓐ ⓑ ⓒ ⓓ	26.	ⓐ ⓑ ⓒ ⓓ
3.	ⓐ ⓑ ⓒ ⓓ	15.	ⓐ ⓑ ⓒ ⓓ	27.	ⓐ ⓑ ⓒ ⓓ
4.	ⓐ ⓑ ⓒ ⓓ	16.	ⓐ ⓑ ⓒ ⓓ	28.	ⓐ ⓑ ⓒ ⓓ
5.	ⓐ ⓑ ⓒ ⓓ	17.	ⓐ ⓑ ⓒ ⓓ	29.	ⓐ ⓑ ⓒ ⓓ
6.	ⓐ ⓑ ⓒ ⓓ	18.	ⓐ ⓑ ⓒ ⓓ	30.	ⓐ ⓑ ⓒ ⓓ
7.	ⓐ ⓑ ⓒ ⓓ	19.	ⓐ ⓑ ⓒ ⓓ	31.	ⓐ ⓑ ⓒ ⓓ
8.	ⓐ ⓑ ⓒ ⓓ	20.	ⓐ ⓑ ⓒ ⓓ	32.	ⓐ ⓑ ⓒ ⓓ
9.	ⓐ ⓑ ⓒ ⓓ	21.	ⓐ ⓑ ⓒ ⓓ	33.	ⓐ ⓑ ⓒ ⓓ
10.	ⓐ ⓑ ⓒ ⓓ	22.	ⓐ ⓑ ⓒ ⓓ	34.	ⓐ ⓑ ⓒ ⓓ
11.	ⓐ ⓑ ⓒ ⓓ	23.	ⓐ ⓑ ⓒ ⓓ	35.	ⓐ ⓑ ⓒ ⓓ
12.	ⓐ ⓑ ⓒ ⓓ	24.	ⓐ ⓑ ⓒ ⓓ		

Reading Subtest

Directions: Read each of the following selections and then answer the corresponding questions. Each question has only ONE correct answer.

> **Read the passage, then answer the six questions that follow.**

Mt. Desert Island

1 The coast of the state of Maine is one of the most irregular in the world. A straight line running from the southernmost coastal city to the northernmost coastal city would measure about 225 miles. If you followed the coastline between these points, you would travel more than ten times as far. This irregularity is the result of what is called a drowned coastline. The term comes from the glacial activity of the Ice Age. At that time, the whole area that is now Maine was part of a mountain range that towered above the sea. As the glacier descended, however, it expended enormous force on those mountains, and they sank into the sea.

2 As the mountains sank, ocean water charged over the lowest parts of the remaining land, forming a series of twisting inlets and lagoons of contorted grottoes and nooks. The highest parts of the former mountain range, nearest the shore, remained as islands. Mt. Desert Island is one of the most famous of all the islands left behind by the glacier. Marine fossils found here were 225 feet above sea level, indicating the level of the shoreline prior to the descent of the glacier.

3 The 2,500-mile-long rocky and jagged coastline of Maine keeps watch over nearly 2,000 islands. Many of these islands are tiny and uninhabited, but many are home to thriving communities. Mt. Desert Island is one of the largest and most beautiful of the Maine coast islands. Measuring 16 miles by 12 miles, Mt. Desert was essentially formed as two distinct islands. It is split almost in half by Somes Sound, a deep and narrow stretch of water seven miles long. For years, Mt. Desert Island, particularly its major settlement, Bar Harbor, afforded summer homes for the wealthy. Recently, though, Bar Harbor has become a burgeoning arts community, as well. But the best part of the island is the unspoiled forest land known as Acadia National Park.

4 Because the island sits on the boundary line between the temperate and sub-Arctic zones, the island supports the flora and fauna of both zones, as well as beach, inland, and alpine plants. It also lies in a major bird migration lane and is a resting spot for many birds. The establishment of Acadia National Park in 1916 means that this natural reserve will be perpetually available to all people, not just the wealthy. Visitors to Acadia may receive nature instruction from the park naturalists, as well as enjoy camping, hiking, cycling, and boating. Or they may choose to spend time at the archeological museum learning about the Stone Age inhabitants of the island. The best view on Mt. Desert Island is from the top of Cadillac Mountain. This mountain rises 1,532 feet, making it the highest on the Atlantic seaboard. From the summit, one can gaze back toward the mainland or out over the Atlantic Ocean and contemplate the beauty created by a retreating glacier.

1. Which of the following lists best outlines the main topics addressed in this passage?

   a. ■ Ice Age glacial activity

       ■ the Islands of Casco Bay

       ■ formation of Cadillac Mountain

       ■ summer residents of Mt. Desert Island

   b. ■ formation of a drowned coastline

       ■ the topography of Mt. Desert Island

       ■ the environment of Mt. Desert Island

       ■ tourist attractions on Mt. Desert Island

   c. ■ mapping the Maine coastline

       ■ the arts community at Bar Harbor

       ■ history of the National Park System

       ■ climbing Cadillac Mountain

   d. ■ the effect of glaciers on small islands

       ■ Stone Age dwellers on Mt. Desert Island

       ■ the importance of biodiversity

       ■ hiking in Acadia National Park

2. Which of the following statements best expresses the main idea of the fourth paragraph of the passage?

   a. The wealthy residents of Mt. Desert Island selfishly kept it to themselves.

   b. Acadia National Park is one of the smallest of the national parks.

   c. There is tension between the year-round residents and the summer tourists.

   d. Acadia National Park has diverse animal and plant life and offers various activities.

3. The content of the fourth paragraph indicates that the writer believes:

   a. The continued existence of national parks is threatened by major budget cuts.

   b. The best way to preserve the environment on Mt. Desert Island is to limit the number of visitors.

   c. National parks allow large numbers of people to visit and learn about interesting wilderness areas.

   d. Mt. Desert Island is the most interesting tourist attraction in the entire state of Maine.

4. In which of the following statements from paragraph 4 of the passage does the author most clearly express an opinion rather than state a fact?

   a. The 2,500-mile-long rocky and jagged coastline of Maine keeps watch over nearly 2,000 islands.

   b. Many of these islands are tiny and uninhabited, but many are home to thriving communities.

   c. Measuring 16 miles by 12 miles, Mt. Desert was essentially formed as two distinct islands.

   d. The best part of the island is the unspoiled forest land known as Acadia National Park.

5. Which of the following words is the best meaning of <u>expended</u> as it is used in the first paragraph of the passage?

   a. spent

   b. created

   c. displayed

   d. instructed

6. Which of the following words is the best meaning of <u>perpetually</u> as it is used in the fourth paragraph of the passage?

   a. exaggeratedly

   b. curiously

   c. continually

   d. magnificently

> **Read the passage, then answer the six questions that follow.**

Eating Disorders

1 Millions of people in the United States are affected by eating disorders. More than 90% of those afflicted are adolescents or young adult women. Although all eating disorders

share some common manifestations, anorexia nervosa, bulimia nervosa, and binge eating each have distinctive symptoms and risks.

2 People who intentionally starve themselves (even while experiencing severe hunger pains) suffer from anorexia nervosa. The disorder, which usually begins around the time of puberty, involves extreme weight loss to at least 15% below the individual's normal body weight. Many people with the disorder look emaciated but are convinced they are overweight. In patients with anorexia nervosa, starvation can damage vital organs, such as the heart and brain. To protect itself, the body shifts into slow gear: Menstrual periods stop, blood pressure rates drop, and thyroid gland function slows. Excessive thirst and frequent urination may occur. Dehydration contributes to constipation, and reduced body fat leads to lowered body temperature and the inability to withstand cold. Mild anemia, swollen joints, reduced muscle mass, and light-headedness also commonly occur in anorexia nervosa. Anorexia nervosa sufferers can exhibit sudden angry outbursts or become socially withdrawn. One in ten cases of anorexia nervosa leads to death from starvation, cardiac arrest, other medical complications, or suicide. Clinical depression and anxiety place many individuals with eating disorders at risk for suicidal behavior.

3 People with bulimia nervosa consume large amounts of food and then rid their bodies of the excess calories by vomiting, abusing laxatives or diuretics, taking enemas, or exercising obsessively. Some use a combination of all these forms of purging. Individuals with bulimia who use drugs to stimulate vomiting, bowel movements, or urination may be in considerable danger, as this practice increases the risk of heart

failure. Dieting heavily between episodes of binging and purging is common. Because many individuals with bulimia binge and purge in secret and maintain normal or above normal body weight, they can often successfully hide their problem for years. But bulimia nervosa patients—even those of normal weight—can severely damage their bodies by frequent binge eating and purging. In rare instances, binge eating causes the stomach to rupture; purging may result in heart failure due to loss of vital minerals such as potassium. Vomiting can cause the esophagus to become inflamed and glands near the cheeks to become swollen. As in anorexia nervosa, bulimia may lead to irregular menstrual periods. Psychological effects include compulsive stealing as well as possible indications of obsessive-compulsive disorder, an illness characterized by repetitive thoughts and behaviors. Obsessive-compulsive disorder can also accompany anorexia nervosa. As with anorexia nervosa, bulimia typically begins during adolescence. Eventually, half of those with anorexia nervosa will develop bulimia. The condition occurs most often in women but is also found in men.

4 Binge eating disorder is found in about 2% of the general population. As many as one-third of this group are men. It also affects older women, though with less frequency. Recent research shows that binge eating disorder occurs in about 30% of people participating in medically supervised weight control programs. This disorder differs from bulimia because its sufferers do not purge. Individuals with binge eating disorder feel that they lose control of themselves when eating. They eat large quantities of food and do not stop until they are uncomfortably full. Most sufferers are overweight or obese and have a history of weight fluctuations. As

a result, they are prone to the serious medical problems associated with obesity, such as high cholesterol, high blood pressure, and diabetes. Obese individuals also have a higher risk for gallbladder disease, heart disease, and some types of cancer. Usually they have more difficulty losing weight and keeping it off than do people with other serious weight problems. Like anorexic and bulimic sufferers who exhibit psychological problems, individuals with binge eating disorder have high rates of simultaneously occurring psychiatric illnesses, especially depression.

_____

7. According to information presented in the passage, all the eating disorders mentioned have which of the following consequences in common?
   a. heart ailments
   b. stomach rupture
   c. swollen joints
   d. diabetes

8. According to information presented in the passage, people who have an eating disorder, but nevertheless appear to be of normal weight, are most likely to have
   a. obsessive-compulsive disorder.
   b. bulimia nervosa.
   c. binge eating disorder.
   d. anorexia nervosa.

9. According to information presented in the passage, glandular functions of eating disorder patients slow down as a result of
   a. lowering body temperatures.
   b. excessive thirst and urination.
   c. protective measures taken by the body.
   d. the loss of essential minerals.

10. According to information presented in the passage, the inability to eliminate body waste is related to
    a. dehydration.
    b. an inflamed esophagus.
    c. the abuse of laxatives.
    d. weight control programs.

11. According to information presented in the passage, bulimia patients
    a. may demonstrate unpredictable violent behavior.
    b. often engage in compulsive exercise.
    c. experience dehydration less than anorexia patients.
    d. frequently experience stomach ruptures.

12. According to information presented in the passage, up to two-thirds of the binge eating disorder population is
    a. older males.
    b. older females.
    c. younger males.
    d. younger females.

> **Read the passage, then answer the six questions that follow.**

The Great Depression

1   The worst and longest economic crisis in the modern industrial world, the Great Depression in the United States had devastating consequences for American society. At its lowest depth (1932–1933), more than 16 million people were unemployed, more than 5,000 banks had closed, and over 85,000 businesses had failed. Millions of Americans lost their jobs, their savings, and even their homes. The homeless built shacks for temporary shelter—these

emerging shantytowns were nicknamed Hoovervilles: a bitter homage to President Herbert Hoover, who refused to give government assistance to the jobless. The effects of the Depression—severe unemployment rates and a sharp drop in the production and sales of goods—could also be felt abroad, where many European nations were still struggling to recover from World War I.

2 Although the stock market crash of 1929 marked the onset of the Depression, it was not the *cause* of it: Deep, underlying fissures already existed in the economy of the Roaring Twenties. For example, the tariff and war debt <u>policies</u> after World War I contributed to the instability of the banking system. American banks made loans to European countries following World War I. However, the United States kept high tariffs on goods imported from other nations. These policies worked against one another. If other countries could not sell goods in the United States, they could not make enough money to pay back their loans or to buy American goods.

3 And while the United States seemed to be enjoying a prosperous period in the 1920s, the wealth was not evenly distributed. Businesses made gains in productivity, but only one segment of the population—the wealthy—reaped large profits. Workers received only a small share of the wealth they helped produce. At the same time, Americans spent more than they earned. Advertising encouraged Americans to buy cars, radios, and household appliances instead of saving or purchasing only what they could afford. Easy credit policies allowed consumers to borrow money and accumulate debt. Investors also wildly speculated on the stock market, often borrowing money on credit to buy shares of a company. Stocks increased beyond their worth, but investors were willing to pay inflated prices because they believed stocks would continue to rise. This bubble burst in the fall of 1929, when investors lost confidence that stock prices would keep rising. As investors sold off stocks, the market spiraled downward. The stock market crash affected the economy in the same way that a stressful event can affect the human body, lowering its resistance to infection.

4 The ensuing depression led to the election of President Franklin D. Roosevelt in 1932. Roosevelt introduced relief measures that would revive the economy and bring needed relief to Americans suffering the effects of the Great Depression. Roosevelt and Congress passed major legislation that saved banks from closing and regained public confidence. These measures, called the New Deal, included the Agricultural Adjustment Act, which paid farmers to slow their production in order to stabilize food prices; the Federal Deposit Insurance Corporation, which insured bank deposits if banks failed; and the Securities and Exchange Commission, which regulated the stock market. Although the New Deal offered relief, it did not end the Depression. The economy sagged until the nation entered World War II. However, the New Deal changed the relationship between government and American citizens, by expanding the role of the central government in regulating the economy and creating social assistance programs.

13. The author's main point about the Great Depression is that
   a. government policies had nothing to do with it.
   b. the government immediately stepped in with assistance.
   c. underlying problems in the economy preceded it.
   d. the New Deal policies introduced by Roosevelt ended it.

14. The author's main purpose for writing this passage is to
   a. provide an account of the causes and effects of a major event.
   b. make a statement supporting the value of federal social policies.
   c. condemn a system of outdated beliefs.
   d. respond to controversial issues politely.

15. The author cites the emergence of Hoovervilles in paragraph 1 as an example of
   a. housing programs sponsored by the federal government.
   b. the resilience of Americans who lost their jobs, savings, and homes.
   c. the government's unwillingness to assist citizens in desperate times.
   d. the effectiveness of the Hoover administration in dealing with the crisis.

16. Which of the following words is closest in meaning to <u>policies</u> as it is used in the second paragraph of the passage?
   a. theories
   b. practices
   c. laws
   d. examples

17. The passage suggests that the 1920s was a decade that extolled the value of
   a. thrift.
   b. prudence.
   c. balance.
   d. extravagance.

18. The example of the human body as a metaphor for the economy, found at the end of paragraph 3, suggests that:
   a. a stressful event like the stock market crash of 1929 probably made a lot of people sick.
   b. the crash weakened the economy's ability to withstand other pressures.
   c. the crash was an untreatable disease.
   d. a single event caused the collapse of the economy.

> **Read the passage, then answer the six questions that follow.**

Light Pollution

1   Light pollution is a growing problem worldwide. Like other forms of pollution, light pollution degrades the quality of the environment. Our ability to see and appreciate the night sky is being steadily diminished by the ever-increasing use of inappropriate night lighting. Where once it was possible to look up at the night sky and see thousands of stars twinkling in the blackness, one now sees little more than the yellow glare of urban sky glow.

2 A basic <u>component</u> of light pollution is glare. Glare occurs when light from a bright source shines directly into the eyes. It is usually caused by an unshielded, or improperly shielded, light source. It can make driving on rainy, slick streets very hazardous. Glare that crosses property boundaries and creates a nuisance is called "light trespass." Light trespass is becoming an important issue in many suburban and rural communities because of the increasing use of cheap, improperly shielded, 175-watt, dusk-to-dawn mercury vapor light fixtures. Typically, they are installed in an effort to improve home security on the theory that more light equals more safety. This is a false belief for two important reasons. First, the excessively bright light creates deep shadows—perfect hiding places for criminals. Second, the light showcases one's possessions and reveals the layout of the property, thus inviting theft. The combined effect of glare from all urban sources creates "sky glow," that yellowish white glow seen in the urban night sky. This is a very recent phenomenon in the history of mankind, beginning with Thomas Edison's invention of the incandescent light bulb. Before this invention, cities were illuminated first by torches and then by gaslight, neither of which contributed much to the overall brightening of the night sky.

3 Not only is light pollution a nuisance, but it is also harmful to life forms whose rhythms depend on celestial events. Birds migrating at night use stars to navigate and can become lost when flying through a heavily light-polluted region that obscures their vision of the night sky. Newly hatched sea turtles have become confused by the urban glow of a nearby coastal city, and instead of moving toward the sea's luminance, crawl toward the city's glow to their death. The circadian rhythms of plants and animals are also affected by a twenty-four-hours-a-day regimen of light. Birds that normally sing at dawn can now be heard singing in the middle of the urban night. Plants will retain their leaves longer near a strong night light and thus will not be properly prepared for the arrival of winter.

4 When we lose the ability to connect visually with the vastness of the universe by looking up at the night sky, we lose our connection with something profoundly important to the human spirit: our sense of wonder. Fortunately, this situation does not have to continue. Unlike other forms of pollution where it may take years to repair the damage, light pollution disappears immediately when corrective action is taken. In the long run, it is cheaper to install and maintain quality lighting that does not waste energy by shining light that is too bright, where it is not needed, and where it is not wanted.

---

19. According to information presented in the passage, light trespass is increasingly a problem
   a. for criminals hiding in shadows.
   b. in suburban and rural areas.
   c. in rainy weather.
   d. for migrating birds.

20. Which of the following lists best outlines the main topics addressed in this passage?
- **a.** ■ Light pollution is a growing problem.
  - ■ Glare and light trespass contribute to light pollution.
  - ■ Light pollution is harmful to life forms.
  - ■ Light pollution can be corrected.
- **b.** ■ A basic component of light pollution is glare.
  - ■ Glare occurs when light shines directly into the eyes.
  - ■ Glare is caused by an unshielded light source.
  - ■ Glare from all urban sources creates "sky glow."
- **c.** ■ Thomas Edison invented the incandescent light bulb.
  - ■ Birds migrating at night use stars to navigate.
  - ■ Glare makes driving on rainy streets hazardous.
  - ■ "Sky glow" is a yellowish white glow in the urban night sky.
- **d.** ■ Before the incandescent light bulb, cities were lit by torches.
  - ■ Plants retain their leaves longer near a strong night light.
  - ■ Newly hatched sea turtles are confused by urban glow.
  - ■ Quality lighting is cheap to install and maintain.

21. Which of the following describes the author's main purpose for writing the passage?
- **a.** to explain why bright exterior lights do not deter burglars
- **b.** to describe the circadian rhythms of plants and animals
- **c.** to highlight the growing problem of light pollution
- **d.** to review the invention and history of the electric light

22. Which of the following statements from the passage expresses an opinion rather than stating a fact?
- **a.** Glare that crosses property boundaries and creates a nuisance is called "light trespass."
- **b.** Not only is light pollution a nuisance, but it is also harmful to life forms whose rhythms depend on celestial events.
- **c.** Unlike other forms of pollution, the damage of which may take years to repair, light pollution disappears immediately when corrective action is taken.
- **d.** When we lose the ability to connect visually with the night sky, we lose our connection with something profoundly important to the human spirit.

23. Which of the following words best defines <u>component</u> as it is used in the second paragraph of the passage?
- **a.** purpose
- **b.** kind
- **c.** appearance
- **d.** element

24. According to information presented in the passage, light pollution affects newly hatched sea turtles by
- **a.** obscuring their vision while they travel during the nighttime.
- **b.** causing them to crawl toward the city's glow rather than the sea's.
- **c.** causing them to be unprepared for the coming of winter.
- **d.** causing them to sing during the night instead of just during the day.

Read the passage, then answer
the six questions that follow.

The Arkwright System

1 The mounting conflict between the colonies
and England in the 1760s and 1770s
reinforced a growing <u>conviction</u> that
Americans should be less dependent on their
mother country for manufacturing.
Spinning bees and bounties encouraged the
manufacture of homespun cloth as a
substitute for English imports. The
manufacturing of cloth outside the
household was associated with relief of the
poor. In Boston and Philadelphia, Houses of
Industry employed poor families to spin for
their daily bread.

2 Such practices rightfully made many pre-
Revolutionary Americans dubious about
manufacturing. After independence, there
were a number of unsuccessful attempts to
establish textile factories. Americans needed
access to the British industrial innovations,
but England had passed laws forbidding the
export of machinery or the emigration of
those who could operate it. Nevertheless, it
was an English immigrant, Samuel Slater,
who finally introduced British cotton
technology to America.

3 Slater had worked his way up from
apprentice to overseer in an English factory
using the Arkwright system. Drawn by
American bounties for the introduction of
textile technology, he passed as a farmer and
sailed for America with details of the
Arkwright water frame committed to
memory. In December 1790, working for
mill owner Moses Brown, he started up the
first permanent American cotton spinning
mill in Pawtucket, Rhode Island. Employing
a workforce of nine children between the

ages of seven and twelve, Slater successfully
mechanized the carding and spinning
processes.

4 A generation of millwrights and textile
workers trained under Slater was the catalyst
for the rapid proliferation of textile mills in
the early nineteenth century. From Slater's
first mill, the industry spread across New
England to places such as North Uxbridge,
Massachusetts. For two decades, before
Lowell mills and those modeled after them
offered competition, the "Rhode Island
System" of small, rural spinning mills set the
tone for early industrialization.

5 By 1800, the mill employed more than 100
workers. A decade later, 61 cotton mills
turning more than 31,000 spindles were
operating in the United States, with Rhode
Island and the Philadelphia region serving as
the main manufacturing centers. The textile
industry was established, although factory
operations were limited to carding and
spinning. This changed when Francis Cabot
Lowell introduced a workable power loom
and the integrated factory in which all textile
production steps took place under one roof.

6 As textile mills proliferated after the turn of
the century, a national debate arose over the
place of manufacturing in American society.
Thomas Jefferson spoke for those supporting
the "yeoman ideal" of a rural republic, at the
heart of which was the independent,
democratic farmer. Foolishly, Jefferson
questioned the spread of factories, worrying
about factory workers' loss of economic
independence. Alexander Hamilton led those
who promoted manufacturing and saw
prosperity growing out of industrial
development. The debate, largely philosophical in the 1790s, grew more urgent after 1830
as textile factories multiplied, and increasing
numbers of Americans worked in them.

25. Which of the following describes the author's main purpose for writing the passage?
- **a.** to account for the decline of rural American society
- **b.** to contrast political views held by the British and the Americans
- **c.** to summarize British laws forbidding the export of industrial machinery
- **d.** to describe the introduction of textile mills in New England

26. Which of the following words best defines *conviction* as it is used in the first paragraph of the passage?
- **a.** sentence
- **b.** boldness
- **c.** belief
- **d.** force

27. Which of the following summaries best captures the most important ideas in the passage?
- **a.** Samuel Slater, a former apprentice and overseer in an English factory, was the person who first introduced British cotton technology to America.
- **b.** The spread of mills across the United States following the turn of the century inspired a national debate over the place of manufacturing in American society.
- **c.** By 1810, 61 cotton mills were operating in the United States, with Rhode Island and the Philadelphia region serving as the main manufacturing centers.
- **d.** Although many pre-Revolutionary Americans were dubious about manufacturing, the Arkwright system eventually helped manufacturing spread throughout the United States.

28. Which of the following statements from the passage expresses an opinion rather than stating a fact?
- **a.** Foolishly, Jefferson questioned the spread of factories, worrying about factory workers' loss of economic independence.
- **b.** The textile industry was established, although factory operations were limited to carding and spinning.
- **c.** England had passed laws forbidding the export of machinery or the emigration of those who could operate it.
- **d.** Thomas Jefferson spoke for those supporting the "yeoman ideal" of a rural republic.

29. Which of the following statements from paragraph 2 of the passage expresses an opinion rather than stating a fact?
- **a.** Such practices rightfully made many pre-Revolutionary Americans dubious about manufacturing.
- **b.** After independence, there were a number of unsuccessful attempts to establish textile factories.
- **c.** England had passed laws forbidding the export of machinery or the emigration of those who could operate it.
- **d.** It was Samuel Slater who finally introduced British cotton technology to America.

30. Which of the following lists best outlines the main topics addressed in paragraph 6 of the passage?

a. ■ Houses of Industry employed poor families to make homespun cloth.
   ■ Slater came to America to introduce textile technology to the country.
   ■ Slater worked for mill owner Moses Brown in December 1790.

b. ■ A national debate about manufacturing in American society arose.
   ■ Thomas Jefferson worried that factory workers would lose independence.
   ■ The debate grew urgent when textile factories multiplied after 1830.

c. ■ Textile mills spread rapidly in the early nineteenth century.
   ■ The textile industry spread across New England.
   ■ The "Rhode Island System" set the tone for early industrialization.

d. ■ The textile industry was established by the year 1800.
   ■ Sixty-one cotton mills were in business by the year 1810.
   ■ Francis Cabot Lowell introduced a power loom and integrated factory.

> **Read the passage, then answer the six questions that follow.**

Chinese Americans in the Gold Rush

1 While there were Chinese in North America before the Gold Rush, documentation from the Gold Rush in the 1850s provides the most reliable starting point for a history of Chinese immigration to America. Most Chinese immigrants entered California through the port of San Francisco. From San Francisco and other ports, many sought their fortunes in other parts of California. The Chinese formed part of the diverse gathering of peoples from throughout the world who contributed to the economic and population <u>explosion</u> that characterized the early history of the state of California. The Chinese who immigrated to the United States at this time were part of a larger exodus from southeast China searching for better economic opportunities and fleeing a situation of political corruption and decline. Most immigrants came from the Pearl River Delta in Guangdong (Canton) Province.

2 Chinese immigrants proved to be productive and resourceful contributors to a multitude of industries and businesses. The initial group of Chinese immigrants sought their livelihood in the gold mines, calling California *Gam Saan*, Gold Mountain. For the mining industry, they built many of the flumes and roads, allowing for easier access and processing of the minerals being extracted. Chinese immigrants faced discrimination immediately upon arrival in California. In mining, they were forced to work older claims, or to work for others. In the 1850s, the United States Constitution reserved the right of naturalization for white immigrants to this country. Thus, Chinese immigrants lived at the whim of local governments with some allowed to become naturalized citizens, but most not. Without this right, it was difficult to pursue livelihoods. For example, Chinese immigrants were unable to own land or file mining claims. Also in the 1850s, the California legislature passed a law taxing all foreign miners. Although stated in general terms, it was enforced chiefly against the Mexicans and the Chinese through 1870. This discrimination occurred in spite of the fact that the Chinese often contributed the crucial labor necessary to the mining enterprise.

3 Discriminatory legislation forced many Chinese people out of the gold fields and into low-paying, menial, and often arduous jobs. In many cases, they took on the most dangerous and least desirable components of work available. They worked on reclaiming marshes in the Central Valley so that the land could become agriculturally productive. They built the stone bridges and fences, constructed roads, and expertly excavated storage areas for the wine industry in Napa and Sonoma counties. The most impressive construction feat of Chinese Americans was their work on the western section of the transcontinental railroad. Chinese American workers laid much of the track for the Central Pacific Railroad through the foothills and over the high Sierra Nevada, much of which involved hazardous work with explosives to tunnel through the hills. Their speed, dexterity, and outright <u>perseverance</u>, often in brutally cold temperatures and heavy snow through two record-breaking winters, is a testimony to their outstanding achievements and contributions to opening up the West.

31. Which of the following statements from the passage states a fact rather than expresses an opinion?
   a. Discriminatory legislation forced many Chinese people out of the gold fields and into low-paying, menial, and often arduous jobs.
   b. The most impressive construction feat of Chinese Americans was their work on the western section of the transcontinental railroad.
   c. They built the stone bridges and fences, constructed roads, and expertly excavated storage areas for the wine industry in Napa and Sonoma counties.
   d. Their speed, dexterity, and outright perseverance, often in brutally cold temperatures and heavy snow through two record-breaking winters, is a testimony to their outstanding achievements and contributions to opening up the West.

32. Which of the following summaries best captures the most important ideas in the passage?
   a. Because they were not allowed to become naturalized citizens, many Chinese Americans had difficulty pursuing their livelihoods, living at the whim of local governments.
   b. Chinese people often took the most arduous, dangerous, and least desirable jobs available outside of gold fields during the Gold Rush.
   c. Most Chinese immigrants came to the port of San Francisco from the Pearl River Delta in Guangdong Province in China.
   d. After immigrating to America during the Gold Rush, many Chinese people contributed greatly to American society even while they were subjected to discrimination.

33. Which of the following words best defines the word explosion as it is used in the first paragraph of the passage?

a. detonation

b. destruction

c. increase

d. outburst

34. Which of the following statements best expresses the author's point of view?

a. The author believes that although they faced some hardships during the Gold Rush, Chinese Americans were basically treated fairly.

b. The author has tremendous respect for the work performed by Chinese Americans during the Gold Rush.

c. The author is surprised that American politicians were not more concerned about making the lives of Chinese immigrants easier.

d. The author admires the United States for allowing Chinese immigrants to come to the country and perform important work.

35. Which of the following words best defines the word perseverance as it is used in the third paragraph of the passage?

a. fearsomeness

b. laziness

c. confusion

d. dedication

36. Which of the following statements provides the best evaluation of the author's credibility?

a. Although clearly sympathetic to Chinese immigrants, the author presents a fact-based account of their hardships during the Gold Rush.

b. The author's bias against the United States government strongly detracts from the credibility of the passage.

c. Despite the fact that the events described in the passage took place over 100 years ago, the author still includes many facts in the passage.

d. The author's misconceptions about the history of Chinese immigrants in America strongly detract from the credibility of the passage.

> **Read the passage, then answer the six questions that follow.**

The Pre-Raphaelite Brotherhood

1 When one thinks of student-led rebellions and the changes they can create, one typically thinks of the struggles of the twentieth century, such as the Civil Rights Movement or antiwar protests of the 1960s. But there have been less dramatic, though no less passionate, rebellions led by young activists in previous centuries—rebellions that had lasting impact on the world around us. One such example is the Pre-Raphaelite Brotherhood.

2 In the mid-1800s, the art world in England was rattled by the initials PRB. The PRB (or Pre-Raphaelite Brotherhood) was founded by William Holman Hunt, John Everett Millais, and Dante Gabriel Rossetti. These three burgeoning artists (the oldest of whom was 21) and their disdain for the artistic

conventions of the time would have a dramatic influence on the art world for generations to come.

3 The PRB was formed in response to the brotherhood's belief that the current popular art being produced in England was lacking in meaning and aesthetic honesty. During the era leading up to the PRB, the Royal Academy dominated British art. The Royal Academy advocated a style that was typically staid and relied heavily on the use of dark amber and brown tones to depict overly idealized landscapes, carefully arranged family portraits and still lifes, and overly dramatic nature scenes, such as a boat caught in stormy seas. By contrast, the PRB believed that art should present subjects that, by their very nature, had greater meaning and more accurately depicted reality. The PRB was committed to bringing greater integrity to art and even went so far as to publish *The Germ*, a journal that extolled the virtues of the PRB's aesthetic principles.

4 To develop subjects with greater meaning, the PRB initially turned to ancient myths and stories from the Bible. Many of the PRB's biblically themed paintings portrayed the religious figures as regular people. This departure from the convention of the time is notable in John Everett Millais's *Christ in the Home of His Parents*. In this painting, Jesus is portrayed as a young boy in his father's carpentry shop. Everyone in the painting, including Christ himself, looks like a common person of that time period, complete with dirty feet and hands. This realism—especially as it related to the Biblical figures—was not well received by many in the art world at the time. Later works done by fellow PRB members, and those inspired by them, utilized themes from

poetry, literature, and medieval tales, often with the aim of highlighting the societal and moral challenges of the time.

5 With the goal of bringing greater honesty to their work, the PRB ignored the convention of painting an imagined or remembered landscape or background. Instead, PRB members would hunt (sometimes for weeks) for locations to incorporate into their paintings and then paint them in exacting detail.

6 The most distinctive aspects of PRB works—both in contrast to the works produced during the early nineteenth century and with the art of today—is their dramatic use of color. By committing themselves to the accurate depiction of nature, the PRB brought a freshness and drama to their work through the copious use of color. Further enhancing their work was a technique they used that involved applying the colored paint on top of wet white paint previously applied to their canvasses. The effect was to make the colors even brighter and more dramatic. Even today, more than 150 years later, PRB paintings have a <u>luminescence</u> beyond those of other works from the same time period. It is believed that their paintings have this quality today because the white layer underneath the colored paint continues to add glowing vividness to the painting.

7 Originally founded by three upstart young men, the PRB had a tremendous influence on an entire generation of artists. William Morris, Ford Maddox Brown, and Edward Burne-Jones are just a few of the significant artists of the time whose work was dramatically influenced by the PRB.

Major Works Created by the Pre-Raphaelite Brotherhood during the 1850s

1850	Dante Gabriel Rossetti's *Annunciation*
1850	Dante Gabriel Rossetti's *Elizabeth Siddal*
1853	Dante Gabriel Rossetti's *First Anniversary*
1854	Dante Gabriel Rossetti's *Found*
1854	Dante Gabriel Rossetti's *Arthur's Tomb*
1854	John Everett Millais's portrait of Ruskin
1855	Dante Gabriel Rossetti's *Beatrice Meeting Dante*
1855	Dante Gabriel Rossetti's *Dante's Vision of Rachel and Leah*
1856	Dante Gabriel Rossetti's *Passover in the Holy Family*
1858	Dante Gabriel Rossetti's *A Christmas Carol*
1858	Dante Gabriel Rossetti's *Seed of David*
1858	John Ruskin's *Rock at Killcrankie*
1859	Dante Gabriel Rossetti's *Writing on the Sand*
1859	Dante Gabriel Rossetti's *Sir Galahad*
1859	Dante Gabriel Rossetti's *Bocca Baciata*

37. According to information presented in the passage, the art world
   a. disliked the PRB's emphasis on realism.
   b. approved of the PRB's choice of subject matter.
   c. appreciated the PRB's attention to detail.
   d. embraced the PRB's style, especially their use of color.

38. Which of the following words best defines the word <u>luminescence</u> as it is used in the sixth paragraph of the passage?
   a. dignity
   b. brightness
   c. beauty
   d. strangeness

39. Which of the following statements best summarizes the main points in paragraph 3 of the passage?
   a. The PRB was so committed to bringing greater integrity to art that they decided to publish *The Germ*, a journal that extolled the virtues of their artistic principles.
   b. The Royal Academy, which dominated British art, advocated a style that depicted carefully posed, overly dramatic scenes, while the PRB wanted to capture reality with greater honesty in their art.
   c. The PRB utilized themes from poetry, literature, and medieval tales, often with the aim of highlighting the societal and moral challenges of the time, in their art.
   d. The PRB used color in a more distinctive and dramatic way than most artists during their time by applying colored paint on top of wet white paint previously applied to their canvasses.

40. According to information presented in the passage, the most distinguishing feature of PRB works is their

   a. surrealism.

   b. contrast to Royal Academy art.

   c. everyday subject matter.

   d. vibrant colors.

41. Which of the following best describes the author's main reason for describing *Christ in the Home of His Parents* in the fourth paragraph of the passage?

   a. to emphasize the reason why the PRB's work did not have a lasting impact

   b. to help readers understand why the PRB was so popular

   c. to illustrate how the PRB's work differed from the art common during their time

   d. to inform readers about the best way to create a painting

42. Information presented in the chart best supports which of the following conclusions?

   a. John Everett Millais's portrait of Ruskin was the most famous painting of the 1850s.

   b. Dante Gabriel Rossetti solely created art based on famous literary works.

   c. John Ruskin preferred posing for portraits by other artists to creating art himself.

   d. Dante Gabriel Rossetti was the most prolific PRB artist during the 1850s.

Writing Subtest

Multiple-Choice Questions

Directions: Read each of the following passages and then choose the one best answer for each of the multiple-choice questions that follow. Each of these passages has numbered parts that are referred to in the associated questions.

> **Read the passage, then answer the four questions that follow.**

(1) A scrapbook is an easy family craft that can reflect the style, format, and contents of its creator's unique personality. (2) All it takes is initiative. (3) Interest and inspiration help, too. (4) Begin by choosing a cover style for your scrapbook which you can purchase premade in a store or create yourself. (5) You might want to use a plastic binder with a clear front cover and decorate it. (6) Next, choose the theme you want for your scrapbook. (7) Is it for your entire family or just you? (8) Do you want it to focus on a single hobby or your life in general? (9) Perhaps you would like it to just be about your career or a memorible vacation.

(10) Do you know what to include in your scrapbook? (11) The more variety you use, the better. (12) How about some photographs, ticket stubs, and postcards? (13) You might want to include personal letters, artwork, or greeting cards. (14) Other probabilities include newspaper clippings, pressed flowers, concert programs, and certificates. (15) I have all of those in mine and it looks fantastic.

1. Which of the following changes would make the sequence of ideas in the passage clearer?

   a. Delete sentence 4.

   b. Delete sentence 10.

   c. Delete sentence 13.

   d. Delete sentence 15.

2. Which part of the passage is missing a comma?

   a. sentence 1

   b. sentence 4

   c. sentence 7

   d. sentence 9

3. Which part of the passage contains a spelling error?

   a. sentence 1
   b. sentence 2
   c. sentence 9
   d. sentence 14

4. Which part of the passage contains an error in word usage?

   a. sentence 5
   b. sentence 11
   c. sentence 13
   d. sentence 14

> **Read the passage, then answer the four questions that follow.**

(1) In a day and age where <u>storytelling</u> is beginning to be considered one of the lost arts, and keeping records means booting up instead of writing down, families may find themselves wondering how to create and preserve their genealogy. (2) Perhaps they want to just save the family stories or trace the most <u>recent</u> generations. (3) Others might want to explore their families' role in history or just put something together to <u>comemorate</u> an anniversary or other important event. (4) Putting together a family tree may sound like a great idea, but how do you even begin to make the first step and how can it be a total family project?

   (5) Investigating the many different people who came before you is a <u>multilayered</u> task that involves asking questions, doing research, combing through real and virtual archives, and even taking a field trip or two to places like cemeteries. (6) After all, a graveyard is really like a museum without walls since it contains fascinating historical artifacts that are hundreds of years old, all in the form of gravestones.

(7) Cemeteries are not the scary places that many horror films try to convey.

   (8) Another great source is the census records that can be found on the Internet. (9) Often, you find out more than just birth and death records. (10) Resources for information include national archives, as well as local family records. (11) Your local library can connect you with basic genealogy guidebooks and reference books as well.

   (12) _____

(13) Grandparents, uncles, aunts, and cousins are often wonderful sources of stories, traditions, facts, and other helpful information. (14) Taking the time to talk to them about family stories can bring all of you closer— another side benefit from a project like this one.

5. Which part of the passage draws attention away from its main idea?

   a. sentence 4
   b. sentence 7
   c. sentence 9
   d. sentence 12

6. Which part of the passage contains an error in comma usage?

   a. sentence 1
   b. sentence 5
   c. sentence 6
   d. sentence 13

7. Which sentence, if added as sentence 12, would be the best topic sentence for third paragraph?

   a. Make sure not to overlook one of the best resources of all—your family.
   b. Grandparents will have the most valuable information for creating a family tree.
   c. Making a family tree is an effective way to bring your family closer together.
   d. The most productive work in creating a family tree will be performed on your own.

8. Which underlined word in the passage is spelled incorrectly?

a. storytelling

b. recent

c. comemorate

d. multilayered

Read the passage, then answer the four questions that follow.

(1) One of the most beautiful resources to inspire any young artist can be found right outside your own front door. (2) The world of nature offers limitless ideas for all the arts—from the beauty of a sunset and the lilting notes of birdsong to the graceful lines of an animal in motion or the starkness of tree limbs against a winter sky. (3) Many of art's most famous masters turned to the world surrounding them to find the inspiration for their masterpieces.

(4) Children can easily become absorbed by nature's beauty, which can be found right outside your own front door. (5) Parents, usually wrapped up in maintaining the daily routine, may not recognize their children's fascination and hurry them along. (6) Cognizant parents can capitalize on these moments and show their children how the purity of a dandelion or the chattering of squirrels can be turned into anything from a sonnet to a sketch to a song.

(7) Best of all, souvenirs from nature are free, bountiful, and inspirational for children, they can use these materials to create incredible works of art. (8) There is a wide variety of artistic mediums, including clay sculpting, charcoal drawing, oil painting, watercolor painting, and photography. (9) Leaves, flowers, seeds, weeds, acorns, bark, and twigs can be brought home and used to create collages, scrapbooks, poems, or ballads, thus preserving nature's beauty indefinitely.

_____

9. Which part of the passage contains a redundant expression of ideas or information?

a. sentence 1

b. sentence 2

c. sentence 3

d. sentence 4

10. Which part of the passage contains an error in apostrophe usage?

a. sentence 3

b. sentence 4

c. sentence 5

d. sentence 8

11. Which part of the passage draws attention away from the main idea?

a. sentence 4

b. sentence 5

c. sentence 8

d. sentence 9

12. Which part of the passage contains a run-on sentence?

a. sentence 4

b. sentence 6

c. sentence 7

d. sentence 9

Read the passage, then answer the four questions that follow.

(1) Snowboarding, often described as a snow sport that combines skateboarding and surfing, is an increasingly common winter sport throughout the world. (2) Snowboarding involves strapping a board to one's feet and sliding down snow-covered mountains. (3) In addition to the snowboard, a snowboarder's

equipment consists of special boots that attach to the board.

(4)Some find snowboarding more difficult to learn than skiing; others consider it easier, requiring the mastery of one board as opposed to two skis and two poles. (5)Other popular snow sports include skiing, bobsledding, and snowmobiling. (6)All agree, though, that once the sport is mastered, it is exciting, stimulating, and fun, and quite similar to both skateboarding and surfing. (7)Those who excel in the sport may even find himself bound for the olympics since snowboarding became medal-eligible in 1998.

13. Which part of the passage contains a redundant expression of ideas or information?
   a. sentence 2
   b. sentence 3
   c. sentence 4
   d. sentence 6

14. Which change is needed in the passage?
   a. Sentence 1: Change "combines" to "combine."
   b. Sentence 2: Change "snow-covered" to "snow covered."
   c. Sentence 6: Change "agree" to "agreed."
   d. Sentence 7: Change "himself" to "themselves."

15. Which part of the passage draws attention away from the main idea of paragraph 2?
   a. sentence 4
   b. sentence 5
   c. sentence 6
   d. sentence 7

16. Which part of the passage contains an error in capitalization?
   a. sentence 1
   b. sentence 3
   c. sentence 5
   d. sentence 7

Read the passage, then answer the four questions that follow.
(Note: An error in paragraph organization has been purposely included in the first paragraph.)

(1) Thanks to advanced techniques, an implanted probe can stimulate individual neurons electrically or chemically and then record responses. (2) Preliminary results suggest that the microprobe telemetry systems can be permanently implanted and replace damaged or missing nerves. (3) The tissue-compatible microprobes represent an advance over the aluminum wire electrodes used in studies of the cortex and other brain structures. (4) Previously, researchers data was accumulated using traditional electrodes, but there is a question of how much damage they cause to the nervous system. (5) Microprobes, since they are slightly thinner than a human hair, cause minimal damage and disruption of neurons when inserted into the brain because of their diminutive width. (6) By using tiny probes as neural prostheses, scientists may be able to restore nerve function in quadriplegics, make the blind see, or make the deaf hear.

(7) In addition to recording nervous system impulses, the microprobes have minuscule channels that open the way for delivery of drugs, cellular growth factors, neurotransmitters, and other neuroactive compounds to a single neuron or to groups of neurons. (8) The probes usually have up to four

channels. (9) Each with its own recording/stim-ulating electrode.

17. Which change is needed in the passage?
   a. Sentence 4: Change "researchers" to "researchers."
   b. Sentence 5: Change "their" to "its."
   c. Sentence 5: Change "than" to "then."
   d. Sentence 9: Change "its" to "it's."

18. Which part of the passage contains a redundant expression of ideas or information?
   a. sentence 1
   b. sentence 4
   c. sentence 5
   d. sentence 8

19. Which of the following would make the sequence of ideas in the first paragraph clearer?
   a. Move sentence 1 after sentence 6.
   b. Delete sentence 1.
   c. Move sentence 6 before sentence 1.
   d. Delete sentence 6.

20. Which part of the passage contains a fragment?
   a. sentence 2
   b. sentence 5
   c. sentence 8
   d. sentence 9

Read the passage, then answer the four questions that follow.
(Note: An error in paragraph organization has been purposely included in the passage.)

---

(1) Loud noises on trains not only irritate passengers but also create unsafe situations and can be extremely annoying. (2) Therefore, such behavior is prohibited by law and by agency policy. (3) A passenger might create a disturbance by playing excessively loud music or making loud noises in some other manner. (4) Therefore, conductors follow a specific list of procedures. (5) In the event a passenger creates a disturbance, the conductor will ask the passenger to turn off the music or stop making the loud noise politely. (6) If the passenger refuses to comply, the conductor will tell the passenger that he or she is in violation of the law and train policy and will have to leave the train if he or she will not comply to the request. (7) If police assistance is requested, the conductor will stay at the location from which the call to the command center was placed or the silent alarm used. (8) Conductors will wait there until the police arrive, will allow passengers off the train at this point, and will not allow passengers on until the situation is resolved. (9) Train conductors are also tasked with checking tickets and collecting fares from passengers.

21. Which part of the passage draws attention away from the main idea?
   a. sentence 3
   b. sentence 5
   c. sentence 7
   d. sentence 9

22. Which of the following changes would make the sequence of ideas in the passage clearer?
   a. Delete sentence 2.
   b. Reverse the order of sentence 2 and sentence 3.
   c. Delete sentence 7.
   d. Reverse the order of sentence 7 and sentence 8.

23. Which part of the passage contains a nonstandard use of a preposition?
   a. sentence 2
   b. sentence 6
   c. sentence 7
   d. sentence 8

24. Which part of the passage contains a redundant expression of ideas or information?
   a. sentence 1
   b. sentence 4
   c. sentence 5
   d. sentence 7

> **Read the passage, then answer the four questions that follow.**
> (Note: An error in paragraph organization has been purposely included in the passage.)

(1) Augustus Saint-Gaudens was born March 1, 1848, in Dublin, Ireland, to Bernard Saint-Gaudens, a French shoemaker, and Mary McGuinness, his Irish wife. (2) Six months later, the family immigrated to New York City, where Augustus grew up. (3) Upon completion of school at age 13, he expressed strong interest in art as a career so his father apprenticed him to a cameo cutter. (4) While working days at his cameo lathe, Augustus also took art classes at the Cooper Union and the National Academy of Design. (5) At 19, his apprenticeship completed, Augustus traveled to Paris where he studied under Francois Jouffry at the renown Ecole des Beaux-Arts. (6) In 1870, he left Paris for Rome, where for the next five years he <u>studies</u> classical art and architecture, and worked on his first commissions. (7) In 1876, he received his first major commission—a monument to Civil War Admiral David Glasgow Farragut. (8) Unveiled in New York's Madison Square in 1881, the monument was a tremendous success; its combination of realism and allegory was a departure from previous American sculpture. (9) Augustus Saint-Gaudens died in 1907 at the age of 59. (10) Saint-Gaudens's fame grew, and other commissions were quickly forthcoming.

25. Which part of the passage requires a comma to separate two independent clauses?
   a. sentence 1
   b. sentence 3
   c. sentence 7
   d. sentence 10

26. Which of the following choices should replace the underlined word in sentence 6?
   a. studied
   b. will study
   c. had been studying
   d. would have studied

27. Which change is needed in the passage?
   a. Sentence 2: Change "where" to "when."
   b. Sentence 3: Change "expressed" to "impressed."
   c. Sentence 5: Change "renown" to "renowned."
   d. Sentence 8: Change "its" to "it's."

28. Which of the following changes would make the sequence of ideas in the passage clearer?
   a. Delete sentence 9.
   b. Reverse the order of sentence 7 and sentence 8.
   c. Delete sentence 10.
   d. Reverse the order of sentence 9 and sentence 10.

> **Read the passage, then answer the four questions that follow.**

(1) Choosing a doctor is an important <u>decision</u>. (2) Here are some things you can do to make the best choice. (3) The single most important thing is to interview the doctors you are considering. (4) Ask questions about the practice, office hours, and how quickly he or

she responds to phone calls. (5) Pay attention to the doctor's <u>communication</u> skills and how comfortable you are with them. (6) The second thing you should do is check the doctors credentials. (7) One way to do this is to ask your health care insurance company how they checked the doctor's credentials before excepting him or her into their network. (8) The cost of healthcare insurance is quite high, and many families have difficulty affording it. (9) Finally, spend a little time talking with the <u>receptionist</u>. (10) Keep in mind that this is the person you'll come into contact with every time you call or come into the office. (11) If he or she is pleasant and <u>eficient</u>, it will certainly make your overall experience better.

29. Which part of the passage contains a redundant expression of ideas or information?
  a. sentence 3
  b. sentence 4
  c. sentence 8
  d. sentence 10

30. Which underlined word in the passage is spelled incorrectly?
  a. decision
  b. communication
  c. receptionist
  d. eficient

31. Which part of the passage contains an error in word usage?
  a. sentence 2
  b. sentence 3
  c. sentence 7
  d. sentence 10

32. Which part of the passage contains an error in punctuation?
  a. sentence 4
  b. sentence 6
  c. sentence 8
  d. sentence 10

Read the passage, then answer the three questions that follow.

(1) _____

(2) Although it is not a particularly long street Dubliners will tell the visitor proudly that it is the widest street in all of Europe. (3) This claim usually meets with protests, especially from French tourists who claim the Champs Elysees of Paris as Europe's widest street. (4) But the witty Dubliner will not surrender bragging rights easily and will trump the French visitor with a fine distinction: The Champs Elysees is the widest boulevard, but O'Connell is the widest street.

(5) Divided by several important monuments running the length of its center, the street is named for Daniel O'Connell, an Irish patriot. (6) An impressive monument to him towers over the entrance of lower O'Connell Street and overlooking the Liffey River. (7) O'Connell stands high above the unhurried crowds of shoppers, businesspeople, and students on a sturdy column; he is surrounded by four serene angels seated at each corner of the monument's base.

33. Which change is needed in the passage?
  a. Sentence 5: Change "running" to "run."
  b. Sentence 5: Change "Irish" to "irish."
  c. Sentence 6: Change "overlooking" to "overlooks."
  d. Sentence 7: Replace the semicolon with a comma.

34. Which sentence, if added as sentence 1, would be the most effective topic sentence for the first paragraph of the passage?

    a. O'Connell Street is the main thoroughfare of Dublin City.

    b. In 1998, Dublin City officials formed a plan to renovate O'Connell Street.

    c. Dublin is Ireland's largest city and capital.

    d. Daniel O'Connell was known in Ireland as "The Liberator."

35. Which change is needed in the passage?

    a. Sentence 2: Insert a comma after "that."

    b. Sentence 2: Insert a comma after "street."

    c. Sentence 3: Replace the comma after "protests" with a semicolon.

    d. Sentence 4: Remove the colon after "distinction."

Short-Answer Questions

Directions: Each of the following seven questions contains two errors in construction, grammar, usage, spelling, capitalization, or punctuation. Rewrite each sentence so these errors are revised but the original meaning remains, without introducing any new errors.

36. At the local community library, Patrons may check out an unlimited number of books, but the overdue fines are more higher than at other libraries.

_____

_____

_____

_____

37. Televisions, which have been a part of American culture for half a century, is more prevalent in American homes than functioning bathrooms.

_____

_____

_____

_____

38. Several award winning authors publish only one book per year, but, due to the ongoing media coverage, appeared to write much more.

_____

_____

_____

39. Ray sat down at his piano, and began playing along with the melody being sung by the sparrow perches outside his window.

_____

_____

_____

_____

40. Paul has a large record collection, the most impressive piece in it is a like-new copy of *The Dark side of the Moon* by Pink Floyd he bought in 1973.

_____

_____

_____

41. Weather I'll be playing on the baseball team this summer depends on what the doctor says about my swolen ankle.

_____

_____

_____

42. While walking to the office Mrs. Mackavey found a silver man's ring lying on the sidewalk.

_____

_____

_____

Writing Summary Exercise

Directions: Use the following passage to prepare a summary of 100 to 150 words.

While a baby is not faced with many serious ethical dilemmas, his or her moral character is formed from the earliest stages of infancy. Recent research has shown that the type of parenting an infant receives has a dramatic impact on the child's moral development and, consequently, success later in life. The renowned childcare expert T. Berry Brazelton claims that he can observe a child of eight months and tell whether that child will succeed or fail in life. This may be a harsh sentence for an eight-month-old baby, but it underscores the importance of educating parents in good child-rearing techniques and of intervening early in cases of child endangerment. But what are good parenting techniques?

The cornerstone of good parenting is love, and the building blocks are trust, acceptance, and discipline. The concept of "attachment parenting" has come to dominate early childhood research. It is the relatively simple idea that an infant who is firmly attached to his or her primary caregiver—often, but not always, the mother—develops into a secure and confident child. Caregivers who respond promptly and affectionately to their infants' needs—to eat, to play, to be held, to sleep, and to be left alone—form secure attachments with their children. A study conducted with rhesus monkeys showed that infant monkeys preferred mothers who gave comfort and contact but no food to mothers who gave food but no comfort and contact. This study indicates that among primates, love and nurturing are even more important than food.

Fortunately, loving their infants comes naturally to most parents, and the first requisite for good parenting is one that is easily met. The second component—setting limits and teaching self-discipline—can be more complicated. Many parents struggle to find a balance between responding promptly to their babies' needs and spoiling their child. Norton Garfinkle, chair of the Executive Committee of the Lamaze Institute for Family Education, has identified four parenting styles: warm and restrictive, warm and permissive, cold and restrictive, and cold and permissive. A warm parent is one who exhibits love and affection; a cold parent withholds love; a restrictive parent sets limits on her child's behavior and a permissive parent does not restrict her child. Garfinkle finds that the children of warm-restrictive parents exhibit self-confidence and self-control; the children of warm-permissive parents are self-assured but have difficulty following rules; children of cold-restrictive parents tend to be angry and sullenly compliant, and the most troubled children are those of cold-permissive parents. These children are hostile and defiant.

While many parents will come to good parenting techniques instinctually and through various community supports, others parents are not equipped for the trials of raising a baby. Are these babies doomed to lives of frustration, poor impulse control, and antisocial behavior?

Certainly not. Remedial actions—such as providing enrichment programs at daycare centers and educating parents—can be taken to reverse the effects of bad parenting. However, the research indicates that the sooner these remedies are put into action, the better.

Open Response: Writing Summary Exercise

_____

_____

_____

_____

_____

_____

_____

_____

_____

_____

_____

_____

Composition Exercise

Directions: Read the following quote below about courage; then follow the instructions for writing your composition.

In his play, *The Admirable Crighton*, J.M. Barrie wrote, "Courage is the thing. All goes if courage goes."

Your purpose is to write a persuasive composition, to be read by a classroom instructor, in which you describe a time in your life when you had the courage to do something or face something difficult, or when you feel you fell short. What did you learn from the experience?

Open Response: Composition Exercise

_____

_____

_____

_____

_____

_____

_____

_____

_____

_____

_____

_____

_____

Reading Subtest Answers

1. b. Choice **b** includes the main points of the selection and is not too broad. Choice **a** features minor points from the selection. Choice **c** also features minor points, with the addition of "History of the National Park System," which is not included in the selection. Choice **d** lists points that are not discussed in the selection.

2. d. Choice **d** expresses the main idea of paragraph 4 of the selection. The information in choices **a**, **b**, and **c** is not expressed in paragraph 4.

3. c. Paragraph 4 discusses the visitors to Acadia National Park; therefore, choice **c** is correct. Choices **a**, **b**, and **d** are not mentioned in the selection.

4. d. The idea that the best part of the island is Acadia National Park is just the author's opinion, while the other answer choices describe inarguable facts.

5. a. The word *spent* makes the most sense if used in place of *expended* in the sentence from paragraph 1, so choice **a** is the best answer. The other answer choices do not make as much sense.

6. c. The word *continually* makes the most sense if used in place of *perpetually* in the sentence from paragraph 4, so choice **c** is the best answer. The other answer choices do not make as much sense.

7. a. See the second and third paragraphs for reference to heart problems with anorexia, the fourth and fifth paragraphs for discussion of heart problems with bulimia, and the last paragraph, where heart disease is mentioned, as a risk in obese people who suffer from binge eating disorder.

8. b. The first sentence of the fifth paragraph tells us that bulimia sufferers are often able to keep their problem a secret, partly because they maintain a normal or above-normal weight.

9. c. In the second paragraph, the thyroid gland function is mentioned as slowing down—one effort on the part of the body to protect itself.

10. a. According to the second paragraph, dehydration contributes to constipation.

11. b. As stated in the opening sentence of the third paragraph, bulimia patients may exercise obsessively.

12. d. See the second sentence of the fourth paragraph. If as many as one-third of the binge eating disorder population are men, it stands to reason that up to two-thirds are younger women, given that we have learned that about 90% of all eating disorder sufferers are adolescent and young adult women.

13. c. According to paragraph 2, *Deep, underlying fissures that already existed in the economy* led to the Great Depression.

14. a. The passage is primarily an account that describes the causative factors (for example, tariff and war debt policies, disproportionate wealth, and the accumulation of debt) that led to the Depression, and its effects (for example, business failures, bank closings, homelessness, federal relief programs).

15. c. Paragraph 1 states that shantytowns were called *Hoovervilles* because citizens blamed their plight on the Hoover administration's refusal to offer assistance.

16. b. Although *policies* can refer to regulations or *laws* (choice **c**) or guiding principles or *theories* (choice **a**), in this context, *policies* refers to the courses of action that are taken, from which a government or business intends to influence decisions or actions. Choice **b** is the only answer that implies action.

17. d. The passage describes the decade as one in which spending dominated over prudent measures like saving (paragraph 3). The wild stock market speculation, also described in that paragraph, is another example of extravagance.

18. b. The analogy depicts the stock market crash of 1929 as a weakening agent to the economy (the way a stressful event may weaken the body's resistance to illness).

19. b. The passage states that light trespass is becoming an important issue in many suburban and rural communities. Choice **a** is refuted in the passage, as light trespass can actually help criminals. Choices **c** and **d** are mentioned in other contexts.

20. a. Choice **a** adequately outlines the main topics addressed in each paragraph of the passage. Choice **b** only outlines paragraph 2, rather than addressing the passage as a whole. Choices **c** and **d** simply gather random details scattered throughout the passage.

21. c. While choices **a** and **b** are topics mentioned in the passage, the main point of the passage is to discuss the growing problem of light pollution.

22. d. In choices **a**, **b**, and **c**, the writer reports facts that can be verified by research. Choice **d** best reflects an opinion of the writer that is difficult or impossible to verify with facts.

23. d. The word *element* makes the most sense if used in place of *component* in the sentence from paragraph 2, so choice **d** is the best answer. The other answer choices do not make as much sense.

24. b. In paragraph 3, the author writes: *Newly hatched sea turtles have become confused by the urban glow of a nearby coastal city, and instead of moving toward the sea's luminance, crawl toward the city's glow and their death.* Choices **a** and **d** describe how light pollution affects birds, and choice **c** describes how it affects plants.

25. d. The passage describes the introduction of *British cotton technology to America* (paragraph 2), specifically to New England.

26. c. Although *conviction* can mean a prison *sentence* (choice **a**) or sense of boldness (choice **b**), or an expression of *force* (choice **d**), in this context, *conviction* refers to the *belief* that Americans should be less dependent on their mother country for manufacturing.

27. d. This is the only answer choice that adequately summarizes the main details of the passage. Although Samuel Slater is an important person in this passage, his life is not its main purpose, so choice **a** is not a good summary of the passage. Choices **b** and **c** also focus on specific details that do not capture the purpose of the passage as a whole.

28. a. This is an opinion because not everyone might agree that Jefferson's questioning of the spread of factories was foolish. The other choices describe inarguable facts.

29. a. The idea that the practices of employing *poor families to spin for their daily bread*, as described in paragraph 1, made pre-Revolutionary Americans *rightful* in their distrust of manufacturing is not an inarguable fact. It is an opinion of the author's that might not be shared by all other people.

30. b. Choice **b** addresses the main ideas in paragraph 6 of the passage. Choice **c** outlines paragraph 4 and choice **d** outlines paragraph 5, rather than 6.

31. a. Choice **a** is the only indisputable fact among the answer choices. Not everyone might agree that their work on the western section of the transcontinental railroad was the most impressive construction feat of Chinese Americans, so choice **b** is an opinion. The same can be said for the opinion that Chinese Americans *expertly* excavated storage areas for the wine industry (choice **c**) and the opinion that Chinese Americans' achievements and contributions to opening up the West are *outstanding*.

32. d. Choice **d** summarizes the main points of the passage better than the other choices, which focus on specific details rather than the passage as a whole.

33. c. Although *explosion* can mean a *detonation* from explosives (choice **a**) that causes *destruction* (choice **b**), or it can mean an angry *outburst* (choice **d**), in this context, *explosion* means the *increase* of economic industries and population in the early history of California.

34. b. By stating that Chinese Americans made *outstanding achievements and contributions to opening up the West* in paragraph 3, the author reveals his or her tremendous respect for the work they performed.

35. d. The word *dedication* is the only choice that makes sense if used in place of *perseverance* in the sentence from paragraph 3, so choice **d** is the best answer.

36. a. Although the author may voice a few opinions in favor of the intelligence, abilities, and work ethic of Chinese Americans, the passage remains a fact-based history rather than a mere opinion piece. Even though the events in the passage did take place a long time ago, there is no reason to believe that era is not well-documented, so choice **c** is not the best one.

37. a. Paragraph 4 states that the PRB's *realism—especially as it related to the Biblical figures—was not well received by many in the art world at the time.*

38. b. The word *brightness* makes the most sense if used in place of *luminescence* in the sentence from paragraph 6, so choice **b** is the best answer. The other answer choices are not as accurate.

39. b. Choice **b** summarizes the most important details in the third paragraph. Choice **a** merely focuses on a single detail without addressing the paragraph as a whole. Choices **c** and **d** focus on details from other paragraphs.

40. d. The topic sentence of the sixth paragraph states that *The most distinctive aspects of PRB works . . . is their dramatic use of color.*

41. c. By describing how *Christ in the Home of His Parents* depicts a Biblical figure as a regular person, the author illustrates how the PRB's work differed from the work of the majority of artists, who portrayed Biblical figures as extraordinary. The author mentions that *Christ in the Home of his Parents was not well received by many in the art world at the time*, so choice **b** is incorrect.

42. d. The overwhelming number of artworks created by Dante Gabriel Rossetti during the 1850s is a testament to his status as a very prolific artist. Although he created a number of works based on famous literature, such as *A Christmas Carol*, the chart does not suggest that he *only* painted works based on famous literature, so choice **b** can be eliminated.

Writing Subtest Answers

Multiple Choice

1. d. Sentence 16 is written from a personal point-of-view that is inconsistent with the rest of the passage, which is informative and impersonal.

2. b. Sentence 2 is a compound sentence and needs a comma to separate its two clauses. The comma should be placed between the words *scrapbook* and *which*.

3. c. The word *memorable* is misspelled in sentence 9 of the passage.

4. d. The word *probabilities* does not make sense in this context. The correct word is *possibilities*.

5. c. This content question asks you to pick the sentence that does not belong in the essay. The only sentence that veers off topic is about cemeteries in scary movies. The rest of the choices are all relevant and relate directly to the main idea.

6. b. Choice **b** requires a comma to separate two of its independent clauses. The comma should be placed between the words *and* and *how*. Choice **a** is incorrect because the commas are used to separate the sentences' independent clauses correctly. Choices **c** and **d** are incorrect because they both use commas to separate listed items correctly.

7. a. The paragraph discusses how one's family is a great resource for putting together a family tree, so choice **a** is the best topic sentence. Although sentence 13 mentions that grandparents may be *wonderful sources of stories, traditions, facts, and other helpful information*, there is no reason to believe that they will always have more valuable information than uncles, aunts, and cousins, also mentioned in the sentence. Therefore, choice **b** is incorrect. Choice **c** merely repeats information from sentence 14, so it is not a good topic sentence. The paragraph discusses the importance of performing work with others, so choice **d** does not make any sense as a topic sentence for this paragraph.

8. c. The word *commemorate* is misspelled in sentence 3. Choices **a**, **b**, and **d** are all spelled correctly.

9. d. The idea that nature's beauty *can be found right outside your own front door* had already been expressed in sentence 1, therefore it is redundant in sentence 4.

10. a. The word *art's* is written in the possessive form, but it should be both possessive and plural. Therefore, the apostrophe should come after the *s* and be written *arts'*. Choices **b**, **c**, and **d** all use apostrophes correctly.

11. c. A list of artistic mediums does not serve any purpose at this point in the passage and it draws attention from the main idea, which is nature as inspiration to young artists. Choices **a**, **b**, and **d** are all relevant to this main idea.

12. c. Sentence 7 is a run-on sentence because it is missing the necessary conjunction to link its two independent clauses. The sentence should contain the word *and*, reading, *Best of all, souvenirs from nature are free, bountiful, and inspirational for children, and they can use these materials to create incredible works of art.*

13. d. Sentence 1 already mentioned the similarity between snowboarding and skateboarding and surfing, so this information does not need to be repeated in sentence 6. Choices **a**, **b**, and **c** are incorrect because they all contain information that is not needlessly repeated elsewhere in the passage.

14. d. This choice provides the plural reflexive pronoun *themselves*, which agrees in number and person with the subject, *Those*. Choice **a** is incorrect because it provides the verb *combine* which does not agree in person or in number with the subject, *snowboarding*. Choice **b** is incorrect because it removes a hyphen necessary to the creation of compound adjectives. Choice **c** is incorrect because it changes the verb to the past tense, which does not agree with the present tense used throughout the paragraph.

15. b. A list of popular snow sports does not contribute anything to the paragraph's main idea, which is the difficulty and rewards of snowboarding. Choices **a**, **c**, and **d** are incorrect because they all maintain focus on this idea.

16. d. The word Olympics in sentence 7 should be capitalized because it is a special event, and therefore, a proper noun. Choices **a**, **b**, and **c** are all capitalized correctly.

17. a. This question calls on the ability to identify standard usage of the possessive form. Choice **a** is correct because the word *researchers* is actually a possessive noun, and so an apostrophe must be added. Choice **b** is incorrect because it contains a faulty pronoun/antecedent—the *microprobes* have a diminutive width, not the brain. Choices **c** and **d** are incorrect because they substitute misused homonyms for the words given.

18. c. The phrases *since they [microprobes] are slightly thinner than a human hair* and *because of their [microprobes'] diminutive width* contain the same information.

19. c. Sentence 6 includes the topic of the passage, and therefore should be placed at the beginning of it. Choice **a** is incorrect because sentence 1 contains information that is further developed in sentence 2. All sentences in paragraph 1 are relevant to its main topic and should not be deleted, so Choices **b** and **d** are incorrect.

20. d. Sentence 9 lacks a subject, so it is a fragment. Sentence 8 may be a short sentence, but it is a complete sentence, so choice **c** is incorrect. Choices **a** and **b** are also complete sentences.

21. d. The main idea of this passage is loud noises on trains, and the fact that train conductors must check tickets and collect fares from passengers has nothing to do with this topic. Choices **a**, **b**, and **c** are incorrect because they all maintain focus on the main idea.

22. b. Sentence 3 develops on the idea of sentence 1 by mentioning how passengers might make loud noises on a train, so it should be placed immediately after sentence 1 as sentence 2. Deleting sentence 2 would not improve the sequence of ideas in the passage, because the fact that loud noises on trains are prohibited by law is useful information, so choice **a** is incorrect. Choice **c** also contains useful information, so deleting it would be incorrect, as well. Sentence 8 develops upon information introduced in sentence 7, so reversing the order of these two sentences would make the sequence of ideas in the passage less clear.

23. b. Sentence 6 contains a nonstandard use of a preposition. The standard idiom is *comply with* rather than *comply to*. Choices **a**, **c**, and **d** do not contain nonstandard uses of prepositions.

24. a. The sentence states that loud noises on trains both *irritate passengers* and can be *extremely annoying*. Because *irritate* and *annoy* basically share the same meaning, this sentence contains an unnecessary repetition of information.

25. b. Sentence 3 requires a comma before the coordinate conjunction *so*. Choices **a** and **c** are incorrect because each contains only one independent clause. Choice **d** is incorrect because it already shows a comma separating the two independent clauses.

26. a. This answer is in the simple past tense, which is the tense used throughout the paragraph. Choices **b**, **c**, and **d** are incorrect because they suggest tenses inconsistent with the tense of the rest of the paragraph.

27. c. The context requires that the noun *renown* be replaced by the adjective *renowned*. Choice **a** is incorrect because the change to *when* makes no sense in the context; it would imply that Augustus grew up before immigrating. Choice **b** is incorrect because it introduces a diction error into the sentence. Choice **d** incorrectly inserts the contraction of subject and verb *it is* in a context where the possessive pronoun *its* is required.

28. a. This passage focuses on the beginning of Augustus Saint-Gaudens's career, so information about his death is irrelevant to this main idea. Moving sentence 9 would not change this fact, so choice **d** is incorrect. Choice **b** is incorrect because sentence 7 discusses an event from 1876 and sentence 8 discusses an event from 1881 and reversing the order of these sentences would not be chronologically correct. Deleting sentence 10 would remove the necessary conclusion from the passage, so choice **c** is incorrect, as well.

29. c. Sentence 8 provides information about the high cost of healthcare insurance. It doesn't give information about the main topic of this passage, which is how to choose a doctor. Choices **a**, **b**, and **d** are incorrect because all these sentences provide information about, and guidelines for, choosing a doctor.

30. d. The word *efficient* is misspelled in sentence 11. Choices **a**, **b**, and **c** are all spelled correctly.

31. c. The word *excepting* means *excluding* and doesn't make sense in this context. The correct word is the homophone *accepting*, which means *welcoming*. Choices **a**, **b**, and **d** do not contain errors in word usage.

32. b. The word *doctor's* requires an apostrophe because the doctor is singular and possesses the *credentials* in this context.

33. c. To make the pair of verbs in the sentence parallel, *overlooking* should be changed to *overlooks* to match the form of the verb *towers*. Choice **a** is incorrect because the word *running* is functioning as an adjective here; the verb *run* would make nonsense of the sentence. Choice **b** is incorrect because *Irish*, as the name of a people, must be capitalized. Choice **d** is incorrect because the change would convert sentence 7 into a run-on sentence.

34. a. Choice **a** adequately sets up the topic of O'Connell Street. The passage does not mention plans to renovate O'Connell Street, so choice **b** is incorrect. Choice **c** suggests that Dublin is the main topic of the passage, not O'Connell Street, so it is incorrect. Choice **d** is incorrect because Daniel O'Connell is not mentioned until the second paragraph, and isn't the main subject of the passage, anyway.

35. b. A comma is required after an introductory dependent clause. Choice **a** would introduce a comma fault, separating a verb from its object. Choice **c** is incorrect because the semicolon would have to be followed by a complete sentence, which is not the case. Choice **d** is incorrect because removing the colon would create a run-on sentence.

Short Answer

36. This sentence should read, *At the local community library, patrons may check out an unlimited number of books, but the overdue fines are much higher than at other libraries.* The word *more* should not be used to modify the comparative form of a word, such as *higher*. Therefore, it should be replaced with *much*. Since the word *patrons* is not a proper noun, it should not be capitalized.

37. This sentence should read, *Televisions, which have been a part of American culture for half a century, are more prevalent in American homes than functioning bathrooms.* In this question, the subject (*televisions*) has been separated from the verb (*is*) by a dependent clause (*which have been a part of American culture for half a century*). Also, the word *prevalent* is spelled incorrectly.

38. This sentence should read, *Several award-winning authors publish only one book per year, but due to the ongoing media coverage, appear to write much more.* There are two verbs in this sentence, and they must be in the same tense. The first verb (*publish*) is present, but the second one (*appeared*) is past. The verb should be changed to *appear*. Furthermore, *award-winning* is a compound adjective, so it needs to be hyphenated.

39. This sentence should read, *Ray sat down at his piano and began playing along with the melody being sung by the sparrow perched outside his window.* There should not be a comma in this sentence because *began playing along with the melody being sung by the sparrow perched outside his window* is not an independent clause. The word *perches* is also incorrect because it is in the present tense while the rest of the sentence is written in the past tense. Therefore, it should be replaced with *perched*.

40. This sentence should read, *Paul has a large record collection, and the most impressive piece in it is a like-new copy of* The Dark Side of the Moon *by Pink Floyd he bought in 1967.* In this question, this is a run-on sentence because it does not have the conjunction *and* needed to separate its two independent clauses. The question also tests your knowledge of capitalization because the word *Side* needs to be capitalized since it is part of a title.

41. This sentence should read, *Whether or not I'll be playing on the baseball team this summer depends on what the doctor says about my swollen ankle.* The word *Weather* refers to atmospheric conditions, which does not make sense in this context. It should be replaced with the homophone *Whether*, which is a conjunction used to introduce an alternative. Also the word *swollen* is misspelled.

42. This sentence should read, *While walking to the office, Mrs. Mackavey found a man's silver ring lying on the sidewalk.* The first error is a missing comma, which is needed to offset the introductory phrase *While walking to the office* from the rest of the sentence. The second error is a misplaced modifier. The question suggests the *man* is *silver*, when the word *silver* should modify *ring*.

Sample Strong Response for Writing Summary Exercise

Research shows that a child's sense of morality forms when he or she is a mere infant. The type of parenting an infant receives affects the child's moral development and success later in life. The best parenting technique is rich in trust, acceptance, and discipline. Parents who respond promptly and affectionately to their infants' needs form strong bonds with their children. Parents must also set limits and teach self-discipline to babies by exhibiting love and affection, as well as self-confidence and self-control. Parents who are cold and permissive tend to raise children who are hostile and defiant. Such children may benefit from enrichment programs at daycare centers and parental education programs, but parents must not waste any time if they intend to use such remedies.

Sample Strong Response for Composition Exercise

Courage and cowardice seem like absolutes. We are often quick to label other people, or ourselves, either "brave" or "timid," "courageous" or "cowardly." However, one bright afternoon on a river deep in the wilds of the Ozark Mountains, I learned that these qualities are as changeable as mercury.

During a cross-country drive, my friend Nina and I decided to stop at a campsite in Missouri and spend the afternoon on a float trip down Big Piney River, 14 miles through the wilderness. We rented a canoe and paddled happily off.

Things went fine—for the first seven or eight miles. We gazed at the overhanging bluffs, commented on the wonderful variety of trees, and marveled at the clarity of the water. Then, in approaching a bend in the river the current suddenly swept us in toward the bank, underneath the low-hanging branches of a weeping willow. The canoe tipped over and I was pulled under, my foot caught for just a few seconds on the submerged roots of the willow. Just as I surfaced, taking my first frantic gulp of air, I saw the canoe sweeping out, upright again, but empty, and Nina frantically swimming after it. I knew I should help but I was petrified and hung my head in shame as I let my friend brave the treacherous rapids and haul the canoe back onto the gravel bar, while I stood by cravenly.

Then came the scream. Startled, I glanced up to see Nina, both hands over her eyes, dash off the gravel bar and back into the water. I gazed down into the canoe to see, coiled in the bottom of it, the unmistakable, black-and-brown, checkerboard-patterned form of a copperhead snake.

Nina was still screaming, but I was calm in a way that must have seemed smug. Gently I prodded it with the oar until it reared up, slithered over the side of the canoe, and raced away—terrified, itself—into the underbrush.

Later that night, in our cozy, safe motel room, we agreed that we each had cold chills thinking about what might have happened. Still, I learned something important from the ordeal. I know that, had we encountered only the rapids, I might have come away ashamed, labeling myself a coward, and had we encountered only the snake, Nina might have done the same. And I also know that neither of us will ever again be quite so apt to brand another person as lacking courage. Because we will always know that, just around the corner, may be the snake or the bend in the river or the figure in the shadows or something else as yet unanticipated that will cause our own blood to freeze.

Scoring Your Subtests

Your scores on the Reading and Writing subtests of the official MTEL Communication and Literacy Skills Test will be scaled scores representing all subareas of each subtest, including all multiple-choice questions, short-answer questions, and open-response assignments. The scaled score for both the Reading and Writing subtest is a conversion of the number of raw points earned on the test to a score in the range of 100 to 300. A scaled score of 240 represents the qualifying, or passing, score for each subtest. You can use the charts on the following pages to find approximate MTEL scores for your performance on this practice test and to help guide your studies with the two review chapters in this book, as well as outside resources. Remember, these are only practice tests and the scores you receive here are only an approximation of what your official scores might be.

Find Your Reading Subtest Score

To find your approximate MTEL score for the practice Reading subtest, you must first figure out how many raw subtest points you earned. Each question answered correctly on this subtest is worth one point, for a maximum of 42 points. Use Table 9.1 to add up your points, giving yourself one point for each correct answer, and zero points for each incorrect answer.

You can also use Table 9.1 to help diagnose your strengths and weaknesses to better focus your studies. The rows in the Objectives column include the MTEL Reading Subtest Objectives that correspond to each question in this practice test. After you have filled in the table, note any particular objective or objectives in which you could use more practice, and then turn to Chapter 7: Reading Skills Review and use the review resources there to help strengthen your skills in that area.

TABLE 9.1 READING SUBTEST SCORING AND REVIEW CHART

QUESTION NUMBER	CORRECT ANSWER	POINTS Correct Answer = 1 Point Incorrect Answer = 0 Points	OBJECTIVE
1.	b		0006 Apply skills for outlining and summarizing written materials and interpreting information presented in graphic form.
2.	d		0002 Understand the main idea and supporting details in written material.
3.	c		0003 Identify a writer's purpose, point of view, and intended meaning.
4.	d		0005 Use critical reasoning skills to evaluate written material.
5.	a		0001 Determine the meaning of words and phrases in the context in which they occur.
6.	c		0001 Determine the meaning of words and phrases in the context in which they occur.
7.	a		0004 Analyze the relationships among ideas in written material.
8.	b		0004 Analyze the relationships among ideas in written material.

(continued)

QUESTION NUMBER	CORRECT ANSWER	POINTS Correct Answer = 1 Point Incorrect Answer = 0 Points	OBJECTIVE
		TABLE 9.1 READING SUBTEST SCORING AND REVIEW CHART (continued)	
9.	c		0004 Analyze the relationships among ideas in written material.
10.	a		0004 Analyze the relationships among ideas in written material.
11.	b		0002 Understand the main idea and supporting details in written material.
12.	d		0002 Understand the main idea and supporting details in written material.
13.	c		0003 Identify a writer's purpose, point of view, and intended meaning.
14.	a		0003 Identify a writer's purpose, point of view, and intended meaning.
15.	c		0004 Analyze the relationships among ideas in written material.
16.	b		0001 Determine the meaning of words and phrases in the context in which they occur.
17.	d		0004 Analyze the relationships among ideas in written material.
18.	b		0004 Analyze the relationships among ideas in written material.
19.	b		0002 Understand the main idea and supporting details in written material.
20.	a		0006 Apply skills for outlining and summarizing written materials and interpreting information presented in graphic form.
21.	c		0003 Identify a writer's purpose, point of view, and intended meaning.
22.	d		0005 Use critical reasoning skills to evaluate written material.
23.	d		0001 Determine the meaning of words and phrases in the context in which they occur.
24.	b		0002 Understand the main idea and supporting details in written material.
25.	d		0003 Identify a writer's purpose, point of view, and intended meaning.
26.	c		0001 Determine the meaning of words and phrases in the context in which they occur.
27.	d		0006 Apply skills for outlining and summarizing written materials and interpreting information presented in graphic form.

QUESTION NUMBER	CORRECT ANSWER	POINTS Correct Answer = 1 Point Incorrect Answer = 0 Points	OBJECTIVE
		TABLE 9.1 READING SUBTEST SCORING AND REVIEW CHART *(continued)*	
28.	a		0005 Use critical reasoning skills to evaluate written material.
29.	a		0005 Use critical reasoning skills to evaluate written material.
30.	b		0006 Apply skills for outlining and summarizing written materials and interpreting information presented in graphic form.
31.	a		0005 Use critical reasoning skills to evaluate written material.
32.	d		0006 Apply skills for outlining and summarizing written materials and interpreting information presented in graphic form.
33.	c		0001 Determine the meaning of words and phrases in the context in which they occur.
34.	b		0003 Identify a writer's purpose, point of view, and intended meaning.
35.	d		0001 Determine the meaning of words and phrases in the context in which they occur.
36.	a		0005 Use critical reasoning skills to evaluate written material.
37.	a		0002 Understand the main idea and supporting details in written material.
38.	b		0001 Determine the meaning of words and phrases in the context in which they occur.
39.	b		0006 Apply skills for outlining and summarizing written materials and interpreting information presented in graphic form.
40.	d		0002 Understand the main idea and supporting details in written material.
41.	c		0003 Identify a writer's purpose, point of view, and intended meaning.
42.	d		0006 Apply skills for outlining and summarizing written materials and interpreting information presented in graphic form.

Total Reading Subtest Points: [   ]

Now, find the number of reading subtest points you earned in the left-hand column of Table 9.2. The corresponding number in the right-hand column is your approximate MTEL score.

TABLE 9.2 READING SUBTEST SCORE CONVERSION CHART	
POINTS	APPROXIMATE MTEL READING SCORE
0–14	100
15–16	101
17–18	116
19–20	131
21–22	146
23–24	161
25–26	176
27–28	191
29–30	206
31–32	221
33–34	236
35–36	251
37–38	266
39–40	281
41–42	296

Find Your Writing Subtest Score

There are a number of steps to finding your total approximate MTEL score for a practice Writing subtest. The first step is to total up the number of raw points you earned for your responses to the multiple-choice and short-answer questions. Like the Reading subtest, each multiple-choice question answered correctly on this subtest is worth one point. Use Table 9.3 to help you add up those multiple-choice points. In Table 9.3, you'll also find each question's related Objective to help focus your studying using Chapter 8: Writing Skills Review.

| | | POINTS | |
QUESTION NUMBER	CORRECT ANSWER	Correct Answer = 1 Point Incorrect Answer = 0 Points	OBJECTIVE
			TABLE 9.3 WRITING SUBTEST MULTIPLE-CHOICE QUESTIONS SCORING AND REVIEW CHART
1.	d		0007 Understand methods for establishing and maintaining a central theme or main idea.
2.	b		0009 Recognize common errors of spelling, capitalization, and punctuation.
3.	c		0009 Recognize common errors of spelling, capitalization, and punctuation.
4.	d		0008 Recognize common errors of sentence construction, grammar, and usage.
5.	c		0007 Understand methods for establishing and maintaining a central theme or main idea.
6.	b		0009 Recognize common errors of spelling, capitalization, and punctuation.
7.	a		0007 Understand methods for establishing and maintaining a central theme or main idea.
8.	c		0009 Recognize common errors of spelling, capitalization, and punctuation.
9.	d		0007 Understand methods for establishing and maintaining a central theme or main idea.
10.	a		0009 Recognize common errors of spelling, capitalization, and punctuation.
11.	c		0007 Understand methods for establishing and maintaining a central theme or main idea.
12.	c		0008 Recognize common errors of sentence construction, grammar, and usage.
13.	d		0007 Understand methods for establishing and maintaining a central theme or main idea.
14.	d		0008 Recognize common errors of sentence construction, grammar, and usage.
15.	b		0007 Understand methods for establishing and maintaining a central theme or main idea.
16.	d		0009 Recognize common errors of spelling, capitalization, and punctuation.
17.	a		0008 Recognize common errors of sentence construction, grammar, and usage.
18.	c		0007 Understand methods for establishing and maintaining a central theme or main idea.
19.	c		0007 Understand methods for establishing and maintaining a central theme or main idea.
20.	d		0008 Recognize common errors of sentence construction, grammar, and usage.

(continued)

TABLE 9.3 WRITING SUBTEST MULTIPLE-CHOICE QUESTIONS SCORING AND REVIEW CHART (continued)			
QUESTION NUMBER	CORRECT ANSWER	POINTS Correct Answer = 1 Point Incorrect Answer = 0 Points	OBJECTIVE
21.	d		0007 Understand methods for establishing and maintaining a central theme or main idea.
22.	b		0007 Understand methods for establishing and maintaining a central theme or main idea.
23.	b		0008 Recognize common errors of sentence construction, grammar, and usage.
24.	a		0007 Understand methods for establishing and maintaining a central theme or main idea.
25.	b		0009 Recognize common errors of spelling, capitalization, and punctuation.
26.	a		0008 Recognize common errors of sentence construction, grammar, and usage.
27.	c		0008 Recognize common errors of sentence construction, grammar, and usage.
28.	a		0007 Understand methods for establishing and maintaining a central theme or main idea.
29.	c		0007 Understand methods for establishing and maintaining a central theme or main idea.
30.	d		0009 Recognize common errors of spelling, capitalization, and punctuation.
31.	c		0008 Recognize common errors of sentence construction, grammar, and usage.
32.	b		0009 Recognize common errors of spelling, capitalization, and punctuation.
33.	c		0008 Recognize common errors of sentence construction, grammar, and usage.
34.	a		0007 Understand methods for establishing and maintaining a central theme or main idea.
35.	b		0009 Recognize common errors of spelling, capitalization, and punctuation.

Multiple-Choice Points Subtotal: [   ]

The short-answer questions in the Writing subtest are worth zero, one, or two points, depending on the success of your response. Use the answer explanations and the following key to figure out how many points you earned for each of your short-answer questions.

SCORING KEY FOR WRITING SUBTEST SHORT-ANSWER QUESTIONS	
POINTS EARNED	DESCRIPTION
2	**Fully Correct:** ■ You successfully corrected both errors in the question and did not introduce any new ones.
1	**Partially Correct:** ■ You properly corrected only one of the two errors in the question. You did not introduce any new errors. ■ You successfully corrected both errors in the question, but introduced a new one.
0	**Incorrect:** ■ You did not correct either of the errors in the question. ■ You properly corrected one of the two errors in the question, but introduced one or more new errors.

Next, use Table 9.4 to add up the number of short-answer points you earned on this subtest.

TABLE 9.4 WRITING SUBTEST SHORT-ANSWER QUESTIONS SCORING AND REVIEW CHART		
QUESTION NUMBER	SHORT-ANSWER POINTS Fully Correct = 2 Points Partially Correct = 1 Point Incorrect = 0 Points	OBJECTIVE
36. 37.		0010 Demonstrate the ability to analyze and revise sentences containing common errors of sentence construction, grammar, usage, spelling, capitalization, and punctuation.
38. 39. 40. 41. 42.		
Short-Answer Points Subtotal:		

Add up the multiple-choice and short-answer point subtotals from Table 9.2 and Table 9.3:

_____ + _____ = _____

Table 9.3 Subtotal   Table 9.4 Subtotal   Total

Next, take that total number and use it in Table 9.5 to find the approximate MTEL score for the multiple-choice and short-answer section of this practice Writing subtest.

Once you have assigned your two open-responses a score between 0 and 4, use Table 9.6 to find your approximate score for the open-response section of the Writing subtest.

TABLE 9.5 WRITING SUBTEST MULTIPLE-CHOICE AND SHORT-ANSWER SCORE CONVERSION CHART	
MULTIPLE-CHOICE + SHORT-ANSWER POINTS	APPROXIMATE MTEL SCORE
0–10	50
11–13	59
14–16	68
17–19	77
20–22	86
23–25	95
26–28	104
29–31	113
32–34	122
35–37	131
38–40	140
41–42	150

TABLE 9.6 WRITING SUBTEST OPEN-RESPONSE SCORE CONVERSION CHART		
SUMMARY RESPONSE POINTS	COMPOSITION RESPONSE POINTS	APPROXIMATE MTEL SCORE
1	1	83
1	2	99
1	3	114
1	4	130
2	1	90
2	2	106
2	3	121
2	4	137
3	1	97
3	2	112
3	3	128
3	4	143
4	1	103
4	2	119
4	3	134
4	4	150

Write your approximate MTEL score for this section here:

MTEL Score for Section 2

The next step is to score your Summary and Composition responses. Of course, you can do this yourself, but it is highly recommended that you ask a professional friend or colleague familiar with the official MTEL writing rubrics to do it for you to get the most accurate gauge of your work. The MTEL writing rubrics you should use to help score your two open responses are available on NES's official website on pages 48 through 51 of the document found here: www.mtel.nesinc.com/PDFs/MA_FLD201_Writing _PRACTICE_TEST.pdf.

Write your approximate MTEL score for this section here:

MTEL Score for Section 2

Finally, to find your overall approximate MTEL writing subtest score, add up your MTEL scores from both sections:

 + =

Section 1 MTEL Score   Section 2 MTEL Score   Overall Writing Subtest Score

COMMUNICATION AND LITERACY SKILLS PRACTICE TEST 2

CHAPTER SUMMARY

This practice version of the Massachusetts Tests for Educator Licensure (MTEL) Communication and Literacy Skills Test is based on the format and content of the official MTEL. See Chapter 4 for a complete description of the official exam. Use this practice test to see how you would do if you were to take the MTEL today, and to diagnose your strengths and weaknesses to help you study more effectively for the official test.

To simulate the test-taking experience, give yourself the time and the space to work. Because you won't be taking the real test in your living room, you might take this one in an unfamiliar location, such as a library. Use a timer or stopwatch to time yourself, allowing ample time for preparing and writing your essay; you'll have four hours to complete your official exam. If you would prefer to take this test for more diagnostic purposes, just take the test in a relaxed manner to find out which areas you are skilled in and which areas will need extra work. After you finish taking your test, you should review the answer explanations found at the end of this test. The answer explanations are followed by information on how to score your exam and diagnose your strengths and weaknesses.

You'll find an answer fill-in sheet for the multiple-choice questions on the following page. You will be writing your answers to the short-answer items on blank lines provided following each question. Lined pages are provided for your answers to the open-response questions following each such item. After you finish taking both subtests, you should review the answer explanations found on page 284.

Reading Subtest

1.	ⓐ	ⓑ	ⓒ	ⓓ
2.	ⓐ	ⓑ	ⓒ	ⓓ
3.	ⓐ	ⓑ	ⓒ	ⓓ
4.	ⓐ	ⓑ	ⓒ	ⓓ
5.	ⓐ	ⓑ	ⓒ	ⓓ
6.	ⓐ	ⓑ	ⓒ	ⓓ
7.	ⓐ	ⓑ	ⓒ	ⓓ
8.	ⓐ	ⓑ	ⓒ	ⓓ
9.	ⓐ	ⓑ	ⓒ	ⓓ
10.	ⓐ	ⓑ	ⓒ	ⓓ
11.	ⓐ	ⓑ	ⓒ	ⓓ
12.	ⓐ	ⓑ	ⓒ	ⓓ
13.	ⓐ	ⓑ	ⓒ	ⓓ
14.	ⓐ	ⓑ	ⓒ	ⓓ

15.	ⓐ	ⓑ	ⓒ	ⓓ
16.	ⓐ	ⓑ	ⓒ	ⓓ
17.	ⓐ	ⓑ	ⓒ	ⓓ
18.	ⓐ	ⓑ	ⓒ	ⓓ
19.	ⓐ	ⓑ	ⓒ	ⓓ
20.	ⓐ	ⓑ	ⓒ	ⓓ
21.	ⓐ	ⓑ	ⓒ	ⓓ
22.	ⓐ	ⓑ	ⓒ	ⓓ
23.	ⓐ	ⓑ	ⓒ	ⓓ
24.	ⓐ	ⓑ	ⓒ	ⓓ
25.	ⓐ	ⓑ	ⓒ	ⓓ
26.	ⓐ	ⓑ	ⓒ	ⓓ
27.	ⓐ	ⓑ	ⓒ	ⓓ
28.	ⓐ	ⓑ	ⓒ	ⓓ

29.	ⓐ	ⓑ	ⓒ	ⓓ
30.	ⓐ	ⓑ	ⓒ	ⓓ
31.	ⓐ	ⓑ	ⓒ	ⓓ
32.	ⓐ	ⓑ	ⓒ	ⓓ
33.	ⓐ	ⓑ	ⓒ	ⓓ
34.	ⓐ	ⓑ	ⓒ	ⓓ
35.	ⓐ	ⓑ	ⓒ	ⓓ
36.	ⓐ	ⓑ	ⓒ	ⓓ
37.	ⓐ	ⓑ	ⓒ	ⓓ
38.	ⓐ	ⓑ	ⓒ	ⓓ
39.	ⓐ	ⓑ	ⓒ	ⓓ
40.	ⓐ	ⓑ	ⓒ	ⓓ
41.	ⓐ	ⓑ	ⓒ	ⓓ
42.	ⓐ	ⓑ	ⓒ	ⓓ

Writing Subtest

1.	ⓐ	ⓑ	ⓒ	ⓓ
2.	ⓐ	ⓑ	ⓒ	ⓓ
3.	ⓐ	ⓑ	ⓒ	ⓓ
4.	ⓐ	ⓑ	ⓒ	ⓓ
5.	ⓐ	ⓑ	ⓒ	ⓓ
6.	ⓐ	ⓑ	ⓒ	ⓓ
7.	ⓐ	ⓑ	ⓒ	ⓓ
8.	ⓐ	ⓑ	ⓒ	ⓓ
9.	ⓐ	ⓑ	ⓒ	ⓓ
10.	ⓐ	ⓑ	ⓒ	ⓓ
11.	ⓐ	ⓑ	ⓒ	ⓓ
12.	ⓐ	ⓑ	ⓒ	ⓓ

13.	ⓐ	ⓑ	ⓒ	ⓓ
14.	ⓐ	ⓑ	ⓒ	ⓓ
15.	ⓐ	ⓑ	ⓒ	ⓓ
16.	ⓐ	ⓑ	ⓒ	ⓓ
17.	ⓐ	ⓑ	ⓒ	ⓓ
18.	ⓐ	ⓑ	ⓒ	ⓓ
19.	ⓐ	ⓑ	ⓒ	ⓓ
20.	ⓐ	ⓑ	ⓒ	ⓓ
21.	ⓐ	ⓑ	ⓒ	ⓓ
22.	ⓐ	ⓑ	ⓒ	ⓓ
23.	ⓐ	ⓑ	ⓒ	ⓓ
24.	ⓐ	ⓑ	ⓒ	ⓓ

25.	ⓐ	ⓑ	ⓒ	ⓓ
26.	ⓐ	ⓑ	ⓒ	ⓓ
27.	ⓐ	ⓑ	ⓒ	ⓓ
28.	ⓐ	ⓑ	ⓒ	ⓓ
29.	ⓐ	ⓑ	ⓒ	ⓓ
30.	ⓐ	ⓑ	ⓒ	ⓓ
31.	ⓐ	ⓑ	ⓒ	ⓓ
32.	ⓐ	ⓑ	ⓒ	ⓓ
33.	ⓐ	ⓑ	ⓒ	ⓓ
34.	ⓐ	ⓑ	ⓒ	ⓓ
35.	ⓐ	ⓑ	ⓒ	ⓓ

Reading Subtest

Directions: Read each of the following selections and then answer the corresponding questions. Each question has only one correct answer.

> Read the passage, then answer the six questions that follow.

Atmospheric Circulation

1 The atmosphere forms a gaseous, protective envelope around Earth. It protects the planet from the cold of space, from harmful ultraviolet light, and from all but the largest meteors. After traveling over 93 million miles, solar energy strikes the atmosphere and Earth's surface, warming the planet and creating what is known as the <u>biosphere</u>, the region of Earth capable of sustaining life. Solar radiation in combination with the planet's rotation causes the atmosphere to circulate. Atmospheric circulation is one important reason that life on Earth can exist at higher latitudes because equatorial heat is transported poleward, moderating the climate.

2 The equatorial region is the warmest part of the Earth because it receives the most direct and, therefore, strongest solar radiation. The plane in which the earth revolves around the sun is called the *ecliptic*. Earth's axis is inclined $23\frac{1}{3}$ degrees with respect to the ecliptic. This inclined axis is responsible for our changing seasons because, as seen from Earth, the sun oscillates back and forth across the equator in an annual cycle. On or about June 21 each year, the sun reaches the Tropic of Cancer, $23\frac{1}{3}$ degrees north latitude. This is the northernmost point at which the sun can be directly overhead. On or about

December 21 of each year, the sun reaches the Tropic of Capricorn, $23\frac{1}{3}$ degrees south latitude. This is the southernmost point at which the sun can be directly overhead. The polar regions are the coldest parts of the earth because they receive the least direct and, therefore, the weakest solar radiation. Here solar radiation strikes at a very oblique angle and thus spreads the same amount of energy over a greater area than in the equatorial regions. A static envelope of air surrounding the earth would produce an extremely hot, uninhabitable equatorial region, while the polar regions would remain inhospitably cold.

3 The transport of water vapor in the atmosphere is an important mechanism by which heat energy is redistributed poleward. When water evaporates into the air and becomes water vapor, it absorbs energy. At the equator, air saturated with water vapor rises high into the atmosphere where winds aloft carry it poleward. As this moist air approaches the polar regions, it cools and sinks back to earth. At some point, the water vapor condenses out of the air as rain or snow, releasing energy in the process. The now-dry polar air flows back toward the equator to repeat the convection cycle. In this way, heat energy absorbed at the equator is deposited at the poles and the temperature gradient between these regions is reduced.

4 The circulation of the atmosphere and the weather it generates is but one example of the many complex, interdependent events of nature. The ever-fascinating web of life depends on the proper functioning of these natural mechanisms for its continued existence. Global warming, the hole in the atmosphere's ozone layer, and increasing air and water pollution pose serious, long-term

threats to the biosphere. Given the high degree of nature's interconnectedness, it is quite possible that the most serious threats have yet to be recognized.

———————

1. Which of the following statements best expresses the main idea of the passage?

    a. The circulation of atmosphere, threatened by global warming and pollution, protects the biosphere and makes life on Earth possible.

    b. If the protective atmosphere around the Earth is too damaged by human activity, all life on Earth will cease.

    c. Life on Earth is the result of complex interdependent events of nature, and some of these events are a result of human intervention.

    d. The circulation of atmosphere is the single most important factor in keeping the biosphere alive, and it is constantly threatened by harmful human activity.

2. Which of the following lists best outlines the main topics addressed in this passage?

    a. I. definition and description of the circulation of the atmosphere
        II. how the atmosphere affects heat and water in the biosphere
        III. how the circulation of the atmosphere works
        IV. what will happen if human activity destroys the atmosphere

    b. I. origin of the atmosphere and ways it protects the biosphere
        II. how the circulation of the atmosphere affects the equator and the poles
        III. how the circulation of the atmosphere interrelates with other events in nature
        IV. threats to life in the biosphere of Earth

    c. I. definition and description of the circulation of the atmosphere
        II. protective functions of the circulation of the atmosphere
        III. relationship of the circulation of the atmosphere to other life-sustaining mechanisms
        IV. threats to nature's interconnectedness in the biosphere

    d. I. the journey of the atmosphere 93 million miles through space.
        II. how the atmosphere circulates and protects the biosphere
        III. how the atmosphere interrelates with weather in the biosphere
        IV. how damage to the biosphere threatens life on Earth

3. Which of the following is closest in meaning to biosphere as it is used in the first paragraph of the passage?
   a. the protective envelope formed by the atmosphere around the living earth
   b. that part of the earth and its atmosphere in which life can exist
   c. living things whose existence is made possible by circulation of the atmosphere
   d. the circulation of the atmosphere's contribution to life on Earth

4. According to information presented in the passage, all temperature changes on Earth are caused by:
   a. variations in the strength of solar radiation
   b. variations in the amount of ultraviolet light
   c. variation of biologic processes in the biosphere
   d. variation in global warming

5. The first paragraph of the passage deals mainly with which of the following effects of the atmosphere on the earth?
   a. its sheltering effect
   b. its reviving effect
   c. its invigorating effect
   d. its cleansing effect

6. In which of the following statements from the passage does the author most clearly express an opinion rather than state a fact?
   a. The atmosphere forms a gaseous, protective envelope around Earth.
   b. The equatorial region is the warmest part of the earth because it receives the most direct and, therefore, strongest solar radiation.
   c. The ever-fascinating web of life depends on the proper functioning of these natural mechanisms for its continued existence.
   d. Given the high degree of nature's interconnectedness, it is quite possible that the most serious threats have yet to be recognized.

Read the passage, then answer the six questions that follow.

Young Mozart

1 The composer Wolfgang Amadeus Mozart's remarkable musical talent was apparent even before most children can sing a simple nursery rhyme. Wolfgang's older sister, Maria Anna, who the family called Nannerl, was learning the clavier, an early keyboard instrument, when her three-year-old brother took an interest in playing. As Nannerl later recalled, Wolfgang "often spent much time at the clavier, picking out thirds, which he was always striking, and his pleasure showed that it sounded good." Their father, Leopold, an assistant concertmaster at the Salzburg Court, recognized his children's unique gifts and soon devoted himself to their musical education.

2 Born in Salzburg, Austria, on January 27, 1756, Wolfgang was five when he learned his first musical composition—in less than half an hour. He quickly learned other pieces, and by age five composed his first original work. Leopold settled on a plan to take Nannerl and Wolfgang on tour to play before the European courts. Their first venture was to nearby Munich where the children played for Maximillian III Joseph, elector of Bavaria. Leopold soon set his sights on the capital of the Hapsburg Empire, Vienna. On their way to Vienna, the family stopped in Linz, where Wolfgang gave his first public concert. By this time, Wolfgang was not only a virtuoso harpsichord player but he had also mastered the violin. The audience at Linz was stunned by the six-year-old, and word of his genius soon traveled to Vienna. In a much anticipated concert, the children appeared at the Schönbrunn Palace on October 13, 1762. They utterly charmed the emperor and empress.

3 Following his success, Leopold was inundated with invitations for the children to play, for a fee. Leopold seized the opportunity and booked as many concerts as possible at courts throughout Europe. After the children performed at the major court in a region, other nobles competed to have the "miracle children of Salzburg" play a private concert in their homes. A concert could last three hours, and the children played at least two a day. Today, Leopold might be considered the worst kind of stage parent, but at the time it was not uncommon for prodigies to make extensive concert tours. Even so, it was an exhausting schedule for a child who was just past the age of needing an afternoon nap.

4 Wolfgang fell ill on tour, and when the family returned to Salzburg on January 5, 1763, Wolfgang spent his first week at home in bed with acute rheumatoid arthritis. In June, Leopold accepted an invitation for the children to play at Versailles, the lavish palace built by Louis XIV, King of France. Wolfgang did not see his home in Salzburg for another three years. When they weren't performing, the Mozart children were likely to be found bumping along the rutted roads in an unheated carriage. Wolfgang passed the long uncomfortable hours in the imaginary Kingdom of Back, of which he was king. He became so engrossed in the intricacies of his make-believe court that he persuaded a family servant to make a map showing all the cities, villages, and towns over which he reigned.

5 The King of Back was also busy composing. Wolfgang completed his first symphony at age nine and published his first sonatas that same year. Before the family returned to Salzburg, Wolfgang had played for, and amazed, the heads of the French and British

royal families. He had also been plagued with numerous illnesses. Despite Wolfgang and Nannerl's arduous schedule and international renown, the family's finances were often strained. The pattern established in his childhood would be the template of the rest of his short life. Wolfgang Amadeus Mozart toiled constantly, was lauded for his genius, suffered from illness, and struggled financially, until he died at age 35. The remarkable child prodigy who more than fulfilled his potential was buried in an unmarked grave, as was the custom at the time, in a Vienna suburb.

---

7. The author's main purpose in this passage is to
   a. illustrate the early career and formative experiences of a musical prodigy.
   b. describe the classical music scene in the eighteenth century.
   c. uncover the source of Wolfgang Amadeus Mozart's musical genius.
   d. prove the importance of starting a musical instrument an early age.

8. According to information presented in the passage, Wolfgang became interested in music because
   a. his father thought it would be profitable.
   b. he had a natural talent.
   c. he saw his sister learning to play.
   d. he came from a musical family.

9. According to information presented in the passage, a consequence of Wolfgang's first public appearance was:
   a. He charmed the emperor and empress of Hapsburg.
   b. Leopold set his sights on Vienna.
   c. Word of Wolfgang's genius spread to the capital.
   d. He mastered the violin.

10. The author's attitude toward Leopold Mozart can best be characterized as
  a. vehement condemnation.
  b. mild disapproval.
  c. glowing admiration.
  d. incredulity.

11. Which of the following words is closest in meaning to <u>lavish</u> in the fourth paragraph of the passage?
  a. wasteful
  b. clean
  c. difficult
  d. extravagant

12. Which of the following statements from the passage expresses an opinion rather than stating a fact?
  a. The composer Wolfgang Amadeus Mozart's remarkable musical talent was apparent even before most children can sing a simple nursery rhyme.
  b. In a much anticipated concert, the children appeared at the Schönbrunn Palace on October 13, 1762.
  c. In June, Leopold accepted an invitation for the children to play at Versailles, the <u>lavish</u> palace built by Louis XIV, King of France.
  d. Wolfgang Amadeus Mozart toiled constantly, was lauded for his genius, suffered from illness, and struggled financially, until he died at age 35.

> Read the passage, then answer the six questions that follow.

What Happened When He Came to America?

1 My parents lost friends, lost family ties and patterns of mutual assistance, lost rituals and habits and favorite foods, lost any link to an ongoing social milieu, lost a good part of the sense they had of themselves. We lost a house, several towns, various landscapes. We lost documents and pictures and heirlooms, as well as most of our breakable belongings, smashed in the nine packing cases that we took with us to America. We lost connection to a thing larger than ourselves, and as a family failed to make any significant new connection in exchange, so that we were left aground on a sandbar barely big enough for our feet. I lost friends and relatives and stories and familiar comforts and a sense of continuity between home and outside and any sense that I was normal. I lost half a language through want of use and eventually, in my late teens, even lost French as the language of my internal monologue. And I lost a whole network of routes through life that I had just barely glimpsed.

2 Hastening on toward some idea of a future, I only half-realized these losses, and when I did realize I didn't disapprove, and sometimes I actively colluded. At some point, though, I was bound to notice that there was a gulf inside me, with a blanketed form on the other side that hadn't been uncovered in decades. My project of self-invention had been successful, so much so that I had become a sort of hydroponic vegetable, growing soil-free. But I had been formed in another world; everything in me that was essential was owed to immersion in that place, and that time, that I had so effectively renounced.

3 Like it or not, each of us is made, less by blood or genes than by a process that is largely accidental, the impact of things seen and heard and smelled and tasted and endured in those few years before our clay hardens. Offhand remarks, things glimpsed in passing, jokes and commonplaces, shop

displays and climate and flickering light and textures of walls are all consumed by us and become part of our fiber, just as much as the more obvious effects of upbringing and socialization and intimacy and learning. Every human being is an archeological site.

—Luc Sante, from *The Factory of Facts* (1998)

13. According to information presented in the passage, the narrator came to the United States when he was

   a. an infant.
   b. a toddler.
   c. in his early teens.
   d. in his late teens.

14. The author's purpose for listing things that he and his family lost when they immigrated to the United States is to

   a. convince others not to immigrate.
   b. show how careless his family was when packing.
   c. show how much he missed his homeland.
   d. show how many intangible and important things were left behind.

15. According to information presented in the passage, our personalities are formed mostly by

   a. our genes.
   b. our education.
   c. our environment.
   d. our caregivers.

16. According to information presented in the passage, when the narrator came to the United States, he

   a. embraced American culture.
   b. rejected his roots.
   c. made sure to keep his heritage alive.
   d. became withdrawn.

17. The author's purpose for writing that "Every human being is an archeological site" is to

   a. suggest that the environment that formed us is a permanent, if buried, part of us.
   b. suggest that we must dig deep within ourselves to discover our past.
   c. suggest that we all have a piece of our past that we would prefer to keep buried.
   d. suggest that only archaeologists understand the impact of our environment.

18. Which of the following statements best summarizes the main points of the passage?

   a. Among other things, the author lost a house, documents, pictures, and heirlooms when he came to America.
   b. The author only half realized that he had lost a number of things when he and his family moved to America.
   c. Offhand remarks, things glimpsed in passing, shop displays, and climate and flickering light help to make us who we are.
   d. Coming to America gave the author an opportunity for self-invention, but resulted in the loss of numerous things as well.

> **Read the passage, then answer the six questions that follow.**

What Is the Author Asking For?

1   The President in Washington sends word that he wishes to buy our land. But how can you buy or sell the sky? The land? The idea is strange to us. If we do not own the freshness of the air and the sparkle of the water, how can you buy them? Every part of this earth is sacred to my people. Every shining pine needle, every sandy shore, every mist in dark woods, every meadow, every humming

insect. All are holy in the memory and experience of my people.

2 We know the sap which <u>courses</u> through the trees as we know the blood that courses through our veins. We are part of the earth and it is part of us. The perfumed flowers are our sisters. The bear, the deer, the great eagle, these are our brothers. The rocky crests, the juices in the meadow, the body heat of the pony, and man, all belong to the same family.

3 The shining water that moves in the streams and rivers is not just water, but the blood of our ancestors. If we sell you our land, you must remember that it is sacred. Each ghostly reflection in the clear water of the lakes tells of events and memories in the life of my people. The water's murmur is the voice of my father's father. The rivers are our brothers. They quench our thirst. They carry our canoes and feed our children. So you must give to the rivers the kindness you would give any brother.

4 If we sell you our land, remember that the air is precious to us, that the air shares its spirit with all the life it supports. The wind that gave our grandfather his first breath also receives his last sigh. The wind also gives our children the spirit of life. So, if we sell you our land, you must keep it apart and sacred, as a place where man can go to taste the wind that is sweetened by the meadow flowers.

5 Will you teach your children what we have taught our children? That the earth is our mother? What befalls the earth, befalls all sons of the earth. This we know: The earth does not belong to man, man belongs to the earth. All things are connected like the blood which unites us all.
—Chief Seattle, from "This We Know" (1854)

19. According to information presented in the passage, what sort of relationship do the author's people have with the land?
a. They own it and do whatever they want with it.
b. They respect it and do not understand how anyone can own it.
c. They are indifferent and can live anywhere.
d. They live there because they have to and would be glad to sell it.

20. The passage was most likely written for an audience of
a. the president only.
b. Native Americans only.
c. all new Americans.
d. all Americans, native and new.

21. The author's main purpose in this passage is to
a. convince the American government not to buy the land.
b. convince American Indians to fight the new Americans.
c. persuade Americans that the land is not worth buying.
d. convince the new Americans that the land is sacred.

22. Former President Ronald Reagan is reported to have said, "If you've seen one tree, you've seen them all." How does this idea compare with the ideas of Chief Seattle?
a. They express essentially the same attitude toward the land.
b. They express essentially opposite attitudes toward the land.
c. Reagan seems to care more about the land than Chief Seattle.
d. We cannot compare them, because Chief Seattle does not talk about trees.

23. Which of the following words is the best meaning of <u>courses</u> as it is used in the second paragraph of the passage?

 a. flows
 b. classes
 c. paths
 d. times

24. Which of the following statements best summarizes the main points of the passage?

 a. The president in Washington has sent a message to Chief Seattle requesting purchase of the land that belongs to the chief and his people, and the chief is considering selling his land.

 b. Chief Seattle believes that the water running in the streams and rivers is not just water, but the blood of his ancestors, and therefore, the water is sacred to him and his people.

 c. The president in Washington wants to purchase land from Chief Seattle's people, but the chief believes the land is sacred and belongs to no man, and therefore, cannot be purchased.

 d. Chief Seattle wants to know whether the president in Washington will teach his children that the earth is their mother, and believes that all things in nature are connected like blood.

Read the passage, then answer the six questions that follow.

The Menu Education and Labeling Act

1 In the past thirty years, Americans' consumption of restaurant and take-out food has doubled. The result, according to many health watchdog groups, is an increase in overweight and obesity. Almost 60 million Americans are obese, costing $117 billion each year in healthcare and related costs. Members of Congress have decided they need to do something about the obesity epidemic. A bill was recently introduced in the House that would require restaurants with 20 or more locations to list the nutritional content of their food on their menus. A Senate version of the bill is expected in the near future.

2 Our legislators point to the trend of restaurants' marketing larger meals at attractive prices. People order these meals believing that they are getting a great value, but what they are also getting could be, in one meal, more than the daily recommended allowances of calories, fat, and sodium. The question is, would people stop "supersizing," or make other healthier choices if they knew the nutritional content of the food they're ordering? Lawmakers think they would, and the gravity of the obesity problem has caused them to act to change menus.

3 The Menu Education and Labeling, or MEAL, Act, would be a significant piece of legislation resulting in menus that look like the nutrition facts panels found on food in supermarkets. Those panels are required by the 1990 Nutrition Labeling and Education Act, which exempted restaurants. The new restaurant menus would list calories, fat, and sodium on printed menus, and calories on menu boards, for all items that are offered on a regular basis (daily specials don't apply). But isn't this simply asking restaurants to state the obvious? Who isn't aware that a supersize order of fries isn't health food? Does anyone order a double cheeseburger thinking they're being virtuous?

4 Studies have shown that it's not that simple. In one, registered dieticians couldn't come up with accurate estimates of the calories found in certain fast foods. Who would have guessed that a milk shake, which sounds pretty healthy (it does contain milk, after all) has more calories than three McDonald's cheeseburgers? Or that one chain's chicken breast sandwich, another better-sounding alternative to a burger, contains more than half a day's calories and twice the recommended daily amount of sodium? Even a fast-food coffee drink, without a doughnut to go with it, has almost half the calories needed in a day.

5 The restaurant industry isn't happy about the new bill. <u>Remonstrations</u> against it include the fact that diet alone is not the reason for America's obesity epidemic. A lack of adequate exercise is also to blame. In addition, many fast-food chains already post nutritional information on their websites, or on posters located in their restaurants.

6 Those who favor the MEAL Act, and similar legislation, say in response that we must do all we can to help people maintain a healthy weight. While the importance of exercise is undeniable, the quantity and quality of what we eat must be changed. They believe that if we want consumers to make better choices when they eat out, nutritional information must be provided where consumers are selecting their food. Restaurant patrons are not likely to have memorized the calorie counts they may have looked up on the Internet, nor are they going to leave their tables, or a line, to check out a poster that might be on the opposite side of the restaurant.

CALORIES OF VARIOUS FAST FOOD ITEMS

McDonald's Big Mac: 540 calories
McDonald's Large Fries: 500 calories
Burger King Double Whopper with Cheese: 990 calories
Burger King Tendercrisp Chicken Sandwich: 790 calories
Taco Bell Beef Gordita Supreme: 310 calories
Taco Bell Fiesta Chicken Salad: 850 calories
Subway 6" Meatball Sub: 580 calories
Subway 12" Sweet Onion Chicken Teriyaki Sandwich: 770 calories

25. According to information presented in the passage, the larger meals now being offered in restaurants
   a. cost less than smaller meals.
   b. add a side dish not offered with smaller meals.
   c. include a larger drink.
   d. contain too many calories, fat, and sodium.

26. Which of the following lists best outlines the main topics addressed in the passage?
    a. ■ Fast food and obesity
       ■ The Menu Education and Labeling Act
       ■ Calorie studies are inconclusive.
       ■ The restaurant industry versus the MENU Act
    b. ■ 60 million Americans are obese.
       ■ the expense of obesity
       ■ Congress versus obesity
       ■ A senate bill affects restaurants with 20 or more locations.
    c. ■ Menus may soon change.
       ■ Milk shakes are unhealthy.
       ■ no virtue in a double cheeseburger
       ■ Obesity and healthcare
    d. ■ Exercise is important.
       ■ chicken breast sandwiches versus burgers
       ■ high levels of sodium
       ■ stating the obvious

27. Which of the following words is the best meaning of remonstrations as it is used in the fifth paragraph of the passage?
    a. champions
    b. questions
    c. statements
    d. arguments

28. Which of the following statements provides the best evaluation of the author's credibility?
    a. The author's misconceptions about obesity and fast food strongly detract from the credibility of the passage.
    b. Although clearly in favor of the MEAL Act, the author presents an informed account of the act and fast-food–related obesity.
    c. Despite confusion about the number of calories in certain fast foods, the author presents a definitive explanation of them in this passage.
    d. The author's bias against the fast food industry strongly detracts from the credibility of the passage.

29. Which of the following statements from the passage expresses an opinion rather than stating a fact?
    a. one chain's chicken breast sandwich, another better-sounding alternative to a burger, contains more than half a day's calories.
    b. many fast food chains already post nutritional information on their websites, or on posters located in their restaurants.
    c. Almost 60 million Americans are obese, costing $117 billion each year in healthcare and related costs.
    d. A bill was recently introduced in the House that would require restaurants with 20 or more locations to list the nutritional content of their food on their menus.

30. Information presented in the chart best supports which of the following conclusions?

a. A Taco Bell Fiesta Chicken Salad has fewer calories than a Burger King Tendercrisp Chicken Sandwich.

b. An order of McDonald's Large Fries has as many calories as a Subway 6″ Meatball Sub.

c. A Taco Bell Beef Gordita is a healthier lunch option than a Burger King Double Whopper with Cheese.

d. A Subway 12″ Sweet Onion Chicken Teriyaki Sandwich is a healthier lunch than a McDonald's Big Mac.

> **Read the passage, then answer the six questions that follow.**

Public Art

1 In Manhattan's Eighth Avenue/Fourteenth Street subway station, a grinning bronze alligator with human hands pops out of a manhole cover to grab a bronze "baby" whose head is the shape of a moneybag. In the Bronx General Post Office, a giant 13-panel painting called *Resources of America* celebrates the hard work and industrialism of America in the first half of the twentieth century. And in Brooklyn's MetroTech Center just over the Brooklyn Bridge, several incredible installations of art are on view at any given time: from an iron lasso resembling a giant charm bracelet to a series of wagons playing recordings of great American poems. The center once displayed a life-sized seeing eye dog that looks so real people are constantly stopping to pet it.

2 There exists in every city a <u>symbiotic</u> relationship between the city and its art. When we hear the term *art*, we tend to think of private art—the kind displayed in private spaces such as museums, concert halls, and galleries. But there is a growing interest in, and respect for, public art: the kind of art created for and displayed in public spaces such as parks, building lobbies, and sidewalks.

3 Although all art is inherently public—created in order to convey an idea or emotion to others—public art, as opposed to art that is <u>sequestered</u> in museums and galleries, is art specifically designed for a public arena where the art will be encountered by people in their normal day-to-day activities. Public art can be purely ornamental or highly functional; it can be as subtle as a decorative door knob or as conspicuous as the Chicago Picasso. It is also an essential element of effective urban design.

4 The more obvious forms of public art include monuments, sculptures, fountains, murals, and gardens. But public art also takes the form of ornamental benches or street lights, decorative manhole covers, and mosaics on trash bins. Many city dwellers would be surprised to discover just how much public art is really around them and how much art they have passed by without noticing.

5 Public art fulfills several functions essential to the health of a city and its citizens. It educates about history and culture—of the artist, the neighborhood, the city, and the nation. Public art is also a "place-making device" that instantly creates memorable, experiential landmarks, fashioning a unique identity for a public place, personalizing it and giving it a specific character. It stimulates the public, challenging viewers to interpret the art and arousing their emotions, and it promotes community by stimulating interaction among viewers. In serving these multiple and important functions, public art beautifies the area and regenerates both the place and the viewer.

6 One question often debated in public art forums is whether public art should be created *with* or *by* the public rather than *for* the public. Increasingly, cities and artists are recognizing the importance of creating works with meaning for the intended audience, and this generally requires direct input from the community or from an artist entrenched in that community. At the same time, however, art created for the community by an outsider often adds fresh perspective. Thus, cities and their citizens are best served by a combination of public art created *by* members of the community, art created with input *from* members of the community, and art created by others *for* the community.

---

31. Which of the following words is the best meaning of <u>symbiotic</u> as it is used in the second paragraph of the passage?
a. harmonious
b. critical
c. destructive
d. intelligent

32. Information presented in the paragraph 3 of the passage is primarily intended to
a. analyze the best and worst qualities of public art.
b. describe how public art affects the community in which it is placed.
c. identify the distinction between public and private art.
d. raise questions about the importance of public art.

33. According to information presented in the passage, one way public art *regenerates* a viewer is by
a. fashioning a unique identity for a public place.
b. personalizing an area and giving it a specific character.
c. creating experimental landscapes.
d. challenging viewers to interpret the art and arousing their emotions.

34. In which of the following statements from paragraph 1 of the passage does the author most clearly express an opinion rather than state a fact?
a. In Manhattan's Eighth Avenue/Fourteenth Street subway station, a grinning bronze alligator with human hands pops out of a manhole cover to grab a bronze "baby" whose head is the shape of a moneybag.
b. In the Bronx General Post Office, a giant 13-panel painting called *Resources of America* celebrates the hard work and industrialism of America in the first half of the twentieth century.
c. in Brooklyn's MetroTech Center just over the Brooklyn Bridge, several incredible installations of art are on view at any given time.
d. The center once displayed a life-sized seeing eye dog that looks so real people are constantly stopping to pet it.

35. Which of the following lists best outlines the main topics addressed in the passage?
- **a.** ■ public art and a healthy city
  - ■ public art as place-making device
  - ■ stimulating the public
- **b.** ■ the relationship between a city and its art
  - ■ how public art affects a community
  - ■ public art: *by* the public or *for* the public
- **c.** ■ the most obvious forms of public art
  - ■ private art found in museums
  - ■ public art and our day-to-day lives
- **d.** ■ All art is inherently public.
  - ■ ornamental benches and street lights
  - ■ Outsiders add fresh perspective.

36. Which of the following words is the best meaning of <u>sequestered</u> as it is used in the third paragraph of the passage?
- **a.** sold
- **b.** generated
- **c.** enjoyed
- **d.** isolated

> **Read the passage, then answer
> the six questions that follow.**

The Great Barrier Reef

1   Coral reefs are among the most diverse and productive ecosystems on Earth. Consisting of both living and nonliving components, this type of ecosystem is found in the warm, clear, shallow waters of tropical oceans worldwide. The functionality of the reefs ranges from providing food and shelter to fish and other forms of marine life to protecting the shore from the ill effects of erosion and putrefaction. In fact, reefs actually create land in tropical areas by forming islands and contributing mass to continental shorelines.

2   Although coral looks like a plant, actually it is mainly comprised of the limestone skeleton of a tiny animal called a coral polyp. While corals are the main components of reef structure, they are not the only living participants. Coralline algae cement the myriad corals, and other miniature organisms such as tube worms and mollusks contribute skeletons to this dense and diverse structure. Together, these creatures compose many different types of tropical reefs.

3   Great Barrier Reef is the world's largest network of coral reefs, stretching 2,010 km (1,250 miles) off Australia's northeastern coast. From microorganisms to whales, diverse life forms make their home on the reef. Over 1,500 fish species, 4,000 mollusk species, 200 bird species, 16 sea snake species, and six sea turtle species thrive in the reef's tropical waters. The reef is also a habitat for the endangered dugong (sea cow), moray eels, and sharks. In addition to the abundance of animal life, the coral reef offers a spectrum of beautiful colors and intricate shapes.

4   Although protected by the Australian government, Great Barrier Reef faces environmental threats. Crown-of-thorns starfish feed on coral and can destroy large portions of reef. Pollution and rising water temperatures also threaten the delicate coral. Located near Queensland in northeast Australia, Great Barrier Reef is so large it can be seen from outer space. But the most preventable of the hazards to the reef are tourists. Tourists have contributed to the destruction of the reef ecosystem by breaking off and removing pieces of coral to bring home as souvenirs. The government hopes that by informing tourists of the dangers of this seemingly harmless activity they will <u>quash</u> this creeping menace to the fragile reef.

37. Which of the following words is the best meaning of quash as it is used in the fourth paragraph of the passage?
   a. influence
   b. highlight
   c. conquer
   d. instruct

38. According to information presented in the passage, the main components of reef structure are
   a. tube worms.
   b. mollusks.
   c. coralline algae.
   d. corals.

39. According to information presented in the passage, a difference between tube worms and crown-of-thorns starfish is that
   a. tube worms help the reef and crown-of-thorns starfish damage it.
   b. tube worms are mollusks and crown-of-thorns starfish are not.
   c. tube worms are food for moray eels and crown-of-thorns starfish are eaten by sharks.
   d. tube worms are beautifully colorful and crown-of-thorns starfish are not.

40. Which of the following statements from the passage expresses an opinion rather than stating a fact?
   a. Coral reefs are among the most diverse and productive ecosystems on Earth.
   b. The coral reef offers the viewer a spectrum of beautiful colors and intricate shapes.
   c. Great Barrier Reef is the world's largest network of coral reefs.
   d. Pollution and rising water temperatures also threaten the delicate coral.

41. Which of the following statements best summarizes the main points of the passage?
   a. Great Barrier Reef is the world's largest network of coral reefs and is home to a diverse range of creatures, including whales, fish species, mollusks, and birds.
   b. Great Barrier Reef provides food and shelter to fish and other forms of marine life and protects the shore from the ill effects of erosion and putrefaction.
   c. Great Barrier Reef looks like it is made up of plants, but actually it is mainly comprised of the limestone skeleton of a tiny animal called a coral polyp.
   d. Great Coral Reef is a large and diverse ecosystem, but it is threatened by certain sea creatures, environmental factors, and the activities of tourists.

42. Which of the following statements from paragraph 4 the passage is least relevant to the main topic?
   a. Although protected by the Australian government, Great Barrier Reef faces environmental threats.
   b. Located near Queensland in northeast Australia, Great Barrier Reef is so large it can be seen from outer space.
   c. Tourists have contributed to the destruction of the reef ecosystem by breaking off and removing pieces of coral to bring home as souvenirs.
   d. The government hopes that by informing tourists of the dangers of this seemingly harmless activity they will <u>quash</u> this creeping menace to the fragile reef.

Writing Subtest

Multiple-Choice Questions

Directions: Read each of the following passages and then choose the one best answer for each of the multiple-choice questions that follow. Each of these passages has numbered parts that are referred to in the associated questions.

> **Read the passage, then answer the four questions that follow.**

(1) Voting is the <u>privilege</u> for which wars have been fought, protests have been organized, and editorials have been written. (2) Some wars have been fought because of religion, land ownership, control of power, and differences in political ideology. (3) "No taxation without representation" was a battle cry of the American Revolution. (4) Women struggled for suffrage, as did all minorities. (5) Eighteen-year-olds <u>clamored</u> for the right to vote, saying that if they were old enough to go to war, they should be allowed to vote. (6) Yet Americans have a deplorable voting history.
(7) Interviewing people about their voting habits is revealing. (8) There are individuals who state that they have never voted. (9) Often, they claim that their individual vote doesn't matter, so they do not vote. (10) Some people blame their <u>absense</u> from the voting booth on the fact that they do not know enough about the issues. (11) In a <u>democracy</u>, we can express our opinions to our elected leaders, but more than half of us sometimes avoid choosing the people who make the policies that affect our lives.

1. Which sentence, if added to the passage, would be the most effective topic sentence of the passage?
   a. Every American is too lazy to vote.
   b. Women and minorities fought for their right to vote.
   c. Americans do not take voting seriously enough.
   d. Americans do not think that elected officials take their opinions seriously.

2. Which part of the passage contains a redundant expression of ideas or information?
   a. sentence 6
   b. sentence 7
   c. sentence 8
   d. sentence 9

3. Which part of the passage draws attention away from the main idea?
   a. sentence 1
   b. sentence 2
   c. sentence 4
   d. sentence 5

4. Which underlined word in the passage is spelled incorrectly?
   a. privilege
   b. clamored
   c. absense
   d. democracy

> **Read the passage, then answer the four questions that follow.**

(1) The vast majority of schools entered the high-tech age years ago by installing computers throughout their libraries and classrooms.
(2) All administrative offices, as well as libraries and classrooms, were equipped with computer

systems. (3) The new trend, however, is taking this one step further at an innovative school in Arizona, which is providing an all-new way for students to do their homework. (4) They provide each student with his or her own laptop!

(5) Instead of using money to buy all new textbooks for Empire High School, the administration used the funds to purchase laptop computers. (6) The teachers commonly select educational materials on the Internet for students to consult to complete homework assignments. (7) To make the laptops feel more personal, students are allowed to store their own music collections on them. (8) Most young people tend to listen to MP3s rather than CDs or records these days. (9) Instead of handing in reports and homework on paper these Arizona students just e-mail it into their individual teachers. (10) So much for that old excuse that the dog ate your homework!

5. Which change is need in sentence 4 of the passage?
   a. Change "laptop" to "laptops."
   b. Change "They" to "Them."
   c. Change "their" to "his or her."
   d. Change "each" to "all."

6. Which part of the passage contains a redundant expression of ideas or information?
   a. sentence 1
   b. sentence 2
   c. sentence 3
   d. sentence 4

7. Which part of the passage draws attention away from the main idea of the second paragraph?
   a. sentence 7
   b. sentence 8
   c. sentence 9
   d. sentence 10

8. Which part of the passage is missing a comma?
   a. sentence 2
   b. sentence 4
   c. sentence 6
   d. sentence 9

> **Read the passage, then answer the four questions that follow.**

(1) Following an overwhelmingly enthusiastic response, the school administration has decided to expand the Community Mural Painting Program—now a part of two high school curriculums—to the middle school level. (2) The program was piloted in the school district last year and it was a successful initiative for students and for the community.

(3) Money to fund the program came from a national grant designed to promote community involvement as well as art appreciation among teenagers. (4) A committee that consists of art teachers, social studies teachers, and school social workers oversees the program.

(5) Studies have shown that young people who have been exposed to similar programs are much less prone to apathy. (6) The same studies state that these programs promote a sense of purpose that serves young people well both inside and outside the academic setting and makes them less apathetic. (7) When the students were interviewed by the program committee. (8) In addition, the community's attitude toward teenagers is improved also.

(9) It is projected that this year more than 150 students will be involved and that more than 20 murals will be painted.

9. Which part of the passage is a nonstandard sentence?
a. sentence 5
b. sentence 6
c. sentence 7
d. sentence 8

10. Which change is needed in sentence 8 of the passage?
a. Delete the word "also."
b. Change "community's" to "communities."
c. Change "teenagers" to "teenagers'."
d. Change "toward" to "according to."

11. Which sentence, if added after sentence 2 of the passage, would best develop the ideas in paragraph 1?
a. The program could benefit other districts, as well.
b. One particularly beautiful mural was painted on a playground wall on the east side of town.
c. Fifty high school students were involved, and they spent five weeks painting ten murals throughout the community in locations that were in great need of some attention.
d. The school district is interested in trying other pilot programs in addition the Mural Painting Program.

12. Which part of the passage contains a redundant expression of ideas or information?
a. sentence 3
b. sentence 4
c. sentence 5
d. sentence 6

> **Read the passage, then answer the four questions that follow.**
> (Note: An error in paragraph organization has been purposely included in first paragraph.)

(1) Over the last decade, a growing number of greyhounds have been adopted to live out retirement as household pets once there racing career is over. (2) Greyhound racing is one of the most popular spectator sports in the United States. (3) Many people hesitate to adopt a retired racing greyhound because they think only very old dogs are available.

(4) People also worry that greyhounds will be hyperactive and need a larger space to run than other breeds. (5) _____.
(6) In fact, racing greyhounds are put up for adoption at a young age even champion racers, who have the longest careers, only work until they are about three-and-a-half years old.
(7) Since greyhounds usually live to be 12 to 15 years old, their retirement is much longer than their racing careers.

(8) Far from being nervous dogs, greyhounds have naturally sweet, mild dispositions, and, while they love to run, they are sprinters rather than distance runners and are sufficiently exercised with a few laps around a fenced-in backyard every day. (9) Greyhounds do not make good watchdogs, but they are very good with children, get along well with other dogs (and usually cats as well), and are very affectionate and loyal. (10) A retired racing greyhound is a wonderful pet for almost anyone.

13. Which sentence, if added as sentence 5, provides the best transition between sentence 4 and sentence 6?

    a. Even so, greyhounds are placid dogs.

    b. These worries are based on false impressions and are easily dispelled.

    c. Retired greyhounds do not need racetracks to keep in shape.

    d. However, retired greyhounds are too old to need much exercise.

14. Which change is needed in sentence 1 of the passage?

    a. Change "there" to "their."

    b. Change "have been adopted" to "have adopted."

    c. Change "growing" to "increasing."

    d. Change "is" to "was."

15. Which part of the passage contains a run-on sentence?

    a. sentence 6

    b. sentence 7

    c. sentence 8

    d. sentence 9

16. Which of the following changes would make the sequence of ideas in the first paragraph clearer?

    a. Delete sentence 1.

    b. Reverse the order of sentence 1 and sentence 2.

    c. Delete sentence 3.

    d. Reverse the order of sentence 2 and sentence 3.

> **Read the passage, then answer the four questions that follow.**

(1) Although eating right is an important part of good health, most experts agree that being <u>physically</u> active is also a key element in living a longer and healthier life. (2) The benefits of physical activity include improved self-esteem, a lowered risk of heart disease and colon cancer, and enhanced <u>flexability</u>. (3) Physical activity, in addition to it's many other rewards, will also help manage <u>weight</u> gain. (4) One of the simplest and most effective ways to increase physical activity is walking; walking requires no special equipment, no particular location, and it can be easily <u>incorporated</u> into even the busiest lives. (5) Add ten minutes or ten blocks to your usual dog-walking routine. (6) Park several blocks away from your destination and walk briskly the rest of the way. (7) Walk up or down the soccer or softball field while watching your kids play. (8) Find a walking buddy who will take a long walk with you once or twice a week. (9) You'll be less likely to skip the walk if someone is counting on you to be there.

    (10) _____.

(11) Before long, it will become a normal part of your daily routine, and you'll hardly notice the extra effort. (12) In addition the increased energy and overall sense of well-being you'll experience will inspire you to walk even more.

17. Which of the following changes is needed in the passage?

    a. Sentence 1: Insert an apostrophe in "experts."

    b. Sentence 2: Insert a comma after "activity."

    c. Sentence 3: Delete the apostrophe from "it's."

    d. Sentence 5: Delete the apostrophe from "You'll."

18. Which sentence, if added as sentence 10, provides the best transition from the first paragraph to the second paragraph?

  a. Physical activity can help strengthen your bones, muscles, and joints.

  b. A walking buddy might be a friend, a neighbor, a family member, or anyone else who shares your desire to attain better health.

  c. Along with increasing your physical activity, eating right is an important way to improve your health and well-being.

  d. Increasing the level of your walking may seem difficult at first, but you may be surprised by how quickly that changes.

19. Which underlined word in the passage is spelled incorrectly?

  a. physically

  b. flexability

  c. weight

  d. incorporated

20. Which part of the passage is missing a comma?

  a. sentence 8

  b. sentence 9

  c. sentence 11

  d. sentence 12

> **Read the passage, then answer the four questions that follow.**

(1) Artist Mary Cassatt was born in Allegheny city, Pennsylvania, in 1844. (2) Because her family valued education and believed that traveling was a wonderful way to learn. (3) Before she was ten years old, she'd visited London, Paris, and Rome. (4) Although her family supported education, they were not at all <u>supportive</u> of her desire to be a professional artist, but that didn't stop her from studying art both in the United States and abroad. (5) A <u>contemporery</u> of artists including Camille Pissarro and Edgar Degas, Cassatt was an active member of the school of painting known as Impressionism. (6) However, in later years, her painting evolved, and she abandoned the impressionist approach with a simpler, more <u>straightforward</u> style. (7) Camille Pissarro was famous for painting portraits of rural and urban life in France, and was particularly fond of painting landscapes depicting the Pontoise community.

(8) Cassatt never married or had children, but her most well-known paintings depict breathtaking, yet ordinary, scenes of mothers and children. (9) Cassatt died childless in 1926 at the age of 82 leaving a large and inspired body of work and an example to women everywhere to break through <u>traditional</u> roles and follow their dreams.

21. Which part of the passage contains a redundant expression of ideas or information?

  a. sentence 1

  b. sentence 5

  c. sentence 8

  d. sentence 9

22. Which underlined word in the passage is spelled incorrectly?

  a. supportive

  b. contemporery

  c. straightforward

  d. traditional

23. Which part of the passage contains an error in capitalization?

  a. sentence 1

  b. sentence 3

  c. sentence 7

  d. sentence 8

24. Which part of the passage draws attention away from the main idea of the first paragraph?
   a. sentence 1
   b. sentence 3
   c. sentence 5
   d. sentence 7

> **Read the passage, then answer the four questions that follow.**

(1) If you have little time to care for your garden, be sure to select hardy plants, such as phlox, comfrey, and peonies. (2) These will, with only a little care, keep the garden <u>brilliant</u> with color all through the growing season. (3) Sturdy sunflowers and hardy species of roses are also good selections. (4) As a thrifty gardener, you should leave part of the garden free for the planting of herbs such as lavender, sage, thyme, and parsley.

(5) If you have a moderate amount of time, growing vegetables and a garden culture of pears, apples, quinces, and other small fruits can be an interesting <u>ocupation</u> that amply rewards your expanded effort. (6) Even a small vegetable and fruit garden may yield radishes, celery, beans, and strawberries that will be <u>delicious</u> on the family table.
(7) _____.
(8) When planting the vegetable garden, you should be sure that the seeds receive the proper amount of <u>moisture</u>, that they are sown at the right season to receive the right degree of heat, and that each seed is placed near enough to the surface to allow the young plant to reach the light easily.

25. Which of the following sentences, if added as sentence 7, provides the best transition from sentence 6 to sentence 8?
   a. When and how you plant is important in producing a good yield from your garden.
   b. Very few gardening tasks are more fascinating than growing fruit trees.
   c. Of course, if you have saved room for an herb garden, you will be able to make the yield of your garden even tastier by cooking with your own herbs.
   d. Growing a productive fruit garden may take some specialized and time-consuming research into proper grafting techniques.

26. Which change is needed in the passage?
   a. Sentence 2: Change "through" to "threw."
   b. Sentence 5: Change "expanded" to "expended."
   c. Sentence 8: Change "sown" to "sewn."
   d. Sentence 8: Change "surface" to "surfeit."

27. Which underlined word in the passage is spelled incorrectly?
   a. brilliant
   b. ocupation
   c. delicious
   d. moisture

28. Which part of the passage contains an error in pronoun-antecedent agreement?
   a. sentence 2
   b. sentence 4
   c. sentence 6
   d. sentence 8

Read the passage, then answer the four questions that follow.

(1) If your office job involves telephone work, than your voice may be the first contact a caller has with your company or <u>organization</u>. (2) For this reason, your telephone manners have to be impeccable. (3) Always answer the phone promptly on the first or second ring, if possible. (4) After answering the phone on the first or second ring, speak directly into the phone, neither too loudly nor too softly, in a pleasant, cheerful voice. (5) Vary the pitch of your voice, so that it will not sound monotonous or uninterested, and be sure to <u>enunciate</u> clearly. (6) After a short, friendly greeting, state your company or boss's name, then your own name. (7) Always take messages carefully. (8) Fill out all <u>pertinant</u> blanks on the message pad sheet while you are still on the phone. (9) Always let the caller hang up first. (10) Do not depend in your memory for the spelling of a name or the last digit of a phone number, and be sure to write legibly. (11) When it is time to close a conversation, do so in a pleasant manner, and never hang up without saying good-bye. (12) While it is not an absolute rule, generally closing with *good-bye* is more professional than *bye-bye*. (13) <u>Verify</u> the information by reading it back to the caller.

29. Which change is needed in the passage?
  a. Sentence 1: Change "than" to "then."
  b. Sentence 2: Change "manners" to "manner."
  c. Sentence 5: Change "they" to "it."
  d. Sentence 6: Change "boss's" to "bosses."

30. Which part of the passage contains a nonstandard use of a preposition?
  a. sentence 1
  b. sentence 2
  c. sentence 8
  d. sentence 10

31. Which part of the passage contains a redundant expression of ideas or information?
  a. sentence 2
  b. sentence 4
  c. sentence 6
  d. sentence 8

32. Which underlined word in the passage is spelled incorrectly?
  a. organization
  b. enunciate
  c. pertinant
  d. Verify

Read the passage, then answer the three questions that follow.

(1) Understand that your boss has problems, too. (2) This is easy to forget. (3) When they have authority over you, it's hard to remember that your boss is just human. (4) Your boss may have children at home who misbehave, dogs or cats or parakeets that need to go to the vet, deadlines to meet, and/or bosses of their own (sometimes even bad ones) overseeing his or her work. (5) If your boss is occasionally unreasonable, try to keep in mind that it might have nothing to do with you. (6) I sometimes get cranky when people don't clean up after themselves in the kitchen of my office. (7) He or she may be having a bad day for reasons no one else knows. (8) Of course if such behavior becomes consistently abusive, you'll have to do

something about it—confront the problem or even quit. (9) But we're all entitled to occasional mood swings.

_____

33. Which part of the passage contains an error in pronoun-antecedent agreement?
   a. sentence 3
   b. sentence 4
   c. sentence 7
   d. sentence 9

34. Which part of the passage draws attention away from the main idea?
   a. sentence 1
   b. sentence 2
   c. sentence 6
   d. sentence 8

35. Which part of the passage contains an error in the use of commas?
   a. sentence 3
   b. sentence 4
   c. sentence 5
   d. sentence 8

Short-Answer Questions

Directions: Each of the following seven questions contains two errors in construction, grammar, usage, spelling, capitalization, or punctuation. Rewrite each sentence so these errors are revised but the original meaning remains, without introducing any new errors. Use the lines following or a separate sheet of paper.

36. A new homeowner comonly struggles to cope with a debt load that far exceeds their actual income.

_____

_____

_____

37. A student cannot get adequate physical rest if you continuously stays up too late gets up too early, and skips meals too often.

_____

_____

_____

38. Studies have shown that the students who turns in careful prepared lab reports do extremely well in science classes such as chemistry and physics.

_____

_____

_____

_____

39. Regular television programming is interrupted last Tuesday because the networks aired the President's State of the Union address.

_____

_____

_____

40. Having finished writing her essay on friday night, the rest of the weekend was totally free to be enjoyed.

_____

_____

_____

41. Before heading to the Laundromat Sayid packed all his dirty clothes over a large, green bag.

_____

_____

_____

42. A bad snowstorm can effect a community by making roads slippery for cars, causing power outages, and producing snow loads that are so heavy they can cause structural damage to poor designed buildings.

_____

_____

_____

_____

_____

Writing Summary Exercise

Directions: Use this passage to prepare a summary of 100 to 150 words.

Among traditional societies of the Pacific Northwest—including the Haidas, Kwakiuls, Makahs, Nootkas, Tlingits, and Tsimshians—the gift-giving ceremony called potlatch was a central feature of social life. The word *potlatch*, meaning "to give," comes from a Chinook trading language that was used all along the Pacific Coast. Each nation, or tribe, had its own particular word for the ceremony, and each had different potlatch traditions. However, the function and basic features of the ceremony were universal among the tribes.

Each nation held potlatches to celebrate important life passages, such as birth, coming of age, marriage, and death. Potlatches were also held to honor ancestors and to mark the passing of leadership. A potlatch, which could last four or more days, was usually held in the winter when the tribes were not engaged in gathering and storing food. Each potlatch included the formal display of the host family's crest and masks. The hosts performed ritual dances and provided feasts for their guests. However, the most important ritual was the lavish distribution of gifts to the guests. Some hosts might give away most or all their accumulated wealth in one potlatch. The more a host gave away, the more status was accorded him. In turn, the guests, who had to accept the proffered gifts, were then expected to host their own potlatches and give away gifts of equal value.

Prior to the tribes' contact with Europeans, gifts might have included food, slaves, copper plates, and goat's hair blankets. After contact, the potlatch was fundamentally transformed by the influx of manufactured goods. As tribes garnered wealth in the fur trade, gifts came to include guns, woolen blankets, and other Western goods. Although potlatches had always been a means for individuals to win prestige, potlatches involving manufactured goods became a way for nobles to validate tenuous claims to leadership, sometimes through the destruction of property. It was this willful destruction of property that led Canadian authorities, and later the U.S. government, to ban potlatches in the late 1880s.

Despite the ban, the potlatch remained an important part of native Pacific Northwest culture. Giving wealth—not accumulating wealth, as is prized in Western culture—was a means of cementing leadership, affirming status, establishing and maintaining alliances, and ensuring the even distribution of food and goods. Agnes Alfred, an Indian from Albert Bay, explained the potlatch this way, "When one's heart is glad, he gives away gifts. . . . The potlatch was given to us to be our way of expressing joy."

Open Response: Writing Summary Exercise

Composition Exercise

Directions: Read this passage about science education, then follow the instructions for writing your composition.

Recently, American students are said to have fallen behind in the sciences. According to results of a worldwide science test administered in late 2007, the performance of American teenagers on the science portion of the exam was poorer than that of students from 16 out of the 30 countries tested. The test focused on real-world application of science knowledge and skills. Some educators believe this is because American teachers are conducting science classes ineffectively.

Your purpose is to write a persuasive composition, to be read by a classroom instructor, in which you suggest ways science classes could be conducted to more effectively challenge students.

Open Response: Composition Exercise

Reading Subtest Answers

1. a. Choice **b** emphasizes only damage to the atmosphere; the passage encompasses more than that. Choice **c** does not mention the atmosphere, which is the main focus of the passage. Choice **d** is too narrow—the final paragraph of the passage emphasizes that the circulation of the atmosphere is but one example of the complex events that keep the earth alive.

2. c. This question assesses the ability to see the organization of a reading passage and to organize material for study purposes. Choice **a** is wrong because the passage does not explain exactly what will happen as a result of damage to the atmosphere and other life-sustaining mechanisms. Choice **b** is wrong because the passage does not explain the origin of the atmosphere. Choice **d** is wrong because it is solar energy that travels 93 million miles through space, not the atmosphere.

3. b. The *biosphere*, as defined in paragraph 1, is a *region* (or part) of the earth; it is not the envelope around the earth, the living things on Earth, or the circulation of the atmosphere (choices **a**, **c**, and **d**).

4. a. This question assesses the ability to see cause and effect. Paragraph 2 deals with how variations in the strength with which solar radiation strikes the earth affect temperature. None of the other choices is discussed in terms of all temperature changes on Earth.

5. a. There is no mention in the first paragraph of any *reviving* or *cleansing* effect the atmosphere may have (choices **b** and **d**). In a sense, enabling Earth to sustain life is invigorating; however, choice **a** is a better choice because the first two sentences mention how the atmosphere *protects* Earth from harmful forces.

6. c. Whether the web of life is *fascinating* is a matter of opinion, because not everyone might agree with this statement. Choices **a**, **b**, and **d** all state inarguable facts.

7. a. The passage is a neutral narration of Mozart's childhood and the beginning of his musical career. Choices **c** and **d** can be eliminated because the author does not take a side or try to provide a point. Choice **b** is incorrect because even though the author *does* make generalizations, they are only incidental to the main purpose of describing Mozart's development as a composer.

8. c. Paragraph 1 clearly states that Wolfgang took an interest in the clavier when his sister was learning the instrument.

9. c. The passage states that Wolfgang's first *public* appearance was at Linz and that after this concert word of his genius traveled to Vienna. The passage states earlier that Vienna was the *capital* of the Hapsburg Empire.

10. b. The author's tone toward Leopold is *mild*—neither strongly approving nor disapproving. In a few places, the author conveys some disappointment, especially in the last lines of paragraph 3, where he or she states that Leopold set an exhausting schedule for Wolfgang.

11. d. *Lavish* means *expended or produced in abundance*. Both *wasteful* and *extravagant* are synonyms for *lavish*, but because it is modifying *palace*, *extravagant* is the more logical choice.

12. a. Whether Mozart's talent was *remarkable* is a matter of opinion, because not everyone might agree with this statement. Choices **b**, **c**, and **d** all state inarguable facts.

13. c. The narrator was most likely in his early teens when he came to America. The author writes that *I lost half a language through want of use and eventually, in my late teens, even lost French as the language of my internal monologue.* This makes it clear that he must have been in the United States several years before he was in his *late teens,* making choice **d** incorrect. He was also old enough to have friends *and stories and familiar comforts and a sense of continuity between home and outside* and *a whole network of routes through life that I had just barely glimpsed,* so choices **a** and **b** are incorrect.

14. d. While some of the things the narrator's family lost were tangible (the house, the heirlooms), most of the list includes intangible things that are very important in establishing our identity and sense of self. He is not trying to convince others not to immigrate (choice **a**); he is not criticizing the United States or his experience since he arrived. There is no evidence that the crates were smashed because his family packed carelessly (choice **b**). In the second paragraph, the author writes that he did not consciously miss his homeland; he *actively colluded* in the losses they suffered and tried to reinvent himself. Thus, choice **c** is incorrect.

15. c. The author writes, *Like it or not, each of us is made, less by blood or genes than by a process that is largely accidental, the impact of things seen and heard and smelled and tasted and endured. . . .* The entire third paragraph lists things in our environment that contribute to who we are. The first sentence in the paragraph contradicts choices **a** and **d**. There is no mention of education (choice **b**).

16. b. The author states that he lost his native language through lack of use and that he not only didn't disapprove of losing his heritage—he often *actively colluded.* In addition, he states that he *had so effectively renounced* the part of him that *had been formed in another world.* This directly contradicts choice **c**. We do not know whether he embraced American culture (choice **a**) or became withdrawn (choice **d**).

17. a. In the third paragraph, the author lists all the aspects of our environment that have an impact on our identity and sense of self. Even if we don't consciously think of these things, or even notice them, they are a part of who we are. We do not necessarily have to dig deep within ourselves to discover our past, so choice **b** is incorrect. We may all have a part of our past that we want to keep buried (choice **c**), but the author doesn't state that anywhere in the passage. The author does not appear to be an archaeologist, and he does not claim that only archaeologists understand the impact of our environment, so choice **d** is incorrect.

18. d. Choice **d** is the only answer choice that adequately summarizes the main details of the passage. Choices **a**, **b**, and **c** focus on specific details that do not capture the meaning of the passage as a whole.

19. b. Throughout the essay, the author expresses his people's respect for the land. *Every part of the earth is sacred to my people,* he states, for example, and *The earth does not belong to man, man belongs to the earth.*

20. c. The author is addressing all new Americans—the people to whom he would be selling the land. There is a clear distinction between the *you* of the new Americans and the *we* of the Native Americans, so choices **b** and **d** are incorrect. Choice **a** is incorrect because he speaks of the president in the third person.

21. d. The questions the author asks and the statements he makes are aimed at convincing the new Americans to treat the land with respect: *you must give to the rivers the kindness you would give any brother; if we sell you our land, you must keep it apart and sacred.* He does not offer any reasons for the new Americans not to buy the land, so choice **a** is incorrect. He does not address the American Indians nor suggest that they fight, so choice **b** is incorrect. He does not state any reasons not to buy the land, and he praises the land rather than pointing out any flaws, so choice **c** is incorrect.

22. b. For Chief Seattle, every part of nature is sacred. *We know the sap which courses through the trees as we know the blood that courses through our veins,* he writes, suggesting that each tree is important and valuable. This directly contrasts the indifference of Reagan's statement, so choice **a** is incorrect. Reagan does not seem to care about the land, so choice **c** is also incorrect. Chief Seattle does talk about trees, as previously noted, so choice **d** is incorrect.

23. a. While *courses* may mean *classes* (choice **b**), *paths* (choice **c**), and *times* (choice **d**), it does not have these meanings in the sentence from paragraph 2. The word *flows* makes the most sense if used in place of *courses* in the sentence, so choice **a** is the correct answer.

24. c. Choice **c** is the only answer choice that adequately summarizes the main details of the passage. Choices **b** and **d** focus on specific details that do not capture the meaning of the passage as a whole. Choice **a** is incorrect because Chief Seattle does not consider selling the land to the president (but he says *if we sell you the land* twice in the passage); in fact, he states numerous times that the land does not even belong to him or any other man.

25. d. The answer is found in paragraph 2: *what they are also getting could be, in one meal, more than the daily recommended allowances of calories, fat, and sodium.*

26. a. Paragraph 1 covers how fast food has caused a rise in obesity, paragraph 3 discusses the MEAL Act, paragraph 4 reveals that *registered dieticians couldn't come up with accurate estimates of the calories found in certain fast foods,* meaning that such studies are inconclusive, and paragraph 5 states that *the restaurant industry isn't happy about the new bill.* Choice **b** outlines the first paragraph without covering the rest of the passage. Choices **c** and **d** merely gather random topics from the passage.

27. d. *Remonstrations* is used to describe a statement that is *against* the bill. Because *arguments* are statements *against* certain things or ideas, choice **d** is the best answer.

28. b. The author says the MEAL Act would be *a significant piece of legislation,* which suggests a favorable attitude toward the act, but does not allow this opinion to detract from the numerous facts in the passage. Nothing in the passage suggests the author has *misconceptions about obesity and fast food,* so choice **a** can be eliminated. The author does present a definitive explanation of calories in fast food, so choice **c** is wrong, as well.

29. a. Whether a chicken breast sandwich is a *better-sounding alternative to a burger* is a matter of opinion, because not everyone might agree with this statement. Choices **b**, **c**, and **d** all state inarguable facts.

30. c. Because a Taco Bell Beef Gordita has 680 fewer calories than a Burger King Double Whopper with Cheese, it is a healthier lunch option. A chicken salad may sound like a relatively healthy lunch option, but Taco Bell's Fiesta Chicken Salad actually has 60 more calories than the Burger King Tendercrisp Chicken Sandwich, so choice **a** is incorrect. A Subway 6″ Meatball Sub has 80 more calories than McDonald's Large Fries, so choice **b** is incorrect, as well. Choice **d** can be eliminated because a Subway 12″ Sweet Onion Chicken Teriyaki Sandwich has 240 more calories than a McDonald's Big Mac.

31. a. The passage describes how public art influences a community in a complimentary and positive way, so the relationship between public art and a community is *harmonious*. Therefore, choice **a** is the best answer.

32. c. Paragraph 3 defines public art as *art specifically designed for a public arena where the art will be encountered by people in their normal day-to-day activities and private art as art that is sequestered in museums and galleries.* The second paragraph is the one that mentions the relationship between public art and communities, so choice **b** is incorrect. Nowhere in the passage does the author discuss the worst qualities of public art, so choice **a** can be eliminated.

33. d. Choice **d** is the only one that explains how public art affects viewers rather than the area in which the art is placed.

34. c. Whether the installations in Brooklyn's MetroTech Center are *incredible* is a matter of opinion, because not everyone might agree with this statement. Choices **a**, **b**, and **d** all state inarguable facts.

35. b. Choice **b** adequately outlines the most important topics in the passage. Choice **a** only focuses on paragraph 5 without addressing the passage as a whole. Choices **c** and **d** merely gather random details from the passage without addressing its most important topics.

36. d. By drawing the distinction that public art is *designed for a public arena where the art will be encountered by people in their normal day-to-day activities*, the author conversely suggests that private art is relatively hidden or isolated from the public in museums and galleries. Therefore, choice **d** offers the best definition of *sequestered*.

37. c. The government intends to end or *conquer* the destruction of the reef by tourists, so choice **c** is the best answer. Although to *quash* something is to *influence* it in a certain way, *conquer* is a much more specific synonym of *quash*, so choice **a** is incorrect.

38. d. Paragraph 2 specifically states *corals are the main components of reef structure.* Tube worms (choice **a**), mollusks (choice **b**), and coralline algae (choice **c**) all participate in formulating reefs, but they are not the main components.

39. a. According to paragraph 2, tube worms contribute skeletons to the reef, which suggests that they help it, while paragraph 4 states *Crown-of-thorns starfish feed on coral and can destroy large portions of reef.* Paragraph 2 states that tube worms and mollusks are found on the reef, but does not suggest that they are the same things, so choice **b** is incorrect. There is no evidence to support choices **c** and **d** in the passage.

40. b. Whether the colors of the reef are *beautiful* is a matter of opinion, because not everyone might agree with this statement. Choices **a**, **c**, and **d** all state inarguable facts.

41. d. Choice **d** adequately summarizes the main topics addressed throughout the passage. Choice **a** only addresses paragraph 3, failing to cover the topics discussed in the entire passage. Choices **b** and **d** mention specific details in the passage, failing to encompass the most important ones.

42. b. The fact that it can be seen from space is more relevant to paragraph 3, which discusses the size of Great Barrier Reef, than to paragraph 4, which focuses on the environmental threats facing it. Choice **a** is relevant because it serves as the topic sentence of the paragraph, while choices **c** and **d** offer relevant details that support that topic sentence.

Writing Subtest Answers

Multiple Choice

1. c. The writer's main point is that Americans do not take voting seriously enough. Answer choices **a** and **d** are not ideas expressed by the writer in this passage. Choice **b** expresses one detail in the passage without addressing the main topic.

2. d. The phrase *so they do not vote* is redundant because sentence 8 already mentioned that these people *state that they have never voted*.

3. b. Although a cause of war is mentioned in the opening sentence, the causes of wars is not the main idea of this passage, so a list of such causes detracts from the passage. Choices **a**, **c**, and **d** all develop the main idea, so they belong in the passage.

4. c. The word *absence* is misspelled in sentence 10 of the passage.

5. c. There is a lack of pronoun agreement in this sentence. The plural pronoun *their* should not be used with the singular *each student*. Only choice **c** replaces the pronoun to make the sentence more understandable.

6. b. That libraries and classrooms were equipped with computers was already mentioned in sentence 1, so this information should not be repeated in sentence 2. Choices **a**, **c**, and **d** are incorrect because they all contain information that had not been mentioned earlier in the passage needlessly.

7. b. The preferred music format of today's students has nothing to do with the main topic of this passage, which is how Empire High School purchased laptops for its students rather than new textbooks. Choices **a**, **c**, and **d** are all on topic.

8. d. The introductory phrase *Instead of handing in reports and homework on paper* needs to be offset from the rest of the sentence with a comma.

9. c. This question tests the ability to recognize a sentence fragment. Although choice **c** does include a subject and a verb, it is a dependent clause because it begins with the adverb *when*. Choices **a**, **b**, and **d** are all standard sentences.

10. a. This question assesses the ability to recognize redundancy in a sentence. Choice **a** removes the redundancy of sentence 8 by taking out the word *also*, which repeats the meaning of the introductory phrase *in addition to*. Choices **b** and **c** involve changing singular nouns to plural and plural possessive nouns, which is not necessary and would make the sentence grammatically incorrect. Choice **d** would change the meaning of the sentence incorrectly. The attitude of the community toward young people is being reported, not what young people have reported about the community attitude.

11. c. Choice **c** provides a fact that supports and expands on the information given in the previous sentences. Sentences 1 and 2 tell us about the program's success and the plans for expanding it. Choice **c** builds on these ideas by providing detailed information about the results of the program and who was involved. Choice **a** changes the subject of this paragraph. This paragraph is about the program in a specific school district and choice **a** makes a comment about other school districts, which may be true, but is not related to the topic of this particular paragraph. Choice **b** adds a detail about the program, but it is a single detail as opposed to a conclusive, summarizing sentence that gives us a clear idea of the program specifics. Choice **d**, which mentions the possibility of other pilot programs, again, changes the subject and veers away from the main topic of this paragraph, which is the Mural Painting Program within this particular school district.

12. d. Sentence 6 needlessly states that mural painting programs make students less apathetic after sentence 5 already stated that *young people who have been exposed to similar programs are much less prone to apathy.*

13. b. Paragraph 2 contradicts the misconceptions potential adopters of racing greyhounds might have about the breed. Choice **b** states that certain popular beliefs about greyhounds are erroneous and acts as a transition to the facts that follow in the paragraph. Choice **a** does not focus on contradicting the misinformation; also, the phrase *even so* appears to agree with the misconceptions rather than contradict them. Choice **c** does not focus on the argument; instead, it repeats information given in the previous sentence. Choice **d**, rather than supporting the main purpose of the paragraph—which is to dispel myths about racing greyhounds—actually contradicts information in sentences 6 and 7.

14. a. The word *there* refers to a direction and does not make sense in this context. It should be replaced with a homophone, the possessive pronoun *their*.

15. a. Without a semicolon between the words *age* and *even* to separate the two independent clauses, sentence 6 is a run-on sentence. Choices **c** and **d** may be long sentences, but they are punctuated properly and are not run-ons.

16. b. Sentence 2 introduces the subject of greyhounds racing while sentence 1 develops on that subject by mentioning that many people have been adopting greyhound racing dogs as pets. Therefore, the two sentences should be reversed. All sentences in this passage are necessary to introduce and develop upon the topic, so none of them should be deleted, which makes choices **a** and **c** incorrect. Choice **d** is incorrect because reversing the order of sentences 2 and 3 would make the paragraph more confusing rather than clearer.

17. c. Choice **c** is correct because the apostrophe in *it's* suggests a contraction of *it is* when the word should be the possessive form of *it*. Choice **a** is incorrect because *experts* is correctly used as the plural form of expert and inserting an apostrophe would make it the possessive form of *expert*. Choice **b** is incorrect because it adds a misplaced comma to sentence 2. Choice **d** is incorrect because it removes the necessary apostrophe from the contraction of *You will*.

18. d. Choice **d** provides a smooth transition between the paragraphs by picking up on the topic of *increasing the level of your walking* from paragraph 1 and introducing the idea that it *may seem difficult at first* but will change quickly in paragraph 2. Choice **a** does not provide such a transition and would fit better with the other benefits of increased physical activity mentioned in sentence 2. Although paragraph 1 ends with a discussion of walking buddies, the topic has moved on by paragraph 2, so choice **b** would not be a good topic sentence for that paragraph. Although it is mentioned briefly in paragraph 1, eating right is not an important idea in this passage, so choice **c** is incorrect.

19. b. The word *flexibility* is misspelled in sentence 2 of the passage.

20. d. A comma is missing after the introductory phrase *In addition* in sentence 12 of the passage. Choices **a**, **b**, and **c** are punctuated correctly.

21. d. Sentence 8 already mentioned that Cassatt never had children, so there is no need to state that she died childless in sentence 9. Choices **a**, **b**, and **c** are incorrect because they all contain information that hadn't already been stated in the passage.

22. b. The word *contemporary* is misspelled in sentence 5 of the passage. Choices **a**, **c**, and **d** are all spelled correctly.

23. a. The word *City* should be capitalized in sentence 1 because it is used as part of the proper noun *Allegheny City*. Choices **b**, **c**, and **d** are all capitalized correctly.

24. d. Choice **d** focuses on the artist Camille Pissarro, who is only briefly mentioned in sentence 5 and is not the main subject of paragraph 1. That paragraph, and the passage as a whole, is mainly about Mary Cassatt.

25. a. This sentence creates a transition between the idea of harvesting food from a garden (sentence 6) and the proper way of planting in order to achieve a good yield of food (sentence 8). Choice **b** is incorrect because it is redundant, repeating information already stated in sentence 5. Choice **c** contains information that is about the subject matter of the first paragraph and is, thus, off-topic in the second. Choice **d** is off-topic and does not match the main idea of the paragraph; in a paragraph on the subject of gardening that takes a moderate amount of time, it mentions time-consuming work.

26. b. The word *expended* should be substituted for *expanded* because *expanded*, meaning *enlarged*, makes no sense in this context.

27. b. The word *occupation* is misspelled in sentence 5 of the passage. Choices **a**, **c**, and **d** are all spelled correctly.

28. d. The singular pronoun *it* does not agree with the plural word *seeds* and should be changed to *them*.

29. a. This sentence requires the adverb *then* in this context. Choice **b** is incorrect because it would introduce a problem in subject-verb agreement. Choice **c** is incorrect because it would introduce a problem of agreement between the pronoun *they* and its antecedent *pitch*. Choice **d** is incorrect because the possessive rather than the plural of the noun *boss* is necessary in this context.

30. d. The verb *depend* is, idiomatically, followed by the preposition *on*; in sentence 10, it is wrongly followed by *in*. Choices **a**, **b**, and **c** are incorrect because none of them contain nonstandard uses of prepositions.

31. b. Sentence 3 already mentioned the importance of answering the phone on the first or second ring, so mentioning it again in sentence 4 is redundant.

32. c. The word *pertinent* is misspelled in sentence 8 of the passage. Choices **a**, **b**, and **d** are all spelled correctly.

33. b. The antecedent of the pronoun *they* in this sentence is *boss*. Since *boss* is singular, the corrected subject pronoun should be *he* or *she*.

30. c. The passage is mainly about understanding that your boss is human, so a sentence explaining one of the author's pet peeves draws attention away from that main idea. Choice **a** is incorrect because sentence 1 is the topic sentence of the passage, so it most certainly does not draw attention away from itself.

35. d. Choice **d** should have a comma after the introductory phrase *Of course*. Choices **a**, **b**, and **c** are all punctuated correctly.

Short Answer

36. This sentence should read, *A new homeowner commonly struggles to cope with a debt load that far exceeds his or her actual income.* This is an example of using a pronoun in the wrong number. The subject (*homeowner*) is singular, and so the pronoun (*their*) should be singular also. The sentence also contains a spelling error; *commonly* is spelled incorrectly.

37. This sentence should read, *A student cannot get adequate physical rest if he or she continuously stays up too late, gets up too early, and skips meals too often.* This is an example of pronoun shift. The sentence begins with a noun and then shifts to the wrong pronoun (*you*). When the noun is used, he, she, or a person must follow it later. The sentence is also missing a series comma between the words *late* and *gets*.

38. This sentence should read, *Studies have shown that the students who turn in carefully prepared lab reports do extremely well in science classes such as chemistry and physics.* This question is an example of a misuse of an adverb (*careful*). It is modifying the verb *prepared* and should have an *-ly* ending (*carefully*). There is also a mistake in subject-verb agreement; since the subject *students* is plural it requires the verb *turn* with an added *s*.

39. This sentence should read, *Regular television programming was interrupted last Tuesday because the networks aired the president's State of the Union address.* The first error is a problem with verb tense. Since the sentence describes an event that took place in the past (*last Tuesday*) the present-tense verb is should be changed to the past tense *was*. The second error is a problem with capitalization. The word *president* should only be capitalized if used as a specific president's title, for example, *President Obama*. This is not the case in this sentence, so *president* should not be capitalized here.

40. This sentence should read, *Having finished writing his essay on Friday night, he was totally free to enjoy the rest of his weekend.* The sentence contains a dangling modifier that needs to be corrected. As written, we do not know who was free to enjoy the rest of the weekend. Adding a specific subject, such as *she*, corrects this problem. The word *Friday* also needs to be capitalized.

41. This sentence should read, *Before heading to the Laundromat, Sayid packed all his dirty clothes into a large, green bag.* A comma is needed to separate the introductory phrase *Before heading to the Laundromat* from the rest of the sentence. There is also an error in preposition usage: he would not pack his clothes *over* a bag; he would pack them *into* it.

42. This sentence should read, *A bad snowstorm can affect a community by making roads slippery for cars, causing power outages, and producing snow loads that are so heavy they can cause structural damage to poorly designed buildings.* The word *effect* is a noun, but this sentence calls for a verb, so it should be changed to *affect*. Furthermore, the word *poor* is an adjective, but it is being used to modify the verb *designed* in this sentence. Therefore, it should be changed to the adverb *poorly*.

Sample Strong Response for Writing Summary Exercise

A potlatch is a traditional gift-giving ceremony central to social life in many Pacific Northwest societies. The ceremony is held to celebrate important events, such as births, marriages, and death A potlatch may last for four or more days during the winter, and involve formal decorations, ritual dances, and feasts, as well as gift-giving. Before the arrival of Europeans to America, gifts included food, slaves, copper plates, and goat's hair blankets. Potlatches also served as ways to lay claims to leadership, which sometimes involved destroying property. This practice led Canadian and U.S. governments to ban potlatches in the late 1880s. Regardless of this fact, potlatches are still important in Pacific Northwest culture.

Sample Strong Response for Composition Exercise

The best way for teachers to boost their students' science test scores is to stop worrying quite so much about the scores and start being concerned about making the students excited about science. Before ever asking students to memorize facts, the teacher should demonstrate a scientific process or, better, teach the students how to experiment for themselves, allowing them to grasp the process with their senses before trying to fix it in their intellect. For example, the teacher might pass around an ant farm in the classroom and let the students observe the little critters skittering behind the glass, going about their complex, individual tasks, before asking the students to read that ants have a rigid social structure, just as people do. If possible, it would be even better to take them on a field trip to observe a real anthill or to see how other kinds of real animals behave, say on a farm or in a zoo. The teacher might allow the students to create a chemical reaction in a beaker—taking care, of course, that they don't blow themselves up—before asking them to memorize the formula. This would help students to witness how science functions in the real world rather than merely as an abstract test question.

When I was small, I had firsthand experience with this kind of teaching. My father built a telescope. The telescope had a clock at its base that kept it fixed on the moon or stars rather than turning as the earth turns. When my father switched off the clock, I remember watching through the eyepiece, fascinated at how quickly the stars drifted out of my field of vision—it took only seconds—and even more fascinated to realize that what I was seeing was us floating so swiftly through space. He told me the magical names of the geological formations on the moon, such as the crater called "The Sea of Tranquility." When I looked through the lens, the pockmarked silvery disc of the moon seemed as close as the hills behind our suburban house.

After that, I became interested in the statistics, such as the rate of the rotation of the earth and the geophysical facts behind the making of the craters that form the moon's laughing face, in a way I never would have if the facts had been the starting point of a lecture. This approach should be begun, not in high school or college, but in grade school or even in kindergarten. The facts are important, of course—without them, we can have no real understanding. But curiosity is as vital to learning as is the ability to memorize—perhaps more so. Curiosity will keep students learning long after they've passed their final test in school.

Scoring Your Subtests

Your scores on the Reading and Writing subtests of the official MTEL Communication and Literacy Skills Test will be scaled scores representing all subareas of each subtest, including all multiple-choice questions, short-answer questions, and open-response assignments. The scaled score for both the Reading and Writing subtest is a conversion of the number of raw points earned on the test to a score in the range of 100 to 300. A scaled score of 240 represents the qualifying, or passing, score for each subtest. You can use the charts on the following pages to find approximate MTEL scores for your performance on this practice test and to help guide your studies with the two review chapters in this book, as well as outside resources. Remember, these are only practice tests and the scores you receive here are only an approximation of what your official scores might be.

Find Your Reading Subtest Score

To find your approximate MTEL score for the practice Reading subtest, you must first figure out how many raw subtest points you earned. Each question answered correctly on this subtest is worth one point, for a maximum of 42 points. Use Table 10.1 to add up your points; giving yourself a one for each correct answer, and a zero for each incorrect answer.

You can also use Table 10.1 to help diagnose your strengths and weaknesses to better focus your studies. The rows in the Objectives column include the MTEL Reading Subtest Objectives that correspond to each question in this practice test. After you have filled in the table, note any particular objective or objectives in which you could use more practice, and then turn to Chapter 7: Reading Skills Review and use the review resources there to help strengthen your skills in that area.

QUESTION NUMBER	CORRECT ANSWER	POINTS Correct Answer = 1 Point Incorrect Answer = 0 Points	OBJECTIVE
TABLE 10.1 READING SUBTEST SCORING AND REVIEW CHART			
1.	a		0002 Understand the main idea and supporting details in written material.
2.	c		0006 Apply skills for outlining and summarizing written materials and interpreting information presented in graphic form.
3.	b		0001 Determine the meaning of words and phrases in the context in which they occur.
4.	a		0004 Analyze the relationships among ideas in written material.
5.	a		0002 Understand the main idea and supporting details in written material.
6.	c		0005 Use critical reasoning skills to evaluate written material.
7.	a		0003 Identify a writer's purpose, point of view, and intended meaning.

(continued)

QUESTION NUMBER	CORRECT ANSWER	POINTS Correct Answer = 1 Point Incorrect Answer = 0 Points	OBJECTIVE
		TABLE 10.1 READING SUBTEST SCORING AND REVIEW CHART (*continued*)	
8.	c		0004 Analyze the relationships among ideas in written material.
9.	c		0004 Analyze the relationships among ideas in written material.
10.	b		0003 Identify a writer's purpose, point of view, and intended meaning.
11.	d		0001 Determine the meaning of words and phrases in the context in which they occur.
12.	a		0005 Use critical reasoning skills to evaluate written material.
13.	c		0004 Analyze the relationships among ideas in written material.
14.	d		0003 Identify a writer's purpose, point of view, and intended meaning.
15.	c		0002 Understand the main idea and supporting details in written material.
16.	b		0002 Understand the main idea and supporting details in written material.
17.	a		0003 Identify a writer's purpose, point of view, and intended meaning.
18.	d		0006 Apply skills for outlining and summarizing written materials and interpreting information presented in graphic form.
19.	b		0002 Understand the main idea and supporting details in written material.
20.	c		0003 Identify a writer's purpose, point of view, and intended meaning.
21.	d		0003 Identify a writer's purpose, point of view, and intended meaning.
22.	b		0004 Analyze the relationships among ideas in written material.
23.	a		0001 Determine the meaning of words and phrases in the context in which they occur.
24.	c		0006 Apply skills for outlining and summarizing written materials and interpreting information presented in graphic form.
25.	d		0002 Understand the main idea and supporting details in written material.
26.	a		0006 Apply skills for outlining and summarizing written materials and interpreting information presented in graphic form.

QUESTION NUMBER	CORRECT ANSWER	POINTS Correct Answer = 1 Point Incorrect Answer = 0 Points	OBJECTIVE
			TABLE 10.1 READING SUBTEST SCORING AND REVIEW CHART (*continued*)
27.	d		0001 Determine the meaning of words and phrases in the context in which they occur.
28.	b		0005 Use critical reasoning skills to evaluate written material.
29.	a		0005 Use critical reasoning skills to evaluate written material.
30.	c		0006 Apply skills for outlining and summarizing written materials and interpreting information presented in graphic form.
31.	a		0001 Determine the meaning of words and phrases in the context in which they occur.
32.	c		0003 Identify a writer's purpose, point of view, and intended meaning.
33.	d		0004 Analyze the relationships among ideas in written material.
34.	c		0005 Use critical reasoning skills to evaluate written material.
35.	b		0006 Apply skills for outlining and summarizing written materials and interpreting information presented in graphic form.
36.	d		0001 Determine the meaning of words and phrases in the context in which they occur.
37.	c		0001 Determine the meaning of words and phrases in the context in which they occur.
38.	d		0002 Understand the main idea and supporting details in written material.
39.	a		0004 Analyze the relationships among ideas in written material.
40.	b		0005 Use critical reasoning skills to evaluate written material.
41.	d		0006 Apply skills for outlining and summarizing written materials and interpreting information presented in graphic form.
42.	b		0005 Use critical reasoning skills to evaluate written material.

Total Reading Subtest Points:

Now, find the number of Reading subtest points you earned in the left-hand column of Table 10.2. The corresponding number in the right-hand column is your approximate MTEL score.

TABLE 10.2 READING SUBTEST SCORE CONVERSION CHART	
POINTS	APPROXIMATE MTEL READING SCORE
0–14	100
15–16	101
17–18	116
19–20	131
21–22	146
23–24	161
25–26	176
27–28	191
29–30	206
31–32	221
33–34	236
35–36	251
37–38	266
39–40	281
41–42	296

Find Your Writing Subtest Score

There are a number of steps to finding your total approximate MTEL score for a practice Writing subtest. The first step is to total the number of raw points you earned for your responses to the multiple-choice and short-answer questions. Like the Reading subtest, each multiple-choice question answered correctly on this subtest is worth one point. Use Table 10.3 to help you add up those multiple-choice points. In Table 10.3, you'll also find each question's related Objective to help focus your studying using Chapter 8: Writing Skills Review.

QUESTION NUMBER	CORRECT ANSWER	POINTS Correct Answer = 1 Point Incorrect Answer = 0 Points	OBJECTIVE
TABLE 10.3	**WRITING SUBTEST MULTIPLE-CHOICE QUESTIONS SCORING AND REVIEW CHART**		
1.	c		0007 Understand methods for establishing and maintaining a central theme or main idea.
2.	d		0007 Understand methods for establishing and maintaining a central theme or main idea.
3.	b		0007 Understand methods for establishing and maintaining a central theme or main idea.
4.	c		0009 Recognize common errors of spelling, capitalization, and punctuation.
5.	c		0008 Recognize common errors of sentence construction, grammar, and usage.
6.	b		0007 Understand methods for establishing and maintaining a central theme or main idea.
7.	b		0007 Understand methods for establishing and maintaining a central theme or main idea.
8.	d		0009 Recognize common errors of spelling, capitalization, and punctuation.
9.	c		0008 Recognize common errors of sentence construction, grammar, and usage.
10.	a		0008 Recognize common errors of sentence construction, grammar, and usage.
11.	c		0007 Understand methods for establishing and maintaining a central theme or main idea.
12.	d		0007 Understand methods for establishing and maintaining a central theme or main idea.
13.	b		0007 Understand methods for establishing and maintaining a central theme or main idea.
14.	a		0008 Recognize common errors of sentence construction, grammar, and usage.
15.	a		0008 Recognize common errors of sentence construction, grammar, and usage.
16.	b		0007 Understand methods for establishing and maintaining a central theme or main idea.
17.	c		0009 Recognize common errors of spelling, capitalization, and punctuation.
18.	d		0007 Understand methods for establishing and maintaining a central theme or main idea.
19.	b		0009 Recognize common errors of spelling, capitalization, and punctuation.
20.	d		0009 Recognize common errors of spelling, capitalization, and punctuation.

(continued)

		POINTS	
QUESTION NUMBER	**CORRECT ANSWER**	Correct Answer = 1 Point Incorrect Answer = 0 Points	**OBJECTIVE**

TABLE 10.3 WRITING SUBTEST MULTIPLE-CHOICE QUESTIONS SCORING AND REVIEW CHART (*continued*)

QUESTION NUMBER	CORRECT ANSWER	POINTS	OBJECTIVE
21.	d		0007 Understand methods for establishing and maintaining a central theme or main idea.
22.	b		0009 Recognize common errors of spelling, capitalization, and punctuation.
23.	a		0009 Recognize common errors of spelling, capitalization, and punctuation.
24.	d		0007 Understand methods for establishing and maintaining a central theme or main idea.
25.	a		0007 Understand methods for establishing and maintaining a central theme or main idea.
26.	b		0008 Recognize common errors of sentence construction, grammar, and usage.
27.	b		0009 Recognize common errors of spelling, capitalization, and punctuation.
28.	d		0008 Recognize common errors of sentence construction, grammar, and usage.
29.	a		0008 Recognize common errors of sentence construction, grammar, and usage.
30.	d		0008 Recognize common errors of sentence construction, grammar, and usage.
31.	b		0007 Understand methods for establishing and maintaining a central theme or main idea.
32.	c		0009 Recognize common errors of spelling, capitalization, and punctuation.
33.	b		0008 Recognize common errors of sentence construction, grammar, and usage.
34.	c		0007 Understand methods for establishing and maintaining a central theme or main idea.
35.	d		0009 Recognize common errors of spelling, capitalization, and punctuation.

Multiple-Choice Points Subtotal: [   ]

The short-answer questions in the Writing sub-test are worth zero, one, or two points, depending on the success of your response. Use the answer explana-tions and the following key to figure out how many points you earned for each of your short-answer questions:

SCORING KEY FOR WRITING SUBTEST SHORT-ANSWER QUESTIONS	
POINTS EARNED	**DESCRIPTION**
2	**Fully Correct:** ■ You successfully corrected both errors in the question and did not introduce any new ones.
1	**Partially Correct:** ■ You properly corrected only one of the two errors in the question. You did not introduce any new errors. ■ You successfully corrected both errors in the question, but introduced a new one.
0	**Incorrect:** ■ You did not correct either of the errors in the question. ■ You properly corrected one of the two errors in the question, but introduced one or more new errors.

Next, use Table 10.4 to add up the number of short-answer points you earned on this subtest.

TABLE 10.4 WRITING SUBTEST SHORT-ANSWER QUESTIONS SCORING AND REVIEW CHART		
QUESTION NUMBER	**SHORT-ANSWER POINTS** Fully Correct = 2 Points Partially Correct = 1 Point Incorrect = 0 Points	**OBJECTIVE**
36. 37.		0010 Demonstrate the ability to analyze and revise sentences containing common errors of sentence construction, grammar, usage, spelling, capitalization, and punctuation.
38. 39. 40. 41. 42.		
Short-Answer Points Subtotal:		

Add up the multiple-choice and short-answer point subtotals from Table 10.2 and Table 10.3:

_____ + _____ = [   ]

Table 10.3 Subtotal   Table 10.4 Subtotal   Total

Next, take that total number and use it in the Table 10.5 to find the approximate MTEL score for the multiple-choice and short-response section of this practice writing subtest.

Once you have assigned your two open-responses a score between zero and four, use Table 10.6 to find your approximate score for the open-response section of the Writing subtest.

TABLE 10.5 WRITING SUBTEST MULTIPLE-CHOICE AND SHORT-ANSWER SCORE CONVERSION CHART	
MULTIPLE-CHOICE + SHORT-ANSWER POINTS	APPROXIMATE MTEL SCORE
0–10	50
11–13	59
14–16	68
17–19	77
20–22	86
23–25	95
26–28	104
29–31	113
32–34	122
35–37	131
38–40	140
41–42	150

Write your approximate MTEL score for this section here: ☐

MTEL Score for Section 2

TABLE 10.6 WRITING SUBTEST OPEN-RESPONSE SCORE CONVERSION CHART		
SUMMARY RESPONSE POINTS	COMPOSITION RESPONSE POINTS	APPROXIMATE MTEL SCORE
1	1	83
1	2	99
1	3	114
1	4	130
2	1	90
2	2	106
2	3	121
2	4	137
3	1	97
3	2	112
3	3	128
3	4	143
4	1	103
4	2	119
4	3	134
4	4	150

The next step is to score your Summary and Composition responses. Of course, you can do this yourself, but it is highly recommended that you ask a professional friend or colleague familiar with the official MTEL writing rubrics to do it for you to get the most accurate gauge of your work. The MTEL writing rubrics you should use to help score your two open responses are available on NES's official website on pages 48 through 51 of the document found here: www.mtel.nesinc.com/PDFs/MA_FLD201_Writing_PRACTICE_TEST.pdf.

Write your approximate MTEL score for this section here: ☐

MTEL Score for Section 2

Finally, to find your overall approximate MTEL Writing subtest score, add up your MTEL scores from both sections:

☐ + ☐ = ☐

Section 1   Section 2   Overall Writing
MTEL Score   MTEL Score   Subtest Score

ADDITIONAL ONLINE PRACTICE

Whether you need help building basic skills or preparing for an exam, visit the LearningExpress Practice Center! Using the code below, you'll be able to access additional MTEL online practice. This online practice will also provide you with:

Immediate Scoring
Detailed answer explanations
Personalized recommendations for further practice and study

Log in to the LearningExpress Practice Center by using the URL: **www.learnatest.com/practice**

This is your Access Code: **7694**

Follow the steps online to redeem your access code. After you've used your access code to register with the site, you will be prompted to create a username and password. For easy reference, record them here:

Username: _____ Password: _____

With your username and password, you can log in and access your additional practice materials. If you have any questions or problems, please contact LearningExpress customer service at 1-800-295-9556 ext. 2, or e-mail us at **customerservice@learningexpressllc.com**

NOTES

NOTES

NOTES

NOTES

NOTES

NOTES